KNOWING AND VALUE

SUNY Series in
Constructive Postmodern Thought
David Ray Griffin, editor

KNOWING AND VALUE

Toward a Constructive
Postmodern Epistemology

FREDERICK FERRÉ

STATE UNIVERSITY OF NEW YORK PRESS

Production by Ruth Fisher
Marketing by Nancy Farrell

Published by
State University of New York Press, Albany

© 1998 State University of New York

For information, address the State University of New York Press,
State University Plaza, Albany, NY 12246

Library of Congress Cataloging-in-Publication Data

Ferré, Frederick.
   Knowing and value   :   toward a constructive postmodern epistemology
   /   Frederick Ferré.
      p.   cm. — (SUNY series in constructive postmodern thought)
   Includes bibliographical references and index.
   ISBN 0-7914-3989-5 (hardcover   :   alk. paper). — ISBN 0-7914-3990-9
(pbk.   :   alk. paper)
   1. Knowledge, Theory of.   2. Postmodernism.   I. Title.
II. Series
BD161.F39   1998
121—dc21   98-14887
                                                                             CIP

10   9   8   7   6   5   4   3   2   1

*To my students, from whom I learned much
about values and knowing*

CONTENTS

PART ONE
DISCOVERING THE EPISTEMOLOGICAL GAP

PART TWO
COPING WITH THE EPISTEMOLOGICAL GAP

PART THREE
DECONSTRUCTING THE EPISTEMOLOGICAL GAP

PREFACE

Philosophy, our most comprehensive way of thinking, rejects fixed boundary lines. Metaphysics and epistemology continually call to each other for explication and support. There is no discontinuous "either/or" separating the great questions of being and knowing. Therefore, it is no surprise that this book is in constant antiphonal partnership with its predecessor, *Being and Value* (Ferré 1996).

Being comes first. What there *is* determines what can be known and how it can be known. But knowing is vital. How we judge we *ought* to think, if we are to think reliably, reflects what kinds of thinkers we think we are. It also determines the map of the world we draw—what is permitted, in principle, to fit on it, and what can claim no logical space. Whether we can know, and what it is we can know, will have consequences for how we live, the technologies we create, and the relations we establish with each other and the world.

This book is about knowing. It is the second part of a trilogy that aims at laying out the elements of a full philosophy, starting with a volume on being, continuing with this volume, and concluding with a volume on living. But putting it this way is more than a little misleading. All three dimensions are present throughout. Living and its values are present in all our thinking about being; knowing is inseparable from living. This is the nub of my thesis for the whole trilogy: values are pervasive in philosophy.

My philosophy is environmental, in the widest sense. It is not simply "environmental ethics," which will appear explicitly only in the final volume, but it is a venture in full environmental philosophy. In it the model of systems ecology—fluid, relational, diversified, evolutionary, value-laden—is crucial both for my view of reality and for my account of knowing. My admiration for Alfred North Whitehead's "philosophy of organism" long preceded my acquaintance with scientific ecology, but Whitehead anticipated what an ecological ontology and epistemology would require, and the marriage is a natural one. Whitehead is the grand environmental philosopher, for whom the environment surrounding even the least occasion of reality is utterly important to it, and for whom the natural selection of self-organizing systems is the story of the universe.

My own story of philosophy, ending with the ecological model, begins with the ancients. I believe that we are currently at a great turning point, comparable in magnitude to the transition between the premodern and modern eras of Western thinking. I tell and retell that sweeping story so that my own views on postmodern metaphysics and epistemology will be understood in context. I realize that there is no single, "absolute" history of Western philosophy; each of us weaves a narrative by choosing to emphasize some threads, to let others remain in the background. Many threads will inevitably be passed over by anyone who approaches the loom. Still, one of the best ways of overcoming incomprehension in the field of philosophy, so fragmented by rival convictions and methods, is to approach our common history with an attentive eye for the choices we make and the patterns we weave as we construct our various histories.

The narratives I tell in this book and in its predecessor are in many ways familiar (as, indeed, they should be, if we have a common history); but in other ways they are nonstandard. I make an unusual effort, for example, to lace the abstract ideas of my protagonists with large dollops of concrete circumstances, human preferences, purposes, hopes, and fears. This makes it obvious that I am systematically interested in the humanity of the philosophies we have inherited. I am delighted that even some professional philosophers, well-versed in the standard histories, have reported finding pleasure in fresh discoveries when approaching the old philosophical story in this way. In the present volume, I am especially glad to think I have narrated the intertwined lives and thinking of Hobbes and Descartes in a way that, so far as I know, is not generally told. Now that I understand their relations better, I understand the origins of modern philosophy more fully. I wish I had been taught these things long ago.

Also nonstandard is my choice of spokespersons, especially in *Being and Value*, from outside the "canon" of "real philosophers." Since in that volume I tried to follow the spark of creative metaphysics wherever it danced, it was necessary to include theologians—Muslim, Jewish, Christian—in the medieval period and scientists in the modern. We simply do not understand premodern metaphysics if we omit Thomas Aquinas, for example, or modern metaphysics if we omit Newton. I make no apologies, therefore, for broadening the range of historical threads I choose to weave.

I do offer a general apology to all the contemporary thinkers whose views have obviously influenced mine but who are not explicitly treated in these volumes. My policy has been to remain unembroiled (allowing a few obvious exceptions) in discussions with living thinkers. Unfortunately, I owe a more specific apology to Frederick Turner for having used his term, "kalogenic," without acknowledgment. I thought I had coined this word from its Greek stems without help, but I was wrong. I had enthusiastically read his *Natural Classicism* (Turner 1985) several years earlier, and had just forgotten. My transgression is doubly painful, since Turner is a personal friend. This lapse is embarrassing, but it vividly illustrates the fact that in a project of this scope, I simply could not begin to do justice to the clamor of current literature. Such discussions are more appropriate, in any case, in professional journals. Once the final volume of this trilogy has been safely brought into port from the great oceans I am navigating, I plan to set sail again on the inland waterways where the journal articles flow.

Mentioning colleagues reminds me to say a word about the readers I have in mind as I send this book to press. No one who knows the field expects to "convince" professional philosophers of anything. Most of us make our living by starting objections and sustaining them, endlessly, no matter how fine the grain of argument. But my broad challenge to modern philosophy is seriously intended, and I hope to debate it on a more detailed scale once the trilogy is complete. The fresh elements in my historical narratives and the comprehensive ecological alternative I recommend for modern philosophic ills ought to be make good grist for philosophical mills, even if persuasion is unlikely.

My intended readers, however, are not my colleagues alone. I want to bring philosophy out of the faculty ghetto, where for the most part it has isolated itself, and into the wider world. This means that I want any readers who are interested in the great issues of being, knowing, and living to be able to read these books with profit. My students, graduate and undergraduate, have been much on my mind during my writing. The first volume was dedicated to "the students of my students." These are not merely hypothetical people. By now, after almost four decades of teaching, I have many former students who have taught many students of their own. These are for the most part not philosophers themselves, but at least some of them have come to realize that philosophy is important for coping with—and shaping—the world they are leading into the new millennium. They would make good readers of these books. This second volume is dedicated to "my students." I have learned much from them, especially about what might be called "applied epistemology." My teaching has been a joy, and this book has been an extension of my teaching. These volumes, consequently, will not be out of place in the classroom, if teachers care to teach with them. Positive reports have already come back about student reactions in courses incorporating *Being and Value*. I hope that these books will be both contributors to their fields and instruments for drawing students into those fields.

Finally, I want to mention certain people who have made special contributions of their own to this enterprise, and to this volume in particular. For some time, my teaching schedule has been designed to parallel the writing of these volumes. For the two years *Being and Value* was in preparation, I was given metaphysics courses to teach. For the next two years, while the present book was being written, I was allowed epistemology courses and seminars. In the next two years, I taught philosophy of technology and ethical theory to help with *Living and Value*. Thanks are due my department head, Donald E. Nute, who has maintained this supportive intellectual environment for my trilogy. Further thanks go to Wyatt Anderson, Dean of the Franklin College of Arts and Sciences at the University of Georgia during the writing of this present book. Dean Anderson, a distinguished geneticist with additional intense interdisciplinary interests in epistemology and ecology, has sustained and encouraged me as Research Professor, helping with both moral and material encouragements.

Embodying the role of "current student from whom I have learned much" is Dr. Bethe Segars McRae, who has read and raised detailed questions about both volumes. In view of her excellent dissertation on Whitehead's theory of moral agency, she gave a particularly penetrating reading to the third part of this book and made suggestions I have gratefully adopted. Another reader to whom I am indebted is John Granrose, philosopher, Jungian analyst, magician, and friend. His gently skeptical view of some of my wilder speculations is as welcome as his encouragement is treasured.

Two others are in many ways beyond thanking. One is Mona Freer, whose blue pencil has repeatedly saved me from solecisms—and worse. She is a reader every author could covet, one who cares about the music of the big picture but also the minutiae of style and form. The other is my wife, Barbara Meister Ferré, who listens to passages when I wonder if they make sense, who encourages me when the voyage seems endlessly long, and who makes life rich and whole.

Frederick Ferré
Athens, Georgia

INTRODUCTION TO SUNY SERIES IN CONSTRUCTIVE POSTMODERN THOUGHT

The rapid spread of the term *postmodern* in recent years witnesses to a growing dissatisfaction with modernity and to an increasing sense that the modern age not only had a beginning but can have an end as well. Whereas the word *modern* was almost always used until quite recently as a word of praise and as a synonym for *contemporary*, a growing sense is now evidenced that we can and should leave modernity behind—in fact, that we *must* if we are to avoid destroying ourselves and most of the life on our planet.

Modernity, rather than being regarded as the norm for human society toward which all history has been aiming and into which all societies should be ushered—forcibly if necessary—is instead increasingly seen as an aberration. A new respect for the wisdom of traditional societies is growing as we realize that they have endured for thousands of years and that, by contrast, the existence of modern society for even another century seems doubtful. Likewise, *modernism* as a worldview is less and less seen as The Final Truth, in comparison with which all divergent worldviews are automatically regarded as "superstitious." The modern worldview is increasingly relativized to the status of one among many, useful for some purposes, inadequate for others.

Although there have been antimodern movements before, beginning perhaps near the outset of the nineteenth century with the Romanticists and the Luddites, the rapidity with which the term postmodern has become widespread in our time suggests that the antimodern sentiment is more extensive and intense than before, and also that it includes the sense that modernity can be successfully overcome only by going beyond, it, not by attempting to return to a premodern form of existence. Insofar as a common element is

xv

found in the various ways in which the term is used, *postmodernism* refers to a diffuse sentiment rather than to any common set of doctrines—the sentiment that humanity can and must go beyond the modern.

Beyond connoting this sentiment, the term postmodern is used in a confusing variety of ways, some of them contradictory to others. In artistic and literary circles, for example, postmodernism shares in this general sentiment but also involves a specific reaction against "modernism" in the narrow sense of a movement in artistic-literary circles in the late nineteenth and early twentieth centuries. Postmodern architecture is very different from postmodern literary criticism. In some circles, the term postmodern is used in reference to that potpourri of ideas and systems sometimes called *new age metaphysics*, although many of these ideas and systems are more premodern than postmodern. Even in philosophical and theological circles, the term postmodern refers to two quite different positions, one of which is reflected in this series. Each position seeks to transcend both modernism in the sense of the worldview that has developed out of the seventeenth-century-Galilean-Cartesian-Baconian-Newtonian science, and modernity in the sense of the world order that both conditioned and was conditioned by this worldview. But the two positions seek to transcend the modern in different ways.

Closely related to literary-artistic postmodernism is a philosophical postmodernism inspired variously by pragmatism, physicalism, Ludwig Wittgenstein, Martin Heidegger, and Jacques Derrida and other recent French thinkers. By the use of terms that arise out of particular segments of this movement, it can be called *deconstructive* or *eliminative postmodernism*. It overcomes the modern worldview through an anti-worldview: it deconstructs or eliminates the ingredients necessary for a worldview, such as God, self, purpose, meaning, a real world, and truth as correspondence. While motivated in some cases by the ethical concern to forestall totalitarian systems, this type of postmodern thought issues in relativism, even nihilism. It could also be called *ultramodernism*, in that its eliminations result from carrying modern premises to their logical conclusions.

The postmodernism of this series can, by contrast, be called *constructive* or *revisionary*. It seeks to overcome the modern worldview not by eliminating the possibility of worldviews such as, but by constructing a postmodern worldview through a revision of modern premises and traditional concepts. This constructive or revisionary postmodernism involves a new unity of scientific, ethical, aesthetic, and religious intuitions. It rejects not science as such but only that scientism in which the data of the modern natural sciences are alone allowed to contribute to the construction of our worldview.

The constructive activity of this type of postmodern thought is not limited to a revised worldview; it is equally concerned with a postmodern world that will support and be supported by the new worldview. A postmodern world will involve postmodern persons, with a postmodern spirituality, on the one hand, and a postmodern society, ultimately a postmodern global order, on the other. Going beyond the modern world will involve transcending its individualism, anthropocentrism, patriarchy, mechanization, economism, consumerism, nationalism, and militarism. Constructive postmodern thought provides support for the ecology, peace, feminist and other emancipatory movements of our time, while stressing that the inclusive emancipation must be from modernity itself. The term postmodern, however, by contrast with *premodern*, emphasizes that the modern world has produced unparalleled advances that must not be lost in a general revulsion against its negative features.

From the point of view of deconstructive postmodernists, this constructive postmodernism is still hopelessly wedded to outdated concepts, because it wishes to salvage a positive meaning not only for the notions of the human self, historical meaning, and truth as correspondence, which were central to modernity, but also for premodern notions of a divine reality, cosmic meaning, and an enchanted nature. From the point of view of its advocates, however, this revisionary postmodernism is not only more adequate to our experience but also more genuinely postmodern. It does not simply carry the premises of modernity through to their logical conclusions, but criticizes and revises those premises. Through its return to organicism and its acceptance of nonsensory perception, it opens itself to the recovery of truths and values from various forms of premodern thought and practice that had been dogmatically rejected by modernity. This constructive, revisionary postmodernism involves a creative synthesis of modern and premodern truths and values.

This series does not seek to create a movement so much as to help shape and support an already existing movement convinced that modernity can and must be transcended. But those antimodern movements which arose in the past failed to deflect or even retard the onslaught of modernity. What reasons can we have to expect the current movement to be more successful? First, the previous antimodern movements were primarily calls to return to a premodern form of life and thought rather than calls to advance, and the human spirit does not rally to calls to turn back. Second, the previous antimodern movements either rejected modern science, reduced it to a description of mere appearances, or assumed its adequacy in principle; therefore, they could base their calls only on the negative social and spiritual effects of modernity. The current movement draws on natural science itself as a witness against the adequacy of the modern worldview. Third, the present movement has even more evidence that did previous movements of the ways in which modernity and its worldview *are* socially and spiritually destructive. The fourth and probably most decisive difference is that the present movement is based on the awareness that *the continuation of modernity threatens the very survival of life on our planet.* This awareness, combined with the growing knowledge of the interdependence of the modern worldview and the militarism, nuclearism, and ecological devastation of the modern world, is providing an unprecedented impetus for people to see the evidence for a postmodern worldview and to envisage postmodern ways of relating to each other, the rest of nature, and the cosmos as a whole. For these reasons, the failure of the previous antimodern movements says little about the possible success of the current movement.

Advocates of this movement do not hold the naively utopian belief that the success of this movement would bring about a global society of universal and lasting peace, harmony, and happiness, in which all spiritual problems, social conflicts, ecological destruction, and hard choices would vanish. There is, after all, surely a deep truth in the testimony of the world's religions to the presence of a transcultural proclivity to evil deep within the human heart, which no new paradigm, combined with a new economic order, new child-rearing practices, or any other social arrangements, will suddenly eliminate. Furthermore, it has correctly been said that "lie is robbery": a strong element of competition is inherent within finite existence, which no social-political-economic-ecological order can overcome. These two truths, especially when contemplated together, should caution us against unrealistic hopes.

However, no such appeal to "universal constants" should reconcile us to the present order, as if this order were thereby uniquely legitimated. The human proclivity to evil in general, and to conflictual competition and eco-logical destruction in particular, can be greatly exacerbated or greatly miti-gated by a world order and its worldview. Modernity exacerbates it about as much as imaginable. We can therefore envision, without being naively uto-pian, a far better world order, with a far less dangerous trajectory, than the one we now have.

This series, making no pretense of neutrality, is dedicated to the success of this movement toward a postmodern world.

David Ray Griffin
Series Editor

1

WHY DO EPISTEMOLOGY?

Sometimes philosophers characterize the modern era as the "age of episte-mology." René Descartes (1596–1650), commonly designated the "Father of Modern Philosophy," is usually credited—or blamed—for this emphasis on establishing some indubitable theory of knowledge as the indispensable starting place for all philosophy. It was his method of beginning from radical doubt that inflated issues of skepticism to the intense level of con-cern with which modern philosophers have approached the problem of knowledge ever since. After Descartes, it seemed that without a completely certain theoretical answer to How do we know anything at all? philosophy could not get started. Without such an answer, any claim could suffer the skeptic's rejoinder: "How do you know that?" Lacking prior ground in a full-blown epistemology, it seemed philosophy could never achieve a se-cure foothold—nor (with any claim to rationality) could science, religion, or even common-sense certitudes.

Over the centuries of the modern era, however, it has become increas-ingly evident that the skeptic's rude rejoinder is no less applicable to episte-mological claims than to any other. All attempts to build fortifications for some indubitable theory of knowledge capable of fending off skepticism fall prey to the arrows of skepticism before the fort can be built. Why, given this endless stand-off, should we continue to worry about epistemology?

Indeed, since the "age of epistemology" more or less coincides with the modern era, and since readers of *Being and Value* (the first volume of this trilogy) will already know that I am convinced that the modern agenda (set

1

by Descartes' unbridgeable dualism between value and nature) is in need of replacement by postmodern ways of thinking, why chew any longer on this quintessentially modern bone? There are plenty of voices declaring the "end of epistemology" (Rorty 1980) and urging us to move on. May we not just ignore theory of knowledge as outmoded and unprofitable?

No, we may not. Knowing, in all its many forms, is too important in human affairs to be bypassed by any philosophy concerned with addressing and making sense of life's richness. It is doubtless true that the Cartesian approach to knowledge is condemned to remain in its frustrating circle: claims to certainty countered by skeptical ripostes. But epistemology need not be identified forever with the modern theories of Descartes, Locke, Hume, Kant, and followers. There may be another approach that can do a better job. That, in a sentence, is what this book is about. The chapters of Part Three will attempt to point the way.

KNOWING AND THE REQUIREMENTS OF THEORY

Epistemology, as one of the primary domains of philosophical theorizing, is properly a locus of philosophy's *comprehensive* and *critical* way of thinking. It is the study (*logos*) of knowledge (*episteme*) in general. It is the disciplined reflection on "knowing *qua* knowing," not just reflection on some particular type or types of knowledge. This does not mean that philosophers must renounce highly specific or technical studies of certain fields of knowing. On the contrary, the critical motive in philosophical theorizing requires intense scrutiny of as many particular claims for types of knowledge as offer themselves for analysis. At the same time (tugging philosophical attention in the other direction), the comprehensive motive in philosophical thinking demands that the many, once sorted out, be considered together.

Such consideration does not necessarily entail that they be reduced to one common denominator. Epistemological pluralism is possible; but this position, if adopted, itself makes a comprehensive claim about knowledge: namely, that different sorts of it cannot be reduced to one sort alone. Its "theory of knowledge" is a theory of "knowledges." Epistemological pluralism needs to account for its readiness to apply the common name "knowledge" to all these irreducible varieties, of course; but that is a different matter.

Similarly, epistemological dualism is possible. Dualism claims that there are exactly two sorts of knowledge, that neither is capable of being reduced to the other, and that the two are incapable of being interpreted within a more comprehensive theory that could account for them both, perhaps as phases or aspects. Dualism, as a minimalist version of pluralism, faces the pluralist's problem with language, that is, of showing how "knowing" can be used meaningfully on both sides of such an unbridgeable duality. But perhaps this can be handled, for example, by reference to "family resemblances," or the like.

More typically, philosophical theories of knowing have attempted to specify what it is that all the special varieties of knowing have in common, uniting them despite specific differences. The general knowledge-making features proposed by competing unitary theories—sense experience, logical consistency, etc.—are subject to vigorous debate, as we shall see in the chapters ahead; but in unitary theories the philosophical drive to comprehensive theorizing has been satisfied to a double degree. First, minimally, they say something about knowing in general (as do pluralist and dualist theories also, in their ways); but second, more daringly, they take the characteristics of all knowing to be internally coherent, making for a single identifiable account of knowing despite the variety of contexts in which real-life claims for knowledge are made.

Having mentioned "coherence," I should now be explicit about the differences I see between *comprehensiveness*, which I have taken as a defining feature of philosophical theorizing, and *coherence*, which is one of the primary functional ideals of all theorizing. Comprehensiveness refers to philosophy's rejection of boundaries. Philosophical thinking is not defined by special subject areas, since all subject areas can in principle be relevant to its questions. For this reason philosophy can be called an "omnirelevant" discipline, no closer in principle to the arts and humanities than to mathematics or the social sciences or the natural sciences or religion. Still, it is a discipline. What disciplines philosophical thought is its commitment to being intensely *critical*, at the same time that it insists on being comprehensive.

This is one of several difficult balancing acts philosophers try to achieve. It is not easy. Historically, philosophies have wobbled on one side or the other between being omnirelevant but largely uncritical, and being highly critical but fragmentary in scope.

"Being critical" itself involves more balancing of polar obligations. The most elementary is *consistency*. Having a clear theory requires avoidance of contradiction, which is destructive of any content. Contradiction within a theory cancels out determinate meaning. But if one fears contradiction so much that any theory found to contain conceptual tensions is immediately condemned, then there will be no opportunity left for theoretical growth through refinement of meaning, making distinctions, or being irritated into solving apparent paradoxes. Socrates made headway (as well as enemies) by exposing contradictions, then going back to work; the temptation is to swat the Socratic gadfly forthwith, but this means the death of dialectical advance.

Likewise, every theory requires *adequacy*. If it is to be more than minimally *applicable* to some domain, it needs to be held open to the whole domain by including as much relevant data as possible about it. It is self-defeating for a theory to achieve a thin consistency at the price of eliminating thick portions of data. Still, this is a hard balance to maintain.

Even harder is the balance between maintaining adequacy to all the relevant evidence and respecting the ideal of *coherence*, that is, the drawing of positive conceptual connections among elements within one's theory. Not only is it much easier to achieve coherence when demands for adequacy are relaxed (and easier to insist on adequacy when coherence is winked at), but also the standards of "relevance" are themselves at least partially provided by the theory in question. In a courtroom the relevance of an item of evidence depends upon the theory of the crime. A blood speck that would be entirely irrelevant on one theory may be crucial on another. This is true in science too. In 1896, in the scientific laboratory of Antoine Henri Becquerel, before X-ray photography was known, the relevance of the location of uranium salt relative to his unexposed photographic plate had yet to be supplied by the theories rising from the work of Marie and Pierre Curie on pitchblende, polonium, barium, and radium chloride.

Still, these are balances that need to be maintained in all theory. It is simply harder to achieve such balances, as philosophers, when our boundaries are neither imposed by external conventions nor required by otherwise delimited special purposes.

KNOWING AND THE VARIETY OF LIFE

Epistemological pluralists may have a strong case, especially if the critical standard of adequacy is heeded and the magnificent variety of contexts in which "knowing" plays a part is given due attention. I make no claim to anything like a complete survey of such contexts in what follows in this section. Nevertheless, at the start of a book about knowing, it is useful to collect and reflect on a range of actual pretheoretical appearances of the concept in actual life.

As I write these words, I have just come in from walking my dog. It is fair to say that I know my dog and she knows me. She also knows her neighborhood, and plunges eagerly to certain favorite spots where she knows that special joys of olfactory richness await. She knows other animals around here and greets them matter-of-factly. She knows with especial eagerness the young neighbor woman with the long, russet hair who always has a special word and pat for her. She also knows my wife, away from home at the moment, and clearly misses her, looking for her every morning in the strangely empty bedroom and sniffing longingly at the pillow where no head has lain for several nights.

I write these words with no linguistic qualms, certainly not intending them as mere metaphorical extensions from human contexts. That would be ridiculously anthropocentric—and more pedantic than even philosophers have a right to be. No, these uses are ground zero for many contexts of "knowing," and these could be multiplied indefinitely. The birds know when it is time to migrate. The sheep know when it is time to mate. The cows know when it is time to come in, and besides, they know the path to the milk shed and the social order in which to walk on it. It is hard to draw a lowermost line to this sort of "knowing" talk: certainly it would be odd to say that spiders do not know how to weave their webs. Do starfish know how to open clams? There must be a level at which we would deny "knowing," or at least declare it analogical, not literal. I would not say, for example, that my thermostat literally knows when the house is cold enough for it to turn the furnace on, though we sometimes talk casually in such ways. And we certainly talk that way about computers—perhaps to the point where the line between the figurative and the literal is increasingly blurred. Living contexts change, as does the "line" between literal and metaphorical, and we had better keep that evolutionary point in view as we proceed.

Most of the contexts of "knowing" I shall next survey are frankly anthropocentric. Not surprisingly, human knowing engages human epistemologists' attention more urgently than other kinds. This fact is perfectly natural; most species are more interested in their own kind for many purposes. But the principle of adequacy to the data should remind us that this anthropocentric focus, though natural, is yet a restriction. Since it restricts us to the most complex and rewarding range of data, however, we need not complain as long as we do not forget.

Like my dog, I know this house, this neighborhood, this territory. I know it to recognize it and to find my way about in it, roughly as she does, though I use different clues, in part because my olfactory powers are so much feebler than hers. Beyond this, I know our home for its significance in ways I do not imagine my dog to know, but in ways my wife can largely share with me (and surpass). Several pieces of our furniture and other important items were once in her mother's apartment in Germany, where we first knew them, before her mother's death. Our dog surely knows the furniture (and which pieces to stay off), but she cannot know the significance they have for us, woven into our own knowing of them and of their previous circumstances. I do not doubt that our dog knows them as somehow important—they loom large for her in our household—but she does not know how they are important for us.

Most of the knowing I have mentioned thus far has been recognitional. Animals and humans recognize places, persons, other animals, features, patterns, and things. Such recognition is essential. Without a recognitional capacity, organisms would be unable to know what to avoid, what to pursue, in their environment. Recognition, whether learned or instinctual, conscious or "hard-wired," makes possible the discriminating behavior that underlies social order of every sort. (It might be added—if we were doing metaphysics—that chemical molecules, too, require some unconscious capacity for mutual recognition if chemical reactions are to occur and structured compounds are to be possible.)

Recognition rests on the yet more fundamental ability to tie the past to the present. If nothing of the past were retained into the present moment, nothing could be familiar. In a totally amnesiac universe, everything would be as if encountered for the first time. But this is not the case. Therefore, memory needs to be added to our inventory of knowings.

Even this one sort of knowing breaks down, under examination, into several sub-types. Dogs know familiar scents remembered from earlier outings; humans know the feel of a familiar pillow as we snuggle down for sleep. These memories seem to be of qualitative features—smells and feels, etc.—that repeat across time. To know a "feature" at all is to be able to pick it out as something encountered before. Without a past, present experience would be literally featureless.

We also know familiar faces that seem not merely collections of features (though features are present) but entities more uniquely individual, personal, concrete. Objects, landscapes, rooms, as well as persons can be recognized before their features are clear.

Memory knowing retains events as well as features and entities. Some of these are happenings of the immediate past that still resonate in the present. I am slapped on the cheek by you and the sting of the blow starts to spread while your angry face and open palm still focus my field of vision. The past is in the present as much as in the past.

But immediacy fades. Some events are only dimly present. Many newer events have intervened. We still may wish to say that we "know" the more remote past event; but at best the knowing is more diluted, distant, and subject to challenge. Memory can play tricks. (This is something else we know by memory.)

Speaking of "immediacy" raises yet another type of knowing. How do I know that I am engaging in an act of recognition when I recognize something? Most of the time, let us grant, we do not know any such thing; and for most of the recognizers in the universe, there is never such knowledge. But under special circumstances (perhaps being challenged by another or puzzled by some unexpected conflict), I attend more carefully than at other times to what is happening. Then I simply am aware of my awareness. I recognize noticingly.

This is usually called "introspective" knowing. I may as well accept that convention, deep rooted as it is. But that word, made up of Latin stems for "inner seeing," is potentially misleading. When I recognize a scent and attend noticingly to this recognition, I am not *looking* at my scent-recognition. I am sniffing more attentively, and attending (perhaps also attending to my attending) to my repertoire of olfactory discriminations; but that is not a kind of vision. There is no visual image there for me to *see*. Likewise, I may be directly aware of my headache, but I do not "see" my headache; rather, I feel it. If I do not feel it, I do not then have a headache; but I can feel it inattentively (when I am too busy with something else to notice it or let it spoil my fun), or I can pay close attention to its baleful qualities as it develops and recedes. There is something essentially direct and unmediated about this kind of introspective knowing. Some have even claimed that it must be infallible. This, if true, would clearly mark it off from memory knowing, which as we saw comes in degrees of assurance.

Still expanding on the epistemological pluralist's case, we might next turn to the great area of perceptual knowing. I know this chair, in which I have been sitting for some time, as hard. I shall soon need to stretch and move around. I also know the bacon as smelling good. I recognize its characteristic odor. But more, I recognize it as no free-floating smell but as an early harbinger of something tempting to eat. Memory knowing underlies my recognitional capacity both of the chair and the bacon; and introspection (abandoning the visual suggestion) assures me of my awareness. Somehow I am convinced, moreover, that the chair and the bacon are not simply qualities of my experience. They are public objects I perceive by way of features I recognize. The chair presses against my back; the bacon odors invade my nostrils.

There will be much more said about sense perception in the chapters that follow. There is no need to develop such issues at this moment. What is interesting from the point of view of pluralism and the sheer variety of "knowings" in real life is the extent to which perceptual knowing escapes complete reduction to other types of knowing. Memory knowing certainly plays a major part, since it makes possible recognitional knowing, and recognition—at least of features—is an essential element in all perceptual knowing. But to the extent that something more than features—something such as a world of objects—is provided through perception (and this seems to be an essential claim of perceptual rather than sheerly introspective knowing), we find the irreducible element.

Completely different from perceptual knowing is what often is called "rational" knowing. There is a qualitative difference between knowing that this chair is getting hard on my back and knowing that if it is hard, then it is not "not-hard." The former I come to know through the pressure of the chair on my body; the latter I come to know in some other way. Is it by inspecting the meanings of "if" and "then" and "not"? Is it by the manipulation of symbols until equivalences appear? Is it by intuiting the coercive authority of some Law of Noncontradiction? Is it by direct awareness of self-evidence? Is it by repulsion from the absurdity of the alternative?

Whatever rational knowing is, memory and recognition must be at work, since meanings (or symbols or concepts or self-evidence or absurdity) need to be recognized for what they are if rational connections are to be made. But there is more going on than simple recognition when an inference is made, a conclusion drawn, a necessity acknowledged. Just as perceptual knowing involves something irreducible, so rational knowing also seems to be a different type from all the rest.

So far, in reviewing the varieties of knowing in life, I have ignored one of the more telling exhibits of the epistemological pluralist: that is, the multiplicity of the very different kinds of knowing that are hallowed and institutionalized in the standard university curriculum. What does history have to do with mathematics? Historical knowing is interested in the establishment of particular occurrences in the past, relying for evidence on records and recollections. Perception and memory, prejudice and venality, are the raw material on which history builds its claims for knowing. Mathematics, in contrast, manipulates formal symbols, universal and necessary, to establish its entirely different mode of knowing. The natural sciences are different again from both history and mathematics. Like history, the sciences attempt to establish individual occurrences with as much accuracy as possible, but unlike history, do so only to suggest or test overarching statements of regularity (laws) or to strengthen or weaken the case for explanatory hypotheses (theories). Historical knowing is of the unique, with secondary reliance on generalities to strengthen plausibility of particular narratives; scientific knowing is of the general, with secondary interest in particular exemplifications of laws and theories. But the "general" in the natural sciences is not the mathematically formal alone; rather, it is general knowledge about the world of perception and its objects. Like mathematics, scientific knowing relies heavily on formal constructs, but (unlike mathematics) this is so only to the extent that these constructs can give form to regularities found in perception.

The curriculum also enshrines other sorts of knowing. Knowing great literature involves quite different things from knowing history or mathematics or natural science. It involves, for one example, cultivating sensibility to qualitative issues in different ways from historical knowing—though knowing history may help—and in ways quite different from mathematical or scientific knowing, though the latter both have a place for knowing the "elegance" or "beauty" of theoretical forms. Again, the curriculum, by sponsoring courses in ethics and religion, suggests that there may be ways of ethical knowing and religious knowing, as well. Music and the visual arts demand still other ways of knowing. There is little wonder that epistemological pluralism is an easy doctrine to grasp for the multiversity-educated of our era.

KNOWING AND BASIC CONTRASTS

Philosophical yearning for order and simplicity is felt in theory of knowledge no less than in other domains. Is there no way to reduce the sheer multiplicity of ways of knowing to some more easily comprehensible form? We shall see in the chapters to follow that one historically important proposal has been dualistic: there are two and only two types of knowing, we are told. One has to do with matters of fact, the other with matters of logic (or "ideas" or "meanings").

This way of organizing thinking about knowing has much to be said for it. In the previous section's collection of ways of knowing, we encountered large differences between the disciplines of universal symbols (e.g., mathematics) and the disciplines of particular events (e.g., history). And in the natural sciences, we noted a significant internal division between the role of formalisms (including mathematics) and the role of data collection and manipulation (including observation, experimentation, and theory development).

Even in my own opening treatment of theory's requirements, I made a point of the difference between the "internal" criteria of theoretical success (consistency and coherence) and the "external" criteria (applicability and adequacy to the data). Is there not the making of a dualism of types of knowing here: a knowing of the relationships between our concepts and a knowing of the relationships between our concepts and the domain of experience they are intended to reflect? I acknowledged the tensions between the two sorts of goals. Does this make me a dualist?

It will take the book as a whole to answer the question properly, but this opening chapter may take at least preliminary note of some strengths and weaknesses of dualism in epistemology. Reducing a welter of differences down to two clearly distinct principles does seem a long step toward simplicity; and simplicity is a desirable theoretical aim. If the two distinct principles are found to be in tension, perhaps this may just be the way things are for cognition. We might need to make sure—if this is so—that we have accommodated both principles as far as possible, and when they clash, might need to use our best judgment without attempting to find a rule for resolving the tension.

Much of modern philosophy, at least until the mid-twentieth century, took for granted a basic dualism between forms of knowing that are either logically necessary or empirically contingent, with nothing in between. "My sister is a sibling" is an example of the first; "my sister is blue-eyed" is an example of the second. To know the truth of the first, all we need is a grasp of language. Since "sibling" means "sister or brother," the predicate of the first sentence repeats the subject and thus makes the sentence as a whole necessarily true but empty of information. It is a tautology. Given an understanding of the words concerned, including the key logical words "is" and "not" and "or," there can be no such thing as a sister who is not a sister or a brother, by virtue of logical consistency.

In contrast, new information is reported by the second sentence, *if* it is true. "Being blue-eyed" is nowhere implicit in the meaning of "sister." Many full-fledged sisters have gray or green or brown or other-than-blue colored eyes; therefore, it could quite well be a mistake to claim blue-eyedness as a fact concerning my sister. Nothing guarantees it. To decide whether it happens to be true in the case of my asserting it requires more than understanding language and deferring to the Law of Noncontradiction; it requires observation.

Thus arises the great duality of "logically necessary" versus "factually contingent," "guaranteed by definition" versus "empirically discovered," "questions of meaning" versus "matters of fact." These contrasts can be summarized in the famous "analytic" versus "synthetic" duality. Analytic truths are defined, roughly speaking, as those statements which can be known to be true simply by "internal" analysis of the concepts concerned. This means, presumably, that they are noninformative, necessary, and (since necessary) thus universally true under all factual conditions. Synthetic truths are those which add on ("synthesize") new information to the formal concepts of the statement concerned. This means, presumably, that they are contingent and particular, dependent on the wayward deliverances of perception.

The great contrast between a priori and a posteriori knowing is also closely related. What can be known "prior" to perception, by virtue of thought alone, can only be of the universal and necessary and is often held to be coextensive with the domain of the analytic; what can be known only "post"-perception must be the contingent facts, thus suggesting an equivalence to the synthetic. If one were to diagram this apparent dualism, it would look like a matrix with four internal boxes, only two of which are occupied.

	A priori	A posteriori
Analytic	occupied with tautological expressions	
Synthetic		occupied with observation-reports

In consequence, any candidate for knowledge that is informative ("factual") will need to arise from perception and must be entirely contingent and particular. Any candidate for knowledge that is necessary or universal will need to be factually vacuous and assured of its truth-status simply by virtue of the internal meanings of the terms that make it up. This implies, of course, that nothing informative about any state of affairs can possibly be affirmed as universally or necessarily true—an outcome which, if accepted, would rule out a great deal of what many philosophers have sought to assert. The sharp duality represented in the above matrix, especially its eliminating any statements from the "synthetic" and "a priori" box at the lower left, therefore may be expected to draw fire, as we shall see in following chapters.

Less often noticed, there is one more box unoccupied: that which would contain the "analytic a posteriori," if such there be. For reasons to be offered later, I am convinced that this final box will reward our attention, too. Tautologies, after all, are linguistic creations, dependent upon relations of synonymy historically established by usage among members of language-communities. What Ludwig Wittgenstein (1889–1951) called "language games" or "forms of life" are prior to the linguistic security claimed for the sort of analytic knowing that depends on substantive definitions (Wittgenstein 1953). Perhaps there are analytic a priori logical truths that rest on entirely timeless formal relations (though even here, in the realm of "if," "and," "or," "not," etc., we may, if we look carefully, find historical changes in definition within the history of logic). But most assuredly, the analytical knowability of "My sister is a sibling," my recent example, depends on much a posteriori knowledge concerning matters such as parenting, sexual reproduction, gender differentiation, and the like. "Getting the words right" itself depends on a posteriori learning of language, whether simply by upbringing within the community of usage or by explicit stipulation. Then, once learned, the "correct" use will be defended by social consensus, and "sibling" will (*shall!*) be taken to mean "children of the same parents, sister or brother" (rendering the tautology secure) rather than, say, "dwells on the Isle of Sibl" or some other tautology-undermining but logically possible alternative.

Once the supposedly exclusive dualisms of "analytic a priori" versus "synthetic a posteriori" (or "truths of reason" versus "truths of experience") are challenged, other important consequences may follow. Different ways of interpreting so called "synthetic a priori" ways of knowing may emerge (Ferré 1961a: 90–94), and the apparent sharpness of epistemological cleavages of all kinds may start to blur (Quine 1980: 20–46). Thus the dualism of "fact" and "meaning" may not be so easy to sustain under close examination. Knowing facts depends on recognizing features that go into the construction of our concepts. But, conversely, recognizing concepts expressed in words and knowing how they should normally be taken to function depends on factual experience both in sense perception and in social-linguistic usage. Much more will be said about these matters in Chapter 9, below.

One more sharp contrast, amounting to a dualism, deserves early notice in this context, though fuller treatment must await later chapters. It is the contrast between great cultural divides over the basic meaning of knowing itself.

In most modern Western thinking about knowing, through and under other deep contrasts such as those between "rational" and "perceptual," or "a priori" and "a posteriori," there is the distinctly Greco-Roman heritage that assumes a sort of *contemplation* in progress. To "con-template" (in the original Latin context) is "carefully" (*con-* derives from the intensifier *com-*) to observe auguries in the *templum* (the sacred space). The same cultural outlook that gave us the visually-oriented Latinism "introspection" for direct awareness of all our thought and experience, provided its philosophical descendants in Rome and Western Europe a reflexlike tendency to equate knowing with some kind of seeing. "I see" in all the modern European languages is a colloquial synonym for "I understand."

What does the model of knowing as seeing carry with it? First, it requires some sort of illumination or some illuminating medium in which the seeing can occur, perhaps a "light of consciousness" that distinguishes knowing beings from unknowing ones. Second, it requires that some degree of distance be placed between the would-be seer and the thing seen. We all know how difficult it is to see something when it is thrust too close to our eyes. One needs a decent separation—a visual distance—in order to focus. Third, to see something, the thing should stand still, as still as possible— absolutely still and unchanging would be best. Fourth, if one hopes to see clearly, one must oneself be calm and still, detached and without anxieties or urgencies.

Given such "perspicuous" conditions (from the Latin for capable of being "seen through"), one may hope to "see" logical relationships, synonymy, entailments, equivalences, etc., with maximum clarity and discrimination. And one may equally hope to "see" sense data of all sorts (not just visual data, though they clearly become paradigmatic for all the senses) with similar distinctness of focus. Knowings of both kinds are types of mental seeing.

A wholly different cultural tradition derives, in a subordinate but traceable lineage, from the Hebrew. The biblical sense of "knowing" includes prominently among its standard uses that of sexual intercourse. Lot, in Sodom, is depicted as horrified that the Sodomite men would surround his house and demand homosexual intercourse with his house guests. Unless one is aware that "knowing" means having sex, the following passage makes no sense:

[The] men of the city, the men of Sodom, both young and old, all the people to the last man, surrounded the house; and they called to Lot, "Where are the men who came to you tonight? Bring them out to us, that we may know them." Lot went out of the door to the men, shut the door after him, and said, "I beg you, my brothers, do not act so wickedly. Behold, I have two daughters who have not known man; let me bring them out to you, and do to them as you please; only do nothing to these men, for they have come under the shelter of my roof" (Genesis 19:4–8).

This use of "know," like the word sodomy, continues to function in our modern culture. We still recognize what "carnal knowledge" means when we hear or read the phrase.

The Hebrew sense carries with it radically different conditions. For visual contemplation, one needs a well-illuminated space; for sexual intercourse, darkness will do. For knowing under the model of vision, there must be distance provided; for sexual intimacy, the exact opposite is required: closeness, contact, penetration are in order. For knowing as seeing, complete repose is desired; for knowing as sexual union, desire gives rise to movement—on the part of the known as well as of the knower—not rest. Finally, the mood implied by the two models is entirely different: seeing seeks clarity and demands calm; sex seeks union and welcomes passion, commitment, urgency, and sweat.

Cool, not warm; distanced, not close; motionless, not dynamic—these key antonyms show how radically the familiar Greco-Roman visual model of knowing stands opposed to its less prominent Hebrew alternative. They are, it seems, completely different and irreconcilable approaches to knowing. And yet, it seems that something vital from each is needed. Too much sheer distance between known and knower may make space for alienation and (ironically) misunderstanding. Too much unrelieved warm intimacy stands in equal but opposite peril of breeding hopeless confusion. Once again sheer dualism seems not to satisfy, though contrasts are certainly present. Working through these real multiplicities and important contrasts is one of the key reasons for doing epistemology. To understand—and make the most of—our powers of knowing requires that we try to grasp how all these diverse elements go constructively together without losing the pungency of their differences.

KNOWING AND BEING

Whatever is genuinely known must somehow "be"—even if only as an idea—in order to be a subject of knowledge. Armed with a good theory of knowledge,

perhaps one can outflank metaphysics and go straight to ontological conclusions from epistemological findings. If so, this would be another good reason
to do epistemology, and to make it prior to the other branches of philosophy.

One way of following epistemology to a theory of being would be to
accept the reality, in some sense, of timeless ideas: for example, "triangularity" (and other geometrical forms), or numbers, or the concept of "equality."
These are all knowable by contemplative reason; therefore, they "are" in
some timeless way. They must be timeless, since it matters not a whit when
(or, perhaps, whether) they are thought about. They are always the same as
themselves. Secure in the mind's eye, they do not change or crumble or blur.
They are in principle indifferent to time. Even "before" the universe and
"after" it (if these are conceivable states), the number *two* is (in a tenseless
sense of "is") the smallest even number and is (in this tenseless sense) always
and everywhere half of *four*. Likewise, ideal *triangularity* can be known in
plane geometry to contain (in the tenseless sense) a total of 180 degrees
within its three interior angles, quite apart from any facts of curved space-
time that might be the basis of different geometries.

A further discovery about the realm of being that might be supposed to
follow from this first epistemological implication is the requirement that there
be "soul" or "mind" capable of knowing these timeless realities. But, if so,
the capacity for dealing with the timeless in human knowers would be fraught
with significance. This would be possible only if something in us is suitable
for making cognitive contact with the eternal. Only the eternal is capable of
the eternal. Therefore it seems that there must be something eternal in or
about us.

But this can hardly be the whole story, since we know by introspection
that other of our ideas are in constant flux. We change our minds, we learn,
we forget, our mood swings. Therefore, it seems we must postulate, following directly evident epistemic facts, that our minds or souls are dynamic as
well as in some part capable of eternity.

What this dynamism deals with, to a large extent, is a huge range of
features or qualities or characteristics that occupy our changing attention.
Colors and sounds and textures and tastes and smells and pressures and
pleasures and pains—all flood through our awareness. Therefore, since these
are known they must somehow have a place in being.

They do not, however, flood through our cognition as a disorganized
flow; features come "bundled" with one another in regular ways. Nor do they
present themselves to us as mere features, but rather as objects in a world.
The world of objects obtrudes itself into our awareness. We seem to know
things and organisms and other persons. Perhaps, as some have argued, these
are "mere appearance"; but at least we know that they appear, and the appearances—at the minimum—need to be included in our accounts of being.

All this (and much more if it were to be developed) derives from the principle that whatever is known deserves recognition as having a place in our theory of reality. This is to see epistemology as taking the lead in determining the general shape of metaphysics. But there is an opposite principle, as well, on which whatever we can know simply *follows* from the way reality is. This is the other side of the coin. Metaphysics determines the knowable.

The negative implication of this principle is that what is unreal is certainly unknowable. If our metaphysics convinces us, for example, that there is no God, then it is futile to seek theological knowledge. If our metaphysics determines that there are no realities except particular things, then it is impossible that we can know universals. If our metaphysics includes only particles in time and change, then whatever it is that we suppose we know, it cannot be timeless entities.

The converse also follows: if there is a God, then knowledge of such a powerful and valuable reality would be of the highest priority. This does not mean that such knowledge is automatically available. Some draw this conclusion, holding that God is of all subjects the most eminently knowable, being the most ultimately real. Others, on different metaphysical grounds, hold to a strong *via negativa*, insisting that the One beyond all multiplicity cannot possibly be known in any of the discursive ways by which alone finite humans know any subject matter. Still others, mediating, argue that God as creator can be known only indirectly, by analogies drawn from the creation. All three of these positions, we note, are epistemological conclusions drawn from metaphysical premises.

With more frequency than may be readily acknowledged in our explicitly non- or anti-metaphysical age, epistemological positions are shaped by theories of reality (or at least by underlying worldviews which shape assumptions that, if worked out, would constitute a metaphysical theory). For many modern philosophers, as we saw in *Being and Value* (chapter 8), the initial premises of epistemological theory self-evidently include key elements of Darwinian theory, itself embedded in the more general materialist conclusions of the modern worldview. These "minimal" ontologies, sometimes acknowledged and sometimes not, are still ontologies; and from them flow much of maximum import to epistemology. If the implicit theory of ultimate reality behind modern science is to be taken as determinative, then mindless matter gave birth by purposeless evolutionary processes to organisms increasingly sensitive to their environments—eventually to cognizing organisms through which thinking and value emerged in a world hitherto without place for either. What "knowing" will be for such organisms will be considered in later chapters. Clearly it will be something quite different from what it would be for "souls" functioning amphibiously in realms of temporal perception and eternal intellection. It will be vastly different yet again, if knowing organisms are considered to be complex evolved societies of self-valuing microentities as portrayed in *Being and Value*.

All these are metaphysical speculations. They (and many others which could be added) all have the profoundest importance for epistemological theory, just as epistemological theory has the deepest importance for validating—or cautioning—metaphysical speculation. Being and knowing are tied with the most intimate threads. Between them they reflect and reinforce our most fundamental values.

KNOWING AND VALUING

With this mention of values, we return at the end of this introductory chapter to the central theme of this book. My thesis is that epistemology, no less than metaphysics, is deeply rooted in judgments of value, explicit and implicit. The rest of the book will be an attempt to explore the many ways in which this is so.

The influence of worldviews and metaphysical theories on theories of knowing is one obvious route through which values impact epistemology. This is readily seen when one's metaphysical stance emphasizes the importance of God, for example, as the source of all being, goodness, and cognitive illumination. Then truth itself becomes a gift of the divine. As we shall see in Chapter 3, for some thinkers truth *is* divine. A theocentric theory of reality influences the *what* as well as the *how* of knowing.

It is less often noticed, but no less the case, that atheistical worldviews, with the radically different epistemic consequences I noted earlier, are nourished by (and reciprocally nourish) profound values of their own. Since in *Being and Value* I pointed out the numerous value-rootings of the modern worldview, it is unnecessary to rehearse all these here; but it may be useful to recall just a few. One of the cleansing values supporting modern mechanistic metaphysics, for example, was its caustic capacity to dissolve the possibility of witchcraft and magic from the conceptual map. If all causal influence is by immediate material contact, then casting spells on one's neighbor's cow or blighting an enemy's crops by satanic ritual is literally unthinkable. To take "action at a distance" to be a metaphysical absurdity, as mechanistic materialism does, has a cleansing effect. Epistemologically, the consequence of this metaphysical axiom is that information is and can be passed only through material sense organs in direct contact with a physical environment, never at a distance by telepathy or other extra-sensory means.

It is not obvious whether metaphysics or epistemology is uppermost here. But such jointly-effective principles as materialism, mechanism, and sensationism are fundamental not only in theory but also in politics. They sailed in part on the refreshing winds of political liberalism (Ferré 1996:

159–69). Metaphysics, with its associated sensationist epistemology, became an effective weapon against an *ancien régime* rotten with tyranny and priestcraft. Opposing modern materialism under such political circumstances put one in the wrong camp. Even the abstract domains of metaphysics and epistemology, drenched as they are with value-implications, cannot avoid partisan considerations. Nor does it take much acquaintance with the sociology of knowledge to realize that something similar holds true today.

Less obviously partisan, but no less value-based, are the decisions (or predeliberative choices) made on how much stock to place in such basic theoretical values as unity, simplicity, and beauty. Other delicate judgments require balancing the values of honesty to the evidence, adequacy to the data, and open-mindedness, on the one hand, with such frequently competing values as loyalty to attained coherences, social concern for publicly announced theoretical commitments, and uncertain levels of hope for the continued viability of imperfectly attained research programs.

Underlying all such judgments is one that determines whether the worldviews behind epistemological theories are made explicit or not: this is a judgment on the importance of exploring theories of the ultimate nature of things in conscious and critical ways. Note that I did not say, "the judgment whether to have worldviews or not," or "the judgment whether one's worldview will have important implications for one's theory of knowing." These latter are not options; they are inevitabilities. Feeling the importance of theorizing carefully about these matters is, however, not an intuition everyone shares. Perhaps this, in turn, reveals crucial variations in epistemological valuation. It could be that those who do—and those who do not—feel the importance of metaphysical theorizing are thereby reflecting different evaluative judgments on what "knowledge" should include and how it should be pursued. At any rate, I now have made the turn from the implications of epistemology in making metaphysical choices to epistemological value-choices themselves.

Metaphysical values, we see, are not the only ones that shape epistemological theories. Profoundly important judgments about the appropriate character of "knowing" lie close beneath the surface, indispensable to epistemological theory.

One of these, noted in the previous section, is the normative judgment on what "knowing" itself should be taken to mean: should it be unitive or separative, Hebrew or Greek? Or should it somehow be a combination of these? Ought we to insist—as an ideal goal at least—that knowing must involve *both* contemplation *and* contact? Or should we choose up sides, discounting the other side, subjecting it to scorn, taking comfort in the company of others who have made the same choice?

I shall call the normative judgment that decides such issues the adoption of an *epistemic norm*. There are others. Shall reason, for example, once in possession of a theory offering valued coherences, be trusted to outweigh perception, if and when the data of perception threaten theory? Which shall be trusted more? The answer will reveal a deep epistemic norm.

There are still more epistemic norms to be considered, of course; but here we need to break off. We are fast approaching the main task of this book, which is to clarify the normative grounds of epistemology. My aim in Part One will be to show the inescapable presence of values in Western epistemology from its premodern founding days until its modern encounter with what I call the epistemological gap. In Part Two, I will take a fresh look at central value-laden modern epistemological strategies for dealing with this gap. Finally, in Part Three, I will suggest fresh epistemic norms (compatible with the ecological worldview advanced in *Being and Value*) that may both deconstruct this paralyzing gap and ground a constructive postmodern concept of knowing.

Before ending this chapter, a few future-oriented "preflections"—offered in reverse order of the expositions to come—might be useful.

Part Three will contain my positive suggestions for a rethought epistemology, emphasizing organismic continuities that tie thinking persons to the eventful universe of evolutionary change. Some readers, well-versed in the problems of modern epistemology and impatient to reap the epistemological consequences of the "kalogenic naturalism" I proposed in the first volume, may wish to start reading there. I would not recommend this for relative newcomers to epistemology, or for those who are entering this trilogy without first having read *Being and Value*; but advanced, or unusually well-motivated, readers should be able to jump in at Chapter 8, and should be able to swim without difficulty.

Part Two will offer my systematic discussion of the main modern epistemological options. Even readers well-acquainted with positivism, coherentism, existentialism, and pragmatism should be able to gain something from my values-oriented examination of their strengths and weaknesses. My "take" is not entirely standard, though all the issues will be familiar to experts. Some, especially those drawn to the cut and thrust of conflicting positions, might therefore like to start reading at Chapter 5. In addition, Part Two will definitely enrich understanding of the new proposals made in Part Three. What is not supplied in Part Two, however, is an account of how modern Western epistemology got itself embroiled in coping with the epistemological gap in the first place. Since this was a contingent (avoidable) matter of history, not the logical necessity it sometimes seemed to the thinkers of Part Two, I urge that at some point every reader should make the acquaintance of Part One.

Part One will provide my account of how modern Western epistemology trapped itself. But these three historical chapters (Ancient, Medieval, and Modern) should not be confused with a standard "history of philosophy." First, I have done my best to focus just on the issues of epistemology, ignoring metaphysics as much as possible. I feel entitled to try this (though it is not always possible to set metaphysics aside) since my fuller account of the struggles of Western philosophy to deal with its metaphysical agenda was given in *Being and Value*. Some of the same central classic voices will need to be heard in both books (e.g., Plato, Aristotle, Aquinas, Kant) but in this book they will not be speaking to the same issues. Some "greats," especially if their greatness was mainly metaphysical, will be omitted; and some (e.g., Locke and Hume) will appear for the first time, especially if their greatness was mainly epistemological. Second, I have enframed these formative epistemological theories in the human lives—the preferences, enthusiasms, and fears—of those who constructed them. My view is that the pervasive value-context of all theorizing provided historically contingent, personal turning points in the path leading from ancient Greece to modern Europe. Things could have turned out otherwise. This is a philosophical thesis that I am attempting to illustrate in these historical chapters. Hence reading these chapters, even for those who are thoroughly versed in the standard facts about the rise of modern epistemology, should not be merely repetitive. For other readers, not expert but merely curious about how modern epistemology got where it is, the historical chapters should be full of fresh interest. For such general readers, for whom the book is meant to be fully accessible, I suggest reading in the order in which the parts are presented.

Read in one way or another, then, the following chapters will contain my best answer to the question, "Why do epistemology?"

Part One

Discovering the Epistemological Gap

2

ANCIENT KNOWERS

Epistemology has not always commanded center stage. Almost from the earliest days, philosophers discussed "knowing," and what it involves, but the full-dress subdiscipline of epistemology is a modern invention. Thus one may speak of the "epistemology" of Plato or Aristotle or St. Augustine, if one likes, but this extension of the word has a slightly anachronistic ring. Likewise, the tone of the skepticism that forced ancient philosophers to devote some attention to their claims for knowledge is not the same tone that epistemologists have had to counter in more recent years.

In the present chapter, I shall try to visit the ancient age without foisting fixed ideas of modernity onto the ancients. I hope to draw important lessons from this visit, especially about the close linkage between what is taken as "knowledge" and what is valued, preferred, embraced—sometimes consciously, sometimes not. My thesis in this chapter is that the standards ancient philosophers laid down as requirements for knowledge rested essentially on value-commitments. Further, my thesis in the book as a whole will be that this value-laden situation is inescapable, though the specific values that have in fact guided the course of Western epistemology were not inevitable. The influence of such values, in my view, is to be carefully considered, but the reality of their presence is not to be wondered at or worried about, though "value-free" modern epistemologists certainly may be expected to wonder and worry. Those moderns, however, omit something of the greatest importance when they try to remove the achievement of knowing from the sea of values—positive and negative—in which it is always immersed.

The power of knowing in humans is the power of getting things right about objects of thought. That is what is meant by calling knowing an achievement. But when there are questions of getting things right or wrong, there are at least implicit standards judging what "right" and "wrong" in this context shall mean. Every achievement is measured relative to a goal. If my goal in tossing horseshoes toward the opposite stake is simply to reach the general area (where they are being collected at the end of the day, for example), my achievement is measured by less stringent standards than if my goal is championship play. The norms of success depend in the first place on defining what game is being played. Thus, to take a different example, the same board with sixty-four squares can be the locus for a game of chess or a game of checkers. Depending on what is decided at the outset, different moves will be allowed or ruled impermissible. So will it be with knowing. The game must be named, the goals defined, the moves approved.

Those who came earliest to the board of human cognitive practice had the broadest scope for making these all-important definitions of what would count as the achievement of knowing. The overall cognitive goal, the legitimate intellectual methods, the shape and variety of the "pieces" to be allowed, and the nature of the "moves" permitted—all were at one time in need of being set up. Here is the usefulness of taking a historical start: by its means we can become better acquainted with the game inherited and modified by modern thinkers. And by its means we may position ourselves to reclaim important degrees of freedom in redefining knowing for our own transitional time, freedoms we might otherwise have overlooked.

PLATO AND HIS PREDECESSORS

When Plato (c. 428–347 B.C.) came of age, philosophically, he found himself in a thought-world in which different proposals for defining knowing were already vying for acceptance. In his more distant past were the works of thinkers including Heraclitus (c. 530–450 B.C.), of Ephesus in Asia Minor, and Parmenides (c. 515–460 B.C.), of Croton in Greek-speaking Italy. Each in practice grounded claims for knowledge in a different paradigm.

As we saw in *Being and Value* (30–31), Heraclitus stressed the ever-changing character of reality. He justified this vision by references to our experience of the flux of things. The flowing river, into which it is impossible ever to step twice, is his most famous example. Because of its constant swirl, the river is not the same river from moment to moment. We can watch its shifting sandbars, its crumbling banks, its ever-restless waters. In knowing the world as changing, we base this knowing on our common experience of the world, through our senses of sight and touch and hearing. *The implicit epistemic norm adopted by Heraclitus was such experience.* This cannot be naive experience, of course, since many things at first look and feel as if they are not changing at all. Naive experience is of both change and stability. But experience also provides a model for undeniable change that is nonetheless manifestly stable in appearance: a candle flame in a draft-free room. The flame burns, it is in constant change, but it retains its form. Even when it flickers, it returns to its shape. In flame we see flux manifesting form, and through it, by speculative extension, we can think the Logos that regulates the changing cosmos.

Parmenides was equally assured in his pronouncements, but as we saw in *Being and Value* (31–33), his assurance was directed to quite the opposite effect. The conceptual impossibility of thinking "nothing"—if there is a thought at all, it must be *of something*—makes certain that all phrases containing or implying negatives must be defective. But every thought of *change* implicitly contains the illicit attempt to think of nonbeing: *not*-any longer this, or *not*-yet that. Reality must be known as changeless (and unitary, indivisible, and eternal), since the contrary involves the impossible contradiction that "It is" can somehow include "It is not."

The implicit epistemic norm in Parmenides' definition of knowing has nothing to do with Heraclitus' reliance on experience. Quite the opposite. If Being turns out to be changeless, then experience does not give us knowledge at all, only what Parmenides called "The Way of Seeming." Knowing, therefore, must be entirely independent of experience; *its success should be judged, instead, on pure reason, the necessary requirements of thought itself.*

Plato was keenly aware of this great either/or—experience versus reason—but in his more recent past still another dispute raged, between his teacher, Socrates, and certain professional thinkers who were called "Wise," or Sophists. These two disputes, taken together, will help to interpret Plato's eventual resolutions on knowing.

SOPHISM

The Sophists rose in Greek society in response to immense cultural changes occurring in the turbulent second half of the fifth century B.C., as the increasingly pluralized organization of society in Greece (and the sustained contact between Greek and foreign cultures at the burgeoning edge of Asia and Europe) led, for the first time, to serious questioning of profound social ideas in religion, politics, and ethics. Such great framework-ideas had hitherto been simply "given," like laws of nature; but now different views could be considered, compared, debated.

Debate, in fact, was increasingly fundamental to prosperity among the citizens of city-states whose courts and legislatures were more and more open to persuasion. It is not surprising, in these circumstances, that teachers offering success in debate should appear, providing their services for hire to benefit the well-born and wealthy. The best known and most highly respected of these was Protagoras (c. 481–21 B.C.) of Abdera, an outpost of high Greek culture in relatively barbarous Thrace; he was an itinerant teacher in various city-states and advisor to Pericles (d. 429 B.C.) during the founding of the great Athenian democracy. His specialty was teaching politics, with particular emphasis on rhetorical powers of persuasion and on winning arguments. Moving from city to city, with different laws and customs, Protagoras had to adapt to his locations in order to achieve his goal.

The goal of knowing, for Protagoras (according to Plato's dialogue named for him), is learning what seems right and proper to a given society, thus *gaining skills in making the local system work*. This is highly relative, of course, but within the framework, there are important distinctions. Going from ignorance of one's political context to knowledge is going from a "worse" to a "better" condition (Plato 1937a: 318a). "And this is prudence in affairs private as well as public; he will learn to order his own house in the best manner, and he will be able to speak and act for the best in the affairs of the state" (Plato 1937a: 318d). Perhaps guided by his itinerant experience, Protagoras generalized a doctrine of complete relativism. His most famous dictum reads: "Man is the measure of all things, of those that are that they are, of those that are not that they are not" (Burnet 1961: Frag. 1; Plato 1937b: 152a). He seems to have been willing to interpret "man" both individually and collectively. On political and ethical matters, what matters is what people agree on, and here one may learn and prudently improve one's knowledge, moving from a worse to a better condition. On sensory impressions, in contrast, it is the individual person who "measures." If the wind appears cold to you it *is* cold; but if it appears warm to me it *is* warm (Plato 1937b: 152). Different measurers determine different outcomes, and beyond this there is no reason to argue. On matters of perception, we can both be right. Indeed, no one can possibly be wrong.

Knowing, for Protagoras, has a practical purpose. The implicit norm is attaining effective citizenship within one's political community. In the knowing-game that Protagoras proposes, there is no point in arguments among different communities. One functions as a citizen, after all, only in a single community. That is the relevant universe of cognition. And there is equally no point in arguing between perceivers who report different qualities of touch or vision or taste or smell. For them the world simply *is* known that way—and what difference could it possibly make? Why, given the goals of knowing set forth by this greatest of the Sophists, should one contend about such matters?

SOCRATES

Socrates (470–399 B.C.), Plato's beloved teacher, offered spirited answers to these rhetorical questions. He was deeply uneasy about any view in which ethics and religion would be taken as simply relative to the conventions of different societies.

As far as we can know the historical Socrates, his mission was grounded in a sense of spiritual calling that he did not take simply as a cultural option. His goal was to seek wisdom, not mere information. The goal of knowing for Socrates was *identifying the underlying common features of whatever was being discussed.* It is thanks to something in common that various instances, partially known, are grouped together. Merely collecting additional instances does not give understanding. Instead, penetrating intellectually to whatever it is they all share, by virtue of which they are all instances of the same thing, is the norm for knowing.

This is Socrates' goal in the dialogue, *Protagoras,* in which Plato depicts his mentor-hero as grappling with the relativizing epistemic norms of the great Sophist. The question begins as a challenge from Socrates as to whether "virtue" can be taught at all, as Protagoras claims to do for a living. Protagoras initially defends the view that the virtues are quite distinct from one another; in particular, he is carried by his pluralistic logic to the assertion that one can possess the virtue of courage without any of the others, such as temperance and justice. But in this sense of "teaching"—in which the various virtues have no intelligible common core (and must be learned not by understanding but merely by imitation and social contagion)—Socrates shows that virtue cannot be taught. Only if they share discussable common properties could they be the subject matter for teaching; but this would make them no longer just relative to different social conventions. Beneath all the superficial clutter of particular instances, this would make them universal.

Socrates enjoys the irony of finally coming around to the view that virtue *is*, in principle, capable of being taught (but only if it is something universal), while Protagoras is forced reluctantly to admit that unless a virtue is based on something *not* merely relative—specifically, a knowledge of "measurement" that can put in proper perspective the immediate appearances of things (what things are "really" larger or smaller, nearer or farther away, more or less painful or pleasurable in the long run)—it is no virtue. But this is to define "knowing" in a radically different sense from his original one. Man may be the "measurer" in Socrates' definition of knowing, but only via a *science* of measurement that orders and culls appearances; man is not the "measure" if that means all appearances must be infallible and accepted without correction.

Socrates puts his strongest riposte against the epistemic relativism of Protagoras in terms of human happiness, not metaphysics:

> Now suppose happiness to consist in doing or choosing the greater, and in not doing or in avoiding the less, what would be the saving principle

of human life? Would not the art of measuring be the saving principle; or would the power of appearance? Is not the latter that deceiving art which makes us wander up and down and take the things at one time of which we repent at another, both in our actions and in our choice of things great and small? But the art of measurement would do away with the effect of appearances, and, showing the truth, would fain teach the soul at last to find rest in the truth, and would thus save our life (Plato 1937a: 356c).

From this it is a short step to extort from the unhappy Sophist another admission: "What would be the saving principle of our lives? Would not knowledge?—a knowledge of measuring, when the question is one of excess and defect . . . ? The world will assent, will they not?" (Plato 1937a: 357a).

Plato's Protagoras does assent, though whether the historical Protagoras would have done so is an open question. The rules for the use of "knowledge" have so changed from those Protagoras would have endorsed that it is little wonder Plato concludes the dialogue showing the distinguished Sophist at first merely nodding, then refusing altogether to reply. In Socrates' knowing-game, the goal is a science of objective measurement in ethical matters. The cognitive rules have shifted again.

PLATO

Plato (c. 428–347 B.C.) was the decisive personality who more than any other established philosophy's rules of knowing, for his time and for centuries to follow. Originally named Aristocles, and noted as a wrestler in his youth, Plato probably earned his famous name from the breadth (*platos* in Greek means "broad") of his powerful shoulders. On those shoulders came to rest the principal knowing-game of Western civilization.

Scion of a wealthy family of aristocrats, whose futile efforts in having opposed a victorious democratic regime undermined their political effectiveness in Athens during Plato's lifetime, he was quick to see and condemn the ephemerality of mere public opinion. The traditional values of Athenian society could surely not, for Plato, be just one more product of political agreement, as easily swept away as the straw arguments tossed together by demagogues intent on currying favor with the fickle public. Something more solidly knowable, timeless, and universal must undergird genuine virtue.

When dealing with one of the great genius figures of all time, it is hard to separate what actually happened from what might have happened to the story of epistemology if Plato had not been born and raised an aristocrat. There were many other contingencies that might have turned the early course of things in different directions. What if the times had not been so turbulent?

What if, that is, the traditions of high Greek culture had not been seriously threatened in Plato's time by the forces of brash, young democrats and hired Sophists? Then no need for elaborate defenses of absolutes would have been felt; or, at least, a lessened sense of "us against them," cast typically in partisan "either/or" attitudes, might have encouraged Plato to pay more attention to shades of gray. What if Plato had not fallen in with Socrates, learning to admire the master's unwavering commitment to conceptual constants beneath the many, conflicting mores of the time? And, still more intriguing: What if Socrates' jury had acted—with the change of just a few votes—to acquit the old eccentric? Then the world-denying overtones of the dungeon cell might not have informed Plato's attitudes toward body versus mind, the senses versus the truth. Instead of discontinuities, Plato might have emphasized continuities. As we shall see, in some moods he actually came close to doing just this.

But as it was, Plato watched with horror as the forces of democracy falsely condemned his beloved Socrates, a great, good man, to death. In the *Apology*, Plato makes it plain that Socrates' hapless legal prosecutors failed to have the least shred of a case. The "old accusers," ignorance and prejudice, were the real danger. The jurors voted to condemn from mere opinion. There was such a thing as the truth of this matter, but the legal system, though formally correct in its procedure, substantively failed to acquire knowledge of it. Proper knowing, use of the "science of measurement" that Socrates had argued for, might have saved a life and prevented tragedy for Athens.

Irony of ironies, Socrates was convicted, in part, because he was ignorantly confused with people like Protagoras! Plato was determined that this confusion would be exposed and corrected, and that his great master would be seen forever as on the side of cognitive ideals completely at variance from those of the Sophists. When he eventually took his stylus to create the dialogues through which we see the Socrates of Plato's maturing ideals, "Socrates," the character, is often drawn even further from the position of the Sophists than he may have been in life.

To highlight these epistemic ideals, we may quickly visit six of Plato's dialogues with a limited set of questions in mind: What did Plato stipulate to be the *goal* of the knowing enterprise? What were the *rules* governing the legitimate *methods* that could be used to reach this goal? What does his text reveal about the key *values* lying behind and expressed through the stipulations he made—values that were thus determinative of the theory of knowing that emerged as his legacy? This account, with its limited purpose, will leave much aside. But raising just these issues to sharper awareness will be important for moderns in quest of a map showing where we have come from and what paths might be open for the future.

1. *Protagoras.* I have already cited the *Protagoras*, in which Plato challenges the Sophist claim that virtue can be taught (in their way) by asking what is really teachable and, consequently, what is knowable. The latter, we saw, could not be reduced to momentary "seemings," as Protagoras' extreme relativism of the present moment would allow. It had to be something more secure, amenable to a *science of measurement* in which the distortions of perspective—what is "really" large and small, more painful or pleasurable— can be corrected. Such a science would be the "saving principle of human life." In that phrase we encounter a value judgment of the more urgent sort. Something more stable than the momentary appearances of things is vital ("saving"!) in the conduct of life. The goal of the knowing activity must be *reliable across time and change*, something that puts the flux of what appears to us in firm perspective. In this, the goal of knowing is that human experience should *be measured*, rather than *being the measure*.

2. *Meno.* The same issue, the teachability of virtue, is also taken up in another dialogue, the *Meno*, dating from what was probably the same relatively early period of Plato's writing. In some ways this encounter with Meno, the handsome young aristocrat, goes considerably farther than *Protagoras* in defining the goal of the knowing-game.

After the initial discussion of the underlying character of virtue, which reminds us of *Protagoras*, the haughty Meno becomes sore about Socrates' repeated successes in exposing him as far from expert on the subject he had assumed himself to be an authority. His tongue, he complains, has been "numbed" by Socrates' touch—as though by the flat-faced electric catfish of the Nile, with which he unflatteringly compares Socrates' appearance. Out of pique he challenges the worth of the very process of inquiry itself. How can one inquire, he asks, unless one already knows the answer one is seeking? If one *does not know* the answer, then how could one ever recognize it as the proper stopping place of the inquiry? But if one *does know* the answer, then what is the point of inquiring, since it is already known?

This challenge to the value of the search for knowledge is so fundamental for Plato that he depicts Socrates as dropping his usual ironic stance and taking a firm position favoring the cognitive quest. At the end of the interlude in which the challenge is considered and met, Socrates declares:

> Some things I have said of which I am not altogether confident. But that we shall be better and braver and less helpless if we think that we ought to enquire, than we should have been if we indulged in the idle fancy that there was no knowing and no use in seeking to know what we do not know;—that is a theme upon which I am ready to fight, in word and deed, to the utmost of my power (Plato 1985a: 86b).

What, then, is the goal that we are told is so important to fight for in word and deed? It is shown by the experiment Socrates conducts with Meno's uneducated slave boy. Socrates leads the youth to come, *by himself*, to the discovery of the Pythagorean Theorem, that the square of the hypotenuse of a right triangle is equal to the sum of the squares of the other two sides. He does this by letting the boy try out wrong answers and discover that they give false results, until finally the youngster tries the correct answer (with corresponding diagram, drawn on the ground) and *sees for himself* that this answer is *necessarily* correct. There is no other conceivable way to create a square containing double the area of a given square but to build the new square with sides equal to the *diagonal* of the original square (the hypotenuse of its internal triangle). True, Socrates suggests various strategies of answering and leads the boy to recognize their failure when they fail. But suggesting is not telling. False trails may be suggested by a stimulating teacher, not just the correct one. The slave boy learns that he cannot lean on Socrates for the answers. He must take responsibility for answering concerning what he himself sees. At the start, the boy is ignorant of the answer he seeks; at the end, he succeeds in knowing, because he has personally seen the necessity, the could-not-have-been-otherwise, of the knowledge he has attained.

This is the goal Plato sets for authentic knowledge and with the goal comes the method. The game is defined in terms of conceptual necessities, truths that could not be false. The certainties involved are not just what we would today call "psychological" certitudes. Meno suffered from this sort of certitude about his understanding of virtue; and his slave boy also felt sure, at the start, that doubling the area of a square could be achieved by doubling the length of the sides. But both turned out to be mistaken. Therefore such "certainty," whether based on inflated ego or complete inexperience, does not count for Plato as the legitimate achievement of knowing. The sort of certainty that is the mark of success must be, rather, the *certainty of being compelled by the idea in question to acknowledge its power of self-evidence.* To contemplate such necessity is to acknowledge it. And to "ac*know*ledge" in this sense is to know. Nothing less will do. The game must be played to the highest standard, Plato insists, or no achievement will be worthy of the laurel crown. Thus *goal* and *method* and *rule* all reflect the same unflinching *valuing* of perfect certainty.

3. *Phaedo.* This dialogue has a somber setting: the prison where Socrates is due to die on that very day, condemned by public ignorance and malice to drink the poison hemlock for no real crime. But Plato depicts Socrates as cheerful, even looking forward to his impending journey to the next world. In such a context, intent on defending love of eternal wisdom even in the face of injustice and impending death, Plato leaned toward discounting

the importance of the body and its organic role in the knowing activity. In such a mood, it is possible to turn with revulsion against bodily experience altogether as a distraction and obstacle to knowing under its ideal definition. As Plato's Socrates says:

> so long as we have the body accompanying our reason in its inquiries, so long as our souls are befouled by this evil admixture, we shall assuredly never fully possess that which we desire, to wit truth. For by reason of the nurture which it must have, the body makes countless demands upon us, and furthermore any sickness that may befall it hampers our pursuit of true being. Then too it fills us with desires and longings and fears and imaginations of all sorts, and such quantities of trash, that, as the common saying puts it, we really never have a moment to think about anything because of the body (Plato 1985b: 66b).

Still, these are only arguments from distraction. The body is indeed a bother. But is this all? No, there is another still more powerful reason to rule out employing the bodily senses in the enterprise of knowing. The necessary, self-luminous object of contemplation that is the goal of the knowing activity can never, in principle, be a product of our imperfect, relative, and changing senses. We have, to use Plato's example, never actually seen a physical object that is *absolutely* equal to another. If we look closely enough, there are always tiny inequalities. Still, we must have a fully functioning conception of "equality," or we could not be aware that every approximate equality falls short of what we have never physically seen.

What we cannot *see*, it turns out, we can nevertheless *think*. We can think about perfect circles even though we can never draw one, certainly not one good enough to withstand scrutiny under all possible magnifications. Therefore, somehow we must have nonsensuous access to such perfect ideas. This might well remind us of Meno's slave boy, who had not been taught the theorem that, under Socratic prodding, he discovered he knew. The kind of learning process that the slave boy went through makes for a mystery. How did he come by his knowledge and how did he eventually know he knew? The boy was not "told" that this was the final answer; when he saw it, the solution simply commended itself to him with indisputable force. It is as though it were something that he had known but forgotten, then once again recognized.

The theory of recollection, only hinted at in *Meno*, now in *Phaedo* returns to give a value-drenched metaphysical account of how the nonsensuous acquisition of certain perfect ideas is possible: through recollection. The soul knew—was in direct contemplative contact with—all these eternal ideas before its birth, then forgot them on entering flesh. Now, when approximations appear in experience, these can bring back to mind the original perfection for our renewed contemplation and acknowledgment. As Plato puts the matter, "So it necessarily follows that we knew the equal at a time previous to that first sight of equal objects which led us to conceive all these as striving to be like *the* equal, but defectively succeeding" (Plato 1985b: 75a). And thus, with one great speculation, Plato defends the desired conclusion that the soul must be immortal (or at least, at this point in the argument, preexistent) and offers an account of the method by which we come to know perfect ideas that could never be acquired by imperfect sense.

4. *Symposium.* The oppressive atmosphere of "death row" carries with it certain value-preoccupations in *Phaedo* that tend, as we have seen, to marginalize the legitimacy of using bodily methods in quest of knowing. This is not Plato's only atmosphere, however. In his *Symposium*, we are introduced to the jolly setting of a wine party and to tipsy praises of the god of love. Death and its overcoming are no longer the intellectual context; life and sex, rather, are on the minds of those gathered for the night's carouse. It is not surprising, therefore, that the place of the body in knowing has a higher value here.

Plato speaks through the wise woman, Diotima, shown as instructing a young Socrates in the nature of love. Erotic attraction, she shows him, is always of and for the beautiful, and ultimately for the eternal Beauty itself. It is not always obvious to the erotically aroused that this is so. They (including animals) may simply lust to mate; but behind even the most primitive urges is the quest for beauty and immortality. "Are you unaware," Diotima asks Socrates,

> that every beast, footed or winged, is so affected, when it desires to beget, that it becomes sick from love? They first want to have intercourse with each other, and next to nurture the offspring which are born (Plato 1985c: 207b–8b).

In the same way, humans seek immortal beauty even when attracted to the particular beautiful bodies around them. The power of eros draws at first toward beautiful individuals and then keeps drawing toward ever higher and more nearly perfect manifestations of beauty as the lover matures in appreciation. First seen as particular, beauty then appears as something present in many bodies, not identical to any of them. "When once he grasps this, he is ordained as a lover of all beautiful bodies and relaxes his passion for any single one. . . . After this, he will come to believe that beauty in souls is more to be valued than bodily beauty. . . . [Next] he may be constrained in turn to contemplate the beauty of laws and practices, and to see that everything itself by itself is akin, in order that he may deem bodily beauty a small thing" (Plato 1985c: 210c).

From the beauty of laws and practices this lover will be lifted still further by the power of eros to appreciate the beauty of various kinds of knowledge. And from this, by philosophical discipline, the lover will at last come to apprehend and appreciate what is meant by absolute beauty itself. "Whoever is tutored in the mysteries of Eros up to this point and learned to contemplate beautiful things in due and proper order, will then, suddenly, in an instant, reach the goal of the mysteries and see a marvelous thing—the nature of beauty. It is that, Socrates, for the sake of which all previous labors existed" (Plato 1985c: 210e).

In neither *Phaedo* nor *Symposium* does Plato take bodily perception as the locus of knowing. The goal remains intellectual contemplation, as in the epiphany of Meno's slave boy. Nor is there any necessary contradiction between Plato of the *Phaedo* and Plato of the *Symposium*, since in both cases physical perception has some role to play: in the former, sense functions to "remind" the soul of what it once knew with perfect clarity; in the latter, sense functions to "draw" the soul toward the ultimate goal. In *Phaedo*, perception offers at best "defective success," though it is a kind of success. In *Symposium*, perception of particulars needs to be left behind and bodily beauty needs to be deemed in comparison "a small thing." But though not strictly contradictory, the values of the two dialogues pull in different directions. The *Phaedo*, with its background the imminence of death, suggests that the body is a prison happily escaped. The *Symposium*, with its atmosphere of wine and love-talk, suggests that through the body (if only the would-be knower is well tutored to contemplate beautiful things in "proper order") a positive path to knowing can be traced. There seems little doubt that both these vectors were present in Plato's approach to knowing at this early point in the history of thought. It should not be surprising, however, that followers later would feel the need to rule more definitively on the legitimacy of perception.

5. *Republic*.   Plato himself further clarifies these tensions in his great *Republic*. Both in his diagram of the Divided Line and in his Parable of the Cave, the relations between the physical, perceptual offerings of experience and the mental, conceptual domain of thinking are laid out in some detail. If we examine both of these with an eye especially for the values implicit in Plato's treatments of these matters, we shall see still more clearly the commitments and preferences implicit in his definition of knowing.

The Divided Line itself is laid out, Plato is careful to specify, in two unequal segments (which I have distinguished with a double line in the diagram below); then each segment is divided again into similarly unequal parts.

I arranged them vertically, since Plato repeatedly refers to the "higher" and "lower" parts of the line and to "rising" or "moving down" levels. The two lower segments together represent the "visible order" of things (Plato 1954: 509e), while the two greater and higher represent the "intelligible." The lowest and least segment of all (A) is stipulated as standing for the direct material of physical perception, that is, images, reflections, shadows (what we might group together as appearances); the next higher and greater segment (B) is let to stand for "the actual things of which the first are likenesses" (Plato 1954: 510a), both natural and artificial objects of all kinds.

Across the great divide between the visible and the intelligible is the important segment (C), at which intellectual objects "high and low" are found,

COGNITIVE OBJECT		COGNITIVE PROCESS	
(D)	pure theory	knowing	
(C)	visualizable models	thinking	
			THE INTELLIGIBLE
(B)	things	believing	THE VISIBLE
(A)	images	imaging	

formal ideas which nevertheless are visualizable or representable in perceptual terms, such as the models and examples used in geometry or in many domains of empirical science. Ultimately, at the top of the scale and greatest of all (since Plato does not specify a ratio, I have felt free to depict it as much larger, in keeping with his extremely high regard for what it contains), we find pure theory (D), beyond the possibility of perceptual representation even by the best of models or diagrams. I have taken a small liberty here by calling the process at this level "knowing," since strictly speaking Plato uses a special technical term of his own, "dialectic"; but my use of "knowing" seems justified, since Plato, too, summarizes by using knowledge-language.

> We shall be satisfied, then, with the names we gave earlier to our four divisions: first, knowledge; second, thinking; third, belief; and fourth, imagining (Plato 1954: 534a).

Plato's low regard for the direct deliverances of perception is evident from one look at this famous diagram. They are relegated to the bottom, and they are least valuable. By themselves they are disorderly, changing, confusing, ephemeral, relatively unclear (though Plato admits of gradations in quality from the merest of shadows to sharply etched reflections on polished surfaces)—in general, they represent the dregs of cognition, shading off indefinitely into utter unintelligibility. Plato's strong negative judgment on unclear experience, as we shall see, persists into modern epistemology and disposes virtually everyone after him to adopt theories that are strongly biased against the physical as opposed to conceptual elements in experience—favoring what human beings are especially good at, demeaning what we share with other animals. (I challenge this value-laden judgment in Part Three, and this challenge forms the basis for my proposed alternative theory of experiencing and knowing.)

Luckily, according to Plato, we humans are able to move up a level from (A) to (B), rising above the murky domain of image-appearances by providing them with the unifying idea of a "something" of which they are the insubstantial appearings. If I simply experience images, for example, of different sides of a coin—appearances of its edge (looking much like a straight line), appearances of it half-rotated (looking like a parabola), straight-on appearances of it from its "heads" or "tails" side (looking much like the full moon)—this provides just a plethora of confusing and inconsistent imagery. But if I add a *belief* that there is also an actual thing, a coin, behind all these images, giving them unity and assuring their stable sequences as the actual thing is rotated, the images are made more intelligible, since they have been drawn together in thought as common effects of one cause.

To the appropriately cautious, just believing in things hardly explains anything. It is only by rising to the next level (C), beyond the visible to the intelligible, that we are able to invoke underlying explanations of the stable sequences of coin-appearances themselves, as they are accounted for by geometrical laws of perspective (for example) taken together with laws about the reflective properties of metals, laws dealing with the rectilinear propagation of light, and so forth. These laws, however, all utilize empirical, visualizable models. What explains and unifies all these laws themselves? To rise to level (D), to the achievement of knowing in the full sense, Plato declares that

> by "unaided reasoning" we mount all the way to something that is not hypothetical, the first principle of all; and having grasped this, may turn back and, holding on to the consequences which depend upon it, descend at last to a conclusion, never making use of any sensible object, but only of Forms, moving through Forms from one to another, and ending with Forms (Plato 1954: 511b).

Knowing in the full sense, then, is achieved through—and is of—Forms alone, the perfect, eternal, self-luminously intelligible objects of intelligence. Perceptual images play a diminishing role in cognition through the first three stages: (1) as merely given, (2) as unified by being attributed to believed-in things, and (3) as made understandable by scientific laws and models of a visualizable sort. But at the acme of knowing, perception disappears from the enterprise. In some ways, the gap between segment (C) and (D) turns out to be even greater than the gap between (B) and (C). And, indeed, in this highest level we come face to face with the ineffable. Concepts and language, not merely images, start also to fail in upper reaches of this rarefied atmosphere.

At this point, we should mix in the rich value-suggestions contained in Plato's closely related Parable of the Cave (Plato 1954: 514–17). The story itself is steeped in, and reinforces, just the values that were implicit in the Divided Line: that is, the physical senses are "low" and degrading, while universal ideas are "high" and ennobling. The parable begins in a cavernous underground chamber in which Plato describes what would, in reality, be a horrifying scene. We discover people in the cave who have been prisoners all their lives, chained at their legs and necks (to keep them from looking around) and forced in this demeaning way to stare straight ahead at shadows projected on the cavern wall before them. The shadows are cast by artificial objects— copies made from wood, etc., of people and animals—moved by concealed puppeteers in front of a fire burning behind a parapet that conceals their own shadows. The puppeteers add dialogue, as appropriate, to their shadow play, and the echo of their voices from the cavern wall makes it seem to the prisoners that the shadows are speaking. They are not only prisoners, they are also victims of systematic deception.

One of these prisoners is suddenly freed and "forced" to stand up and turn around. His eyes, accustomed to darkness, ache in the dazzle of the fire, and of course he fails to recognize the objects whose shadows he had previously followed. He is confused and longs to escape back to his chains. But instead he is dragged "forcibly up the steep and rugged ascent" (Plato 1954: 515d) until he is pushed out of the cave and into the sunlight above. Here he is even more dazzled, at first blinded by the sun and able at best to make out shadows and reflections. But gradually his eyes adjust. He can make out real things, of which he previously had only seen the shadows of imitations. In due course he is able to look at the heavenly bodies at night and, finally, to discover the sun itself shining, full of warmth and light, in its own domain. Now he is aware of the source of life, warmth, and visibility itself, and of the realities that are merely being copied in the cave. At last he realizes the deception that had been foisted on him and all the others.

If the former prisoner should be generous enough to go down again into the cave to tell his former comrades what he has discovered, it is unlikely they would receive him well. They have focused on the shadows all their lives; in their society they are esteemed for their capacity to predict the sequence of these changing shadows. The returning visionary is handicapped by having been in the sun. He is now less adept at the knowing-game the prisoner community has defined. The others mock and reject his reports of another possible definition. "They would laugh at him and say that he had gone up only to come back with his sight ruined; it was worth no one's while even to attempt the ascent. If they could lay hands on the man who was trying to set them free and lead them up, they would kill him" (Plato 1954: 517a).

Plato's epistemic values lie entirely exposed in this parable. Sense perception is deceitful, likened to the mere shadow of a cutout copy. The knowing-game most people play, merely predicting empirical events with maximum possible accuracy, is based on ignorance enforced by imprisonment in our flesh. People ought to be far more interested in what lies behind the events, and still more in what is responsible for and explanatory of all events—what is beyond all events. This can only be attained by disentangling oneself from the flickering shadows of sense perception and rising to appreciate the steadiness of the heavens, especially the single effulgent source of life and illumination itself. Knowing is contemplation and acknowledgment of the necessary, the eternal, the perfect, the One.

At this point, we are reminded strongly of Parmenides, whose views, we noted, were part of Plato's philosophical heritage. Plato, however, has here moved beyond Parmenides in a crucial way, insisting on something Parmenides himself did not supply: a place in the cognitive universe for what

Heraclitus identified as constant flux. Since, as we saw in *Being and Value* (32), the only possible true assertion for Parmenides is limited to "It is," he had been forced to remain silent on the question how the Way of Seeming could even *seem* to be. Worse, Parmenides could make no attempt to link the Way of Seeming—full of plurality and change—with the Way of Truth— single, immutable, eternal. The two Ways had no connection with one another, and the vital goal of unity in knowing was thereby lost. Plato, at least, offered a diagram and a parable to connect the eternal One with the shifting multiplicity of experience. We may well wonder, however, whether the appearance of connectedness is real or illusory. Perhaps Plato's effective emphasis was more on "divided" than "line." In giving homage to Parmenides at the top of the line, the bottom of the line becomes once again outside the scope of understanding.

This is because at the top of the line the Form of the Good is beyond discourse; it is the unifier of all multiplicity, the Form of all Forms. Therefore at its fullest, knowing is ineffable. Words break thoughts up; sentences distinguish subjects from predicates, nouns from adjectives. The vision of the ultimate, if it is to be perfect, eternal, and absolutely one, cannot be communicated in words. This ineffability theme in Plato's epistemology will become important in the Middle Ages, as we shall see. But the more the Parmenidean side of Plato is victorious, the less ordinary perception can be seen to play a coherent role in human knowing.

6. *Theaetetus.* Later, in his *Theaetetus*, Plato struggled again with the problem of defining the notion of the "account" needed to distinguish genuine knowledge from mere right opinion. He came to no positive conclusion on that score, though he made headway on other issues important to his successors. Under no circumstances, he shows, could perception be confused with knowledge. That is reinforced. Those epistemic rules stand. None the less, Plato struggles to avoid making the distinction an absolute separation. We perceive through organs suited for specific objects, that is, colors for the eyes, sounds for the ears, smells for the nose, etc.—and yet we are able to compare the different senses in regard to shared attributes, like vividness, difference, multiplicity, etc., which are not given through any particular sense alone. They are the "common" sensibles, which seem to be more at home in thought than sense, and yet to be present throughout the sensible world, as well. Sense perception is not thoughtless; thought seems not entirely senseless. With such themes Heraclitus could have been comfortable; Parmenides did not, after all, wholly triumph.

Continuing to wrestle with the interplay between bodily perception and mental contemplation, and continuing to puzzle over differing degrees of dignity on the "lower" end of the epistemic ladder—these were Plato's undying epistemic bequests to his successors. The first was his student, Aristotle.

ARISTOTLE AND HIS SUCCESSORS

Aristotle's early years were spent, like Plato's, in the company of nobility; but unlike Plato, Aristotle was the scion not of a ruling family but of a court physician. His father, Nicomachus, was a prominent medical doctor in Stagira, a Greek-speaking city in Macedonia, where Aristotle was born in 384 B.C. During Aristotle's childhood, Nicomachus moved the family to Pella, the royal seat of the Macedonian king, Amyntas II, to become the king's physician. There Aristotle came to know Amyntas's son and heir, Philip. On his parents' untimely death, the youthful Aristotle returned to guardians in Stagira until he was sent, at about age seventeen, to Plato's Academy in Athens.

He was a member of the Academy for twenty years, until Plato's death in 347 B.C., but was not one of those to share Plato's penchant for the absolute, mathematical side of knowing. When the Academy's leadership passed to the mathematicizers, Aristotle left Athens for the island of Lesbos, where he engaged for several years in biological research, more in keeping with his temperament. While on Lesbos, he was called by Philip II of Macedonia, who had meanwhile succeeded his father to the throne, to return to Pella as tutor for Philip's teen-aged son, Alexander. After three years tutoring the future Alexander the Great, Aristotle returned to Stagira for five more years of quiet research before moving back to Athens in 335 B.C. to found his own school, the Lyceum. The welcome in Athens for those with Macedonian associations, however, became quite cold in 323 B.C., when emperor Alexander died. Aristotle felt the need to withdraw for his own safety and died an exile in the next year at the age of sixty-two.

The value attached to knowing, for Aristotle, is second to none. He opens his great *Metaphysics* with the declaration: "All men by nature have a desire for knowledge" (Aristotle 1951a: 67). But clearly, "knowing" must have a different set of overtones in this new context, since in the next sentence Aristotle goes on to use sense perception, not contemplation of mathematical truths, as the first instance of the natural desire for knowledge. He writes:

> An indication of this is the joy we take in our perceptions, which we cherish for their own sakes, quite apart from any benefits they may yield us. This is especially true of sight, which we tend to prefer to all the other senses even when it points to no action, and even indeed when no action is in prospect; a preference explained by the greater degree to which sight promotes knowledge by revealing so many differences among things (Aristotle 1951a: 67).

Here is no looking askance, as Plato would have preferred, at the body's sensory access to the world of becoming. We take joy in perception; we cherish the senses for their own sakes; we like it best when we are able to discriminate the greatest multitude of differences within our sensory fields.

Aristotle goes even further to ground human knowing in the same soil as animals, who also have perception and in some cases memory, allowing learning. It is this combination of perception and memory that gives rise to experience (*empeiria*) in humans, and to a certain degree this capacity is shared by some of the beasts. Humans can go beyond such experience to art (*technē*) and reason (*logismos*), but experience remains an important cognitive phenomenon. Here Aristotle calls on one of many characteristic examples from medicine.

> To make the judgment that when Callicles was ill of a certain disease a certain remedy was beneficial, and to make a similar judgment about Socrates, and so on, is a matter of experience. Art would consist rather in judging that the remedy is beneficial for all persons of a given type who are suffering from a given disease—e.g., for phlegmatic or bilious people suffering from fever. From a practical standpoint experience may well be quite as good as art; indeed we often see men of experience succeeding better than those who have theory [*logos*] without experience. The reason for this is that experience is knowledge of particulars, art of universals, and that actions and their effects are always particular (Aristotle 1951a: 68).

Here writes the loyal son of a doctor, who has seen what he has seen in the successful practice of a skilled empiric, however orthodox or not it might be to refer to "knowledge of particulars."

Still, those who know both universal truths and particular cases are still more to be admired. Aristotle, after all, is an adopted son also of Plato's Academy. The knowledge of particulars may be of value, especially practically, "Nevertheless we think of knowledge and understanding as belonging rather to art than to experience, and we judge artists [*technitēs*] to be wiser than mere empirics on the ground that wisdom must always involve some knowledge. Empirics know *that* something is, but not *why* it is; artists, on the other hand, know the why and the reason [*aitia*]" (Aristotle 1951a: 68). This is the superiority of the educated over mere laborers, since "in any craft we regard master-craftsmen as more estimable and as having a wiser understanding of their craft than manual workers because they know the reasons why things are done, whereas we look on manual workers as analogous to those inanimate things which act without knowing what they do, as fire burns for instance, the only difference being that inanimate things behave as they do by nature, manual workers by habit" (Aristotle 1951a: 68–69).

Quite aside from snobbery (something that might be anticipated in slave-supported Athens), this passage does show a tension with Aristotle's earlier apparent desire to remain fair to empirics. But certainly physicians who work case by case cannot be confused with drone laborers who "act without knowing what they do," mere habituated imitators of inanimate forces. Empirical medicine's "knowledge of particulars" may not be up to the level of genuine "art," but it is a respectable variety of knowledge. Perhaps we see here a tension in Aristotle's own value-intuitions: between, on the one side, his acknowledgment of the importance of concrete experience in cognition, and, on the other, his learned admiration for the unique power of the universal. It is through the universal that we teach, as Plato held in *Meno*, *Protagoras*, and elsewhere. "Broadly speaking," Aristotle agrees, "what distinguishes the man who knows from the ignorant man is an ability to teach, and this is why we hold that art and not experience has the character of 'genuine knowledge' [*epistēmē*]—namely, that artists can teach and others . . . cannot" (Aristotle 1951a: 69).

Still, the standards of inquiry are for Aristotle quite flexible. The mark of an educated person is to demand only the appropriate degree of precision in any area of study. In his *Nicomachean Ethics*, he contrasts what should be the cognitive goals in, say, statecraft as contrasted with subject areas with more perfectly luminous starting points. "Excellence," and "justice," and even "good" are so filled with uncertainty in ordinary discourse, he points out, that "they come to be looked on as mere conventions, having no natural foundation" (Aristotle 1951b: 159).

> In such matters, then, and starting from such premises as we do, we must be content with a rough approximation to the truth; for when we are dealing with and starting out from what holds good only "as a general rule," the conclusions that we reach will have the same character. Let each of the views put forward be accepted in this spirit, for it is the mark of an educated mind to seek only so much exactness in each type of inquiry as may be allowed by the nature of the subject-matter (Aristotle 1951b: 159).

But this principle of flexibility works both ways. Where circumstances prevent the fullest degree of cognitive precision, there we must show our education by accepting the best we can get. Where circumstances allow maximum rigor, however, we are remiss if we do not insist on a maximal definition of knowing. "It is equally wrong to accept probable reasoning from a mathematician and to demand strict demonstrations from an orator" (Aristotle 1951b: 159).

When it comes to defining maximal knowing, Aristotle shows himself a faithful son of Plato's Academy. The very words he uses for theoretical knowledge, *epistēmē theōrētikē* (Aristotle 1951c: 147), carry the flavor of vision. The Greek *theōría* has as its primary meaning "a looking at, viewing, beholding, observing (Liddell & Scott 1953: 317). The mental vision that is full knowing is self-luminous, necessary, universal, and perfect.

Aristotle never doubts that we can in fact have such knowledge, but how do we make the transition from lesser approximations—from experience to art and finally to this highest achievement of full knowing? Aristotle cannot accept Plato's account, invoking the soul's supposed prior direct contemplation of the ideal Forms, before birth, since (as we saw in *Being and Value* (58–59), he gives no credence to independent, absolute existence of the Forms at all. How then? In reply, Aristotle provides what might today be called a "naturalized epistemology." He gives an account of the process by which information from the world turns to knowledge in the mind.

All such accounts rest on a view of what is and is not real. As I showed in some detail in *Being and Value* (60), Aristotle accepted Plato's key doctrine, developed in *Timaeus*, that the world is made up of universal qualities embodied and particularized in the receptacle of space-time. Without Plato's mythic context, the important things remain for Aristotle. The universal Forms, including sensory qualities (like the color red) as well as more abstruse characters (like "equality" and "circularity") are real *in* the things they characterize. Real things are *hylomorphic*, made up of a matter-component and a form-component. This is as much the case for perceivers and thinkers, like us, as it is for all other particular substances. Our defining qualities—as living beings capable of self-nourishment, reproduction, locomotion, sensation, and reason—constitute our real essence, our soul. But that is the same as our form, expressing our primary characteristics. Our form is nothing other than our soul; and our soul is nothing other than our personal form, embodied in the living flesh that gives it its definite character.

Among its characteristic functions, the living (ensouled) human body receives information from the world around it through its sense organs. In his *Psychology*, Aristotle adopts Plato's advance in *Theaetetus*, agreeing that the various sense organs receive qualities unique to themselves. The eyes are capable of light and colors, the ears pitch and tone, the nose odors, the tongue sweet and salty flavors, the touch temperature and textures. These are the "special sensibles" appropriate to the different organs. These "sensibles," whatever they may be, are all both particular (in their embodiment here and now) and universal (in their capability of being present at indefinitely many places and times). The very same foul odor, yesterday, today, or tomorrow can cause our nose to wrinkle in disgust. The very same shade of red can be present in limitless numbers of apples at the same time.

This capacity of universals to be independent of specific times and places allows them to enter our bodies—without leaving the substances that continue to embody them in the world around us—through the organs capable of receiving them. This is the foundation of Aristotle's theory of sensation. The *very same* form—a particular shade of red in an apple, for example—is in the external substance *and* in the living sense organ of the perceiver. This means that there can be a qualitative identity despite nonidentical embodiments. The specific shade of red, R, is the same shade whether it is in the apple, where it exists as R_{apple}, or in the eye, where it exists as R_{eye}. In general, Aristotle says, "we must understand by 'sense' [*aesthēsis*] that which can receive the sensible forms of things without their matter, as wax receives the imprint of a signet-ring without receiving the iron or gold of which it is made" (Aristotle 1951c: 134). The difference between wax and a sense organ, however, is that wax takes on the form of what impresses it in a wholly insentient way; what makes sense organs special is that theirs is a living matter capable of receiving forms that are perceptible by the organism. Air, for example, must be acted on by odors if odors are to be wafted to our waiting noses. But air is "merely" acted on by odors. The difference between the two sorts of acting-upon, Aristotle says, is "that smelling is simultaneously an act of perceiving, whereas air, when acted upon by an odor, does not itself perceive the odor but is merely thereby made perceptible to sense" (Aristotle 1951c: 136). The crucial difference, then, is in the immediate experience in living perceivers, equipped with sense organs empowered with the capacity for sensing the disembodied characteristics of things. Air and wax do not have such experience; perceivers do.

But mere "immediate experience" of sensible qualities falls considerably short of the rich sort of encounter that human beings have with their world, filled with recognizable objects and predictable happenings, memories, and expectations. The next step toward full knowledge comes, for Aristotle, with the recognition of the place of mind in sense perception. As we saw above, Plato before him had noticed elements of perception that seem not to be limited to the "special sensibles" of the individual senses. Aristotle builds on this insight, identifying "common sensibles" as movement and rest, figure and magnitude, number and unity (Aristotle 1951c: 137). These are not themselves colors, odors, textures, tastes, or sounds, but they are perceived in conjunction with these special sensibles. We can perceive motion, for example, through sight and touch and sound. We can perceive magnitude by taste and smell as well as by the other three. We notice these distinct characteristics just because we have a number of different special senses through which the same forms are experienced, though they are not the exclusive objects of sight or of hearing or of any other particular organ.

At the level of simple sensation, while it lasts, the perceiver is not likely to err, Aristotle holds. But falsity enters the picture with the higher perceptual capacities. The common sensibles of motion or magnitude, for example, can be and often are wrongly perceived, as when we are deceived by a trick of lighting or perspective. Here "perceiving *as*" has overtaken mere perceiving, and it becomes clear that imagination and thought are mixing with sensation.

So long as each sense merely perceives its own special objects, its perception is true, or subject to a minimum of falsity. But when we take the further step of perceiving these special sensibles as attributes belonging to certain actual things, we reach the stage at which deception becomes possible (Aristotle 1951c: 144).

Imagination is simply the continuation of the physical processes of sensation in the perceiver beyond the actual perceptive encounter with the world. In this it is a faculty shared with the higher animals. But humans have the additional power to imagine at will, to call up memory images and think about them, "seeing them in our mind's eye" (Aristotle 1951c: 143). With this we take yet another step toward genuine knowledge.

All objects of sense and imagination are formal. They are universal qualities that can exist separate from their original place in the matter of the perceived object and become additionally embodied in the receptive matter of the sense organ. Even though they may mislead us if we perceive them, in unguarded ways, "as" other than they are, it must be remembered that in themselves they are essentially the identical quality, the same Form, as exists in the object perceived—at least while it is being perceived.

When the rational mind attempts to understand and have knowledge, the process of *theōría* ("seeing") involved is held by Aristotle to be analogous in structure to the process of sensation. The universal that has been abstracted by the sense organ is a Form capable in principle of being thought as well as being sensed. Its particular locus or manner of embodiment is irrelevant to its essence. Therefore the mind must be able to embody Forms abstracted from the sense just as the sense embodies Forms abstracted from the original object. "In short, as the faculty of sense is related to sensible objects, so thought [*nous*] must be related to intelligible objects" (Aristotle 1951c: 145). This will supply a route from the world via sense perception to unblemished knowledge, since the Forms we think of are the *very same* Forms that exist in the substances around us. Continuing our earlier example, a particular apple is characterized by a specific shade of red. The red that exists in the world, R_{apple}, and that we enjoy aesthetically by sense, R_{eye}, is also the same redness that can be an object for thought, R_{mind}.

This means that the mind must be infinitely impressionable, since the world is populated by indefinitely many qualities, and every one of these must in principle be able to be imprinted in the receptive matrix provided by the mind. This capacity for utter acceptance Aristotle calls "passive intellect," since its function is simply to receive Forms. But here Aristotle notices an extremely interesting consequence: that this infinite hospitality to form requires the passive intellect to have no definite character of its own. Anything with a specific set of qualities will be more accepting of some qualities—ones that "fit" better with its own—than others. If everything, by definition, must fit equally well, the passive intellect cannot allow bias and must be characterless except for its capacity to accept characters. Alien to nothing, the passive intellect can have no physical organs, since these are hostages to circumstance. The physical sense organs are disturbed when overstressed by too much of their particular sensibility. Having been made with specific structures, the ear can be deafened by sounds and the eye can be blinded by too much light. But the intellect is spared this vulnerability. "Mind, on the contrary, when it has been reflecting on objects of an unusually rational character, is thereafter not worse but all the better equipped to deal with lesser matters. This is because the faculty of sensation is dependent upon the body, whereas mind is separable from it" (Aristotle 1951c: 146). (We shall see how the seeds of discontinuity planted here by the supposed "separability" of mind from body grow into a tangled harvest for medieval and modern epistemological theory. Since I consider these to be weeds, I shall try to root them out in due course.)

Besides this "separable" passive aspect of mind, which functions as the receptive matrix of intellect, assuring an unbroken link between the formal aspect of the world and the contemplating knower, there is also an active aspect of mind. Aristotle does not have much to say about this active intellect, though his medieval followers found his rather cryptic remarks intensely interesting for metaphysical reasons; Aristotle hints, however, sounding more than a little Platonic, that this aspect of the soul might be capable of breaking free both from the material body and from the passive, receptive aspect of the intellect itself. The metaphysical issues need not detain us here, but for epistemology the portentousness of the discontinuity can hardly be overstated. Especially noteworthy is not only Aristotle's acknowledgement that the mind is in part active but his judgment that this, indeed, is the part still more to be honored. The active intellect represents the "creative" (*poiētikos*) side of thinking, in which mind "makes" all things (Aristotle 1951c: 147). It is the power we have to recall experience, to imagine, to focus attention—in sum, to put thoughts together as the "poet" of contemplative knowing. It is our special glory.

However much *epistēmē* may finally be a matter of *poiēsis*, that is, however much knowing is the product of constructive intellection, for Aristotle it is in the end a creation that is, above all, not fiction but a discovery (contemplative *theōría*) of what is universal and given by the formal structures of the universe itself. Plato's ruling on what is to count as knowing is not overturned or even seriously challenged. It must be the Forms, ideal, universal, necessary, and perfect, that are to count as the objects of knowing. Aristotle challenges the independent existence of those Forms, but not their status as the goal and fulfillment of the cognitive "game." He simply offers an alternative account of how we may come to contemplate them, through a two-stage process of their reduplication, first into sense and thence into thought.

In this Aristotle "naturalizes" Plato's epistemic commitments, thus assuring that the mainstream of Western thinking—in which Plato or Aristotle remained the principal choices—down to, and including much of modern times, will remain faithful to Plato's basic insistence that authentic knowing must achieve certainty, necessity, universality, perfection, and timeless truth.

At the same time, Aristotle left the seeds of problems destined to grow over the centuries. His own experience-oriented temperament, as we saw, was inclined to give medical empirics their due and to acknowledge a whole range of modes of knowing, granting a far more respectable place for sense experience than Plato, even in his most relaxed moods (as in the *Symposium*), ever would have acknowledged. As we saw, Aristotle even used the phrase "knowledge of particulars" in connection with the success-rate of medical practice. But in his developed theory of knowledge, this is an oxymoron. Only universals—Forms—are able to take the route through sense to intellect that in the end provides us knowledge. Particulars, strictly speaking, cannot be known. Particularity is provided by matter, and matter is unknowable except through the universals that characterize it and can also, because of their universality, characterize sense and intellect as well. Aristotle's inclination to grant empirics their due is blocked by his theoretical commitment to the rules of the Academy.

Another problem with huge consequences for the future of epistemology was never addressed by Aristotle, perhaps because his value commitments and those of Plato's Academy did not allow him to consider it seriously. It is the question whether the universal characters of objects in the world are in fact perfectly reduplicated in sense and then in intellect. Aristotle is keenly aware that they must be—absolutely must be—so replicated *if* there is to be assurance of knowledge in Plato's sense through the sequence he describes. He goes to the theoretical lengths of insisting that the passive intellect can have no positive characteristics of its own. Why? Simply to assure that there can be cognition of all Forms received without the distortion that would be caused by some preexistent trait interacting with and altering incoming Forms. If this were to happen, we would never have reason to be confident that the very same Form that is in our mind is the Form that is in the world. In a revealing passage, Aristotle declares that the "authority" of the soul is at stake in this ruling. "And since everything is a possible object of thought, Anaxagoras was right in declaring that this aspect of the soul, in order to have authority over the things it knows, must be unmixed with any of them; for its functioning is hindered and impaired by the intrusion of anything alien. Accordingly, the intellectual faculty, like the sensitive, has no other intrinsic nature than that of being a certain capacity . . ." (Aristotle 1951c: 145).

The assurance of knowledge as a given is so strong in Plato and Aristotle that it is worth stipulating what is quite an odd view: that the passive intellect must be declared to lack all characteristics of its own, except the capacity to receive any and all characteristics. Still less plausibly (and unexplained) the senses—if they are not to introduce "alien" elements—must also, according to this passage, be credited with the same sort of unresisting hospitality to at least their specific range of sensible Forms, even though Aristotle admits that our sense organs are made of meat. He makes an attempt to distinguish the sensible "capacity" from the sense organs, but since he acknowledges that the senses can be stunned and distorted by overload and disease, and that "the faculty of sensation is dependent on the body" (Aristotle 1951c: 146), it is obscure how he can defend the perfect passivity of the *capacity* given the imperfection of the materially particularized *organs* on which the capacity depends.

Aristotle was apparently not bothered by these questions. His assurance of knowledge was too powerful, and too precious, to be jeopardized by them. These seeds of doubt, however, were to grow.

In the time after the deaths of Alexander the Great and Aristotle, which is traditionally designated the Hellenistic—in contrast to the classical Hellenic—age, three major philosophical traditions flourished, each with a different set of epistemic norms. I shall deal with these, briefly, as variations on the normative themes we have been considering. Epicureanism then becomes recognizable as Aristotelian empiricism without commitment to Plato's certainty or to Plato's Forms. Stoicism emerges as an attempt to define knowing no less without recourse to Forms but with continued commitment to classical certainty. Skepticism appears as a sustained effort to liberate thinkers from the quest for knowing itself, seen as a soul-disquieting activity.

EPICUREANISM

Epicurus was born in 341 B.C., on the island of Samos. In youth he was evidently influenced by the great Atomist philosopher, Democritus, whose view, that only particular atoms and emptiness are real, ruled out at once the possibility that universals or Forms exist, either "by themselves" in a Platonic realm, or "in things," as Aristotle maintained.

But if all existence is strictly particular, the issue remains how we come to know the world beyond our material minds and bodies. Epicureans cannot allow appeal to immaterial qualities of things—qualities that can be instanced both in things and in ourselves, sense organs and thought processes—as Aristotle had maintained. Still, knowledge is affirmed. But how is this possible in a world without Forms?

The Epicurean answer is to postulate the mediation of a new category of individualized and materialized messenger-forms, structures made of fine atoms constantly flying off from the surfaces of things and retaining their features. These effluences, called *eidōla*, are everywhere about us. Some strike the atoms of our sense organs and are thence transmitted to the still finer atoms of our minds. There they cause conscious images, *phantasía*, which are particular arrangements of soul-atoms that correspond, under proper circumstances of transmission, to the structures of the things we thereby represent. There is no need for universal realities; each image is quite particular, but since these images resonate in our minds longer than the actual physical sense experience that causes them, they can be named by our words and be used meaningfully even later, in the absence of their perception.

Admittedly, distortions can occur in this process. Epicurus was well aware that distant square towers, for example, may appear round. In transit, the *eidōla* may be abraded, their rough edges knocked off, as it were. But that is simply the way of the world. Clearer and nearer perceptions are less likely to suffer such distortions. Those perceptions can correct the others.

What Epicurus would not allow was any generalized challenge to the reliability of sense perception as a route to knowing. What else do we have? "If you fight against all sensations, you will have nothing by reference to which you can judge even those which you say are deceptive" (Epicurus 1974a: 21). At the center of Epicurean theory of knowing is the commitment to the normal trustworthiness of sense, to the self-evidence that those sensations are caused by a real world, and to the regularity of this outer world, in which we and others like us experience structurally similar sense perceptions, the better to ground community, language, and ultimately friendship. Diogenes wrote of Epicurus: "He starts from the fact that all men have sensations (*aisthēseis*), and asserts, without proof, that these must be caused by something other than themselves" (Diogenes Laertius 1974: 21). Epicurus himself wrote: "We must suppose that it is when something enters us from things which are external that we perceive . . . their shapes" (Epicurus 1974b: 21).

This supposition is indeed required if there is to be knowledge of the world within a rigorously atomist theory of that world. Both the presumption of knowledge and the atomistic theory are strongly valued by Epicurus. These he will find ways to defend. But by temperament and training he does not feel the need to embrace Plato's demand that knowing be absolute and certain.

Like Aristotle, he is a voice for moderation in all things; but unlike Aristotle, he did not spend twenty years studying with Plato in the Academy. Therefore Epicurean knowing is a more relaxed game, with less stringent rules, than we have been accustomed to in this chapter.

STOICISM

The Stoics did not agree. They agreed with their rival Epicureans on some basic things about knowing: in particular, on the nonexistence of immaterial Forms and in large part on how to account for the cognitive relationship without recourse to any such realities. But they could not agree to the abandonment of the basic stipulation—so dear to the classical Hellenes—that knowledge, to be knowledge, must be completely certain.

Stoicism as a philosophical movement began at almost the same time as Epicureanism. The founding figure, Zeno of Citium, was born on the island of Cyprus in 333 B.C., later moving to Athens while Epicurus was finding his house and garden. Unlike Epicurus, who remained secluded behind garden walls at the edge of the city, Zeno began his lectures in the very heart of town, on the "Painted Porch," or "Stoa," which gave its name to the movement, a colonnade overlooking the main public buildings of ancient Athens. This was good symbolism, since Stoicism was to be associated with public life for its entire history in both Greece and Rome.

Zeno, and Stoicism generally, had a temperamental inclination toward either/or distinctions. The founder of Stoicism early had been influenced by the image of Socrates, the indefatigable martyr seeking wisdom, particularly (as we saw) precise and infallible ethical wisdom. This uncompromising philosopher-hero would not have been one to settle for "good enough," and neither would Zeno. For him there existed simply the wise and the ignorant. There was no comfortable middle ground. "Comfort" itself was suspect. Zeno's other early admiration had been for the Cynics, Diogenes and Crates, whose radical asceticism and wholesale rejection of lax "normal" standards were already legendary. The same tendency to sharp dichotomies also expressed itself in Stoic views of virtue. Here, too, was an all-or-none attitude. There is no such thing as a "moderately virtuous" condition; one is either virtuous or not.

This either/or epistemic attitude toward knowing resulted in many difficulties for the Stoics, but—difficulties or not—it was a non-negotiable demand. The main source of difficulty is this: by rejecting the existence of immaterial Forms, they denied themselves epistemic accounts that had been available to Plato and Aristotle on how such perfect contemplative *theōría* could be achieved. They were committed to this end, however, and insisted they could have it by other means.

The most famous account of the Stoic's progress toward knowing is Zeno's own, symbolized by four gestures of the hand. The first gesture is the *open hand*, representing the accepting mode in which our bodies are influenced by the outside world in sense perception. Objects cause disturbances in the surrounding air and these disturbances influence our sense organs. The sense organs, in turn, transmit influences to our inner receptor (located, it was thought, in the heart). So far, as the symbol suggests, the perceiver is passive in the process.

The second gesture is the *partially closed hand*. This symbolizes the perceiver's active assent to the initial influence, or sense impression. With this the perceiver has gone beyond mere awareness—which could in principle be illusory or hallucinatory—and has started to affirm that something is out there causing the impression. Error is possible at this point, which thus far is strikingly close to the Epicurean account of perception, though missing a developed doctrine of *eidōla*.

The third hand gesture, however, marks a significantly new stage. Some impressions, Zeno maintained, are "cognitive." That is, there is a type of impression which, as Cicero later put it, is "stamped and moulded out of the object from which it came with a character such as it could not have if it came from an object other than the one which it did come from" (Cicero 1974: 127). This stage of "cognitive impressions"—impressions that carry with them the mark of their objective origin—is symbolized by the *closed fist*, which represents our "grasping" (*katalēpsis*) of the cognized thing. The partially closed hand represents receipt of concepts that we assent to; the fully closed hand is cognitive grasp. We know the difference directly, by experience.

And yet, even firmly grasped beliefs eventually can be proven wrong. There may have been unusual circumstances, of which we were ignorant at the time, that tricked us into feeling falsely certain about even our clearest cognitive impressions. Here Zeno's fourth hand gesture is made: the tightly closed fist is *held firmly by the other hand*. This symbolizes the certainty that comes from successfully defending cognitive sense impressions with arguments to fend off all such later surprises. Finally, at this fourth stage, real knowing is achieved, according to the Stoics. It is totally secure: both argumentatively defended and intuitively convincing.

Such knowing, the Stoics held, is strictly infallible. This is how the wise person knows; compared to this, all else is mere ignorance. Quite clearly these are provocative claims, especially in view of the empirical, error-prone pathway that Stoic metaphysics required Stoic epistemology to take. For hundreds of years to come, the Skeptics would merrily pepper sober Stoics with their objections.

SKEPTICISM

At the opening of this chapter I remarked that the tone of the Skeptics in ancient times was different from that of their modern namesakes. The modern side of the comparison will be developed in Chapter 4; for now it is enough to place the Skeptics into the general thought world of Hellenistic society.

The spiritual leader of the Skeptics was Pyrrho, born about 360 B.C. in the Peloponnesian town of Elis. It may sound odd to refer to a skeptical figure as offering "spiritual" leadership, but in the Hellenistic context, this was exactly Pyrrho's role. He grew up during an era of vast change. An older mentor was Anaxarchus, a disciple of the Atomist philosopher, Democritus. The Atomists had radically challenged the easy assumption that sense experience reveals the world as they held it to be, that is, nothing but colorless, soundless, odorless atoms falling forever in a void. This is not how things *look*. Our senses must be systematically fooling us. Socrates, too, was remembered to have said that the only thing he knew was that he was ignorant. And Plato had compared the sensory world to mere shadows.

Anaxarchus and Pyrrho both became court philosophers with Alexander the Great and accompanied him on his daring campaigns to Egypt and India. While on campaign in India they are reported to have taken an interest in the "naked philosophers" (the "Gymnosophists"), with their devotion to ascetic and meditational practices. This created a heady brew.

On his return to Elis after Alexander's sudden death, Pyrrho turned to teaching a comforting message for turbulent times. The clash of contradictory views, he declared, need not cause alarm or disquiet. Peace of mind, *ataraxia*, is best obtainable by suspension of judgment, not by claim and counterclaim. Nothing need coerce our consent. Pyrrho lived a simple, honorable life and was in return greatly honored by his city, even being exempted for life from paying taxes.

Pyrrho wrote nothing, so far as is known, but his preachments are remembered through the writings of his disciple, Timon. Timon's writings, themselves, have disappeared but are known through later quotation and commentary. Early in the fourth century A.D., Bishop Eusebius (c. 260–340 A.D.) cites a second-century A.D. document, for example, as follows:

> His pupil Timon says that the man who means to be happy must consider these three questions: 1. what things are really like; 2. what attitude we should adopt toward them; 3. what the consequence of such an attitude will be. According to Timon Pyrrho declared that things are equally indistinguishable, unmeasurable and indeterminable. For this reason neither our acts of perception nor our judgments are true or false. Therefore we should not rely upon them but be without judg-

ments, inclining neither this way nor that, but be steadfast saying concerning each individual thing that it no more is than is not, or that it both is and is not, or that it neither is nor is not. For those who adopt this attitude the consequence will be first a refusal to make assertions and second, freedom from disturbance (Long 1974: 80–81).

The point is, for Pyrrho, that no one can justly claim knowledge in the sense either of sensory or theoretical certainty. Sense experience carries no assurance, despite the insistence of the Stoics to the contrary. All we get from perception is what *seems*, under certain circumstances, to *us*. That is entirely relative. Our sense organs, our point of view, changing environmental conditions—all justify our refusal to move from "it seems" to "it is." And since ultimately all our concepts rest on such shaky ground, there can be no cognitive certainty at all. Better that we maintain a determined refusal to make or accept any claims whatever. The symbol of Pyrrhonian Skepticism was the evenly balanced scale. Suspending judgment, *epochē*, is the way to personal peace.

After Pyrrho, many years of struggle between the disciples of suspended judgment and the advocates of positive doctrine ensued. Shortly after Pyrrho's death in 270 B.C., the leaders of the Academy, though acknowledging no debt to Pyrrho, themselves became spokesmen for the *epochē*. Arcesilaus (316–241 B.C.), taking the helm of the Academy about 265 B.C., admired the cut and thrust of Plato's depiction of Socrates at work, and urged return to the humility of Socratic ignorance and the brilliance of Socratic dialectic. He and the Academy, mainly in opposition to Stoic claims, turned to stressing the Platonic themes of sensory uncertainty, while ignoring the Platonic affirmations of contemplative certainty. Adopting Plato's commitment to what the goal of knowing must be—absolute self-evidence—but concentrating not on reaching it but on the impossibility of attaining such a goal from the empirical starting-place of the Stoics, the Academic Skeptics served a constant critical function against the "believers" of their era.

3

MEDIEVAL BELIEVERS

As we begin this chapter, spanning the 1,000 years from the birth of Augustine in A.D. 354 to the death of William of Ockham in 1349, we should bear in mind that our narrative dips into only a tiny sampling from the rich swirl of views on knowing that actually filled the great transition between classical and modern times. In *Being and Value* (Chapter 4), I sketched more of this variety—Jewish, pagan, Muslim—than I intend to pursue here. Even those sketches were highly selective; but selection is inevitable. The trick is to select what is crucial and leave the rest—with apologies, no doubt—hoping that the main story lines are clear enough to serve the purpose at hand.

My purpose is to illuminate background values and commitments in Western theories of knowing, and no value-phenomenon was more important to the history of Western thought than the rise of Christianity. In some ways this is a rather odd fact, since the humble people who were the first Christians were far from intellectuals. Jesus of Nazareth was an itinerant preacher of obscure origins who never in his brief life left a small corner of the great Roman Empire. He did not theorize about knowing; instead he reached out to the sick and the poor with generous acts of love and parables suited to simple folk. He objected to legalisms of all kinds, ritual or ethical. After his cruel death, his followers became certain that he had been the promised Messiah sent from God and were certain, too, that he had triumphed miraculously over sin and death and could overcome their sin as well, offering eternal salvation. The earliest collections of his sayings were woven into canonical texts, the three Synoptic Gospels, in which "following Jesus," and his generous, uncalculating way of life was emphasized as important above all. Belief was not at first emphasized. In the Synoptics, occurrences of various forms of the word "believe" are minimal, averaging only ten each. Later, under the influence of the former Pharisee, Saul of Damascus (renamed Paul, the Apostle, after his dramatic conversion), legalisms of ritual and ethics continued to be opposed, but a new emphasis on belief was instituted in their place. This was echoed in the last of the four Gospels, the *Gospel According to John*, composed after Paul's ministry, in which "belief" in its various forms appears almost one hundred times.

Holding the correct beliefs—orthodoxy (from *orthos* for straight, upright, or just, and *dóxa* for belief or opinion)—became extremely important to the integrity of the church founded to organize the followers of Jesus in the centuries after his death. Innumerable cults competed in the Roman world for the spiritual allegiance of masses in turmoil. Standards of Christian belief, even to the point of imposing a new legalism of the mind, were considered vital to the unity of the Christian community and thus for the effective salvation of souls. Belief in the reality of God, the Creator, Law Giver, Lord of History; belief in the seriousness of sin; and belief in access to salvation from sin and death through Jesus, the Christ—these had to be incorporated in a common framework of commitment for members of the Christian community. Arguments were fierce over the details within this framework. Councils were held, dangerous formulations were identified and denounced, creeds were adopted and enforced, heretics were excluded. The spirit of the first three or four centuries of the Christian age in the Roman Empire was far removed from the quest for *ataraxia* or *apatheia*, "peace of mind" or "passionless unconcern," that had so strongly attracted Hellenistic seekers, "dogmatists" and "skeptics" alike.

Among the thinkers within the Christian community, however, unbroken links with the Hellenic knowers, Plato and Aristotle, remained. In *Being and Value*, I showed how echoes of the metaphysical views of these towering figures continued to reverberate, modified by Jewish, Muslim, and Christian contexts, for many centuries. In this chapter we shall see that the same phenomenon—themes with variations—holds for epistemology as well.

AUGUSTINE

Aurelius Augustinus was born in A.D. 354 in what is now Algeria, North Africa, in the city of Thagaste. His mother, Monica, was a strongly committed Christian and his father, Patricius, a pagan. Monica was extremely eager to have her son, Augustine, become a Christian; but she did not approve of infant baptism and instead wanted him to come to Christianity knowingly and voluntarily. She would have to endure a long, painful wait.

Her son was more naturally drawn to temptations of the flesh. At fifteen he left home for education, first at Madaurus and, after a dissolute year at home, on to Carthage for advanced work in rhetoric and legal studies. His father died soon thereafter, and in Carthage at age eighteen Augustine fathered an illegitimate son.

It was in the next year that Augustine had his first real introduction to philosophy, through Cicero's *Hortensius*, now lost. For Augustine it was like a first conversion. As he described it later,

> [T]his book altered my affections, and . . . made me have other purposes and desires. Every vain hope at once became worthless to me, and I longed with an incredibly burning desire for an immortality of wisdom. . . . I was thereby strongly roused, and kindled, and inflamed to love, and seek, and obtain, and hold, and embrace not this or that sect, but wisdom itself, whatever it were . . . (Augustine 1961: 34).

Augustine took up Manichaeism, whose sharply dualist philosophy of flesh against spirit must have challenged his style of life even as it purported to account for the nature of things. Augustine, now teaching rhetoric in Carthage, had serious questions about the intellectual adequacy of this account, however, and in due course raised his issues in person with Faustus, a Manichaean Bishop in the region. The answers Faustus gave him seemed weak and evasive, certainly not up to the epistemic standard that his reading of Cicero had inspired him to demand. Augustine felt disillusioned with Manichaeism and turned for solace to Skepticism in its Academic form, particularly as argued by Arcesilaus and Carneades. He also attempted, at his mother's importuning, to give Christian scriptures another chance, but he found the behavior of some Old Testament patriarchs objectionable and was generally not impressed by the literal faith Monica urged on him.

At age twenty-nine, Augustine made a bold career move from Carthage to Rome, where he established a school of rhetoric. At this point he found himself continuing in the Skeptic modes but still searching for something more satisfying. In the next year he won the important post of public orator in Milan and moved to that city, where he was joined by his mother and other friends from Africa. In Milan he came to appreciate, at first simply professionally and then in much more personal ways, the famed rhetorical skills of Bishop Ambrose, a Christian with a markedly different approach to his faith. Unlike Monica, Ambrose interpreted scripture allegorically. He also knew and appreciated Stoic ethics and the pagan neoplatonist philosophy of Plotinus (205–70), described in *Being and Value* (82–84). Augustine was enthralled. The uncompromising cognitive standards of Cicero seemed—perhaps—compatible with this reading of Christianity.

Augustine later described his eager, turbulent studies of "the Platonists," and of the Scriptures, as leading to the turning point of his life. He was becoming intellectually convinced that in Christianity, properly understood, is to be found the complete "wisdom" he had been seeking. He could not bring himself to make (or even, quite, to want) a whole-hearted personal commitment, since this would mean deep changes in his life, including parting with his mistress; but in his mind, though not yet in his will, he was convinced. He felt stuck. He had been stuck a long time. He wanted to want—but could not bring himself to want enough—the purity that was the necessary condition both of real philosophical wisdom and of genuine Christianity.

> For many of my years (some twelve) had now run out with me since my nineteenth, when upon the reading of Cicero's *Hortensius*, I was stirred to an earnest love of wisdom; and still I was deferring to reject mere earthly felicity, and give myself to search out that, whereof not the finding only, but the very search, was to be preferred to the treasures and kingdoms of the world, though already found, and to the pleasures of the body, though spread around me at my will. But I wretched, most wretched, in the very commencement of my early youth, had begged chastity of Thee, and said, "Give me chastity and continency, only not yet." For I feared lest Thou shouldest hear me soon, and soon cure me of the disease of concupiscence, which I wished to have gratified, rather than extinguished (Augustine 1961: 139–49).

When the conversion event then occurred, in 386, he could not believe that he had brought it about by his own powers. He gave credit instead to the power of God, working graciously in his soul, for having achieved this convergence of philosophical belief and living conviction which alone he could not have accomplished.

Augustine's theory of knowing rests on the two main conversions that shaped his life: his conversion to philosophy and his conversion to Christianity. The first came early in his life via the writings of Cicero; the second came in Milan only after his understanding of "philosophy" had become Platonic, and Christianity had become reasonable to him. He never considered the two conversions, one to an uncompromising search for wisdom, the other to complete dedication to God, to be incompatible. On the contrary, he took Christianity as the eternal spring which could finally provide the wisdom that could slake the thirst of his youth.

Faith and reason work reciprocally, for Augustine. Our capacity for reason is the distinguishing mark of human superiority, but its "priority" depends on the level of analysis. Chronologically, opinions and beliefs come first; but, logically, if it were not for our God-given capacities for reason, we would be neither capable of language nor able to entertain beliefs of any kind. God approves of human reason. As Augustine put it,

> God forbid that He should hate in us that faculty by which He made us superior to all other living beings. Therefore we must refuse so to believe as not to receive or seek a reason for our belief, since we could not believe at all if we did not have rational souls (Augustine 1964 c: 47).

At the same time, it is reasonable to acknowledge that there are various religious beliefs concerning human salvation that our present sinful mortal condition prevents us from knowing by reason—yet—making belief without knowing appropriate in this case. Not only is such belief a reasonable response to our limited condition but also it cleanses and opens the soul to God, the great light that can illuminate our reasoning faculties.

> So, then, in some points that bear on the doctrine of salvation, which we are not yet able to grasp by reason—but we shall be able to sometime—let faith precede reason, and let the heart be cleansed by faith so as to receive and bear the great light of reason; this is indeed reasonable (Augustine 1964b: 47).

> As he matured, Augustine reasoned his way far from the Skepticism of his earlier years, even anticipating Descartes' famous "I think, therefore I am" argument. In early philosophical writings, following his final conversion to Christianity, he grappled directly with the Academic positions he had previously advocated. Still in Italy, in seclusion with friends in Cassiciacum during the autumn and winter of 386–87, Augustine wrote *Against the Academics*. In a pleasant dialogue form, he surveys Epicurean and Stoic theories of knowing as opposed by the Skeptics of the New Academy and concludes that Skeptic scruples are ludicrous. At least it is indubitably true that *appearances do present themselves* to us. This much can count as firm knowledge. The world may not be "like" these appearances, but that need not be what is claimed if one is wisely restrained in one's assertions.

> "But," he [the Academic Skeptic] asks, "how do you know that the world you speak of exists at all? The senses may deceive." No matter how you argued, you were never able to repudiate the value of the senses to the extent that you could convince us that nothing appears to us to be. Indeed, you have never in any way ventured to try to do so. But you have done your very best to convince us that the reality could

be different from the appearance. By the term "world," then, I mean all this, whatever kind of thing it be, which surrounds and nourishes us and which presents itself to my eyes and seems to me to hold earth and sky or quasi earth and quasi sky. If you say that nonreality presents itself to me, I shall still be free from error. It is he who rashly judges that which presents itself to him to be actual reality that falls into error (Augustine 1964a: 155).

This holds, Augustine continues, even if the Skeptic worries that one might be asleep or insane. Appearances will be just as much appearances whether they are presented in dreams or awake. And even if I am deceived on how many worlds there really are, mathematical truths are not subject to doubt. Perhaps, for the sake of argument, I am asleep.

But it is manifest that no matter in what condition I am, if there is one world and six worlds, there are in all seven worlds, and I unhesitatingly assert that I know this. Now, then, convince me that this combination . . . can be not true by reason of sleep, madness, or the unreliability of the senses; and if being awakened from my slumber I recall them I shall allow that I am vanquished (Augustine 1964a: 156).

This helps to narrow the field of uncertainty. It is the field of *sense perception* that is most insecure. Mathematics is exempt.

The key point for Augustine is that on Plato's theory of knowing (here operating in the background), the deliverances of the senses, though adequate for the pursuit of daily affairs, *never were claimed to provide more than opinion*. On this view, sense perception and mathematical truths are in quite different cognitive positions on the divided line. For all the difficulties started by the Skeptics, a Platonist like Augustine can remain serene about what really counts. He closes his discussion of sense perception with the observation, "Certainly, their arguments against sense perception are not valid against all philosophers. There are some philosophers [Platonists], for example, who maintain that whatever the spirit receives by way of bodily sense can generate opinion, indeed, but not knowledge. They insist that the latter is found only in the intelligence and, far removed from the sense, abides in the mind" (Augustine 1964a: 157).

Much later in his writings, Augustine as Bishop of Hippo, once again in Africa, returned more than once to refute Skepticism, this time anticipating Descartes. In *The Trinity*, completed in A.D. 416, he repeats his earlier defense of the genuineness of appearances as at least really appearing—and then goes on to one more conclusion we can draw from this, namely, that we *know we are alive* as we experience these appearances.

The knowledge by which we know that we live is the most inward of all knowledge, of which even the Academic cannot insinuate. Perhaps you are asleep and do not know it, and you see things in your sleep. For who does not know that what people see in dreams is precisely like what they see when awake? But he who is certain of the knowledge of his own life does not therein say, I know I am awake but I know I am alive; therefore, whether he be asleep or awake, he is alive. Nor can he be deceived in that knowledge by dreams; since it belongs to a living man both to sleep and to see in sleep (Augustine 1964f: 167).

And in his most famous work, *The City of God*, written during the same period and finally completed in A.D. 426, Augustine discovers the cognitive certainty of his own existence, supported by the very fact that he doubts. In this he rejoices in his final triumph over the Academic Skeptics:

But without any delusive representation of images or phantasms, I am most certain that I am and that I know and delight in this. In respect of these truths, I am not at all afraid of the arguments of the Academicians, who say, What if you are deceived? For if I am deceived, I am. For he who is not, cannot be deceived; and if I am deceived, by this same token I am. And since I am, I am deceived, how am I deceived in believing that I am? For it is certain that I am, if I am deceived. Since, therefore, I, the person deceived, should be, even if I were deceived, certainly I am not deceived in this knowledge that I am. And, consequently, neither am I deceived in knowing that I know. For, as I know that I am, so I know this also; that I know (Augustine 1964d: 166).

We *know*, and we *can know that we know*. Augustine is a faithful follower of Plato in these convictions even while he pioneers a new argument in their support. This argument—or something close to it—will reappear in a modern version when in the next chapter we reach René Descartes, by whom it is used to ground a whole system. For Augustine the argument was used in a simpler way, philosophically, and in a different spirit, valuationally. Philosophically, it was simply a way of establishing that the Skeptics were foolish to raise their many doubts about our cognitive powers. We can, on the contrary, know many things. Valuationally, Augustine "delights" in his discovery. Interestingly, the main point he draws from his argument for the certainty of his existence has more to do with affection than epistemology. The delightful realization that he has both *knowledge of his existence* and *knowledge that he can know something* with such perfect security gives him joy. He loves his discovery!

And when I love these two things, I add to them a certain third thing, namely, my love, which is of equal moment. For neither am I deceived in this, that I love, since in those things which I love I am not deceived; though even if these were false, it would still be true that I *loved* false things. For how could I justly be blamed and prohibited from loving false things, if it were false that I loved them? But, since they are true and real, who doubts that when they are loved, the love of them is itself true and real (Augustine 1964d: 166–67)?

The loving, living being who knows these things about itself is essentially a soul, Augustine believed, temporarily inhabiting a body in a fallen world of sin and change.

This value-drenched worldview made a difference. Augustine's epistemic posture reaches toward Descartes in the future, and even more obviously toward Plato in the past, but his functioning epistemic norms, steeped in his religious values, gave his theories a distinctive twist. On the positive side, Augustine's joy in human reason as God's greatest gift pulled him, as we saw, to favor our rational powers as making our species "superior to all other living beings." On the negative side, his strong revulsion against the vileness of the body further pushed his epistemological preferences away from considering organic continuities between thought and perception. Although I shall later argue that such antiorganicism is profoundly mistaken and epistemically harmful, we should admit that Augustine had a number of motives for stressing discontinuity. Perhaps his early immersion in Manichaean dualism helped form his low esteem for the body. Perhaps his pious mother's disapproval—and certainly his own struggle against his strong sexual urges—together with his Christian anticipation of an afterlife completely freed from bodily taints, reinforced the side of Platonic tradition which, as we saw earlier, took a negative view of the soul's relation to its "prison" in the body. For Augustine, the soul alone is active, relative to its body; the instrument cannot under any circumstances operate on its operator. Augustine concluded that the soul is so superior to the body that it is impossible for the body even to influence it. This value-judgment mandates quite distinctive conclusions about perception.

In *The Trinity*, for example, Augustine distinguishes three distinct elements in perception which must work seamlessly together in the perceptive process. In vision, for example, there is, first, the *object seen*. That this object is entirely distinct is proven by its capacity to persist quite apart from being seen. We can hold it in the dark and know that it has an existence separate from the visual event. Second, there is the temporally limited *act of sensation*, which did not exist before we started seeing the object, and which comes to an end when the object is no longer seen. Of course we have a capacity for sight before the event (or "we should not differ from the blind" [Augustine 1964f: 170]), but the visual event itself occurs only when this capacity is activated in the living body of the perceiver, which proves it a second distinct thing. Third, there is in the visual event a *mental awareness*, the "attention of the mind," that is also distinct from the other two. If the bodily capacity is destroyed, as when a person is blinded, the mental effort— the hope or wish or straining to see—remains, exposing the fact that it is a quite different thing. As Augustine sums the matter: "These three, then, the body that is seen and vision itself and the attention of mind which joins both together, are manifestly distinguishable not only on account of the properties of each but also on account of the difference of their natures" (Augustine 1964f: 170).

In Augustine's value-world only the soul, however, is worthy of perception itself. The external object, though necessary, merely supplies its Form; the living sense organ, though also necessary, would not perceive anything— it would just be another piece of meat—were it not for a "commingling" of soul with body. The *soul in the organ*, not the bodily organ itself, is what actually sees: "and although an inanimate body does not perceive, yet the soul commingled with the body perceives through a corporeal instrument, and that instrument is called sense" (Augustine 1964f: 170). This means that perception is an act of soul, proceeding from the perceiver, not from the perceived.

What the senses sense is Form. The Form of a perceived object is taken on by the sense organ, just as the form of an object is taken by water when immersed. But just as water ceases to hold that form when the object is removed, so a sense organ tends to lose the impressed Forms of its perceived objects, usually so fast that we fail even to distinguish between the Form of the object in itself and the Form that is produced by it in sense. If the senses were like wax, which retains the imprint of the signet ring long after the ring is removed, we might be more alert to the fact that the Forms are in distinct locations. Sometimes, though rarely, we do have clues to this phenomenon, as in after-images left in our eyes by bright lights—images that linger and change color as they fade.

More important, however, is the retentive power of the conscious mind, which can hold on to Forms, attend to them lovingly, recall them at will, and even incorporate them in guiding behavior in the absence of the entities entertained in thought. Augustine explores three types of knowing in *The Literal Meaning of Genesis* (written during the same years as *The Trinity*), where he distinguishes between *perceptual* knowing of objects in presence, *imaginative* knowing of objects in their absence, and *conceptual* knowing of what are not objects and are not capable of being imaged. Characteristically, he uses love as his example of the third, and most important, kind. We know love; but since it is not an object, we do not know love in the same way we know apples. We know it directly from internal intellectual illumination. Other Forms are capable of being sensed, Augustine writes. "But love can neither be seen in its own essence with the eyes of the body nor be thought of in the spirit by means of an image like a body; but only in the mind, that is, in the intellect, can it be known and perceived" (Augustine 1964e: 178).

For Plato, too, genuine success in knowing comes only in the intellect, soaring high above the realm of sensory images, up where the eternal Forms are contemplated in their perfection and unity. But Plato's theory of reminiscence, his attempt to account for the mind's capacity to recognize perfect Forms that never appear in the imperfect world of Becoming, was not available to Augustine. It flattered human souls too much. The rational soul is indeed the source of human superiority to all other living beings. That is the good news. But the bad news is that all beings, most especially human beings, are creatures fallen into sin. Our souls, he believed, are not eternal but were created at some point in time by God. To consider them eternally preexistent would be to give them too high a status; it would even bring God's sovereignty into question. On these values, an alternative account of our knowledge of pure Forms was urgently needed.

Augustine's answer combined three solutions into one grand, theocentric proposal. First, God is the living repository of the Forms (no more need to ask "where" they are); second, God is constantly within our souls, allowing us gradual cognitive access to the perfect Forms (no more need to postulate a preexistent state); and, third, God is the illuminating light of the mind, without which we could have no cognition at all, and in embrace of which, ultimately, we find the saving knowledge that is the goal of wisdom-lovers.

Augustine's commitments on what counts as the marks of genuine "knowing" echoed Plato's on the norms of certainty, necessity, eternality, unity, and perfection. He strongly reinforced one tendency in Plato, stressing the complete discontinuity between body and mind, percept and concept. What he subtracted—on the basis of other commitments that are central to Christian worship of a perfect, sovereign, creator God—was the Platonic hypothesis of an eternal, preexistent, cognizing soul. In this altered framework he was able to interpret our knowledge of necessary truths by substituting an immanent God for a transcendent Realm of Forms; a significant change, metaphysically, but a minor adjustment epistemologically. All the while he was able to avail himself of much Platonic imagery, as from the Allegory of the Cave, in which the Form of the Good, represented by the blazing Sun, provides both being and illumination for the finite world below.

On this note, we may take our leave of Augustine, the Platonist Christian. The epistemic norms he embraced formed a powerful, mutually supportive network. They would endure across the ages we call Dark.

BETWEEN AUGUSTINE AND AQUINAS

By far the largest tract of time spanned in this chapter occurs in this section. From the death of Augustine in A.D. 430 to the birth of Thomas Aquinas, approximately 800 years would need to elapse—more total time than separated the Delphic call of young Socrates from the conversion of Augustine. Those years were not entirely barren, as I have tried to show in *Being and Value*, but in terms of theories of knowing and their bearing on the values of the Western mind, there is not much that rises to prominence. Insofar as there was reflection on the character of knowledge, the Platonized Christianity of Augustine served—along with other mainly Platonizing Church Fathers and an anonymous neoplatonic work attributed to Dionysius the Areopagite—as the dominant influence.

JOHN SCOTUS ERIUGENA

At the half-way mark of this long span, however, a thinker of considerable power and originality emerged. Born in A.D. 810, John Scotus Eriugena was one of few in his time to master the Greek language. This, during the Carolingian Renaissance period, must have been accomplished in Ireland, where Greek scholarship in the monasteries was advanced far beyond the level of the rest of Europe. ("Eriugena" means "of Erin," and Ireland was shown as *Scotia Maior* on the maps of the period.) Before age forty, Eriugena made his way to Paris, to direct the Court School of King Charles II, and to translate Greek works that had been sent in 827 to the Carolingian court by Byzantine Emperor Michael II. Among these works was the corpus attributed to "Dionysius the Areopagite," whom St. Paul was reported in the New Testament (*Acts* 17:34) to have converted on the Areopagus in Athens. In fact, this material was written around A.D. 500 by an unknown Christian mystical thinker who was heavily under the influence of neoplatonic literature, specifically that of Proclus (410–85), the last of the great pagan neoplatonists; but its attribution to Dionysius gave the works quasi-Apostolic prestige and enormous influence.

The treatises by pseudo-Dionysius (as the pseudonymous author is now known) were especially concerned with knowledge of and language about God. In them, especially in *Divine Names* and *Mystical Theology*, the latent Platonic vector toward an epistemology of ineffability was followed to its fullest. Considering the causal flow "downward," flowing from the One to the world, according to pseudo-Dionysius, there is much to be said about God, reflected in God's self-manifestations. On this "downward path," the One is first expressed through the great Forms that (in Plato's Divided Line) are ultimately unified by the Form of the Good at the "top" of the line. Still moving "down" the line, "below" the intelligible realm of Forms, the world lamely manifests these ideal archetypes in space and time, and thus many names become available for attribution back "upward" toward the One from which all flows. The image of the Sun, for example, or words like "good" and "wise," even the word "one"—all these and many more (as, for example, in the biblical metaphors of "rock" and "shield") can be spoken regarding God in affirmative theology. But God is of course really not *like* what any of these words mean to us. Therefore, more important to pseudo-Dionysius than affirmative theology (the *via affirmativa*) was negative theology (the *via negativa*), which comes from moving conceptually "up" the divided line from the world of becoming to its intelligible unification in the Forms and then on to the realm beyond conceptual intelligibility, where unity transcends and erases the differences between even the most fundamental Forms. There, at the "top," words or thoughts, which are necessarily diverse—which therefore cannot but analyze and divide—are simply not applicable. Thus none of the names we use for God can suit God in the ultimate divine Unity.

John Scotus Eriugena was more than translator of this material from Greek to Latin. He accepted it, wholeheartedly, as canonical and orthodox, and consequently created a system motivated by the attempt to synthesize the three strands that meant the most to him: Christian doctrine, the views of Augustine, and pseudo-Dionysius. In his mid-fifties he wrote *De Divisione Naturae*, to bring all these together. His confidence was in reason's ability to give such convincing arguments that recourse to "proof texts" would be unnecessary. Every authority not backed by good reasons is weak, he argued; and the power of true reason needs no authority (Eriugena 1962: 132).

Eriugena's approach rests on an Augustinian interpretation of Christianity, already Platonic, as we have seen; but it pushes so strongly beyond Augustine toward neoplatonist descriptions of our ontological and epistemological situation that Augustine might well have rejected it, as did later Church authorities, who ordered it burned in 1225. The primary problem for Pope Honorius III, who instituted the ban, was a metaphysical one: viz., the suspicion of pantheism (since neoplatonic emanationism strongly suggests that the world is somehow "made out of" God). But Eriugena's epistemology is especially interesting to us for its extreme emphasis on cognitive discontinuities.

The issues of perceptual knowing do not arise in Eriugena's work, as they do in Augustine. Rather, the key question is whether the "top" of the cognitive scale is or is not open in principle to humans. Eriugena closely follows pseudo-Dionysius in the treatment of affirmative and negative theology. Affirmations may be made about God, but only on the recognition that every affirmation is no more than a figure of speech. None of the words we possess, no matter how "purified" or abstract, can be attributed to the One who is beyond the distinctions of subject and predicate. If we say things about God, this is well and good; but what we say has nothing to do with God's own reality. We have no knowledge through our affirmations. Negations, on the other hand, saying that God is *not*-this or *not*-that, are the literal truth. God is not material and not cruel (for example), but those are easy negations. We need to learn to say that God is not good (as we are "good" and as we know the "good") or that God is not wise (as we can understand "wisdom"). God is not even "powerful" or "one" in any way we can comprehend. Thus we have the literal truth when we deny predicates of God, but this, too, gives us not the least morsel of positive knowledge.

Eriugena recognized that there is a great difference, however, between negations. To deny that God is "material" or "evil" is one thing; to deny that God is "spirit" or "good" is another. Both types of negation are literally true; but they have a different force. The former are simply false. The latter are false, too, but in a more complex way: they point to predicates beyond which we would find God if we could. Thus Eriugena urged that we speak of God as "super-good" or "super-wise," using superlative language in ways permitted by orthodox doctrine and scripture. These superlative expressions, he proposes, can reconcile literally false affirmation with literally true negation. Their grammatical form is affirmative; but since they do not classify or attribute anything, they remain logically negative. Thus ultimately, even with the appearance of affirmation, we remain appropriately cut off from knowledge, which must end when one gazes upward, beyond the Forms.

Eriugena's remarkable ninth-century synthesis shows the latent tension within the Platonic set of epistemic commitments as well as the tension between Platonism and Christianity. Is the goal of knowing really attainable once the "game" is defined as requiring perfect certainty of a complete whole? Or must all hope of knowing in this way eventually surrender to ineffable, wordless ecstasy—confidence without conceptual content? Likewise, if perception is to be entirely discontinuous from pure thought, can thought be more than vacuous? Finally, must all Ideas themselves be unified in a single Idea of Ideas beyond all differentiation and plurality? To follow that vector seems to abandon all thought, language, and comprehension.

Anselm

If modern nations had existed in his time, Anselm would have been a truly international figure. He was born in the Alpine region of northern Italy to a wealthy family in 1033, crossed the Alps in search of education at age twenty-three, and three years later found himself in Normandy, at the Abbey of Bec, where he began studies with a fellow Italian, the scholarly Lanfranc. During the four following years, Anselm blossomed in piety and learning, becoming a monk of the abbey and a leading younger member of the community. When Lanfranc left Bec in 1063 to become abbot at Caen, Anselm was chosen Prior of Bec and began to teach. He was filling this position when, in 1066, William of Normandy launched his invasion against Britain and successfully added England to his kingdom as William I, the Conqueror. Four years later King William induced Lanfranc to become Archbishop of Canterbury and about the same time, still at Bec, Anselm was asked by his fellow monks to write what he had been teaching as guidance for them, both for their understanding and for their spiritual life. In response Anselm wrote what he at first called *Exemplum meditandi de ratione fidei* (*An Example of Meditating on the Rationale of Faith*) and later, in 1076, it was published as *Monologium de ratione fidei* (*Monologue on Reasons for Faith*). In 1078 Anselm was chosen Abbot of Bec and in the same year wrote for his monks his most philosophically influential treatise, first known as *Fides quaerens intellectum* (*Faith Seeking Understanding*) and then published as the *Proslogion* ("Address"). His "address" was directed to God alone, as we shall see, though after publication it reached a wide audience and stimulated much controversy, as it does to this day.

Philosophically, this is all the background we need for Anselm's contribution to the theory of knowing, but it is of human interest to observe that this prayerful teaching monk was to become embroiled in much more worldly controversy. After his teacher, Lanfranc, died in Norman England in 1089, the new king, William Rufus, attempted to take over Church revenues and refused for four years to appoint a new Archbishop of Canterbury who might oppose his will. In 1093, however, William agreed to appoint Anselm, despite—or perhaps because of—Anselm's deep reluctance to accept the post. Four years of mounting controversies ended with Anselm's departure (without royal permission) to visit Pope Urban II, whom William Rufus refused to recognize. This led to exile for Anselm from 1097 to 1100, during which he wrote another of his most famous works, *Cur Deus Homo* (*Why the God-Man?*) and other significant theological treatises. On the accession of Henry I to the throne in 1100, Anselm was welcomed back to Canterbury, but a new struggle immediately began over this king's claimed right to appoint the clergy to their posts. This led to yet another trip to a new pope, but no resolution could be reached and Anselm found himself once again in exile from 1103 to 1106. Finally, in Normandy, king and archbishop found a compromise formula and Anselm returned to Canterbury, where he died peacefully in 1109.

The embattled archbishop of later years, however, is not the relevant figure for our narrative. It is, instead, the wise teacher and leader of monks, the writer of spiritual guide books, who interests us. Anselm was a person of intensity, both in his spiritual devotion and in his intellectual penetration. It may have been this intense quality that troubled kings later in his life; but, while still quietly at Bec, Anselm's intensity of faith and intelligence drove him up hitherto unscaled heights in search of a way to weld them indissolubly together in heart- and mind-satisfying ways.

In this quest, Anselm was completely Augustinian. He used Augustine's famous phrase: *credo ut intelligam*, "I believe in order to understand," as his often-repeated motto. In the context of the abbey, belief could be taken for granted. The quest for understanding was the driving concern.

The principal avenue to Anselm's theory of knowing and to the value commitments that shape it, is his *Proslogium*. The *Proslogium*, a "Discourse" or "Address," is addressed to God, in a way that echoes in unmistakable ways Augustine's great *Confessions*. This point is often overlooked when philosophers today debate the ontological argument it contains. The prayerful literary form of the *Proslogium*, originally titled *Faith Seeking Understanding*, must itself show to every reader that Anselm is deeply, passionately, a believer in God. In his opening preface, Anselm himself explains his adoption of this form: "I have written the following treatise in the person of one who strives to lift his mind to the contemplation of God, and seeks to understand what he believes" (Anselm 1958b: 2). Chapter 1, often omitted from modern readings, shows the heat of Anselm's motives:

> Speak now, my whole heart! speak now to God, saying, I seek thy face; thy face, Lord will I seek (Psalms xxvii. 8). And come thou now, O Lord my God, teach my heart where and how it may see thee, where and how it may find thee. . . . What, O most high Lord, shall this man do, an exile far from thee? What shall thy servant do, anxious in his love of thee, and cast out afar from thy face? He pants to see thee, and thy face is too far from him. He longs to come to thee, and thy dwelling-place is inaccessible. He is eager to find thee, and knows not thy place. . . . Finally, I was created to see thee, and not yet have I done that for which I was made.
>
> O wretched lot of man, when he hath lost that for which he was made! O hard and terrible fate! Alas, what has he lost, and what has he found? What has departed, and what remains? He has lost the blessedness for which he was made, and has found the misery for which he was not made (Anselm 1958b: 4).

Only God, as Augustine taught, can really empower the vision of God that is ultimate wisdom. For this reason Anselm prays to be taught how to seek this knowledge. "Teach me to seek thee, and reveal thyself to me, when I seek thee, for I cannot seek thee, except thou teach me, nor find thee, except thou reveal thyself" (Anselm 1958b: 6). His heart is securely grounded in passionate belief, but in painful truth this is not balanced by a corresponding assurance of the head. In this imbalance he cannot rest content. Of course perfect knowledge is impossible in this life; but surely if God approves our reasoning capacities (as Augustine taught), there should be something available to the intellect worthy of the passion of faith.

> I do not endeavor, O Lord, to penetrate thy sublimity, for in no wise do I compare my understanding with that; but I long to understand in some degree thy truth, which my heart believes and loves. For I do not seek to understand that I may believe, but I believe in order to understand. For this also I believe,—that unless I believed, I should not understand (Anselm 1958b: 6–7).

Anselm's main epistemological achievement is finding (or being "given"), to his satisfaction, an argument for God's existence that is intellectually worthy of his prior confidence of heart. The great ontological argument we examined in *Being and Value* (88–90) begins—as exactly appropriate if belief should precede understanding—from the Christian community's definition of God. Anselm uses the simple pronoun "we" for the Catholic Church of which he is a faithful member:

> And so, Lord, do thou, who dost give understanding to faith, give me, so far as thou knowest it to be profitable, to understand that thou art *as we believe*; and that thou art *that which we believe*. And, indeed, *we believe that thou art a being than which nothing greater can be conceived* (Anselm 1958b: 7, emphasis supplied).

Anselm is not claiming to have invented the famous phrase on which the argument hangs. On the contrary, he explicitly indicates that Christian faith down the ages, from biblical times to his age, has been distinct in taking God to be holy, perfect, most high, beyond every conceivable flaw or blemish. He does not claim that all peoples or all religions have so held. He is perfectly aware that devotees of Moloch had a different idea of their god; so did the worshipers of brazen images; so did the Greeks and Romans. But "we" believe that God must mean a being than which nothing greater can be conceived. If conceived with a defect, then not "our" God, says the Catholic tradition. And if it were not for God's self-revelation, "we" would not have this belief. Faith, made possible through the Church, comes first.

Now, finding this belief in place among "us," what does this signal to the understanding? If we meditate prayerfully and with a receptive mind about the rational implications of what "we" believe, what do we find? Amazingly, Anselm rejoices, we find *knowledge* of God's existence—knowledge clad in necessity worthy to match the certainty of our faith. Nothing less than the greatest can be allowed as God; this is given by "our" faith. But if we compare a conception, (1) of God as having all perfections *except* existence, with a conception, (2) of God as having all perfections *including* existence, it is clear than (1) describes God as less great than (2). Therefore (1) cannot be thought as pertaining to "our" God, since to conceive "our" God is to conceive a being than which nothing greater can be thought. The result is that necessarily we cannot think "our" God's nonexistence (Anselm 1958b: chapters 2 and 4).

Another reflection provides a second, subtly different, argument to a similar conclusion: if God's quality of existence is conceived as necessary and as the source of the existence of everything else, this is greater than if God's existence were subject to contingency like all finite things—that is, than if it were even *possible* that God not exist. Therefore, on the same principle—that we think carefully in accordance with "our" belief—God must be thought as having necessary existence and the creative power of giving existence to whatever else exists (Anselm 1958b: chapters 3 and 5).

This line of argument does not work for any other gods, or God conceived in any other way than according to the Christian tradition. Anything conceived as other than "that than which nothing greater can be conceived" has no claim on necessary existence. As Anselm notes, "[Indeed], whatever else there is, except thee alone, can be conceived not to exist" (Anselm 1958b: 9). One could not prove the gods of Olympus, for example, by this argument. They are conceived as far from perfection. No one is forced to think about God in "our" way. Those outside the faith do not. But if one does think in accordance with "our" tradition, one is permitted a quality of understanding that at last can satisfy the mind with a rational certainty equal to our passionate intellectual longing.

Belief came first, as we saw, through revelation, scripture, tradition, the Church, and personal acknowledgment; but through rational reflection and the grace of God, now understanding has penetrated to the point where the mind can fend for itself. Anselm rejoices in the argument that has come to him, and thanks God for this gift:

I thank thee, gracious Lord, I thank thee; because what I formerly believed by thy bounty, I now so understand by thine illumination, that if I were unwilling to believe that thou dost exist, I should not be able not to understand this to be true (Anselm 1958b: 10).

This is a fascinating claim. Anselm, in that exclamation of gratitude, is not denying that belief was for him the necessary condition for understanding God's necessity; but he is now affirming that he has established firm understanding beyond simple belief—with God (in Augustinian fashion) the divine "illuminator" of the mind. Anselm also is not claiming that his mind somehow has penetrated God's perfect nature, contrary to the warnings of pseudo-Dionysius or John Scotus Eriugena. No, what the understanding grasps is a definition of God that, while it sounds quite positive, is actually comparative. God is that *than which nothing greater* can be conceived. We need not arrogantly suppose we can conceive God's essence. We simply say, in the tradition of negative theology, that anything that can be shown to contain a flaw or imperfection is *not* God as "we" understand "God."

Finally, we should note that Anselm, in expounding this argument, never considers the crucial epistemological-cum-metaphysical question whether our concepts are real beyond our acts of thinking—whether when we contemplate a great, general idea we are or are not directly in touch with something that transcends the thinker. The Platonic tradition was so strong, reinforced from all sides but especially from Augustine, whom he revered, that for Anselm the objective reality of Ideas was never in question, never in doubt. The primary foundation of his argument is that "whatever is understood, exists in the understanding." This is not a weak sense of "exists." Thus, when a necessity for thought is discovered, this ipso facto uncovers a necessity of reality. It is not merely that Christians cannot consistently think (or meaningfully say) that their God is nonexistent, but that the universal, perfect, and necessary Christian God, encountered in meaningful contemplation, must actually be. The struggle that was to commence immediately after Anselm over the status of ideas, therefore, was of the utmost significance both for epistemology and for religion.

ROSCELLINUS, WILLIAM OF CHAMPEAUX, AND ABELARD

It is not the case, of course, that what came to be called Nominalism was first invented in the Middle Ages. We have seen already that the reality of Forms was firmly denied in classical times by Epicureans and Stoics as well as Skeptics. We have also noted the epistemological consequences of such denials, both when linked to and released from Platonic rulings on the ultimate standards of knowing. But in the era between Augustine and Anselm there had been few voices raising objections to the consensus that concepts and qualities exist as universal realities. A tiny trickle of thinking may have reflected an Aristotelian resistance to the independent existence of formal realities, preferring the notion that universals exist only as manifest in concrete substances; but evidence for this in Europe is slight, and most of Aristotle's work was not yet known. The mainstream flowed with Augustine, Eriugena, and Anselm.

This accented the shock that Roscellinus administered to the thought-world of Anselm's time when, in a most uncompromising way, he boldly called all that in question. Roscellinus (also called Rucelinus, Roscelin, and Roscelin de Compiègne), a somewhat younger contemporary of Anselm, was born in Lower Brittany around 1045 and studied at Soissons and Rheims. He was attached to the cathedral of Chartres and became canon of Compiègne. Not much is known about his life; and, unfortunately, we have nothing that he himself wrote. Everything we hear about his doctrines we glean from outraged refutations by his opponents, including most notably Anselm himself and Roscellinus' own former student, Peter Abelard, on whom more soon.

Evidently, from all the horrified reactions, Roscellinus flatly denied that there is any reality besides particular realities. Only individuals exist. There is no such thing as "whiteness" that is shared between several white objects, there are only the white objects. "White" is just a word we apply to each. When we talk about "qualities" and "concepts" we are doing exactly that: we are just talking. A universal is a mere *flatus vocis*, a breathing of a word, a puff of air sounding for a moment, then gone like any individual event.

What drew attention to Roscellinus' radical rejection of real universals was, in keeping with the values of the time, application of his theory to religion. In 1090 Anselm, offended that Roscellinus seemed to think himself allied with himself and his teacher, Lanfranc, thundered back against the implied doctrine of the Trinity that would follow from Roscellinus' position on universals. In 1092 his view was denounced at the Council of Soissons.

Although he recanted at the time, he continued unabashedly to teach his nominalistic views, and two years later he was again denounced by a council and fled to England just as Anselm was getting settled into his new position as Archbishop of Canterbury. This did not bode well for a happy stay and it was not long before Roscellinus returned to France, to teach for a while at Tours and then at Loc-menach (Loches), where among his students was the young Peter Abelard. It is from Abelard's refutations that we learn much of what Roscellinus is reputed to have held about the particular nature of all ideas. The intellectual ground was not prepared at that time, however, for these views. Roscellinus died without many converts sometime after 1121, when he was last heard attacking Abelard's doctrine of the Trinity; but his name was remembered ever-after as the founder of the so-called "*moderni*" (Moderns) who dared to deny the reality of Forms. As we shall see in the next chapter, this Nominalist tradition, though born in abstruse theological controversy over orthodox interpretations of the Trinity and Incarnation, was destined for wider epistemic fields to conquer.

Roscellinus' diametrical opposite was soon to rise, and to rise from among Roscellinus' own students of dialectic. William of Champeaux, born in 1070, began his own teaching career at Paris soon after the turn of the twelfth century. In 1108 he voluntarily retired himself from teaching at the Notre Dame cathedral school (where among his students was Peter Abelard) to enter a priory nearby. His students and friends, however, implored him to return to teaching, and soon he did, continuing even after his move to Châlons in 1113, until his death in 1121.

William was a devoted disciple of Anselm, but took his master's Platonic views of universals even further; and in the face of Roscellinus' extreme Nominalism, he founded a partisan school of no less extreme Realism. As in the case of Roscellinus, we have no first-hand writings of William and must gather his views from others, particularly from the copious polemics of Abelard. It seems that young Peter Abelard attended his lectures at the cathedral school of Notre Dame. After a while Abelard could not refrain from disputing what he heard, beginning in that first classroom and continuing in different venues for many years.

What Abelard heard was the view that individuals do not exist as such, except as accidents of one universal substance. Only the participation of different Forms (properties, qualities, characteristics—all universals) differentiates what we call "individuals" from one another. If it were not for their different qualities, Socrates and Plato, to use William's example, would not differ from one another. They are just "man" modified by properties that combine to make them who they are. Anything meaningful we might wish to say about them that might differentiate them from one another, or from any other men, or from anything else at all, would be expressed in concepts capable of being thought. And only the intelligible, the formal, can be thought.

The story of William and his Realism is so intimately entangled with that of Peter Abelard, his student, expositor, and scourge, that it makes most sense at this point to bring Abelard himself directly to the fore. Abelard was born the first son of a noble Breton household at Pallet, near Nantes, in 1079. He was extraordinarily gifted in quickness of mind and opted early for a life of learning rather than for the military or political activities that might have been more normal for one of his breeding. As a youth he wandered freely in search of teachers, stopping a while with Roscellinus at Loc-menach, as noted earlier, and eventually moving on to attend the lectures of William of Champeaux during the latter's first teaching career at the cathedral school of Notre Dame in Paris. In William's classroom the battle began, with the agile young mind of Abelard (as Abelard tells it) besting his teacher from the beginning.

After his education was complete, Abelard established a school of his own. At first it was at Melun, some distance from Paris, because, it seems, William (who was by then established in reputation and well-connected in important circles) worked vigorously to oppose the school. In due course Abelard was able to move the school closer to the city, to Corbeil, where he carried on his debate even more vigorously than was good for his health. After a pause for recuperation, he returned to the fray, finding William now teaching in the nearby priory of St. Victor, but still capable of blocking Abelard's hopes to teach in Paris itself. The situation changed, however, after Abelard gained a great public victory over William, forcing him to amend his central position in an embarrassing way. William never quite recovered, and Abelard was able to set up his school in Paris, on the heights of St. Geneviève overlooking Notre Dame. There his brilliance won him all the honors he could wish, and in 1115 he was appointed chair at the cathedral school, and canon in the cathedral itself. He taught to the adulation of throngs of students and was at the top of his academic world. And there, at this pinnacle moment, lived also within the precincts of the cathedral, another canon, whose beautiful niece (and ward), Héloïse, turned fourteen in the year of Abelard's appointment. Their torrid romance was destined in the next four years to knock Abelard from his pinnacle. But this sub-story, alas, falls outside the context of Abelard's epistemological values, and must remain off-stage.

Abelard's epistemological values themselves were those of mediation and moderation. He was committed to the norms of unity and coherence at the very time when extreme Nominalism and extreme Realism were becoming self-conscious partisan movements. Neither of his former teachers— neither the Nominalist Roscellinus, with his doctrine of the general term as a mere *flatus vocis*, implying that similar things have nothing in common, nor William of Champeaux, with his opposite view that everything is a mere accidental modification of a single substance—could possibly be correct. Instead, Abelard argued, even if we clear away the extravagances of William's (and Anselm's) Realism by assuming that existence in the full sense can be admitted only for concrete particular entities, we still need not fall into the radical individualism of the extreme Nominalists. General ideas are not just particular puffs of breath. Particular things are genuinely related by meaningful universal concepts. Such a concept is not merely a particular word (*vox*), but is or carries a general meaning (*sermo*); and this general meaning, emergent in our minds, allows unification in our thought, since it can be predicated of indefinitely many particulars. The *sermo* is not itself an entity subsisting somehow in a realm of Form, but neither is it an individual sound with no more capacity to relate, predicate, or illuminate than any other purely individual event.

Abelard's mediating position, often called Conceptualism, was at once classified by the Realists with Nominalism; but this classification was not fair, if by Nominalism is meant the view that general terms are mere "names" and nothing more. It is important to separate the metaphysical from the epistemological stakes here. Metaphysically, indeed, Abelard sided with the view that universals do not have existence prior to particular entities, except, perhaps, as ideas in the mind of God; but epistemologically, he stressed the importance of generality in human experience and thought, as well as in our language. This whole area of inquiry, as we shall see, was destined to become enormously important in modern times. I deal with it, too, as part of my proposed postmodern philosophy of language in Part Three. I suspect Abelard would have been pleased by my approach.

Abelard's heritage—his irenic epistemic norms, his dialectical brilliance, his quest for subtle distinctions, and (after his disgrace and mutilation) his new-found spiritual modesty, his stress on ethical intentions and on the morality and love of God—stirred his students to intense enthusiasm, even when he tried to become a hermit. They followed him with tents and begged for his lectures. They even built an oratory for him, which he called "The Paraclete."

But others followed him, as well, with less benign intent. Abelard possessed in abundance what today might be called a "liberal" spirit in what were increasingly illiberal times. He was dogged by heresy-hunters, particularly by Bernard of Clairvaux (1090–1153), who brought him repeatedly to trial in his latter years. It was on the road to Rome in 1142, to appeal his latest condemnation, that Abelard collapsed and died. His body was returned (in secret) to the Paraclete, which in the meantime had become a convent presided over by Héloïse. After her death, their bones were interred together, and remain so today.

The next years were not kind to original thinking, but an event of immense philosophical importance was to occur during the eighty-five years between the death of Abelard and the birth of Thomas Aquinas: the complete works of Aristotle were to be translated into Latin and to make their way into the thinking of European Christians. In or about 1150, Raimund, archbishop of Toledo, ordered the *Physics*, the *Metaphysics*, the *Nicomachean Ethics*, the *Psychology*, and other treatises, to be translated from Arabic through Castilian into Latin. Frederick II (1194–1250), who reigned as Holy Roman Emperor from 1215 until his death, ordered fresh translations of Aristotle directly from Arabic. At first these works, which arrived through, or were associated with, the Islamic philosophers, Avicenna (980–1037) and Averroës (1126–98), were looked on with great suspicion. But gradually the resistance faded. First the logical books, some of which had long been known, were allowed in the universities; then, by 1231, Pope Gregory IX permitted all but the *Physics* to be taught; and by mid-century everything was not only available, it was required. It was into this fresh climate, bubbling with new (and possibly dangerous) ideas that Albertus Magnus and his brilliant follower, Thomas Aquinas, entered the history of thought.

THOMAS AQUINAS

Seldom in thinking about thinking do we come upon a phenomenon so remarkable as the achievement of Thomas, who was born in Aquino, Italy, around 1225, and died only forty-nine years later, in 1274. The principal biographical facts were presented in *Being and Value* (94–95). I need here only reemphasize the importance to Thomas of his much longer-lived teacher, Albert ("the Great," often Latinized as Albertus Magnus), who with good reason was called the "Universal Doctor." Albert's life spanned that of Thomas. He was born in Swabia, Germany, as early as 1193 (though perhaps as late as 1206), studying in Padua and entering the Dominican order there in 1223, two years before Thomas' birth. He received his doctorate from Paris and taught there from 1245, just at the time that Thomas reached that haven, freshly escaped from the recent kidnapping by his family (which had been designed to keep him out of the Dominican order and safely in the family's Benedictine tradition). The young man was immediately drawn to Albert's powerful lectures, and when Albert left Paris for larger responsibilities in founding what was to become the distinguished Dominican school at Cologne, Thomas followed him. There he stayed to teach, as well, until in 1257 he received his own doctorate from Paris and was appointed to the Dominican chair at that extraordinary center. In the same year, Bonaventure (1221–74), the great mystic theologian, who had been recently appointed to the Franciscan chair at Paris, received his doctorate, too. For a time the University of Paris had at once the "Angelic Doctor," Aquinas, and the "Seraphic Doctor," Bonaventure, teaching from rival chairs. By all reports the men themselves were well-disposed toward one another. After Thomas' death, the "Universal Doctor," Albert, returned to the scene in 1277 to defend the views of Thomas, which by then had come under attack. Albert himself, whose thought had been the quarry from which Thomas had cut his fine building materials, did not die until 1280.

Albert's greatness came, in part, from fearlessness. He was not intimated by the philosophy of Aristotle, as some of his contemporaries were. Though not wholly consistent in his language, which was drawn in part from the neoplatonic sources of his time—especially Augustine—as well as from newly recovered Aristotelian documents, Albert firmly set himself against the temptation to shrink from this new knowledge. In his view, that would have been a form of faithlessness. Truth is truth; and since Christian beliefs are true, he held, there is nothing less needful than to shield faith behind a curtain of prohibitions and condemnations. With these confident values, he set out to show that one's thinking can be freshly Aristotelian and stoutly Christian at the same time.

These were the basic values also embraced by young Thomas, and they formed the framework for his far more comprehensive, systematic, and powerful synthesis. The *unity of truth* is the underlying epistemic commitment of all his work. This does not mean that everything, even in principle, is open to human reason or subject to rational proofs. Thomas, following Albert, parted company with those in the neoplatonic camp who argued that a beginning for time, for example, could be demonstrated. He also declared that certain other great elements of Christian thought, like the doctrine of Trinity and of the Incarnation of God in Jesus, are simply matters of faith: "mysteries" found—rightly—outside the domain of reason. This does not in the slightest mean, to Thomas, that the mysteries of faith are true in any different sense than are the demonstrations of logic. On the contrary, truth is one and indivisible, but the reach of the human mind, during this life at least, has limits which deserve acknowledgment and respect.

The mind, however, is a wonderful gift from God. There is no need for special acts of illumination from the divine; none are required, at least, beyond the sheer sustaining in existence of the mind itself in the same way that God sustains all that is created. For the first time within Christian thinking, Thomas thus provided, in this way, the basis for a wholly independent philosophy by affirming the potency of natural reason. The division of labor between philosophical thinking and theological thinking is not in the quality of the thinking or in the character of truth. It is grounded in the difference between what depends on revelation from beyond nature and what can be discovered without the provision of extra-natural sources of information.

Where, then, does our *natural* knowledge come from? Here Thomas is completely committed to the Aristotelian answer: it comes initially from abstraction—from abstracting universal Forms found in the world by way of the senses. The human intellect is midway between two extremes. Animals, equipped only with senses, can "know" only particularized items of information. Angels, granted complete freedom from matter, can know universal truth but can know individuals only indirectly. But human minds reap universal qualities from the material entities in which they reside and then can know them in their universality.

> [Sensing] is the act of a corporeal organ. And therefore the object of every sensitive power is a form as existing in corporal matter. . . . Therefore we must needs say that our intellect understands material things by abstracting from phantasms; and that through material things

thus considered we acquire some knowledge of immaterial things . . .
(Aquinas 1958: 402).

In this straightforward embrace of the Aristotelian epistemology, Thomas
accounts for how we can have genuine knowledge, as specified by Plato's
standard, but without Plato's free-floating Forms. He distinguishes his position sharply from the latter: "But Plato, considering only the immateriality of
the human intellect, and not that it is somehow united to the body, held that
the objects of the intellect are separate Ideas, and that we understand, not by
abstraction, but rather by participating in abstractions. . . ." (Aquinas 1948:
402).

Plato might not have cared for that characterization of the Forms as
abstractions, but this was Thomas' Aristotelian rendering. For Thomas, the
source of all human knowledge is rooted in the soil of individual things; and
matter is what provides the individuation. Such orthodox Aristotelian
hylomorphism was to cause him trouble, as we shall see in a moment. But
the position is intended to pay proper honor both to the ancient ideal of
knowing, as contemplating universal and necessary objects before the mind,
but—rejecting Plato-inspired radically discontinuous views of mind and body—
also to the reality of the living, sensing body and its positive links with
nature. For Thomas, the natural world is God's created gift, as are our minds.
We should therefore rejoice in finding ways that it can offer us footholds for
higher knowledge, even up to the highest possible knowledge about God.

Thomas' famous proofs for the knowledge of God, based on various
experienceable aspects of nature, show his epistemological commitments.
First, to know God's *existence*, start with what is humanly experienceable
(e.g., facts of change or of order), then point out the need for a cause or
ground for such a phenomenon, then argue that only an ultimate cause can
account for the whole range of these phenomena without calling for still more
accounts, and finally stipulate that this ultimate cause is uncontroversially
given the name "God." Starting from lowly abstractions from the senses, that
is, we can rise to demonstrative certainty concerning the existence of God.

What, though, of our supposed knowledge of God's *nature*? Bare existence of an unqualified "something" is not enough to satisfy religious values, much less the mind's craving for understanding ultimate things. Can a
cognitive process that is required, by Aristotelian rules, to rise from sense
perceptions provide adequately for the hungers of soul and intellect?

Thomas was fully aware of the negative answers that might be offered
to this even more challenging question on our knowledge of God's nature.
The author he knew as Dionysius (whom we call pseudo-Dionysius) strongly
opposed, with apparent apostolic authority, every sort of positive theology

and was frequently cited—and wrestled with—by Thomas as he worked out his position. This position would need to accommodate several commitments. First, Thomas was committed, both by his faith and by his Aristotelian view of God as Pure Actuality, to the principle that God is ultimately intelligible to the highest degree. Despite Dionysius, Thomas affirms that *in God's own nature*—though not relative to our own cognitive powers—we must acknowledge God's intrinsic knowability in the highest degree: "Since everything is knowable according as it is actual, God, Who is pure act without any admixture of potentiality, is in Himself supremely knowable" (Aquinas 1948: 71).

Second, Thomas is committed to the rationality—to what, in *Being and Value* (20 ff.), I earlier called the "decent order"—of the created *kosmos*. There are no genuine needs which are not satisfied by the universe. The world was not made to tantalize us. "But if the intellect of the rational creature could not attain to the first cause of things, the natural desire would remain vain" (Aquinas 1948: 71–72).

Religiously, too, ultimate beatitude is for the intellect to dwell in the knowledge of God forever. And if that were to be ruled impossible, then the intellect "would either never attain to beatitude, or its beatitude would consist in something else beside God; which is opposed to faith" (Aquinas 1948: 71).

But, fourth, Thomas is precluded by his Aristotelian commitment to sense perception from holding that we can gain anything besides natural, philosophical knowledge from normal abstraction and manipulation of concepts derived from the material world. This means that all likenesses between finite, perceptible essences and God's infinite essence are ruled out.

Thomas found himself in a difficult position, mediating between the epistemic consequences of too much stress on discontinuity, leading to a *via negativa*, and the *via affirmativa* demanded by contemplation of the legitimate expectations of epistemic completion, both from faith and from reason. His response was to attempt a middle way, the way of responsible, or grounded, analogy. Such analogies, being a type of "likeness," cannot in principle refer to or illuminate God's essence, as we have seen. But if we take them as governing our "names" for God, and if we realize that we are naming God from the creaturely side, as cause of ourselves and all things, rather than attempting to lay bare God's essence itself, then we may proceed a long way toward the affirmations that are craved and yet seem to be forbidden. "In this way therefore [God] can be named by us from creatures, yet not so that the name which signifies Him expresses the divine essence in itself . . . " (Aquinas 1948: 98).

Analogies are taken as epistemic gatekeepers, shutting the door on overweening claims to knowledge but opening again, in guarded ways, to certain expressions and not to others. There are two basic principles that will allow the gate to open. The first is the metaphysical principle that God is the ultimate cause for all finite things. This means, as a first approximation, that *analogies of attribution* may legitimately be made of God, as cause, in the way we use the word "healthy" to refer to the air at a mountain spa. The air is "healthy" in an analogical way because it contributes causally to helping the organisms who breathe it become "healthy" in a primary, literal way. But we need more epistemic restrictions than this, Thomas points out, because otherwise there would be no way to assign a reason "why some names more than others should be applied to God. For He is assuredly the cause of bodies in the same way as He is the cause of good things; therefore if the words *God is good* signified no more than, *God is the cause of good things*, it might in like manner be said that God is a body, inasmuch as He is the cause of bodies" (Aquinas 1948: 100).

A more stringent principle of responsible gatekeeping is required. This Thomas supplies by inverting this first rather primitive analogy of attribution. Instead of taking the primary significance of a quality (like "healthy") from the *caused* entity, which would make all language about God meaningful only in a secondary sense, one should turn this around, taking God, the *cause*, as the primary analogate and taking created things as secondary analogates. Then, since "God prepossesses in Himself all the perfections of creatures, being Himself absolutely and universally perfect" (Aquinas 1948: 101), creatures will be *analogies of God* insofar as they have received their positive qualities from their divine maker.

> Therefore, the aforesaid names signify the divine substance, but in an imperfect manner, even as creatures represent it imperfectly. So when we say, *God is good*, the meaning is not, *God is the cause of goodness*, or *God is not evil*; but the meaning is, *Whatever good we attribute to creatures pre-exits in God*, and in a higher way (Aquinas 1948: 101).

The second principle of responsible epistemic gatekeeping, Thomas argues, is that qualities and characteristics always relate to their owners *relative to their natures*. If we were to call a horse intelligent, we would not be taken as implying anything about its mathematical prowess; equine intelligence is proportional to equine nature, just as human intelligence is proportional to human nature. Therefore, by *analogies of proportionality*, when we are asked to consider a "name" for God, it will signify only proportionally to the divine nature, not to a creaturely nature. If a king is wise and powerful, this is proportional to human nature; if we use the words "wise" and "powerful" in connection with God, they will mean something relative to divine nature, not just to ours.

Does this mean that when we use the same word of God and of humans, that we are merely equivocating on our terms? It might appear so, since we are forbidden direct knowledge of the divine nature by which to explicate our analogy, but Thomas resists this conclusion. The application of our terms is certainly not univocal, that is, flatly literal. But it is not just an exercise in equivocation, either, since (harking back to the earlier analogy of attribution) we are allowed as a starting point the knowledge—demonstrated by the experience-based arguments discussed earlier—that God is the *cause* of everything we can perceive and from which we can abstract our concepts.

> And in this way some things are said of God and creatures analogically, and not in a purely equivocal nor in a purely univocal sense. For we can name God only from creatures. Hence, whatever is said of God and creatures is said according as there is some relation of the creature to God as to its principle and cause, wherein all the perfections of things pre-exist excellently. Now this mode of community is a mean between pure equivocation and simple univocation (Aquinas 1948: 108).

This is certainly a compromise. If one were to lack the metaphysical and religious commitments strongly affirmed by Thomas, one might judge it fragile. It affirms the importance of knowing God, but pulls back from univocal language each time it is offered. It honors the mystic sensibility of pseudo-Dionysius (and John Scotus Eriugena), but it shrinks from assuming the full consequences of utterly negative theology. It offers analogy as a supposed gatekeeper for faithful language about God, but the principles that would open or close the epistemic gate are made extremely difficult—perhaps impossible—to apply. We are told that "God's qualities are to God as human qualities are to humans," but we cannot solve this proportion, given two unknowns. That is, we may assume that we know well enough human nature and human qualities, but if we try to discover what meaning is conveyed by words expressing God's qualities, we are told that they are proportional to God's nature—which is another unknown. If we complain that this leaves us with pure equivocation, we are told that a causal relation grounds the analogy. But causality, alas, is too promiscuous a principle, since it would open the door to everything. Therefore we are told to shift the analogy so as to take the Creator as the prime analogate, but if we do this while holding that God is absolutely One, we must deny all distinctions between qualities—taken in some unexplained "higher way"—distinctions that alone make finite concepts meaningful.

Whichever way we go, we come up empty, cognitively. Still, given the metaphysical and religious commitments central to Thomas and his followers, the theory of analogy helped at the time. It helped to bridge Platonic discontinuity with Aristotelian continuity between perception and understanding. It helped to reconcile the diametrically opposed epistemic norms of

Platonic mysticism and Aristotelian empiricism. It helped to argue that humans can have knowledge "enough" for our finite condition without claiming "overweening" comprehension of the ultimate. It helped to give some standard, even though a logically circular one, for authorizing speech about the divine.

With Thomas we have reached the apex of the tendency toward synthesis between Plato and Aristotle, theology and philosophy, faith and reason. The brilliance and sweep of the Angelic Doctor's achievement remains one of the monuments of all time to the capability of human thought.

Thomas' epistemology rested on an almost seamless weaving together of his religious and his philosophical values. One of the most crucial—both religiously and philosophically—was his commitment to unity and coherence, to the value of synthesis-making itself. Since this value is not universally compelling, it would not be long before the Thomistic tapestry would begin to unravel.

Scotus and Ockham

John Duns Scotus

John Duns, the Scot (usually Latinized to Scotus), was born in 1265 or 1266. Little is known about his life; there is dispute even about which side of the Scottish Duns family can claim him. He was ordained a priest in 1297, after having received his childhood education in a Franciscan monastery in Dumfries. Soon afterward, he began to lecture, reaping much acclaim. Reports of his lectures at Cambridge are uncertain, but by 1300 he was teaching at Oxford; and two years later he turned up to lecture for a year at Paris. In 1303 he was banished for siding with the pope against the king in a dispute over church taxation, but was back again in a year. In 1307 he was transferred to a Franciscan center in Cologne, where he died the following year. In this short life he established, by force of personality and fineness of distinctions, a following that made Scotism a major alternative to Thomism for centuries to come.

Duns, the Subtle Doctor, "*Doctor Subtilis*," disagreed with the Thomistic-Aristotelian epistemic rules in one profoundly important respect: he did not accept the view that all our knowledge must come from abstraction of clear Forms from sense perceptions. If this were true, he argued, then the only proper objects of our knowledge would be universals. Qualities, characteristics, features, and traits are doubtless of great moment in knowing things, but these can attach to indefinitely many subjects. Besides all the universal aspects, there is also for cognition *the thing itself*, the being that we know. If we did not somehow, in some vague or confused way, first know the thing itself, how could we ever know that those clear and discussable qualities we abstract are qualities of *it*? Worse, if we love some particular person, we certainly know more than a cluster of abstract characteristics—color of hair, height, weight, shape of nose, moral habits, and the like. We know the object of our love as the very individual, the particular *thisness*, that is before us. The *whatness* (or *"quidditas"*) is much more easily communicated, thought about, imagined in absence; but *thisness* (or *"haecceitas"*) is also directly known.

Duns consequently distinguishes between two kinds of knowledge. The first is knowledge by abstraction, in which he agrees for the most part with the familiar Aristotelian tradition. The second is knowledge by intuition, which he defines as cognition of the immediate presence of an individual when it is present. This also involves abstraction of the Forms from the essence of the thing, but underlying this formal abstraction is the immediate awareness of the "thisness" of the known thing's presence. This unique thisness is not in principle provided or providable by mere, unqualified matter alone, as Aristotle and Thomas had asserted. It has too much quality for mere matter, but too much particularity for mere Form. Thus genuine intuitive knowledge entails contact with the actual presence of the thing intuited, since "it is against the nature of intuitive knowledge that it should be of something which is not actually existent and present" (Scotus 1962: 22).

There are strong value-considerations in rejecting the previously hallowed rule that only universals can be known by the intellect and adopting in its stead this alternative epistemic norm. One motive, of course, to which I have already alluded, is the protest against losing the particularity of the object of one's affection. No collection of loose-fitting concepts will substitute for the unique individual with whom one is united in love. And love was important to Duns. He rejected the Thomistic view that salvation consisted in the *knowledge* of God. That is too intellectual, too speculative. Beatitude consists in the *love* of God. This is a union of the soul with its object that goes beyond the mere contemplation of essence. It is the burning intuition of being itself.

Another important epistemological motive for insisting on intuitive contact with the thisness of unique particulars is to ground the possibility of objective knowledge itself. If all we ever immediately knew were formal qualities, then what would happen to the concrete world itself? It would systematically escape our immediate awareness; it would become a cognitive vacuity. No skeptic he, such consequences Duns took as patently absurd. In the next chapter we shall watch a different outcome unfold under the guidance of different values.

Additional motives, more specifically theological but no less value-driven, reinforced Duns' support of an account of experience in which unclear feelings are just as important as clear conceptions. We need not go into these more technical points, which involve Duns' views on human knowledge in the afterlife, the knowledge of angels, and the credibility of Christ's Incarnation. But all his arguments drew him in the same direction: to rejection of the overwhelming prior consensus that only universals can be known.

A further (more general) harmful implication of that consensus, and Thomas' acceptance of it, according to Duns, is that on those grounds we could not possibly know even our own minds in their particularity. Everything we can know turns out to be a *quality* that might as well be characterizing indefinitely many other selves. The uniqueness of our own particular self vanishes. Thomas actually acknowledged that our self-knowledge must be indirect, by way of acts of intellection clear enough to characterize and put words to. But for Duns, once having broken with the key rule of the Platonic-Aristotelian knowledge game, there was no such limitation. Surely, he held, we *just do* have self-knowledge of more than the formal contents of our intellects—we *just can* know ourselves directly, intuiting our intellects as the unique individual entities they are.

Admittedly, for Duns, our knowledge of such being—direct, intuitive knowledge—is far from clear and far from perfect. We cannot in this life have direct natural knowledge of God's being, though that is our ultimate end. This, he speculated, is due to original sin, our fallen state blinding us to the ultimate intuition. Only God could overcome this blindness with a loving act of self-revelation. "Our infirmity" also makes intuitions even of finite objects much less clear than they would be apart from our sinful condition, and this makes them far less clear than they will be in the afterlife. Being, however, which is the proper object of the intellect, is in principle available for immediate contact even now.

This offers yet another epistemic benefit. *Being*, Duns held, is a term we use univocally, even when we are talking about God at one moment and creatures at another. Without a univocal anchor, the Thomist analogical ship drifts aimlessly. "Being," however, provides this anchor, something basic that both God and creatures have in common. This does not minimize the difference between infinite and finite being, he argued. But while admitting that there is no such thing as a being that is both infinite and finite, there is a real basis for grouping both together, since being of either sort has in common the radical *opposition to nothingness*. Since this is so, thinking of God is grounded in more than equivocation.

John Duns Scotus was clearly a believer. His arguments assumed Christian doctrine, and his epistemic norms were deeply shaped by his religious priorities, including his Franciscan loyalties as well as appreciation for close logical distinctions. But while undoubtedly a believer in the strongest sense of the term, Duns did not put his first priority on matters speculative. As I noted earlier, love, not contemplative knowledge, was the highest goal for him. This makes theology not primarily a speculative science, as it was for Thomas Aquinas, but a practical one. The main thing should be to guide right conduct and affection; and this, for Duns, is a matter of the will, not the intellect. Were we to delve into metaphysical questions, we would see how important to Duns was the absolute freedom of God's will. He found abhorrent the notion, accepted by Thomas, that God's will could in any way be subordinate to principles. That would make the principles prior, not God. For God's omnipotence to be defended, the will of God must be absolutely unmotivated by anything prior, even by God's contemplation of the good. What is good is so because God wills it, not the reverse. So, likewise, Duns emphasized the importance of the human will, and of theology as not derivative from metaphysics, but, rather, from God's gracious decision to offer theology its first principles through revelation.

Theology, as a practical science dependent on God's voluntary revelation, does not derive its first principles from metaphysics; but—conversely— metaphysics, as a theoretical science dependent on self-evident first principles of reason, does not depend on theology, either. The two are independent sciences operating in different domains for different ends. Duns saw no great conflict between them; he engaged in them both. But if they are each free-standing, it does not matter so much whether or not the first principles of theology are capable of being demonstrated by reason. In this area Duns was hard to convince. It is not clear exactly what his position was on the proofs, since some of the more radically negative documents purporting to be his may well be spurious. But it is quite clear that he did not think highly of any of the proofs for God. No a priori arguments, he held, could prove anything about actual existence. And the causal arguments used by Thomas only proved, at most, that there is a supreme cause of the phenomena they explain. They do not prove that this supreme cause is worthy of worship, is divine, or is the God of Christian theology. Therefore the Scotists, following Duns in years to come, were among those who placed comparatively little stock in the efforts of natural theology. For them, as for Duns himself, belief was secure without proofs. There were too many flaws in the logic of the dominant Dominicans to satisfy reason; but why bother? Belief was secured on a different footing.

In later centuries the Scotists, by then a major movement, became a thorn in the fleshy optimism of the Renaissance establishment. The followers of Duns were always making distinctions and raising objections to the new learning. They were perceived as obstinate, cranky, impervious to liberal learning. Their opponents, in exasperation, coined the epithet, "dunces," against them, in "honor" of Duns, their founder. Duns, of course, was no dunce. In his time he offered both principled opposition to the novel teachings of Thomas and his Dominican followers and a systematic, constructive alternative. The alternative, however, was a system of belief running on a track parallel to, rather than joined with, the norms of general knowledge. In this Duns Scotus inserted a significant wedge into the medieval synthesis of faith and reason. And into the crack thus believingly begun, others would continue to drive their intellectual wrecking bars.

WILLIAM OF OCKHAM

William of Ockham, a firm believer in Christian revelation and in logically demonstrable truth—but also a critic, a theological, logical, and political controversialist, and at the end a fugitive from the vengeance of his Church— was the principal wrecker of the medieval synthesis. He was born in England, probably in the town of Ockham, near London, sometime between 1280 and 1290. It seems likely that he studied at Oxford from 1310 to 1315, strongly influenced by the continuing echoes left reverberating by John Duns Scotus after his departure for Paris a decade earlier. He, like Duns, joined the Franciscans, who were continuing Duns' cause, and by 1317 he was himself lecturing at Oxford on the Bible and on the influential *Sentences* of Peter Lombard. By 1324 Ockham received his credentials as Master of Theology and was ready to start his teaching career, but at just that point he became the subject of charges of heresy and was summoned to the papal seat at Avignon. The former Chancellor of Oxford, a Thomist, had brought fifty-six articles of accusation against Ockham, which he was obliged to answer in person. A Papal Commission was appointed, and a trial was conducted; but it continued without result for three years, during which Ockham (at Pope John XXII's initial request) became involved with the controversy over poverty for the Franciscan order. This controversy was soon entangled in the political struggle between the Pope and the Holy Roman Emperor, King Louis of Bavaria. When the head of the Franciscan order, also in Avignon facing discipline, decided in 1328 to flee to the protection of King Louis, Ockham fled too. The rest of his life was spent in Munich, under the Emperor's protection, where he wrote polemics against the papal position on Church and State. Finally, when King Louis died, Ockham had no choice but to apologize and submit; but it is unclear whether he ever signed the document of submission, since the Black Death, raging around Munich in 1349, seems to have taken him first.

This brilliant "otherwise thinker," known as *Venerabilis Inceptor* (called "Venerable Beginner" because, though qualified, he never received a regular teaching post) was stimulated by, but no mere follower of, John Duns Scotus. Some of the principal points—with vital epistemological repercussions—that he took (and retained) from Duns were: (1) the emphasis on the absolute, untrammeled centrality of the *will* of God the Omnipotent (I shall shortly explain why this is epistemologically important); (2) the *non-speculative* character of theology; and (3) the *univocality* of the language of being, guarding the continuity of our talk about God with other talk to save it from mere equivocation and to rescue our thought about God from agnosticism; and the distinction between *intuitive and abstractive* knowing. The spirit of his thinking, too, like Duns, was unflinching when it came to ladling out boiling criticism against received opinions. This applied, of course, to the entrenched Thomists; for Ockham, however, it was to be generously poured onto the Scotists as well.

Ockham, we must remember, was a passionate religious believer. His name, associated with his so-called "Razor," is often invoked today as though he had been a skeptic, but that is a historical misreading. His influence, we shall see, led to much skepticism. Many moderns feel quite comfortable with his arguments. How surprising, then, to learn that his criticisms were all in the cause of rigorous religious belief!

The troubles with Duns, he argued, were twofold. First, he had allowed himself to be taken in, without adequate justification, by the doctrine of the Forms. And, second, he had not gone far enough in following the full epistemological implications of Christian belief in the omnipotence of God.

First, on the question of universal entities, Ockham simply had no patience or sympathy. For him it was simply self-evident that everything must be particular. Things are things. We never encounter anything that is not singular, located in time and space, either in the world or in our mental experience. To suppose that general predicate words refer to something besides particular properties of things is to be misled, to postulate an odd sort of entity—a universal Form—without any reasonable necessity at all. Duns was guilty of this, along with the Thomists and virtually everyone else. But the following epistemic rule, he insisted, is sound: one should not multiply "entities" without some reason sufficient to make it necessary to do so. This is just to apply the discipline of sufficient reason to our thinking. It is not so much a metaphysical prejudice as a rule of clean procedure. This, then, was Ockham's famous "Razor." It was not sharpened as an ontological weapon but was an epistemic rule. His usual way of expressing this rule was: *Pluralitas non est ponenda sine necessitate*, or "Plurality is not to be posited without necessity" (Ockham 1957: xxi). If we can get along perfectly well with the domain of particular existences, then there is no necessity to postulate the additional mysterious terminology of universal existences. It is not needed. It causes troubles.

If we follow this rule, then we need not speculate endlessly, for example, about what "individuates" particular things, since there is nothing strange to explain. Individual things are just that, and to explain their individuality is just to explain what caused them to be. There is no need for hylomorphic "prime matter," or for wonderment about how disembodied angelic intellects can know particularity. Particularity is all there is. This is true for God as well. If we want to translate what *universalia ante rem* could mean, it refers to the singular fact that God's mind knows all the things that ever have been or could be. But these are all individual acts of the divine mind, about individual actual or possible entities.

Our own thoughts, too, are particular events. When we have intuitive knowledge, we are engaged causally with a particular entity and our senses perceive this entity both in its existence (as Duns said) and in its particular features. When we sense a second such entity with similar features, our minds make an automatic act of recognition and comparison. Our words then can be predicated of these similar things. But there is nothing universal in all this. The acts of mind that occur are all singular; the entities themselves are all singular; the terms we use, as we use them, are all singular. The fact that a given term can refer to a number of similar particular things is what allows us to group many particulars together in useful ways. Ockham's early followers were called "Terminists" to reflect the importance of the particular *terminus* or predicable, as against the supposedly universal Forms of either Plato or Aristotle. Later the position came to be called Nominalism, and that is what I shall call it, too, though there are many varieties of Nominalism that need to be crowded under that elastic word. Ockham's Christian variety was only one kind, and not the first, as we have seen. But as he developed and defended it, it became a powerful lever to pound into the crack in Thomism begun by Duns Scotus, splintering also much of Duns' own position along with the medieval synthesis.

Ockham's second main criticism of Duns was that he had not taken in the full implications for *epistemology* of the radical *omnipotence of God.* Only God is necessary. Everything else is as it is only because of a completely free, thus entirely arbitrary, act of God. What does this imply for knowledge? Above all *it follows that everything in the created universe is utterly contingent.* No matter of fact is necessary. Nothing that exists could have been deduced from anything, since God might equally freely have chosen otherwise. And this means, importantly, that the only way to gain knowledge about how things happen to be is to look and listen and touch and taste and smell how God made them. This is a theological motive for an inductive spirit. It is not simply empirical philosophy, of the sort we shall explore in the following chapter. Rather, it is a religiously motivated call to give up all deductive thinking about the actual world.

Deductive thinking has its important place, however, for Ockham. From absolutely necessary first principles we can deduce how things must be in any possible world. God's omnipotence does not entail that logical impossibilities become possibilities for God. A genuine contradiction is radical impossibility, total nonentity, unmeaning. And it is no limitation on God's perfect freedom that God "cannot do" what has no standing in possibility or meaning. Therefore, we can dismiss the old chestnuts such as whether God, the necessary being, if omnipotent, can commit suicide. And we can reject as nonsense the question whether God can create stone so heavy that even omnipotence cannot lift it. These are silly questions, based on logical confusions. But interesting questions of logic follow from deducing what is and must be possible in all contingent circumstances. For this Ockham developed powerful modes of argument.

Epistemology under such norms, emphasizing the omnipotent freedom of God, contains two interesting twists. One new one is that even intuitive knowledge, which involves (by definition) the actual existence of the object known (as Duns, too, had insisted) can under one, but only one, circumstance be false (as Duns had not seen). Since any effect that is able to be caused by contingent causes is *ipso facto* shown to be a genuine possibility, there is no obstacle to God's producing that same effect by direct action, without use of any of the normally intervening contingent causes. That means that, in principle, even intuitive knowing does not guarantee the external object's presence—*if* God should please to take direct action in this case.

A second twist that was not so new, since it was anticipated by Duns, is that moral knowledge cannot in principle be derived from any eternal principles of right or good. What is good is so because of the arbitrary decision of God. We must learn what God decided through the sources of revelation. And these results must be reverently accepted, not deduced. Nothing intrinsic in our acts makes them good or right.

In thus driving a wedge between the norms of behavior and human reason, Ockham furthered a still-wider thesis on the separation of faith from even the best and most powerful reasoning. Theology itself, as for Duns, is a practical discipline. But for Ockham, theology, in opposition to Duns, is no "science" at all. Theology offers no logically necessary first principles; consequently, nothing in it follows deductively from such first principles, as would be needful for any genuine knowledge worthy of being called "scientific." Theology is a matter of faithful belief, and nothing about it can claim (or should want to claim) the additional authority of reason. Reason, for Ockham, is therefore free to follow its own bent, stopping only when contradicted by still higher authority, revelation itself. The two run not only on separate parallel tracks, as Duns held, but sometimes the tracks may cross one another. At such points, revelation has the right of way. As Ockham put it:

> I consider it to be dangerous and temerarious to force anyone to fetter his mind and to believe something which his reason dictates to him to

be false, unless it can be drawn from holy scripture or from a determination of the Roman Church or from the words of approved doctors (Ockham 1957: xviii).

With this, however, the harmony of faith and reason at last turns dissonant. Truth as *reason* dictates may come into conflict with truth as *faith* (interpreted by "approved doctors") dictates instead. Himself a victim of the *Realpolitik* of Church "fetters," Ockham noted the possibility of forced submission long before his own.

He left no disciples, in the literal sense. He died in exile and humiliation. But his work was noticed, and it caught fire in the tinder of the fourteenth century, just waiting for conflagration. At first "Ockhamism" was condemned and forbidden. But by the end of his century and through the fifteenth, even a Cardinal of the Church, Pierre d'Ailly (1350–1425) and a Chancellor of the University of Paris, Jean Charlier de Gerson (1363–1429), could thrive as leading Nominalists. Gerson and d'Ailly were both also pious mystics, providing satisfaction, *by turns* (though not simultaneously) to entirely discontinuous cravings of the secular mind and the religious spirit. The divorce, however, was nearly complete; it became so as soon as Renaissance humanism, and then modern science, came to preoccupy the best minds of the fifteenth and sixteenth centuries. The Nominalists had long called their path the *via moderna*, the "modern way," as against the "old way," the *via antiqua*. In many ways William of Ockham, though always thinking of himself as a committed believer, opened wide the gates to modern doubt.

4

MODERN DOUBTERS

Modern doubt has a peculiarly keen edge to it, though it is not all of the same sharpness, as we shall see. In important ways, this edge was honed during the two centuries between Thomas Hobbes (born 1588) and Immanuel Kant (died 1804). Awareness of an unbridgeable epistemological gap between the knower and the known—hinted at (for other motives) by Ockham and others—was forced into modern consciousness during those years. This situation was not always clear, even to the main players. Hobbes, for all his Ockhamite Nominalism and Epicurean doubts about the qualitative sensory world, was not especially worried about his assurance that there *is* a material world "out there" to be known. The plight of the would-be knower, however, became increasingly evident, until its final, absolute formulation by Kant. Since then, ways of coping with the epistemological gap have preoccupied modern philosophers, as we shall see in Part Two; but none of these ways have been satisfactory. In Part Three I shall offer suggestions that can, I hope, deconstruct the modern impasse to which this chapter leads.

All students of philosophy will have studied the six thinkers to be reviewed here. If readers feel inclined to skip directly to Part Two, there is nothing to prevent that. Still, although these are the most familiar figures of modern philosophy (with good reason!), they are not usually treated quite as I plan to do. I am, of course, interested in their finished theories of knowledge, but I am no less interested in the norms and values, commitments and preferences (often unnoticed), that led the human thinkers concerned to these theories. Making preferential choices in philosophy did not occur only in ancient and medieval times. Moderns, even if embarrassed by them, make their value-judgments, too. Some include premodern commitments reaffirmed. Some are new. Together they make a mighty network of norms—what I earlier called "rules of the knowing game"—hugely effective for some enterprises (especially the mathematical sciences) but deeply frustrating for the other aspects of the wider human quest for knowing. I hope that most of my readers, no matter how familiar with Hobbes, Descartes, Locke, Berkeley, Hume, and Kant, will take yet another look at them as purveyors of epistemic norms as well as epistemic theories.

HOBBES AND DESCARTES

The lives and thinking of Hobbes and Descartes were interestingly intertwined, though this is hardly ever indicated in standard treatments. My own treatment will be resolutely nonstandard in this respect since I intend to show how their careers twined around one another like two live wires, growing closer until, in 1640, they met intellectually, though not yet in person, producing a shower of sparks. Then nothing remained but wariness.

HOBBES, FROM 1588 TO 1620

Although Thomas Hobbes (1588–1679) was born eight years earlier than René Descartes (1596–1650), the younger man published first in philosophy. Conventionally, Descartes is awarded the title of "Father of Modern Philosophy"; but it is hard to deny Hobbes' equally strong claims to paternity. Examining the face of today's dominant Anglo-American philosophy, indeed, one finds Hobbesian family resemblances—the strong nose and piercing eyes—particularly striking. What is biologically impossible is nevertheless true for modern philosophy: it has not one, but two, "Fathers." In significant ways, these two Fathers were at loggerheads, as we shall see, over the nature of knowledge; but in still more determinative ways, they shared the fears and hopes—the basic commitments—that after them came to define the modern game of knowing.

Hobbes, in his mid-eighties, wrote his autobiography in Latin verse, in which he portrayed himself with a striking metaphor. He said that his mother, terrified of the approaching Spanish Armada in the fateful year, 1588, gave birth to twins: himself and fear. The metaphor is apt, since insecurity is the dominant motive for all of Hobbes' thinking, political and epistemological; but as pointed out in the splendid biographical study by Arnold Rogow (Rogow 1986: 17 ff.), Hobbes was taking poetical liberties with the facts. His birth in Malmesbury, England, occurred on April 5, but the Armada did not even set sail for the first time until the middle of May. When it did sail it was blown south, away from England, and was forced to regroup for a second try in July. By August 2 it was defeated.

Still, insecurity was a vital theme in Hobbes' life. During his boyhood years, his father, the Reverend Thomas Hobbes, Sr., was a highly controversial village clergyman, subject of many complaints and lawsuits from his parishioners and others for neglect of duty and public drunkenness, as well as violent and vulgar behavior. Legal records indicate that Hobbes' mother took the side of the parishioners against her husband in at least some of these cases. In 1604, the ne'er-do-well senior Hobbes got into a violent brawl with another clergyman from a neighboring village and fled to London, never to return to his family.

It was in this anxiety-ridden context that the teen-aged Hobbes, aided by his uncle, a prosperous glove-maker, attended Magdalene Hall at Oxford and continued a good classical education begun at Malmesbury. There was no family wealth. Young Hobbes would need to struggle for his life and win whatever he could by his wits.

To his good fortune he was chosen in February 1608, by the great Cavendish family—one of England's richest—to become tutor for the young William Cavendish, then eighteen and disqualified for University education because already married. William had requested a tutor of roughly his own years, rather than some venerable sage, and the Principal of Magdalene Hall recommended Hobbes, who was then (at his graduation from Oxford) still not quite twenty. William's father, the first Baron Hardwick, was to become the first Earl of Devonshire in 1618. On his death, Hobbes' pupil was to become the second Earl of Devonshire. For the next seventy years, with only brief intermissions, Hobbes was to be in the employ of the Cavendish family, the Devonshires. In consequence, he was provided a livelihood, an excellent library, opportunities for travel, and extended contacts with the leading intellectuals of his day. In 1610, only two years after taking up his duties, Hobbes took William on a visit to the Continent, a standard "grand tour" for the education of the nobility. Then only twenty-two, Hobbes had his first opportunity to travel in Europe; it would not be the last.

DESCARTES, FROM 1596 TO 1620

At that time, René Descartes, fourteen, was in study at La Flèche, a Jesuit College recently founded by King Henry IV for the sons of gentlemen, where he had been enrolled since the age of eight. Descartes was the third child in his family, and his mother, who had never been strong, died in giving him birth. Descartes inherited his mother's rather delicate constitution, and as a result was given special privileges from an early age, such as remaining in bed long hours after most people were required to be at work. He was raised by a grandmother. His father, a lawyer and a judge, was a member of the local parliament at Rennes.

After eight years at La Flèche, where he showed academic talent, especially in the area of mathematics, Descartes was given a year in the country to learn fencing and horsemanship, then allowed to go to Paris with a valet and a modest but adequate income from his father. In Paris, on his own, Descartes tasted the pleasures of the city, especially gambling, but in moderation. He also made the acquaintance of leading French mathematicians and reestablished a close friendship with an older alumnus and acquaintance from La Flèche, Marin Mersenne (1588–1648), who had in the meantime become a member of the Minim Friars and a talented mathematician in his own right. When Mersenne was reassigned in 1614 to the provinces, Descartes lost interest in society and went into many months of seclusion at a Paris address he kept secret, working on mathematical issues. Eventually his location was discovered, however, and social pressure reasserted itself. Unable to continue his mathematical research, he was bored and restless. Leaving Paris, he obtained his law degree from the University of Poitiers in 1616. The next year, age twenty-one, with no taste for the practice of law, restless and at loose ends, he travelled to Holland where he volunteered for military service in the army of Prince Maurice of Orange, who was fighting in Spanish Belgium to defend Holland's new independence from Spain. While there he met Isaac Beeckman (1588–1637), Principal of the College of Dort and an established man of science and mathematics, who encouraged Descartes to continue his mathematical research. In July 1619, Descartes left Holland, now at peace, and volunteered his military services to the Bavarian army, which was rumored to be engaging soon against the Protestant princes. Descartes at twenty-three that winter, encamped at Neuburg on the Danube in Swabia, and, finding himself in a quiet, stove-heated room, engaged in solitary thoughts that two decades later were to be the central inspiration of his *Meditations* (1641)— on which Thomas Hobbes was to express his Objections.

HOBBES, FROM 1620 TO 1629

Back from the first European travels with William Cavendish (simultaneous with Descartes' tours of military duty), Hobbes had been teaching his aristocratic pupil and improving his own circumstances. He made the acquaintance of Francis Bacon (1561–1626), following Bacon's retirement from the Lord Chancellor's position, disgraced by convictions for petty bribery. Hobbes, still primarily a classical scholar, ingratiated himself with Bacon by translating some of his writings into Latin. He was not particularly enthusiastic about Bacon's recommendations of a highly empirical approach to science, but he was impressed by the rhetorical fanfares Bacon was playing for the new age

of post-Aristotelian thought. Hobbes had not been especially taken with
Aristotle's philosophy while at Oxford, and Bacon's criticisms struck him as
thoroughly justified. In the same years, Hobbes became acquainted also with
William Harvey (1578–1657), whose discovery of the circulation of the blood
was in the making. The idea of the body as a closed hydraulic system and the
heart as a mechanical pump was fascinating to Hobbes. In the year after
Harvey published his epoch-making *On the Circulation of the Blood* (1628),
Hobbes, then forty-one, published his own first work, a translation of
Thucydides' great *History of the Peloponnesian Wars*. The book, which Hobbes
titled *Eight Bookes of the Peloponnesian Warre, Written by Thucydides, the
Sonne of Olorus: Interpreted with Faith and Diligence Immediately out of the
Greeke by Thomas Hobbes, Secretary to the Late Earle of Devonshire* (1629),
was an immediate success. It was dedicated to the memory of William
Cavendish, Hobbes' long-time pupil, the second Earl of Devonshire, who had
already died (from what was called excess of good living) at the age of thirty-
eight. Christian, William's widow, saw no further reason to retain Hobbes;
thus, at this moment of triumph, he was cast loose. He did not know it was
to be a temporary separation. The insecurity of life reasserted itself.

DESCARTES, FROM 1620 TO 1629

During the same span of years, Descartes had made several momentous decisions. He had left military service in the summer of 1621, after seeing a
variety of scenes in middle Europe. He was present, for example, at the
important Battle of Prague in 1620, but after the death of his commander, he
resigned and made his way back to his father's home at Rennes in Brittany.
There he sold property and arranged for a comfortable permanent income for
himself. After some travels in June of 1625, he settled again in Paris, where
he found his friend Mersenne once more in place. During this period Descartes
and Mersenne engaged in exciting work on the refraction of light, but he
could not fully shake the conviction that he had a more profound contribution
to make. After his meditation in the stove-heated room in the winter of 1619,
he had experienced in one night three remarkable dreams, suggesting to him
a special life-mission. These continued to haunt him. He travelled restlessly,
but continued to return to Paris. In November 1628, he expressed himself
forcefully in a salon debate with a gentleman remembered only as Chandoux,
who had been maintaining that knowledge should and must settle for probability. Descartes overwhelmed Chandoux with arguments why only absolute
certainty could count as knowledge. Then, after so distinguishing himself, he
was approached by someone who had been present and was much impressed.
This was the Cardinal Pierre de Bérulle (1575–1629), a leading follower of
Duns Scotus. Cardinal Bérulle drew Descartes aside to urge him in the strongest

terms that someone with his views and talents had an obligation to spend the rest of his life with more focus on exploring and defining that "truth and knowledge" about which he had spoken so fervently. The advice hit its mark, reminding Descartes of his epiphany in the stove-heated room and his subsequent dreams. Convinced he had an overwhelmingly important mission to fulfill, Descartes decided to exile himself from the distractions of Paris and to take up residence in peaceful Holland. In 1629, just as Hobbes' translation of Thucydides appeared, Descartes departed for the Low Countries, never again to live in Paris.

HOBBES, FROM 1630 TO 1640

Hobbes, however, was at this point ready to head back to Paris and to the rest of the Continent, this time with a new pupil in tow. With his many connections, cultivated during the Cavendish years, and with new fame from the Thucydides translation, he had quickly found employment with Sir Gervaise Clinton as tutor to Clinton's son, who was ready for his Grand Tour.

It was during this visit to the Continent that Hobbes had his own "revelation," on the possibilities of knowing. Somewhere in Europe, very likely in Geneva during a pause in peregrinations with his pupil, Hobbes chanced upon a copy of Euclid's *Elements of Geometry*, opening it idly to Proposition 47. At first blush, the proposition seemed quite implausible to Hobbes. As William Aubrey, his much younger friend and first biographer, described the event (retaining Aubrey's expurgations), Hobbes exclaimed:

> "By G—, this is impossible!" So he reads the demonstration of it, which referred him back to such a proposition; which proposition he read. That referred him back to another, which he also read. Et sic deinceps, that at last he was demonstratively convinced of that trueth. This made him in love with geometry (Aubrey 1898 in Rogow 1986: 100).

Hobbes indeed "fell in love" with geometry from that moment, a mid-life infatuation that did not fade. He had been much concerned with arguing politics—apparently much engaged, while living and working among the nobility, in private debates over the rights of kings and the need for an all-powerful sovereign during the turbulent, frightening years leading to increasing instability and portents of revolution—and he had almost despaired of the possibility of convincing people of anything. But geometry! That method could, by simple arrangement of clearly defined terms, force assent from beginning to end. Here was a model for genuine knowing. Here was an epistemic norm by which all serious claims for knowing can be judged. Is it self-evident, or is it demonstrated from self-evident principles by self-evident deductive steps? If so, it is admitted as knowledge; if not, then it is merely probable or prudential or dogmatic, but is not truly up to standard.

Hobbes was in his early forties when he first appreciated the charms and power of geometry. A decade earlier, Descartes had already made his epoch-making invention of analytical geometry, the synthesis of geometry with algebra. This had been achieved during the peaceful years in the Dutch army, in the company of stimulating scientific and mathematical companions gathered into his officers corps by the enlightened Maurice of Nassau. Descartes, at the time, had been in his early twenties. There was never any real comparison between the mathematical skills of the two Fathers of modern philosophy. Descartes was an authentic mathematical genius; Hobbes was just a lover of Euclid's method. Later in life, to his cost, Hobbes tried his hand at original work and convinced himself that he had squared the circle. Alas for him, he convinced no others, and his reputation in old age suffered for his mathematical pretensions, especially among the members of the recently founded Royal Society who took up their acid pens against him (and excluded him from membership). But in 1631 this was all far in the future. The second visit to the Continent is best remembered for budding new love for geometric method.

On his third tutorial visit to Europe, a leisurely stay from 1634 to 1637, Hobbes added substantive premises to his method. He spent much time in Paris, developing on this visit warm relations with Father Marin Mersenne, Descartes' closest friend, and with Mersenne's circle of intellectuals. Included in this circle was Pierre Gassendi (1592–1655), a priest convinced that Christian faith could be harmonized with the atomism of Democritus and Epicurus. In addition to his discussions with this enthusiastic atomist, Hobbes was able to arrange a visit to see Galileo in Italy. Galileo's *Dialogo sopra i due massimi sistemi del mondo* (the *Dialogue Concerning the Two Chief World Systems*) had been published in January 1632 and had already been condemned by the Church in 1633, before Hobbes' visit. Galileo himself was living under house arrest in Arcetri, near Florence, when Hobbes called on him. There is no record of their conversation, but it seems likely that Galileo encouraged Hobbes to continue developing his vision of the world, in which the geometrical method of Euclid could be harnessed to the atomism of Epicurus to create a coercively convincing demonstration of what human nature and human society must be—and what sort of government such beings must have to avoid destruction by their own abrasive impacts on one another. An early work by Hobbes, his *Short Tract on First Principles* (unpublished during his lifetime and not published until 1889), written during this time of philosophical emergence, attempts to lay out the foundations for such a worldview by offering geometry-like definitions and, through these, to link everything in the universe to matter in motion. This "everything" includes sensation and thought, in proper Epicurean manner. The "phantasms," by which we perceive the world, are also nothing but particular bits of matter in motion; and the world itself, apart from subjective experience, is entirely without color, taste, sound, texture, or odor. Hobbes, though not fully engaged in philosophy to this point, and still unpublished in the field, had clearly developed for himself at least a sketch of an entire worldview—firmly nominalist, materialist, and atomist—by the mid-1630s. It was in the same spirit, and with an obvious evocation of Euclid's *Elements of Geometry* in his title, that Hobbes wrote his first treatise in political philosophy, back once again in England during the increasingly bitter debates between king and Parliament. This was his *Elements of Law*, written (but not published) in 1640. When in November 1640 the strains between the factions in English politics reached what seemed to Hobbes their inevitable snapping point, he fled back to Paris, this time not as tutor but as exile. Always insecure and timid, Hobbes imagined himself in danger of his life because of his "little treatise" (the *Elements of Law*), which strongly defended the sovereignty of the king. Later he boasted that he had been "the first of all who fled" (Hobbes 1986: 124). It seems that Hobbes took his danger much more seriously than was actually warranted, but, however this might be, he found immediate welcome and safe-haven in Paris with Father Mersenne and his circle of intellectuals.

Hobbes' philosophical ideas, both political and metaphysical, were well known to this circle, within which Hobbes was by then accepted as a respected—even a leading—member. Because of this connection, through which Hobbes was at last, to his evident gratification, "numbered among the philosophers" (Hobbes 1986: 111), Father Mersenne (who had through correspondence maintained constant contact with Descartes in Holland) invited Hobbes to respond to Descartes' *Meditations*, then being circulated in manuscript. Descartes had requested Mersenne to collect opinions from leading thinkers of the day. These "Objections," after being bundled with others, answered by Descartes, and published with the *Meditations*, were to be Hobbes' first public expression of views that had been gestating for some years.

DESCARTES, FROM 1630 TO 1640

Descartes, meanwhile, had been busy in Holland. Prior to his arrival he had sketched *Rules for the Direction of the Mind*, though this manuscript was not published in his lifetime. He also wrote an extensive manuscript on physical reality simply called *Le Monde*, or *The World*. Just as it was ready for publication in 1634, however, disturbing news reached him of the condemnation of Galileo's *Dialogue* (1632). Since his views on nature were closely akin to Galileo's, and because he did not want to offend the Church or risk the troubles befalling the great Italian physicist, he suppressed the manuscript, sending it to a friend for safe-keeping. Unfortunately, that manuscript disappeared forever. The *Discourse on Method of Rightly Conducting the Reason and of Seeking for Truth in the Sciences*, however, was successfully published in 1637, together with three earlier scientific essays intended to illustrate the method at work: "Optics," "Meteorology," and "Geometry." It seems likely that Hobbes had read this important work in England, after his return from the third tutorial visit to Europe and before his precipitate self-exile in 1640. The *Discourse on Method* thus turned out to be Descartes' first publication, and—thanks to its being published in French rather than Latin—it was a work directed to the widest educated readership of his time. It was a huge success, and justified the high opinion of Descartes' many admirers in Paris, some of whom had much earlier started a rumor that his philosophy was already completed. Descartes himself wryly comments that one of the reasons he felt it necessary to retire to Holland and write the book was "to try by all means to make myself worthy of my reputation" (Descartes 1960: 23).

The *Discourse* itself was written boldly, but not in a brash tone. Descartes was forty-one in 1637, and had until then been unpublished. He begins with great modesty, referring to his talents as no more than average. But if all of us, as a species, are equally endowed with "good sense" (Descartes 1960: 3), then the way in which we use our minds—the *method* of thinking we adopt—makes all the difference to our success in knowing. That is why he rejoices in having had the "luck" to find a reliable method, one he hopes to share. He grants that human intelligence, within the species, is equally distributed, but a fortunate method can give extra power to even mediocre talent.

> For I have already had such results that although in self-judgment I try to lean toward undervaluation rather than to presumption, I cannot escape a feeling of extreme satisfaction with the progress I believe I have already made in the search for truth (Descartes 1960: 4).

This happy outcome, as Descartes reflects, was not really thanks to, but rather despite, the efforts of his Jesuit teachers at La Flèche. Through them he had come to learn all too well the uncertainty of every doctrine. "For I found myself saddled with so many doubts and errors that I seemed to have gained nothing in trying to educate myself unless it was to discover more and more fully how ignorant I was" (Descartes 1960: 5). This was not due to second-rate schools, half-hearted effort, lack of intelligence, or poor intellectual climate. On the contrary, Descartes felt that he had been offered the best education available, had voluntarily gone far beyond his assignments, and could safely therefore decide that there was simply no such wisdom in the world as he had previously hoped to find.

Descartes' proffered method was thus at first motivated by a personal dissatisfaction, but a dissatisfaction he felt entitled to universalize. But his frustration and disappointment were fortunate for him since they allowed him to "stumble upon" the maxims that constituted his new method.

According to the *Discourse*, the occasion for his formulation of these maxims was the crucial day of solitude in the warm room in Germany in the winter of 1619. "There was no conversation to occupy me, and being untroubled by any cares or passions, I remained all day alone in a warm room. There I had plenty of leisure to examine my ideas" (Descartes 1960: 10). The context of the warm room is important for us, interested in noticing underlying values. It offered isolation from the world of affairs. It provided seclusion from the intrusion of any other persons. Its quiet comfort insulated Descartes from "cares or passions." The maxims shaping the modern epistemological enterprise thus were born from (1) *pure theory*, disconnected from pragmatic issues; (2) *pure individuality*, withdrawn from community; and (3) *pure neutrality* of feeling, safe from turbulent emotion or concern.

The maxims themselves were few. On the principle that too many rules "furnish an excuse for vice" (Descartes 1960: 15), Descartes offered only four, briefly enough for me to quote in full:

Rule One

The first rule was never to accept anything as true unless I recognized it to be certainly and evidently such: that is, carefully to avoid all precipitation and prejudgment, and to include nothing in my conclusions unless it presented itself so clearly and distinctly to my mind that there was no reason or occasion to doubt it (Descartes 1960: 15).

This first rule might be called the "All or none" maxim. Something is either absolutely certain or not to be accepted at all. This was the issue in the Descartes' Paris salon debate with Chandoux, the one that impressed Cardinal Bérulle so much that it led to Descartes' withdrawal from the Parisian social bustle—a man conscious of a mission. It had been the basic ground for Descartes' youthful dissatisfaction with all he had been taught at La Flèche: nothing was absolutely certain, and absolute certainty must be insisted upon (as Plato had done) for epistemic success.

Rule Two

The second was to divide each of the difficulties which I encountered into as many parts as possible, and as might be required for an easier solution (Descartes 1960: 15).

This second rule might be called the "Divide and conquer" maxim, or the "Analytic imperative." It was to become the unquestioned strategy of modernity, underlying the specialized curricula and departments of modern higher education.

Rule Three

> The third was to think in an orderly fashion when concerned with the search for truth, beginning with the things which were simplest and easiest to understand, and gradually and by degrees reaching toward more complex knowledge, even treating, as though ordered, materials which were not necessarily so (Descartes 1960: 15).

This third rule is the "Start from the simple" maxim. We should think our way from the simplest and clearest to the more complex, from the understandable to the obscure. Even though our subject matters may not actually be so ordered, we should treat them as though they were.

Rule Four

> The last was, both in the process of searching and in reviewing when in difficulty, always to make enumerations so complete, and reviews so general, that I would be certain that nothing was omitted (Descartes 1960: 15).

This fourth and final rule is the "Check your work" maxim. Not only should relevant considerations not be left out, but also our steps from the easily understandable to the complex need to be examined for logical certainty.

To these maxims Descartes immediately appended a comment on geometry that must have pleased Hobbes when he read it in England. "Those long chains of reasoning, so simple and easy, which enabled the geometricians to reach the most difficult demonstrations, had made me wonder whether all things knowable to men might not fall into a similar logical sequence. If so, we need only refrain from accepting as true that which is not true, and carefully follow the order necessary to deduce each one from the others, and there cannot be any propositions so abstruse that we cannot prove them, or so recondite that we cannot discover them" (Descartes 1960: 15–16). It is following the right method, which we might in this context call the "geometrical" one, that warrants certainty even in mathematics. Given the right method, even a child can achieve the same certainty as a sage (Descartes 1960: 17).

One more topic in the *Discourse* would have been important to Hobbes: Descartes claims to derive moral rules, as well, from his method. This, as I noted earlier, was one of Hobbes' primary motives in adopting the geometric method: a way of thinking that could coerce consent even in political contro- versies. However, Descartes would have fallen short, from Hobbes' point of view, in the actual rules that he derives. "Derives," indeed (though the word is used by Descartes), is too strong. His are, instead, minimal practical rules offered, not deduced, in the context of radical intellectual reforms. Descartes looks at his moral maxims as defining a comfortable dwelling place where we can stay while the work of rebuilding goes on. Morality is not seen as the end result of geometrical chains of reasoning so much as a prudent way of living while theory is being reconstructed from the ground up. Obedience to the local laws, prudent acceptance of the local religion, moderation, avoidance of binding contracts that might later limit freedom—these are the substance of Descartes' first moral rule. But none of this seems to be epistemically certain. The uncertainties implicit in the first moral rule are admitted in the second, which was to be as resolute in action as he could be. This makes *practical* good sense, as illustrated by Descartes' example of how someone lost in the woods is better off being resolute—following even an uncertain course straight ahead—rather than wandering about, "now turning this way, now that" (Descartes 1960: 19). Still, from Hobbes' point of view, this would be dis- appointing, rising at best to the level of good prudential counsel rather than to knowledge. In some ways, Hobbes' thirst for certainty was even more urgent than Descartes'.

Since we know exactly what Hobbes thought about other points in Descartes' epistemology, thanks to the objections he raised to them, and since the next book, the *Mediations on First Philosophy*, restated and enlarged on many of the key themes of the *Discourse on Method*, we may usefully turn directly to it at this point.

Descartes wrote his *Meditations*, not at first in French (though a later French edition was soon provided), but in Latin, with an eye to gaining the official support of key opinion-makers of his day, the Dean and the Faculty of Theology at the Sorbonne, to whom he dedicated the work. He wanted the world of scholars and, above all, established Catholic scholars, on his side. He saw no incompatibility between his approach and sound Christian doc- trine; and in his Dedication to the "Most Wise and Illustrious, the Dean and Doctors of the Sacred Faculty of Theology," he stressed the usefulness of intellectually coercive proofs—for the existence of God and for the indepen- dence of the human soul from the physical body—for use against infidels and atheists who understandably dismiss arguments from revelation as based on circular reasoning. It was his eagerness to enlist the leading thinkers of the Church, at least as much as his view that questions of "such moment" deserve being dealt with "more than once" (Descartes 1958: 167), that led to his writing and circulating the second book that Hobbes would read in manuscript.

We are not now so much concerned about the metaphysical doctrines of the *Meditations*, which occupied us in *Being and Value*, as about the epistemological. But nowhere in the history of philosophy is there a better illustration of the intertwined character of epistemology and metaphysics than in this work. Descartes begins, as in the *Discourse* (but with much increased emphasis and many more illustrations), with the doubtfulness of virtually everything. Sense experience is untrustworthy; there is no clear criterion to prove that we are not dreaming; we are capable of making mistakes even in arithmetic and geometry (e.g., by adding sums incorrectly or miscounting the sides of a figure). Whatever *can* be doubted *should* be doubted, since knowledge as absolute certainty is our aim. And whatever has let us down once should never be trusted. All these are relatively straightforward epistemic observations and resolutions. Then Descartes adds a metaphysical hypothesis to heighten the epistemic stakes: suppose that there exists a malevolent demon, a sort of anti-God, omnipotent in trickster powers, intent on universal deceit, assuring that sums are *always* falsely added and geometrical figures *constantly* miscounted. What, if anything, is left to know with certainty? Descartes' famous answer (anticipated, as we saw, by Augustine) is that at least one truth about reality can nevertheless be known with absolute conviction: that "I am" whenever I think or say this. Even on the terrible supposition of the deceiving demon, a thinker must be admitted—someone to be deceived—whenever there is a successful deception. "I am," whenever I affirm this, is an unconditionally certain judgment, just the sort Descartes was seeking when he began by adopting the epistemological resolution to doubt whatever is even remotely possible to doubt.

But all one can know with this level of certainty, at this point, is that the thinker exists *qua* thinking thing, and nothing more. One cannot know, on the strength of this argument (so far) that one has a body or that there is a world beyond one's field of consciousness. Everything one has to work with, in rebuilding one's epistemological inventory, is contained within one's solitary field of awareness. Still, within this field there are important resources. There now is one instance of an indubitable truth, "I am," and by examining it one can discover the epistemological characteristics that make it certain. Its certainty commends itself directly to the mind by its clarity and distinctness. As Descartes argues:

> I am certain that I am a thinking thing. But do I thereby know also what is required to render me thus certain of anything? In the first knowledge there is indeed nothing save the clear and distinct apprehension of what I am affirming; yet this would not suffice to render me certain of its truth, if it could ever happen that anything which I apprehend thus clearly and distinctly should yet prove false; and accordingly [since this

is evidently impossible] I would now seem to be able to adopt as a general rule that everything I apprehend in a genuinely clear and distinct manner is true (Descartes 1958: 194).

Equipped with an instance of absolutely certain knowledge and the criterion for recognizing more, Descartes—in the interest of epistemology—immediately moves to remove the worst metaphysical ground for doubt (the hypothesis of the malevolent demon) by establishing the best metaphysical ground for taking at least some of our ideas as trustworthy: the existence of a perfect, thus non-deceiving, God. His specific proofs are not central to the interests of this book (see Ferré 1967b: chapter 5), but it is of interest here to note the interplay of epistemology ($_e$) with metaphysics ($_m$) in Descartes' thinking. God_m can be $known_e$ to $exist_m$ with $certainty_e$ if we have $ideas_e$ requiring the divine $existence_m$ that are characterized by the same marks of $clarity_e$ and $distinctness_e$ that we find in the $idea_e$ that our own $existence_m$ is certainly $true_e$ each time we affirm it. Suffice it to say that Descartes was completely satisfied by his proofs for God, and held that they were even *more* secure than the certainties of arithmetic and geometry, since the logically prior assurance of a perfectly good God removes any nagging reservation based on the possibility of a malevolent deceiver who might cloud our minds each time we turn to mathematical calculation.

HOBBES AND DESCARTES, IN 1640

Thomas Hobbes, reading these arguments in 1640, was far from satisfied. His grounds for objection, no less than Descartes' grounds for satisfaction, were thoroughly intertwined metaphysical preferences and epistemic norms. By this time in his life, at age fifty-two, although he had as yet published nothing explicitly philosophical, Hobbes was well launched in his philosophical direction. The sixteen objections which he offered Descartes, anonymously, through the intermediacy of Father Mersenne, reflected his own positive doctrines then taking shape and already sketched, though not published, in his *Short Tract on First Principles*.

It would be tedious to take up each of the sixteen objections in turn. Instead I shall distill the main epistemological points of Hobbes' complaints and the main lines of Descartes' replies. It is impossible to eliminate metaphysics altogether, but I shall hold it to a minimum.

The first objection shows that Hobbes is prepared to out-radicalize the purportedly radical position of Descartes. He starts by admitting—insisting on—the dubitability of all the old apparent reliabilities. Asserting the impossibility of finding a criterion to distinguish dream experience from waking experience, he adds that "the images present to us when we are awake and using our senses are not accidents inhering in external objects, and fail to prove that such external objects do as a fact exist" (Hobbes 1955 in Kaufmann 1962: vol. 2, 76). But then, pointing out that Plato "and other ancient Philosophers" had long ago said as much about the world of sense, he expresses his wish that Descartes, "so distinguished in the handling of modern speculations, had refrained from publishing those matters of ancient lore" (Kaufmann 1962: vol. 2, 76). "What's new or exciting about this?" seems to be his challenge.

Descartes defends his reworking of these "old" arguments, not claiming novelty or credit for them, but pointing out that "while I have sought no praise from their rehearsal, I believe that it was impossible for me to omit them, as impossible as it would be for a medical writer to omit the description of a disease when trying to reach the method of curing it" (Kaufmann 1962: vol. 2, 76–77). The opening skirmish is indecisive; it is more a matter of atmospherics, and a wrestle for the high modern ground, than of substance. But Descartes is already on the defensive.

Next, Hobbes attacks what he regards as the confusion between "thinking" as a *process* done by a subject or agent and "thinking" as a *substance* in itself, spiritual, non-extended, immaterial. It is interesting to see how Hobbes restates Descartes' famous *cogito* argument:

> From the fact that I think, or have an image [sic!], whether sleeping or waking, it is inferred that I am exercising thought; for *I think and I am exercising thought* mean the same thing. From the fact that I am exercising thought it follows that *I am*, since that which thinks is not nothing.

For something to engage in *any* process, dreaming or imagining, understanding or leaping, the something so engaged must exist.

> But where it is added, *this is the mind, the spirit, the understanding, the reasons*, a doubt arises. For it does not seem to be good reasoning to say: *I am exercising thought*, hence *I am thought*; or *I am using my intellect*, hence *I am intellect*. For in the same way I might say, *I am walking*; hence *I am the walking* (Kaufmann 1962: vol. 2, 77).

Hobbes had already come to the firm conclusion, essential to the ancient atomists and his friend Gassendi, that to be is to be a particular material thing or a complex of particular material things, located somewhere in space and characterized by motion or rest. Just as we cannot conceive of leaping without something leaping, so we cannot conceive of thinking without something thinking. And "something," for Hobbes, means a material something. He uses the terms "substance" and "matter" interchangeably. That is a given for him. This makes it an analytic truth. Something that is supposed to be spatially nowhere could never be sensed, therefore is utterly unimaginable. Consequently he can write: "Hence, since the knowledge of this proposition, *I exist*, depends upon the knowledge of that other, *I think*, and the knowledge of it upon the fact that we cannot separate thought from a matter [sic!] that thinks, the proper inference seems to be that that which thinks is material rather than immaterial" (Kaufmann 1962: vol. 2, 78).

Descartes at once denies the parity between walking and thinking, since the former is always understood as merely the action of something else, the body, but the latter is sometimes understood to be the faculty itself. Again he puts himself into alliance with ancient and medieval usage. He agrees that subjects of all activities are to be understood as substances and therefore (here is a suggestion of Aristotle) "as wearing the guise of matter, vis. metaphysical matter" (Kaufmann 1962: vol. 2, 78–79); but substances are not merely on that account always to be classified as *bodies*. Appealing to received scholarship and common consensus, he points out that "both logicians and as a rule all men are wont to say that substances are of two kinds, spiritual and corporeal" (Kaufmann 1962: vol. 2, 79), distinguished by their characteristic activities. Corporeal substances engage in motion or rest, and are characterized by figure and shape, always presupposing extension in space; spiritual substances, in contrast, engage in entirely different activities, "thought, perception, or consciousness" (Kaufmann 1962: vol. 2, 79), which do not presuppose spatial extension. The two give rise to very different concepts. There is no logically necessary link between "substance" and "body."

Hobbes deeply disagrees. He insists, as we saw, that there is indeed such a necessary link. A substance that is not a body is unimaginable. But here lies an even deeper disagreement. The real root of the metaphysical disagreement between Hobbes and Descartes, on whether there can be incorporeal substance, rests on an epistemological impasse over the meaning of "ideas." It gradually emerges in Hobbes' objections, that he equates "having an idea" with "imagining." Since all imagining, no matter how lofty, uses the materials of prior sensory experience, we can have no ideas that have not initially come to us as particular perceptions. Descartes makes much of the distinction between "imagining," based on prior sense perception, and "conceiving," intuiting a meaning by direct intellectual intuition. A piece of wax, for example, is not understood, Descartes argued, by "imagining" it in all its different states—solid, liquid, etc.—but by "conceiving it by the mind alone" (Kaufmann 1962: vol. 2, 80). Hobbes seems at first to agree, but he uses the word "conceiving" in a quite different sense: "There is a great difference between imagining, i.e. having some idea, and conceiving with the mind, *i.e. inferring, as the result of a train of reasoning, that something is, or exists*"

(Kaufmann 1962: vol. 2, 80, emphasis added). Then he adds, in proper nominalist fashion:

> But what shall we now say, if reasoning chance to be nothing more than the uniting and stringing together of names or designations by the word is? It will be a consequence of this that reason gives us no conclusion about the nature of things, but only about the terms that designate them, whether, indeed, or not there is a convention (arbitrarily made about their meanings) according to which we join these names together.

Then, warming to his hypothetical suggestion, Hobbes lets fly his own hypothesis about what "thinking" must be, grounding his epistemological nominalism in metaphysical materialism again:

> If this be so, as is possible, reasoning will depend on names, names on the imagination, and imagination, perchance, as I think, on the motion of the corporeal organs. Thus mind will be nothing but the motions in certain parts of an organic body (Kaufmann 1962: vol. 2, 80).

Descartes, however, is adamant. "Conceiving" is not merely inferring, but is, rather, inspecting meanings, or pure intellection. In the *Meditations* he had given an example of the difference between understanding the meaning of a pentagon ("five-equal-sided figure," etc.) which takes a little effort of mind, and going to the additional trouble of trying to picture—to construct in the imagination—what a pentagon actually looks like. "Now in thus imaging its shape," Descartes wrote, "I am plainly aware of having to make a certain special effort of the mind, an effort not required in merely thinking of it; and this special effort of the mind makes clear to me the difference there is between imagination and pure intellection" (Descartes 1958: 231). In his reply to Hobbes he reiterates this phenomenological distinction. Further, "reasoning" is not merely stringing names together. Rejecting Hobbes' nominalism, he continues: "Moreover, in reasoning we unite not names but the things signified by the names . . ." (Kaufmann 1962: vol. 2, 81). And what are these "things signified"? They are deeper than words—they lie behind and are independent of the particular words that we use. "For who doubts whether a Frenchman and a German are able to reason in exactly the same way about the same things, though they yet conceive the words in an entirely diverse way?" (Kaufmann 1962: vol. 2, 81).

Firmly committed to his idea of "idea," however, Hobbes plunges a knife into the heart of Descartes' epistemological security: his proof of the existence of God, who then becomes the warrant for confidence in the existence of the external world, other minds, and even mathematics. For Hobbes, there can be no idea of God, since God is beyond sense and imagination.

> When I think of a man, I recognize an idea, or image, with figure and colour as its constituents; and concerning this I can raise the question whether or not it is the likeness of a man. . . . But, when one thinks of an Angel, what is noticed in the mind is now the image of a flame, now that of a fair winged child, and this, I may be sure, has no likeness to an Angel, and hence is not the idea of an Angel. . . . It is the same way with the most holy name of God; we have no image, no idea corresponding to it. Hence we are forbidden to worship God in the form of an image, lest we should think we could conceive Him who is inconceivable (Kaufmann 1962: vol. 2, 81).

The best we can do is to acknowledge that something (unknown) must have caused the whole universe in which we find ourselves; but this is a far cry from knowing that God is a perfect, infinite substance who would never allow a malevolent demon to deceive us all the time.

To this Descartes replies that of course there is no *image* of God, but that his proof rests on the *idea* of God. At this point he explains further his use of the term "idea": "I take the term idea to stand for whatever the mind directly perceives; and so when I will or when I fear, since at the same time I perceive that I will and fear, that very volition and apprehension are ranked among my ideas" (Kaufmann 1962: vol. 2, 82). Hobbes reject this wider use of the word, arguing instead that "idea" should be reserved for a representation of something and that fear is no thought, just the experienced effects of a thought. If a lion rushes at us, we have the thought of the lion plus the effect of the thought of the lion, which is the natural impulsion to escape.

Be this as it may, the question of whether there can be an idea of God is too important, epistemologically and metaphysically, to be dropped. Hobbes puts the issue succinctly: "If there is no idea of God (now it has not been proved that it exists), as seems to be the case, the whole of this argument collapses" (Kaufmann 1962: vol. 2, 83); and Descartes responds in kind: "If there is an idea of God (as it is manifest there is), the whole of this objection collapses" (Kaufmann 1962: vol. 2, 83).

Hobbes cannot let the matter rest. Descartes uses the term "infinite" about God, and argues that this is a positive (indeed, supremely positive) idea. But is this so? Hobbes analyzes the matter differently:

> This substance is *infinite* (i.e. I can neither conceive nor imagine its boundaries or extreme parts, without imagining further parts beyond

them): whence it follows that corresponding to the term *infinite* there arises an idea not of the Divine infinity, but of my own bounds or limitations (Kaufmann 1962: vol. 2, 85).

A similar negative analysis is offered of "all-powerful" and "independent" and so forth. But Descartes, who holds that we can *think* many things we cannot *imagine*, replies that we can think God's infinite properties by extending indefinitely the universal ideas we have of our own spiritual powers. We all know from personal experience what the general form of mental action is. This is something quite positive, and to magnify it to the limit is an equally positive idea.

> [By] idea I mean whatever is the form of any perception. For does anyone who understands something not perceive that he does so? and hence does he not possess that form or idea of mental action? It is by extending this indefinitely that we form the idea of the intellectual activity of God; similarly also with God's other attributes (Kaufmann 1962: vol. 2, 86).

Here Descartes might be understood as holding that there is univocal knowledge of God's nature, but that is not an inevitable interpretation. The answer is not developed. He could have intended the "way of eminence," in which God's nature is thought in terms of what is always eminently more than the human side of the analogy. It is clear, however, that Hobbes— whether piously or not—has clothed his position in the familiar *via negativa*, and that Descartes' position, in contrast (for the rescue of his epistemological certitudes), must be allied with medieval defenders of the *via affirmativa*.

Hobbes' negations do not stop with the idea of God, but continue to raise doubts about the possibility of any idea regarding soul or even substance. "For substance (the substance that is a material, subject to accidents and changes) is perceived and demonstrated by the reason alone, without yet being conceived by us, or furnishing us with any idea" (Kaufmann 1962: vol. 2, 84). Descartes grows increasingly weary and short in his replies. "I have frequently remarked," he says, "that I give the name idea to that with which reason makes us acquainted just as I also do to anything else that is in any way perceived by us" (Kaufmann 1962: vol. 2, 85). And, later, "For the rest, I am tired of repeating how it is that we can have an idea of God" (Kaufmann 1962: vol. 2, 87).

The clash between the two Fathers of modern philosophy winds down with mutual incomprehension but without surrender on either side. Hobbes, toward the end, raises the skeptical question whether God, even if perfect, might not have sufficient motives to deceive us or allow us to be deceived.

Parents and doctors do it all the time, and "no fault is committed" (Kaufmann 1962: vol. 2, 90). Descartes merely repeats that cognitive errors occur but not by God's intent, and that any such deceiving intention "is contradictory to impute to Him" (Kaufmann 1962: vol. 2, 90). But he does not meet the actual point, or show why benevolent deception is a contradiction, merely adding, wearily, "Once more this is bad reasoning on my critic's part" (Kaufmann 1962: vol. 2, 90).

HOBBES AND DESCARTES, FROM 1641 TO 1650

Hobbes' initial anonymity as "my critic" was soon lost. Still in exile, he published *De Cive* in 1642, the year after Descartes' *Meditations* had appeared. Then it became clear—from style and substance—who the "critic" of the Third Set of Objections had been. Descartes read Hobbes' book and recognized his tormentor. He did not think highly of the book, and (through Mersenne) accused Hobbes of plagiarizing his ideas on subjective sense phenomena (Rogow 1986: 148). Indeed, Descartes then resolved to have nothing more to do with the Englishman, though eventually they did meet. Descartes visited Paris in 1648 and, perhaps with misgivings, consented to the meeting. According to Charles Cavendish, scion of the family once more supporting Hobbes, they "had some discourse." Their areas of agreement went unspecified, but Cavendish reported that they disagreed "extreamelie" on the nature of "hardness" (Rogow 1986: 148).

This meeting between the two Fathers came toward a time of endings for both men. For Hobbes it came as his exile in France was about to end. King Charles I was executed in the following year. Hobbes became seriously ill and was forced to discontinue tutoring mathematics to the exiled Prince of Wales, who in 1660, after the rule of Cromwell, would become King Charles II. As health allowed, Hobbes worked on his greatest book, *Leviathan*, in which his epistemological and metaphysical views (fully foreshadowed in his "Objections") were finally expressed and in which he argued for the political necessity of an absolute sovereign. Since it did not matter, in Hobbes' political physics, whether the pressure-producing ruler at the top of society is a King or a Lord Protector, Hobbes was able to arrange safe return to England despite Cromwell's approach to power.

For Descartes, endings were more final. First, his long sojourn in Holland came to its end when his friend, Chanut, the French ambassador to Sweden, persuaded him to take an interest in Queen Christina, the daughter of the late King Gustavus Adolphus. Queen Christina was a most remarkable person, a brilliant and energetic monarch who, in turn, was interested by Chanut in Descartes' thought. Christina began to read his works and to correspond with him. Soon he was invited to come to Sweden to convey his philosophy at firsthand to the royal pupil and to help her organize a Swedish Academy, to be modeled after the distinguished French Academy. In October 1649, Descartes arrived in Stockholm, at the start of winter. Christina was an enthusiastic student, but had time for her philosophical studies only at 5:00 o'clock in the morning. Descartes, who by age fifty-three had established a lifetime habit of late rising, nevertheless accommodated the royal schedule; but the cold morning air was too much for his always delicate constitution. He contracted pneumonia, and in the depth of a particularly severe Swedish winter, on February 11, 1650, he died.

HOBBES, FROM 1651 TO 1679

After his return to England in the year after Descartes' death, Hobbes had almost three decades left of life. They were his prime philosophical years, full of fame and controversy. The *Leviathan* was published in the year of his return, and stimulated much notoriety. It was an open challenge not only to traditional "softer" ways of thinking about politics but also of thinking about thinking. In it, Hobbes makes clear and systematic the spare materialist epistemological and metaphysical foundations that had lain beneath his objections to Descartes. There is no need for me to develop these any further. They are already familiar, not simply from the foregoing sections of this chapter but also from earlier treatments of Atomism and Nominalism. Even Hobbes' language of "phantasms" directly echoes Epicurus' *phantasía*; and his nominalistic razor is familiar from Ockham's shaving of Forms from the world. But Hobbes presented these premodern ideas in a new spirit: welcoming a dawning age shorn of sentiment and superstition, both in public affairs and in a new, tough-minded approach to human nature and human capacities for knowledge.

Happily, Hobbes was an enthusiastic controversialist. He enjoyed his encounters, whether with outraged bishops on free will (which he utterly denied) or scornful mathematicians on squaring the circle (which he stubbornly affirmed). He wrote prolifically, publishing *De Homine* in 1657, and *De Corpore* in 1665. At one point his works were investigated for atheism and heresy by a parliamentary committee; and although his former student, King Charles II, apparently deflected the committee from making a report, further publications were banned. Rejected for membership in the Royal Society, he continued, nevertheless, to write and argue. His history of the English civil war, *Behemoth*, was completed in 1668. In 1672 his Latin verse autobiography was completed. Through the latter we know that he unfailingly considered himself to have routed all opponents, freely employing military idioms of the most vivid sort. Life was a zestful, if strenuous, battle against all comers. He exercised regularly, ate and drank sparingly, and had the satisfaction of outliving virtually all his enemies. Bedridden at ninety-one, Hobbes was about to be left (comfortably, with servants) by the Cavendish family, who were moving for the winter from Chatsworth (one of their grand estates) to Hardwick (another great house about ten miles away); but Hobbes loudly expressed his characteristic timidity of empty houses and was taken along, despite his age and condition. Within a few days, safe again at the site of his first tutorial assignment, Hobbes suffered a stroke; and on December 3, 1679, he died.

REFLECTIONS ON HOBBES AND DESCARTES

At first it seems that the differences between these two Fathers of modern philosophy outweigh their similarities. Surely the differences are great—and obvious.

The most glaring difference between them is the thoroughgoing monistic materialism of Hobbes and the equally complete mind-matter dualism of Descartes. These are metaphysical positions, of course, to which I attended, in *Being and Value*. But these are metaphysical commitments with enormous epistemological import since Hobbes' materialism required him to account for thinking, knowing—all mental phenomena—as activities solely of unthinking matter in motion; while, conversely, Descartes' dualism gave him the problem of accounting for the evident but mysterious connections between physical stimuli and mental receptions, mental intentions and bodily actions.

There is no need to rehearse the various aspects of this enormous issue, which—as I put it in the previous volume—set the never-fulfilled "modern agenda." What is important epistemologically is to note the implications of these respective metaphysical commitments for what an "idea" can be. For Descartes, an idea can be anything "perceived by the mind," including the entire field of consciousness, from fears and hopes, through sensory and memory images, to mathematical theorems and thoughts of God. The mind, as he understands mind, is nonspatial. It is not limited to the here-and-now character of particular things. It can intuit general meanings, quite independent of any localized or visualizable image. His best example, from the *Meditations*, comes from geometry. In the sixth and final Meditation, he opens with an explicit treatment of the difference between the imagination and what he calls "pure intellection" (Descartes 1958: 230). If we think about a triangle, he points out, it may be easy to suppose that our thought is merely a picture in our heads of a closed three-sided figure, the definition or meaning of "triangle" is of such a simple construction, requiring only three lines, that it is easy to "intuit them as present, this being what I term imaging" (Descartes 1958: 230). But make the figure much more complex, and the situation changes.

Think instead of a chiliagon, that is, a plane figure defined as having one thousand equal sides. The definition is simple to understand. That is "pure intellection." But what do we picture, if we try to imagine one? It is impossible to count one thousand equal sides in our mind's eye. We simply imagine a figure with "lots and lots" of sides, a sort of prickly circle. And even though "it may happen that I confusedly represent to myself some shape, it is yet evident that this shape is not a chiliagon," still, we can *think* perfectly clearly of the *meaning* of a chiliagon. Now, while imagining a chiliagon, contrast its idea with that of a myriagon, which is clearly defined as a plane figure enclosed by ten-thousand equal sides. How does our image change? Is it not still a vaguely prickly circle with "lots and lots" of equal sides, but "ten times more"? The "ten times more" makes clear and precise sense in terms of intuited abstract meaning, but it makes no sense at all if it must be derived from a mental image already overstrained.

This is one of the places where Descartes has a clear advantage over Hobbes. It does seem that there are many things we can think that we cannot imagine. Many enjoy thinking about astronomy, for example. We get used to thinking in terms of light-years as a measure of distance. The concept, "light-year," is reasonably clear. It is the distance in which a ray of light will travel in a year at roughly 186,000 miles per second. We can imagine the interval required for one second. We can pretty well imagine a mile, perhaps from walking or from looking at a landmark. But I, at least, cannot *imagine* precisely 186,000 miles, though I can *think* such a quantity to any number of decimal points required. Now, to *think* a light-year, one merely needs to multiply the number of seconds in a year by 186,000 miles. Perfectly clear. But this is *unimaginable*, except vaguely, by imagining a miniature solar system, perhaps, and something else "very far" beyond. In astronomy, however, light-years are considered quite small, relative to the distances we must think, and can think, beyond where we can usefully imagine. Similar comments might be made about thinking, versus imagining, in geological time frames. We can pretty well imagine a year, though that takes quite an effort; but I wager no one can imagine a million years, or by imagination alone distinguish a million from ten million years. But ten million years is just yesterday, relative to the age of the earth. These are matters, fortunately, at which geological science is adept in thinking, with excellent results. Descartes seems to have been right. We have many more ideas than we can image.

Hobbes' insistence that all our ideas must be images came from a rather primitive theory, in which the only things that can possibly be are tiny bits of inert stuff endowed with shape, hardness, and motion. If one begins with this as a master hypothesis, then ideas, too, must be particular reverberations of tiny bits of stuff, since there is nothing else allowed in the theory. It follows deductively, with the certainty of geometrical demonstration, that ideas can only be particulars. Within this framework, it is required by the premises that sensations will be the putting into motion of body-atoms by object-atoms, and that ideas afterward will be residual motions left from these sensations. There is nothing else they could be, since there is nothing else at all. This follows with perfect, coercive assurance, in the way admired by Hobbes in geometry. He opens the *Leviathan* with these fundamentals:

> Concerning the thoughts of man, I will consider them first singly, and afterwards in train, or dependence upon one another. Singly, they are every one a *representation* or *appearance*, of some quality, or other accident of a body without us, which is commonly called an object. Which object worketh on the eyes, ears, and other parts of a man's body; and by diversity of working, produceth diversity of appearances.
>
> The original of them all, is that which we call SENSE, for there is no conception in a man's mind, which hath not at first, totally, or by parts, been begotten upon the organs of sense. The rest are derived from that original (Hobbes 1839: vol. 3, 1).

From this is follows, deductively, that imagination can be nothing other than "decaying sense." In this, memory and dreams are in the same category.

> IMAGINATION therefore is nothing but *decaying sense;* and is found in men, and many other living creatures, as well sleeping, as waking. . . . And any object being removed from our eyes, though the impression it made in us remain, yet other objects more present succeeding, and working on us, the imagination of the past is obscured, and made weak, as the voice of a man in the noise of the day. From whence it followeth, that the longer the time is, after the sight or sense of any object, the weaker is the imagination (Hobbes 1839: vol. 3, 4–5).

It is interesting to note that "it followeth" whether in fact our actual *experience* accords with this deduction or not. We all know that vividness of imagination is not cleanly proportional to temporal remove. The snake I saw years ago is more vivid in my imagination than the leaf I saw this morning. Hobbes, however, is more interested in what "followeth" than in what actually happens. In this respect it is a mistake to consider Hobbes the Father of the British Empiricists. He wants geometrical certainty rather than messy inductive approximations. He was not much impressed with Francis Bacon's methods. Euclid, instead, was his model. Of course Hobbes held that the only material we can think with is whatever originates in sense, and this much is good empiricist doctrine; but in this he is not especially set apart (Aristotle and Thomas Aquinas, as we have seen, held that much)—and, more important, his grounds for holding this "empiricist" position were not themselves empirical but deductive. It is an odd reversal of usual stereotypes to note Descartes appealing to our experience in imagining and conceiving, while Hobbes deduces what "followeth" without much regard for experience, but so it is. Still, Hobbes does not thereby cease to be British, nor does Descartes rank as an empiricist.

Other obvious differences between Descartes and Hobbes were less important than their argument over the character of thinking itself. Descartes thought that he could prove God's existence by the otherwise inexplicable greatness of the idea of God, and Hobbes flatly rejected this. But this apparently large difference comes down again to their incompatible ideas on what an idea can be, and so is simply part of the same quarrel. Remaining differences were mainly temperamental. Descartes wanted the approval of the Church, while Hobbes was happy to tweak clerics in tender places. Descartes felt the need to have a proof of the external world, while Hobbes was content to postulate, in the first paragraph of the *Leviathan*, that our thoughts are representations of "some quality, or other accident of a body without us, which is commonly called an *object*" (Hobbes 1839: vol. 3, 1). In this Hobbes showed more common sense, but less sensitivity to the problem of the epistemological gap that was to block the modern philosophy he fathered. Descartes really respected the danger of skepticism, although he approached it in the manner of a game, ruling that he would doubt whatever could possibly be doubted so that its limits could be soundly demonstrated. Hobbes, though the child of fear, really did not worry about skepticism, although he courted it happily with his radical negations about God's nature, the self, and even substance. In these temperamental matters, Descartes deserves, more than Hobbes, his traditional title as Father of modern philosophy; though Hobbes, perhaps more than Descartes, led the way toward the abyss of the epistemological gap itself.

Still, the similarities between Hobbes and Descartes are yet more important than their differences. These are what made them both genuinely generative of modern philosophy.

It would be "temerarious," and no less unseemly, to attempt psychoanalysis of such figures at such long temporal and cultural remove. I am neither qualified nor interested in so doing. It may be enough, I hope, simply to note that both of these men—one motherless from ill-health and the other fatherless from desertion—were by much evidence insecure at inner depths, probably to a greater than the average extent. Hobbes was notoriously full of fears and anxieties, and self-consciously so. He was the "first who fled." He was, as he said in his old age, born a twin to fear. His political philosophy, which I have not attempted to describe, was based on mutual fear of the "war of all against all" in a theoretical state of nature he abhorred as the worst possible condition imaginable. Descartes, though not economically insecure, was strangely fearful of normal social intercourse. He hid in Paris for many months at an undisclosed address, until discovered. He attained his philosophical heights in utter solitude, symbolized by the stove-heated room in the middle of winter, entirely without "conversation" and without practical cares. He remained long hours in bed, thinking and working out of reach of the prying eyes of others, and when he could no longer do so, it killed him. In Holland, itself a place of remote self-exile, he moved his household repeatedly to keep his whereabouts secret, and, in order not to reveal his location, carried on his correspondence with Mersenne through intermediaries. He was haughty to those he took to be his intellectual inferiors, cutting off relations with those (like Hobbes) who challenged him too much; but he was obsequious toward the establishment, and longed for official stamps of approval. He even suppressed an important book, *Le Monde*, rather than take a chance of sharing the fate of Galileo. And when he was finally admired by royalty, even at the cost of comforts and ultimately his health, he could not resist the lure.

It would be reductive and wrong to treat such personal insecurities as sufficient reasons for Hobbes' and Descartes' strong insistence on absolute certainty as the primary hallmark of genuine knowing. There is in the Western tradition a noble tradition, as we have seen, leading back at least to Plato, which demands nothing less as the mark of cognitive success. Still, there can be no question that the Fathers of modern philosophy were united in this ideal. After them, certainty, absolute indubitability, clarity, distinctness, and coercive persuasive power have been the standard epistemic norms of modern philosophy.

For this reason, among others, mathematics has been supremely honored by the heirs of Hobbes and Descartes. Both were, in William Aubrey's phrase about Hobbes, "in love with geometry." For Hobbes, this was a love for method, more than substance; for Descartes, who was a creative mathematical genius in his own right, it must have been both. In neither case, however, was the love of these men for mathematics quite the same as the loves announced by Kepler and Galileo for the same beloved. As we saw in *Being and Value* (120–31), in Kepler's case, the mathematical properties of things could alone be known, because they are uniquely clear and capable of precise handling, thus revealing the numerological mysteries of creation; in Galileo's, the "book of nature" itself was written in the language of geometry. Descartes and Hobbes shared some of these views. For Hobbes, only the mathematically treatable features of things—size, shape, velocity, and the like—were genuinely real, the rest being only subjectively produced by the vibrations of our mental atoms. For Descartes, the same could be said for extended substance, that is, material reality; and since only these properties could be "clearly and distinctly" known, God is not deceiving us (we are deceiving ourselves) when we take mind-dependent secondary qualities, like color and taste and texture, as inhering in the extra-mental world. Descartes even thought Hobbes had plagiarized these views from him, though they were clearly expressed in Galileo well before the *Discourse on Method* (and by the Epicureans long before that); thus, deeply counter-intuitive philosophical theories were well on the way to solidifying into modern rhetorical platitudes like, "If a tree falls in the forest and no one is there, does it make a sound?" Beyond the substance of mathematical problems and the clarity of mathematical properties, for both Hobbes and Descartes, lay the power of mathematical method. This method, deduction from clear principles—the "Start from the simple" maxim—was the highroad from cognitive insecurity to assured certainty for both the Fathers. Both men were dedicated deductivists in pursuit of coercive conclusions. Hobbes liked the idea of forcing his conversation partners to political conclusions they might prefer to avoid. Descartes commended his method to the theologians of the Sorbonne as a way of grinding away the doubts and objections of infidels and atheists.

Another immensely significant common preference for both Descartes and Hobbes was for the analytical method. Descartes announced it first, and most clearly, in his "Divide and conquer" maxim: to "divide each difficulty which I encountered into as many parts as possible . . ." (Descartes 1960: 15). Hobbes, in his practice, was no less a true Father of analytical philosophy, analyzing the meaning of terms into smaller components derivable from supposedly clear grounds in sense perception, from which the meaning of all words must come. The "Analytic imperative" is maximally strong in both these Fathers.

Finally, beyond the demand for clarity, certainty, the use of analysis, the "All or none" maxim, the "Start from the simple" and "Check your work" maxims, on which they fully agreed, and the many-faceted love for mathematics, both Hobbes and Descartes shared a common contempt for the old doctrines of premodern times—especially for scholastic Aristotelianism—and a common confidence in their new age rising. They both admired Copernicus, Kepler, and Galileo, the founders of a new science and a revolutionary new worldview. The present was not inferior to the tried and traditional. The Age of Gold was not in the past. Quite the reverse; the best was on its way, rising among them, perhaps from them. Both men were in their prime when Isaac Newton was born in 1642, just a year after the publication of Descartes' and Hobbes' exchange in the *Meditations*. Nothing would have fit better into their attitudinal framework, if only they could have foreseen the Newtonian triumph, than the idea of modern progress.

Progress there was to be. It would come in the sciences, in exploration of the world, in technology and economics. Much of this was powered by the love of mathematics, the commitment to analysis, the conception of inert matter, and the spirit of optimism. In philosophy there was a kind of progress, as well. It was a progression, as we shall see, from the Fathers toward the recognition of the epistemological gap.

LOCKE AND BERKELEY

JOHN LOCKE

In 1632, the year that Descartes completed his missing book, *The World*, and Hobbes fell in love with geometry, John Locke (1632–1704) was born in Somerset, England, near Bristol. The political persuasion of Locke's family was quite the opposite of Hobbes'. His father, a liberal Puritan attorney, fought on the parliamentary side against King Charles I. Locke himself, in later life, was to be on the enemies list of the Catholic Stuarts until James II was overthrown in the Glorious Revolution of 1688. Locke had a hand in this overthrow, conspiring in Holland with William of Orange, who—with his wife Mary, daughter of James II—took the throne in the bloodless coup that introduced to England the Bill of Rights and constitutional monarchy.

As this suggests, Locke was not simply an abstract thinker; he was a man deeply engaged in events. The spirit of British Empiricism, which comes more from Locke than any other figure, is steeped in the moderation, tolerance, practicality, and concreteness of this man's upbringing and life experiences. He was enrolled first at Westminster School (whose methods of rote learning were later sharply criticized in Locke's writings on education), then at Christ's Church College, Oxford, where he was elected to a studentship in 1652. Oxford was in the grip of the driest of premodern scholasticism during this period, and Locke was repelled. In his spare time he read Descartes, and though he was never a Cartesian, he admired the clarity and order of his method. He earned his Bachelor of Arts degree in 1656, then stayed on for a master's degree. During this time he enjoyed the friendship of Robert Boyle (1627–91) and his circle of scientific experimentalists, engaging also in experiments of his own. From 1660 he taught Latin and Greek at Oxford for a time, and in 1664 was appointed Censor in Moral Philosophy. During this time he also busied himself in medical studies, though he did not complete his medical degree until 1674 and never entered medical practice.

There were many practical affairs in which he became involved during those years. In 1665 he had his first taste of diplomatic service, as secretary in a mission to the Elector of Brandenburg. In the next year, he was employed by the soon-to-be Earl of Shaftsbury (with whom he earlier had formed a friendship) as medical advisor to the Earl and as tutor to the Earl's son. In 1672, when Shaftsbury became Lord Chancellor, he appointed Locke Secretary for Ecclesiastical Benefices, then, in 1673, Secretary to the Council for

Trade and Plantations. After Shaftsbury's political downfall in the following year, Locke returned to his haven at Oxford to complete his medical degree; but after that (himself in ill-health), he left in 1675 for the gentler climate of France. In France, where he remained for four years, he reactivated his earlier interests in Descartes' philosophy, becoming especially close to the followers of Gassendi (the Christian atomist), who were critical of many aspects of Descartes' thought. Locke shared these criticisms and developed them further in his own way.

On his return to England in 1679, Locke rejoined the Earl of Shaftsbury, who was busily plotting against the future James II. The plot was discovered, and in 1683, Shaftsbury was forced to flee to Holland. Later in the same year Locke thought it prudent to follow. During his absence, King Charles II expressed hostility to Locke by requesting Oxford to cancel Locke's remaining positions there; and after James II ascended to the throne, the younger Stuart demanded of the Dutch authorities that they arrest and return Locke to England. This did not happen, perhaps because the Dutch were not interested in cooperating; but this was enough to prompt Locke to live under an assumed name. He lived in constant contact, despite this, with an intellectually stimulating group of friends; and it was during this semi-underground period of exile that he had time to write and rewrite his great contribution to epistemology, his *Essay Concerning Human Understanding*.

In 1687, or perhaps before, Locke became an advisor to William of Orange, as a new plot to replace James II was brewing. A few months after William's success in 1688, Locke escorted William's wife, Mary, back to England when she joined her husband in February 1689, on the way to becoming joint monarchs. Later in that year, the *Essay Concerning Human Understanding* was published. In the following year Locke's other major publication, *Two Treatises of Government*, appeared.

The new regime of William and Mary offered Locke an ambassadorship to the Elector of Brandenburg, but his health was not good enough for him to accept it. Instead, he lived as a guest of the prominent Masham family in Oates, outside London in Essex. There he received visits from such luminaries as Samuel Clarke and Isaac Newton. There also he wrote his works on education, revised his primary works, and composed his anonymous treatise, *The Reasonableness of Christianity*. Eventually, in 1696, he did accept the duties of Commissioner of Trade, which he fulfilled (despite an unsuccessful request to resign on health grounds) until 1700. In 1704, at peace with himself, and listening to Lady Masham read him the Psalms, he passed away.

This life of liberal engagement with the world provided the varied context for Locke's theory of knowing. This is clearly one of the reasons Locke's work is notoriously "loose" in style and structure—and even in logical consistency. The virtues of tight, rigorous, coercive argumentation were not of great importance to Locke, though he admired them in Descartes. Little as he agreed with Descartes in substance, still less did he consider it important to emulate him in form. In other words, his was not a mathematical approach. There was no "falling in love with geometry" in his background. Instead, there were many worldly tasks to accomplish—diplomatic, administrative, and personal—and only limited time and energy left to pursue purist ideals of theory that, in practice, were really not his norms at all.

The way the *Essay* was begun (probably in the winter of 1670–71), and the manner of its composition, give clues to Locke's modest and easy-going theoretical posture. He describes, in his opening "Epistle to the Reader," how it happened that he wrote the work at all.

> Were it fit to trouble thee with the history of this Essay, I should tell thee that five or six friends meeting at my chamber, and discoursing on a subject very remote from this, found themselves quickly at a stand by the difficulties that rose on every side [difficulties, according to a note left by one of these friends, James Tyrrell, concerning principles of morality and revealed religion]. After we had a while puzzled ourselves, without coming any nearer a resolution of those doubts which perplexed us, it came into my thoughts, that we took a wrong course; and that, before we set ourselves upon enquiries of that nature, it was necessary to examine our own abilities, and see what objects our understandings were or were not fitted to deal with (Locke 1956: 4).

Locke volunteered to write something as a conversation-starter for the next meeting of the group, which was consented to; and then as opportunity warranted, he added to it. As he put it:

> Some hasty and undigested thoughts, on a subject I had never before considered, which I set down against our next meeting, gave the first entrance into this discourse, which having been thus begun by chance, was continued by entreaty; written by incoherent parcels; and, after long intervals of neglect, resumed again, as my humour or occasions permitted; and at last, in a retirement, where an attendance on my health gave me leisure, it was brought into that order thou now seest it (Locke 1956: 4–5).

The history of its writing was thus entirely unsystematic. It was catch-as-catch-can, quite in harmony with its undogmatic, empirical conclusion that we must, in all knowing, wait for the deliverances of experience. This very casualness about redundancy and inconsistency in technical terms—maddening to some scholars—is perceived as charming by others. Alfred North

Whitehead, for example, finds Locke's work admirable precisely because it does not attempt to force experience into predetermined molds. It is open. It strives for maximal adequacy, the inclusion of whatever knocks for admission, rather than maximal coherence. As I noted in Chapter 1, the quest for coherence may tempt one to exclude data, in the interest of a neater "fit" for theory. But Locke declined to exclude, even when it made his theories messier. As Whitehead wrote: "The enduring importance of Locke's work comes from the candour, clarity, and adequacy with which he states the evidence, uninfluenced by the bias of metaphysical theory. He explained, in the sense of stating plainly, and not in the more usual sense of 'explaining away'" (Whitehead 1978: 145).

All this rests easily within Locke's life and values as a busy, practical man. He admits, as he continues his opening "Epistle," that there are many "redundancies" (his way of defusing the more acid charges of "inconsistencies" that were made in his time); but these, he replies, can be put down to the history of his writing and to the other demands on his time.

> I will not deny but possibly it might be reduced to a narrower compass than it is; and that some parts of it might be contracted: the way it has been writ in, by catches, and many long intervals of interruption, being apt to cause some repetitions. But to confess the truth, I am now too lazy or too busy to make it shorter (Locke 1956: 5).

And in all this, Locke did not consider himself to be engaging in high-flown philosophical theory (what Whitehead called "metaphysics"). Rather, he draws attention to the usefulness of his project, sorting out the possibilities and limitations of human knowing; but he sees it as a humble labor. His image for his own status is amusing and revealing: "It is ambition enough to be employed as an under-labourer in clearing the ground a little, and removing some of the rubbish that lies in the way to knowledge . . . " (Locke 1956: 7). As he portrays it, his work as "under-laborer" is actually *pre*philosophical, unsophisticated, and wholly lacking in grandiose airs. Epistemology, at his time, had clearly not come to dominate the field. But, in the irony of things, Locke's under-laboring would lead exactly to that result.

Despite its importance in the development of British Empiricism, Locke's theory of knowing—at this point in our narrative—is easily grasped. Readers have become well aware of the arguments given and the positions taken by Aristotle and Epicurus, Thomas Aquinas and John Duns Scotus. Locke adds his own flavor to these experience-centered theories, but his views are neither unprecedented nor especially refined. Against the backdrop of Oxford scholasticism, however, which had sprouted a dense beard of technical terms, his common-sense reaffirmation of Aristotle's old dictum—that nothing reaches the mind save through experience—felt new and radical. It was widely welcomed as the necessary sharp razor to give philosophy a youthful, clean face, fit for modernity.

And although it was not in the broader perspective particularly original, Locke's philosophy was in the literal sense genuinely radical. It went to the root, the "radish" of things. Most simply expressed, it asked *what our ideas are* and *where they come from*. My treatment of his thought, correspondingly, will content itself with four topics of central importance to Locke, all grounded in these root questions. I shall briefly examine (1) Locke's understanding of "idea"; (2) his stalwart rejection of the notion that any such ideas are innate; (3) his way of analyzing the origins of key ideas; and (4) his attempt to show that all genuine knowledge can be analyzed into combinations of ideas so defined and so structured.

What are ideas? Locke's definition of "idea" is offered early in the *Essay*, in the Introduction, where he writes:

> [Before] I proceed on to what I have thought on this subject, I must here, in the entrance, beg pardon of my reader for the frequent use of the word *idea* which he will find in the following treatise. It being that term which, I think, serves best to stand for whatsoever is the object of the understanding when a man thinks, I have used it to express whatever is meant by *phantasm, notion, species*, or whatever it is which the mind can be employed about in thinking; and I could not avoid frequently using it (Locke 1956: 15–16).

This is an endlessly debated definition. Can it mean "whatever is before the mind," including perceptions of emotional states like fear or hope? Descartes took that line in his debate with Hobbes, as we recall. At first it seems that Locke is following this same broad path. But doubts emerge when we note that Locke twice repeats that ideas are the object "when a man *thinks*," and are whatever it is that the mind is "employed about in *thinking*." The more we contemplate this, the cloudier it gets. When we feel fear, are we "thinking"? Hobbes certainly thought not. We are instead, Hobbes declared, experiencing a mere causal effect, that is, a tendency to flee from the object imaged. Where in this debate is Locke?

In practice, Locke leans toward the broader, more inclusive approach of Descartes. Since for him awareness is the source of all our ideas, it may be fair to paraphrase Locke as holding that an idea is anything of which we can be aware—thus be able to name and think about. He seems allied more to Descartes (and the medievals), too, in accepting that ideas can be general.

By including "species" as one synonym for "idea," he accepts that we are aware of general sensible qualities like "redness" or "middle C," and of general intelligible species like "equality" or "greater than." His is an empiricism without the extremes of nominalism. Still, by including "phantasm" as another synonym for "idea," Locke raises the sharp problem whether he intends his key word to refer to modifications of *consciousness alone* or, as he sometimes implies, to meanings that refer to an *object beyond* them. As an astute commentator put it, regarding Locke, "discussion of ideas is sometimes discussion of our *ideas* of things and sometimes of the *things* of which we have ideas" (Copleston 1962: vol. 5, part 1, 82, emphasis supplied). Similarly, Whitehead takes particular satisfaction in Locke's having observed that, "there is scarce any particular thing existing, which, in some of its simple ideas, does not communicate with a greater, and in others with a less, number of particular beings. . ." (Locke 1956: bk. 3, chap. 9, sec. 14, quoted in Whitehead 1978: 147). Whitehead finds this important since, in contrast to Locke's opening passages tending to define "idea" as simply a mental state, "This passage . . . illustrates Locke's habit of employing the term 'idea' in a sense other than particular content of an act of awareness" (Whitehead 1978: 147).

Are any ideas innate? Because—to put it kindly—he valued adequacy over coherence (or, perhaps, because of "laziness" and being "too busy"), Locke's position on the character of "ideas" is not crystal clear, to say the least. But on one matter there is no ambiguity: he does not at all allow that ideas of any kind can be "innate."

Locke is convinced that all our ideas have a history of arrival in our minds. His method will be to analyze our knowledge into its component ideas and our ideas into the circumstances of their arrival in our awareness—the "historical, plain method" (Locke 1956: 10), as he named his crucial invention. But if this method is to be comprehensive for all knowing, if nothing is to escape it, it is imperative that no ideas can be "ahistorical," outside the scope of the method. Sometimes commentators express surprise at the length of Locke's polemic against innate ideas at the beginning of his *Essay*; but innate ideas posed a potentially fatal threat to his method as a whole. Here we see an excellent example of a methodological commitment at work. The whole effectiveness of his chosen enterprise as "under-laborer," clearing out mental rubbish that has been carelessly strewn into our minds, depends on none of our ideas being "innate" in the sense of having no history of arrival and thus escaping the "historical, plain method."

This stress on tracing facts about the genesis of ideas draws attention to one of the key problems in his empiricism, namely, that epistemological issues are not clearly distinguished from psychological ones. By so insisting,

Locke makes the *history* of an idea count more heavily than the *character* of the idea. His methodological commitments limit him to a clumsy way of distinguishing between the *logical* and the *psychological* issues involved. The latter are purely factual, and would apply equally well to the origins of hallucinations as those of normal perceptions, to ideas resulting from obsessions as well as to conclusions drawn from valid demonstrations. The historical, plain method of Locke is suited to tell us *where in fact* our ideas came from, but not *how well warranted* they are. His historical empiricism is thus positioned to be strong on description of our opinions and their origins, but it is weaker in handling their justification, if they are justified.

Where do our key ideas come from?   Still, Locke is greatly interested in sifting our ideas in hopes of getting to the foundations of such knowledge as we can hope to attain. The bulk of his large *Essay* is devoted to this, detailing the sources of ideas (either from sense or from reflection on the operations of our minds) and their kinds (simple or complex, in either simple modes or mixed); and ruminating about the important consequences that follow from a proper appreciation of their histories. My sketch of the highlights in the following paragraphs of this subsection can hardly aim at completeness. It will concentrate on Locke's moderation: his deep desire to hold to the middle ground of common sense and his readiness to report what he finds without dogmatic concern for the consequences in theory.

Book 2 of the *Essay* begins with a discussion of the only alternative left, once innate ideas have been firmly rejected. Locke puts it as follows:

> Let us then suppose the mind to be, as we say, white paper, void of all characters, without any ideas; how comes it to be furnished? Whence comes it by that vast store, which the busy and boundless fancy of man has painted on it with an almost endless variety? Whence has it all the materials of reason and knowledge? To this I answer, in one word, from EXPERIENCE; in that all our knowledge is founded, and from that it ultimately derives itself (Locke 1956: 42).

Experience comes from just two sources: deliverances of the five senses, with all their variety of appropriate ideas (color and shape from the eyes, tastes from the tongue, etc.), and nonsensory awareness of the operations of our own minds. Locke toys with the idea of classifying these as "external" versus "internal" sense (Locke 1956: 44), but rejects this usage as potentially confusing. Instead he calls the source of the first sort of ideas "sensation" and the source of the second sort "reflection." Through the former we gain our ideas of external objects in the world; through the latter we gain our ideas of everything else.

Here Locke is within common sense. He assumes the existence of external material things causing sensations in our bodily sense organs, and he assumes the existence of minds (sometimes he calls them "souls" or "spirits") in which operations occur. These minds are not, by the way, purely "thinking things." Instead, Locke is quite willing, again in his common-sense way, to grant that minds need not think (or be conscious) all the time. What they are while unconscious, as in deep sleep, he does not worry about; but clearly they are something more, for Locke, than their functions (Locke 1956: 47–48).

If all our ideas come from sensation or reflection, then what are they like? We are used to experiencing blends of many ideas at once, as in a snowball being round and white and cold and hard all at the same time. But it is important, Locke urges, to remind ourselves that: "Though the qualities that affect our senses are, in the things themselves, so united and blended that there is no separation, no distance between them; yet it is plain the ideas they produce in the mind enter by the senses simple and unmixed" (Locke 1956: 53). *Simple, clear* ideas are the foundation. Vision provides the clear and distinct ideas of roundness and whiteness; touch gives us coldness and hardness. These enter our minds through their respective sense organs quite separate and simple, however much they may be "blended" in our perceptions (and originally in the thing itself). Here Locke is giving an analysis of what "must be," not a historical treatment of our actual blurry experience. In so doing, he shows, like Hobbes and Descartes, strong epistemic preference for those aspects of experience that are clear and distinct—open (in the language of Chapter 1) to "Greek" contemplation—rather than warm and intimate—open to "Hebrew" embrace. I plan to challenge this preference in Part Three. But, interestingly, Locke himself (as we shall see) backs away from insisting on this preference when it becomes epistemologically awkward. He has still wider values—loyalty to common sense and to the actual facts of experience—that trump the traditional norms of clarity and distinctness.

Given the initial preference for clarity, Locke's principle of analysis is that some ideally clear ideas, as in white or cold, are just discovered not to be subject to further breakdown, though of course there may be indefinitely many shades of white and indefinitely many degrees of cold. A specific shade of white, encountered in a specific snowball with a specific degree of coldness is the end of the line, at which we stop in tracing the origins of our ideas. They are also what we just receive, passively, prior to doing anything with them in our minds. In both these respects, therefore, they are the "earliest" of our ideas, even though we should not imagine that as infants we experienced pure, unmixed simple ideas. We cannot create these; we depend on receiving them. If we had been brought up in a room with only black and white objects, we would never be able to manufacture for ourselves the idea of red. The same passivity is shown in our reception of ideas of reflection, simply registering the experience of our own mental states.

> In this part the understanding is merely passive; and whether or no it will have these beginnings and, as it were, materials of knowledge, is not in its own power. . . . These simple ideas, when offered to the mind, the understanding can no more refuse to have, nor alter when they are imprinted, nor blot them out and make new ones itself, than a mirror can refuse, alter, or obliterate the images or ideas, which the objects set before it do therein produce (Locke 1956: 52).

Simple ideas are the foundation, then, because they are indivisible, uncreatable, indestructible, and not under our power. It is a contingent reality that we happen to have only five senses; we can imagine that God might have created us with more or fewer. But when we do try to imagine this, it is an empty or abstract imagining; we cannot imagine what the ideas proper to such an additional sense would have been like; and if we were deprived of a sense from birth, we could not imagine the ideas proper to that sense.

Simple ideas, whether originally from sensation or from reflection, combine in complex ways. Some ideas, like pleasure and pain, can come from both sensation and reflection. Most come from only one source, but after their arrival, they become associated with one another. They are involuntarily mixed in actual perception of the world of objects, as we have seen; but what is different about complex ideas is that they are also open to voluntary combination and modification (Locke 1956: 93).

We can by combining simple ideas in new ways come up with complex ideas of substances we have never experienced; or we may think about substances with ideas drawn from daily life. Either way, the idea of "substance" is omnipresent—but problematic.

> [The] ideas of substances are such combinations of simple ideas as are taken to represent distinct particular things subsisting by themselves, in which the supposed or confused idea of substance, such as it is, is always the first and chief (Locke 1956: 94).

"*Supposed*" idea? Unfortunately, the ever-present "supposed" idea of substance is quite defective, judged by the ideal of clarity. This is a problem Locke feels keenly, but he is unable to justify giving up the idea merely on this account. It is far too important to be sacrificed to an epistemic norm.

Locke was not the first to worry about the idea of substance. We saw earlier that Hobbes flatly denied the possibility of having such an idea at all.

Descartes no less flatly (and impatiently) affirmed the possibility. Here Locke, characteristically, prefers a middle course. Where does the idea of "substance" come from? Locke answers that experience gives us a great number of simple ideas that go constantly together, and that "not imagining how these simple ideas can subsist by themselves, we accustom ourselves to suppose some *substratum* wherein they do subsist, and from which they do result, which therefore we call *substance*" (Locke 1956: 154–55). Substance, so conceived, is always behind the scenes, never on stage.

> So that if any one will examine himself concerning his notion of pure substance in general, he will find he has no other idea of it at all, but only a supposition of he knows not what support of such qualities which are capable of producing simple ideas in us; which qualities are commonly called accidents (Locke 1956: 155).

In this sense, Hobbes was right that we have no idea of substance; "thus here, as in all other cases where we use words without having clear and distinct ideas, we talk like children; who being questioned what such a thing is which they know not, readily give this satisfactory answer, that it is *something*; which in truth signifies no more, when so used, either by children or men, but that they know not what; and that the thing they pretend to know, and talk of, is what they have no distinct idea of at all, and so are perfectly ignorant of it, and in the dark" (Locke 1956: 155–56).

Perfectly ignorant? This is one verdict to which Locke is drawn by his doctrine that the only ideas we can possibly have must come from primitively clear elements in experience. But, at the same time, such a conclusion is too extreme for Locke. Surely there is more to say. Our ideas may be confused and inadequate when it comes to dealing with substance, and we may literally be without a *good* (read "clear") idea of what we are talking about. "Only we must take notice, that our complex ideas of substances, besides all these simple ideas they are made up of, have always the confused idea of something to which they belong and in which they subsist" (Locke 1956: 156). Clarity may be preferred, but one must take what one can get. A *confused* idea is not the same as *no* idea. We seem to speak intelligibly about objects possessing properties. We say "a body is a thing that is extended, figured, and capable of motion; a spirit, a thing capable of thinking" (Locke 1956: 156), and these locutions, so widely used, must mean something. Locke proposes a compromise:

> These and the like fashions of speaking intimate that the substance is supposed always something besides the extension, figure, solidity, motion, thinking, or other observable ideas, though we know not what it is (Locke 1956: 156).

Furthermore, it would be irrational give up the idea of substances—as irrational as to deny the idea of the self. We must hold the mind to be a substantial reality because of all the mental operations we experience, steadily going together, even though we obviously cannot experience the mental substance "behind" such operations. Locke concludes that it would be no less absurd to deny material substance:

> [By] supposing a substance wherein thinking, knowing, doubting, and a power of moving, &c. do subsist, we have as clear a notion of the substance of spirit as we have of body; the one being supposed to be (without knowing what it is) the *substratum* to those simple ideas we have from without; and the other supposed (with a like ignorance of what it is) to be the *substratum* to those operations which we experiment in ourselves within (Locke 1956: 157).

The ironic consequences of this argument for common-sense acceptance of material and mental substances will become apparent in due course.

I mentioned, in passing, that the qualities of sense objects may—or may not—be "like" our ideas. In holding this, Locke was in distinguished company, including Galileo, Descartes, and Hobbes; while their own ancestors were Democritus and Epicurus. There was nothing particularly novel, therefore, in Locke's distinguishing between the "primary" qualities, which do resemble, and the "secondary" qualities, which do not resemble, the ideas we have of them. There was one significant twist, however: since Locke did not want to suggest that qualities are merely something in our minds alone, he distinguished, in his moderating way, between the *qualities*, which, he asserted, are in the things themselves, and the *ideas* of these qualities, which are in our minds. Or, to put it still more carefully, there are *powers* in objects which we speak of as "qualities" when these powers modify our sense organs and bring about ideas in our minds. The same powers we speak of as "mere powers" when they bring about changes in non-percipient things. The power in a fire to melt wax is exactly the same power as the power to give us the sensory ideas of golden radiance and warmth. The latter powers, when working on us, are the fire's qualities of being yellow and warm.

But are these qualities *like* the ideas of yellowness and warmth they generate in us? No, these qualities are neither constant nor inseparable from the objects qualified. It may at first seem so, "And yet he that will consider that the same fire that at one distance produces in us the sensation of warmth, does at a nearer approach produce in us the far different sensation of pain, ought to bethink himself what reason he has to say, that his idea of warmth which was produced in him by the fire, is actually in the fire, and his idea of pain which the same fire produced in him the same way is not in the fire"

(Locke 1956: 69). Locke's solution is that both ideas, the warmth and the pain, are present only in us, while the power to heat (to produce in us to the ideas of comfort or pain, or to bring a piece of wax to the melting point) is present in the fire itself—but *not as resembling* either of our ideas. The same is true for the vast bulk of our sensory ideas, all of which depend upon our bodily organs and mental constitutions. Were it not for our perception of them, they would not exist at all.

If there are qualities *always* present in and inseparable from objects, however, Locke holds that they can be counted on to resemble our ideas. They would be primary qualities, as distinct from fickle secondary ones. And since the very concept of material objects requires that such objects must have bulk, figure, quantity, location, and motion or rest, we can rely on these ideas to give us accurate representations of things in themselves. As to such qualities, Locke asserts: "Those are in them, whether we perceive them or no; and when they are of that size that we can discover them, we have by these an idea of the thing as it is in itself, as is plain in artificial things. These I call *primary qualities* (Locke 1956: 71).

Locke here refers cautiously to the "size" of the primary, natural (non-"artificial") things in themselves, since he takes for granted that the vast majority of these are too small to be perceived alone. In this he shows his appreciation for the atomism of Gassendi, with whose followers he spent much time in France. And at this point Locke is fully in tune with Hobbes, whose mechanistic materialism rules the world of physical sense perception. When Locke asks himself "how bodies produce ideas in us," his answer is "manifestly by impulse, the only way which we can conceive bodies operate in" (Locke 1956: 67–68).

The correlation between the "insensible impulses" of objects in themselves (purely bulk, figure, and motion) and our many-splendored universe of sensory ideas (all our visual hues, all odors, sounds, etc.) is entirely arbitrary. There is no natural similarity at all. God simply willed the correlation when he made us. We look in vain for a reason "that a violet, by the impulse of such insensible particles of matter of peculiar figures and bulks, and in different degrees and modifications of their motions, causes the ideas of the blue colour and sweet scent of that flower to be produced in our minds. It being no more impossible to conceive that God should annex such ideas to such motions with which they have no similitude, than that he should annex the idea of pain to the motion of a piece of steel dividing our flesh, with which that idea has no resemblance" (Locke 1956: 68).

Locke's views about ideas and qualities attempt a delicate balance. Most of our ideas do not resemble the qualities in things; but even the secondary qualities in things are not merely subjective, since in themselves they are real powers, which can be relied upon under normal circumstances to give us our regular palette of sensations, however arbitrary and nonresemblant they may be. The whole theory depends, of course, on there being a useable idea of *causal power*. Without such an idea, the concept of qualities as powers in things, and with it the theory of perception as based on causal influence from the world outside, would collapse. Where, on the historical, plain method, do we find such an idea emerging into experience?

Locke's answer here contrasts significantly with his position on substance. Though he begins by noting that our experience of material substances fails to give us any clear, direct awareness of the *power* to change or to be changed—but only the *fact* of constant change in the conjoined simple ideas that make up substances—he does not from this conclude that we lack an idea of causal power. Instead, he turns from ideas of sensation to ideas of reflection. "But yet, if we will consider it attentively, bodies by our senses do not afford us so clear and distinct an idea of active power as we have from reflection on the operations of our minds" (Locke 1956: 137). In the external world, we can never see a power, only its effects. But the power to initiate effects is directly, if not clearly, experienced in acts of willing.

> The idea of the beginning of motion we have only from reflection on what passes in ourselves, where we find by experience, that, barely by willing it, barely by a thought of the mind, we can move the parts of our bodies which were before at rest (Locke 1956: 138).

Locke is not a dogmatist, however, and he wants to hold the door open for those who might claim to have experience of active powers in the world of sensation: "But if, from the impulse bodies are observed to make one upon another, any one thinks he has a clear idea of power, it serves as well to my purpose, sensation being one of those ways whereby the mind comes by its ideas: only I thought it worth while to consider here by the way, whether the mind doth not receive its idea of active power clearer from reflection on its own operations, than it doth from any external sensation" (Locke 1956: 138).

Assured of the idea of cause and finding the idea of spiritual substance no less rational than the idea of material substances, Locke affirms the possibility of an idea of the first spiritual cause, God. In this he adopts a compromise position between Hobbes, who simply denied the possibility of any idea of God, and Descartes, who claimed a positive innate idea of God's infinity and perfection. There is no need for such extremes, for Locke. God is incomprehensible, of course; but even to say this much requires an idea of *what* is incomprehensible. And this idea enters our minds in the same way as all the others being traced by the historical, plain method.

For if we examine the idea we have of the incomprehensible Supreme Being, we shall find, that we come by it the same way; and that the complex ideas we have both of God and separate spirits are made up of the simple ideas we receive from reflection: v.g., having, from what we experiment in ourselves, got the ideas of existence and duration, of knowledge and power, of pleasure and happiness, and of several other qualities and powers which it is better to have than to be without; when we would frame an idea the most suitable we can to the Supreme Being, we enlarge every one of these with our idea of infinity; and so, putting them together, make our complex idea of God (Locke 1956: 172).

Such an idea of God depends, quite obviously, on the idea of infinity, and that for Locke is a compromise, too. Hobbes held that infinity is a purely negative idea; Descartes argued that it is the most positive idea we can conceive, since so full of perfection. Locke strikes for the middle ground. There is something positive in the idea and something negative. On the positive side, "When we would think of infinite space or duration, we at first step usually make some very large idea, as, perhaps, of millions of ages or miles, which possibly we double and multiply several times. All that we thus amass together in our thoughts is positive" (Locke 1956: 130). At the same time, "infinite" does not mean simply "very great." It means *without* any bound or limit. I am reminded of my theologian father's favorite joke: a sailor is hauling up and coiling a rope that trails into the water from the stern of his ship. He coils and coils, then hauls and coils some more. Finally, after a long, long time, he wipes his brow and moans, "By Jumpin' Jimminy, the end must be cut off!"

"Infinite ropes" would be those for which any idea of an end would be deleted. Is infinity a positive or a negative idea? Is it an idea at all? If the idea of God depends on it, is there, after all, any idea of God? Locke strove hard to bring sensible balance to such questions, and many more. His down-to-earth values led him to seek to embrace as much as possible; but, as we shall see, his well-intended compromises were not to last.

What can we know? Finally, the question which motivated all of the above— What is the extent of human knowledge?—needs to be answered. In his answer, offered in Book 4 of the *Essay*, Locke, though he begins by adopting the full-fledged requirement of Plato and Descartes for genuine knowing (absolute certainty), ends by allowing a considerably more relaxed standard of success.

It follows from everything that has gone before, Locke believes, that human knowing must be a matter of ideas alone. Ideas are all we have. If we can successfully claim knowledge, therefore, it must be "nothing but the perception of the connexion and agreement, or disagreement and repugnancy, of any of our ideas" (Locke 1956: 255). There are four sorts of agreements (or disagreements). These are: (a) the *identity* of ideas (e.g., "p is p"), (b) the *relation* of ideas (e.g., "if all p's are q's and this is a p, then it is a q"), (c) the *coexistence* of ideas (e.g., "if this is gold it is highly malleable"), and (d) the *real existence* of what our ideas represent (e.g., "I exist"). These four categories can be judged against three degrees or standards of knowing. These degrees are (i) *intuitive* knowing, (ii) *demonstrative* knowing, and (iii) *sensitive* knowing of particular existence. If we place the categories against the standards, what do we find?

First, if we define intuitive knowing as the highest level, we will discover that only *identity of ideas* can reach this standard of certainty. Intuitive knowing, according to Locke, is "irresistible." It is a direct, unmediated perception by the mind of the agreement or disagreement between ideas. Locke celebrates this kind of knowledge, which "like bright sunshine, forces itself immediately to be perceived as soon as ever the mind turns its view that way; and leaves no room for hesitation, doubt, or examination, but the mind is presently filled with the clear light of it" (Locke 1956: 261). All other knowledge ultimately depends on this for its own support. One cannot demand a higher certainty than this. The question of the identity of ideas, or their necessary incompatibility (nonidentity) falls into this intuitive domain.

Below the highest, but still high enough to warrant the great title of knowledge, is knowing by demonstrative proof. Here the relation between our ideas is seen, but not directly. Other ideas, which constitute the demonstration, intervene. The result is just as coercive, as Hobbes saw to his satisfaction, but it is not as easy or direct as intuitive knowing; it allows of doubt prior to the demonstration (as intuition, being immediate, does not), and— being at several steps remove—it is not so clear as intuition. But, since each step in a demonstrative proof depends on and is validated by a direct intuitive awareness of its necessity, demonstrative reasoning qualifies fully for knowing in the strong sense Locke officially embraces. Here the relations of ideas, the second kind of knowledge, can be validated or definitively found wanting.

And below this, Locke says, there is no more "knowing," *strictly speaking.* "These two, viz., intuition and demonstration, are the degrees of our knowledge; whatever comes short of one of these, with what assurance soever embraced, is but *faith* or *opinion,* but not knowledge, at least in all general truths" (Locke 1956: 265).

And yet this sounds too rigid, too dogmatic, for Locke. He immediately begins to qualify and compromise. There are other sorts of relations between ideas—the coexistence of properties of substances and the real existence of things—that people also do their best to know. This domain of ideas, dealt with in the empirical sciences and common sense, "going beyond bare probability, and yet not reaching perfectly to either of the foregoing degrees of certainty, passes under the name of knowledge" (Locke 1956: 265). Our ideas of the qualities of material substances do in fact coexist nearly all the time in notable regularities, which we call laws of nature. It would be foolish to refuse the honorific title, "knowledge," where there is so much confidence. Cartesian doubt need not be taken seriously. Descartes worried that he might be dreaming, but to this Locke offers a reply midway between the jocular and the acid:

> If any one say, a dream may do the same thing, and all these ideas may be produced in us without any external objects; he may please to dream that I make him this answer: (1) That it is no great matter whether I remove his scruple or not: where all is but dream, reasoning and arguments are of no use, truth and knowledge nothing. (2) That I believe he will allow a very manifest difference between dreaming of being in the fire, and being actually in it. But yet if he be resolved to appear so sceptical as to maintain, that what I call being actually in the fire is nothing but a dream; and that we cannot thereby certainly know that any such thing as fire actually exists without us; I answer, that we certainly finding that pleasure or pain follows upon the application of certain objects to us, whose existence we perceive, or dream that we perceive, by our senses; this certainty is as great as our happiness or misery, beyond which we have no concernment to know or to be (Locke 1956: 266–67).

On this pragmatic note, Locke concludes this discussion, departing from his uncharacteristically narrow earlier resolution to allow nothing to be called knowledge except intuition or demonstration. "So that, I think, we may add to the two former sorts of knowledge this also, of the existence of particular external objects by that perception and consciousness we have of the actual entrance of ideas from them, and allow these three degrees of knowledge, viz., *intuitive, demonstrative,* and *sensitive . . .*" (Locke 1956: 267).

The inventory of knowable items under these three heads is worth noting. For Locke, there are indefinitely many general truths that can be known by immediate intuition and demonstration—the whole of existing logic, arithmetic, geometry, and what is yet to be discovered in such fields. But when it comes to knowledge of existence, truths pertaining to reality rather than simply to the agreement of abstract ideas, Locke concludes that one and only one item can be *known* to exist under each of the two "genuine knowledge" headings. Oddly, every knower is aware of a *different* truth under the strongest and simplest heading of "intuitive" knowing, but each knower can reason to the *same* truth under the heading of "demonstrative" knowing.

The one matter of existence that one can know in the absolute, intuitive way Locke describes is one's own reality. Without mentioning Descartes, Locke is obviously happy to join in fully affirming the *"cogito ergo sum"* argument. He puts his own cheerfully pragmatic stamp on it, however, as follows:

> He that can doubt whether he be anything or no, I speak not to, no more than I would argue with pure nothing, or endeavour to convince non-entity that it were something. If any one pretends to be so sceptical as to deny his own existence (for really to doubt of it is manifestly impossible), let him, for me, enjoy his beloved happiness of being nothing, until hunger or some other pain convince him of the contrary (Locke 1956: 311).

But of course "one" is a variable covering many different existences. What "one," each one, can know is that he or she exists; and this is a different specific truth in each case. I have certain and indubitable knowledge that *I* exist, but I have no such certain knowledge that *you* exist, even though you affirm your own reality with just as much claim to perfect assurance as I do mine.

Given these individual intuitive knowings, however, we can each, according to Locke, move by demonstrative steps to knowing a common truth about existence: that is, that God exists. This cannot, of course, be done through Descartes' primary proofs, which depend on our finding an innate idea of a perfect God among the inventory of ideas that constitute us as thinking things. There are, Locke has argued at length, no innate ideas. But we are capable of knowing intuitively, thus certainly, the abstract and general truth that nothing comes from nothing, that nothing makes nothing, that out of nothing, nothing comes. This proves that there has never been a state of pure nothing, since we already know with perfect intuitive certainty that something (i.e., one's self) exists. But this means that from all eternity something has existed, namely, the necessary creator-God.

Each can know God with *deductive* certainty; each can know self-existence with *intuitive* certainty. But these are the only two items of existence that can be "known"—strictly speaking—under the traditional epistemic norm of certainty that Locke feels obliged (much of the time) to affirm. All other claims to knowing pale in comparison. Locke muses (sounding almost Cartesian):

> From what has been said, it is plain to me we have a more certain knowledge of the existence of a God, than of anything our senses have

not immediately discovered to us. Nay, I presume I may say that we more certainly know that there is a God, than that there is anything else without us. When I say we *know*, I mean there is such a knowledge within our reach which we cannot miss, if we will but apply our minds to that, as we do to several other enquiries (Locke 1956: 313).

All other claims to knowledge of existence, then, whether from common sense or from the sciences, will be subject to suspicion. Locke wavers on the degree of suspicion he recommends. When feeling loyal to the ideals of knowing that have been dominant in Western philosophy since Plato, he warns that even natural science is incapable of genuine knowledge. It is, however, capable of providing us with high degrees of probability; and in the end that may be all we should ask for. "Our knowledge, as has been shown, being very narrow, most of the propositions we think, reason, discourse, nay, act upon, are such as we cannot have undoubted knowledge of their truth; yet some of them border so near upon certainty, that we make no doubt at all about them, but assent to them as firmly, and act according to that assent as resolutely, as if they were infallibly demonstrated, and that our knowledge of them was perfect and certain" (Locke 1956: 335).

Locke ends, then, by examining probability and its degrees. "[Having], as I think, found out the bounds of human knowledge and certainty," it remains only "to consider *the several degrees and grounds of probability, and assent or faith*" (Locke 1956: 335). "Faith?" Is this all that science can offer if "knowledge" is taken so strictly? At this point we may close our account, since Locke has brought the story to a crossroads for modern thinking: Must everything, besides the infallible awareness of one's simple ideas, the intuitive knowledge of one's solitary finite existence, and the deductive knowledge of God, be classified as one sort of "faith" or other? Should we remain committed to the epistemic norm of certainty, as Locke insists in his more stringent moods, even if it leads to these alarming consequences? Or should we, with Locke in some of his more latitudinarian moods, look at assorted probabilities with a wink and a nod and call it knowledge?

GEORGE BERKELEY

George Berkeley (1685–1753), Bishop of Cloyne, was no despiser of faith, under the right religious circumstances; but he saw no need to invoke faith in science or daily life for things we can perfectly well know. His mission was to warn against straining credulity, as Berkeley believed Locke did, by claiming too many wooly things as goals of knowledge that cannot be substantiated—or even properly thought. As we shall see, Berkeley accepted the same inventory of knowable realities as Locke had done: self, God, and immediate ideas. Taking the limits of this inventory more rigorously than Locke had done, Berkeley drew some radical conclusions that led ever more swiftly to the full awareness of a looming epistemological gap.

Berkeley was born in Ireland to an English family at the time Locke, while exiled in Holland, was helping to plot the overthrow of James II and arrange his replacement by William and Mary. They never met, since the much younger man was still studying in Trinity College, Dublin, when Locke died. But Berkeley was born into an astonishing age of intellectual excitement. Newton's *Principia* was published just two years after his birth; Locke's *Essay* first came out when he was five. He grew surrounded by the awareness of profound novelty in the air, and with a sense of unlimited possibilities for radical rethinking.

It seems that Berkeley availed himself of these possibilities quite early. Soon after his appointment at age twenty-two as Fellow of Trinity College (for more biographical information see *Being and Value*, 191–94), he set to writing his *New Theory of Vision* (1709). Already by this time, according to his notes, he was privately convinced (though he does not mention it in this first book) that the material world is an otiose assumption. At any event, he argues forcefully and explicitly for immaterialism in his next book, *Treatise Concerning the Principles of Human Knowledge* (1710), published at age twenty-five; and his highly popular *Three Dialogues Between Hylas and Philonous* followed only three years later, while Berkeley was on an extended trip to London in 1713, still not yet thirty.

All this radical writing was done long before Berkeley was appointed Dean at Derry Cathedral in 1724, still longer before he was made Bishop a decade after that. It may be significant, from the point of view of Berkeley's values, that the young man who wrote the intense polemics against abstract ideas and the intelligibility of material substrates turned into the clergyman who, with equal intensity, worked for multi-ethnic education in America, criticized Newton's vision of nature as hopelessly abstract, and preached universal cures in his latter years. When he first wrestled with Locke, however, he was a clear-headed youth with the idealism (and naiveté) needed to follow an argument to its conclusion. He was not afraid to march to his own drummer. Indeed, he expected others to drop ancient muddle and march along with him. He put a high value on reason and saw absolutely no conflict between reason and his religious faith. He experienced the perceptible world vividly in all its immediacy; and through his perceptions he understood himself to be in the active presence of God.

It must be emphasized that Berkeley's positive view was a cleaned-up, consistent interpretation of Locke's analysis of the human epistemic situation into (1) ideas of one kind or another and (2) mind aware of these ideas. If easygoing Locke, as we saw, occasionally slipped from his "nothing but ideas" position and wrote as though it is independent things of which we have ideas, Berkeley did not. The opening sentence of the youthful *Principles of Human Knowledge* makes it manifest that all we can have before our minds is ideas, or other kinds of ideas or . . . still other kinds of ideas.

> It is evident to anyone who take a survey of the objects of human knowledge, that they are either ideas (1) actually imprinted on the senses, or else such [ideas] as are (2) perceived by attending to the passions and operations of the mind, or lastly (3) ideas formed by help of memory and imagination, either compounding, dividing, or barely representing those originally perceived in the aforesaid ways (Berkeley 1962: 276–77).

In this sentence, though without using the technical terms, Berkeley takes for granted Locke's division between (1) ideas of sensation and (2) ideas of reflection, and Locke's further distinction (3) between simple and complex ideas. Still in the same opening paragraph, Berkeley further takes for granted Locke's analysis of substances as the coexistence of ideas in steady or regular ways:

> Smelling furnishes me with odors, the palate with tastes, and hearing conveys sounds to the mind in all their variety of tone and composition. And as several of these are observed to accompany each other, they come to be marked by one name, and so to be reputed as one thing (Berkeley 1962: 277).

Completing the inventory, still quite in harmony with Locke, Berkeley quickly adds mind, which does the perceiving. "This perceiving being is what I call *mind, spirit, soul*, or *myself*. By which words I do not denote any one of my ideas, but a thing entirely distinct from them wherein they exist, or which is the same thing, whereby they are perceived; for the existence of an idea consists in being perceived" (Berkeley 1962: 277).

None of this should shock Locke or his followers. It is essentially straight out of the *Essay*. But Berkeley did shock many readers by taking the implications of these principles with utmost rigor. By so doing he thought he was urging that accepting Locke's fundamentals, without flinching from the consequences, would lead to a much simplified epistemic outcome, in which dead matter is unknowable—unthinkable—and what is left to know is much more vivid and saturated with meaning. Others, however, interpreted him as snatching away our ability to know the real, objective world.

The Berkeleian position is entirely straightforward and quintessentially the product of earlier modern thinking. If, as Descartes and Hobbes had agreed, the existence of ideas depends on their being perceived; and if, as they further agreed, it is the nature of minds to perceive (and only minds perceive); and if, as Locke had shown, all that is directly experienceable is ideas; then all that is experienceable depends upon minds perceiving. This is not so shocking when applied to experiences of pain or hope or jealousy, Locke's "ideas of reflection"; but Berkeley saw no escape, logically, from applying it also to his "ideas of sensation," to experiences of apples and books as well.

Locke had come close to admitting as much in his discussion of substance, the unperceivable and therefore unknowable "*je ne sais quoi*" that lies under all the sensible qualities we experience as coexisting in the things we name as things. But, as Berkeley saw it, Locke lacked the courage of his convictions. He retreated to the merely negative view that it would be just as irrational to doubt material as spiritual substance and to the compromise position that we have a shadowy, confused concept of "material substrate" despite the absence of any clear idea on the subject. Hobbes, to his credit, had followed his argument to the end, denying any idea of "substance" in the sense of substrate; but then Hobbes contradicted himself by nevertheless postulating unperceiving (and never, as such, perceived) material atoms as behind all our phantasms. Locke, less clearly but no less illegitimately, had accepted the prevailing materialism without argument and without noticing that his own epistemology had completely undermined it.

Berkeley's diagnosis of the disorder that allowed even major thinkers to make such mistakes was the pernicious influence of abstract ideas. The process of mental abstraction is pulling ideas apart from one another and thinking some while ignoring others. We are accustomed to separating ideas from one another in imagination. We can think an apple that is not red. Separating the apple's color from other imagined ideas of it in our thoughts is a legitimate abstraction, since apples really need not be red. They can be green or brown or yellow or mottled. Thus we can think of apples and for some purposes simply not assign them specific colors, though in the back of our minds we know that every actual apple must have some specific color or other.

Unfortunately, many have confused themselves by misusing this power of abstraction. They have attempted to abstract ideas from the fact that ideas must always be perceived by some specific mind or other. Just as it would be arrant nonsense to take seriously the phrase, "an absolutely colorless apple," so it is literally meaningless to use the phrase, "an absolutely unperceived idea." But this is what is entailed in supposing that one can think about inert, unperceived, and unperceiving material things beyond, behind, or underneath our ideas. We can of course imagine a book on a table in a room where no one is imagined perceiving it. But this is simply to overlook the fact that these imagined ideas are still being perceived by some mind—our own, by imagining the situation. Such harmful abstracting becomes systematic and endemic in theories of a world of things existing entirely apart from some perceiver.

But what of the long-standing distinction between the "primary" and "secondary" qualities of things, which had been stock in trade for modern thinkers ever since Galileo, who accepted the mathematical characteristics of things as objectively real but, as we saw in *Being and Value* (129), likened tastes and colors to feelings of being tickled, namely, that they are in the perceiver alone rather than in the feather? Locke, we saw, followed in this tradition, insisting on the subjective, or mind-dependent, character of most sensory ideas—all colors, textures, tastes, smells, sounds, etc.—but (like Galileo, Descartes, and Hobbes) reserving the quantifiable ideas—size, shape, motion, etc.—as genuinely representative of the objective world. The standard argument was that unlike the unstable and therefore mind-dependent ideas of secondary qualities, our ideas of "bulk, figure, quantity, location, and motion or rest" are constant and inseparable in thought from sensory objects, and are therefore both in our minds and in the things so characterized.

Berkeley would have none of this distinction. For one thing, our ideas of size and shape are just as fickle and relative to our perceptions as our ideas of color or warmth. If we are at a distance from some object of sense, the size seems smaller than if we are close at hand; shapes, too, change as an object is rotated and seen from different angles. Motion or rest is highly relative to the circumstances of the perceiver. If it is answered that at least *some* size or other, *some* shape or other, *some* condition of motion or rest, is inseparable from our thought of an object of sense, Berkeley can counter that at least *some* color or other, *some* temperature or other, is just as inseparable. It is illicit abstraction to suppose that we can imagine shape without all the attendant qualities of color or (if in the dark) texture or the like. If our ideas of the so-called "secondary" qualities are (rightly) considered mind-dependent, then by exactly the same token our ideas of the so-called "primary" qualities are dependent on subjectivity as well.

Does this make the world a more unstable, dreamlike place than a world "grounded" in matter? Not at all. All experience is just what it is: its regularities are utterly unaffected by Berkeley's simplification. The so-called "hypothesis" of a stable, material substrate is not only unnecessary, since subjectivity is in any case required for *all* ideas, as much for shape as for color, it is also not explanatory at all—it is not even a genuine hypothesis, since it cannot be meaningfully formulated. We cannot, on this pseudo-hypothesis, imagine *how* the (unimaginable!) inert substrate would "support" or "underlie" the qualities it supposedly stabilizes. There can be no thinkable relation between a thinkable and an unthinkable thing. Nothing is provided by this supposition.

But how, then, can the obvious stability and regularity of the sensory world—the world of natural science—be understood? For Berkeley the answer is both obvious and wholly in keeping with his scheme of values: the answer lies in the faithfulness of a supreme Mind, whose wisdom and general providence is manifested in our every perception. It is God's role to offer the predictability that we call the "laws" of nature, but which are nothing in themselves but our descriptions of the ways God chooses (normally) to present the ideas that are the objects of sense. This does not mean that God is forbidden to act otherwise if divine wisdom so dictates. But most of the time God is patient and constant in supporting the natural universe in highly predictable ways. If we put a book on a table and leave the room unoccupied and secure, we can count on finding it there when we return. Such mundane daily experiences give constant evidence of God's faithfulness. A pair of anonymous limericks puts the incredulous question and the calm rejoinder in classic form:

> There was a young man who said, "God
> Must think it exceedingly odd
> If he finds that this tree
> Continues to be
> When there's no one about in the Quad."

> Dear Sir: Your astonishment's odd:
> *I* am always about in the Quad.
> And that's why the tree
> Will continue to be,
> Since observed by, Yours faithfully, God.

Can we, though, claim any *idea* of God? If, in accounting for the stability of the natural world, the God-hypothesis is to replace the matter-hypothesis, it had better not fall into the same meaninglessness that prevented the so-called inert substratum from doing any conceptual work. It seems, however, that on Berkeley's understanding of "idea," we can have no ideas of God. Ideas are passive; God is supposed to be active. Ideas are limited; God is supposed to be infinite. Indeed, even finite minds or spirits allow of no ideas, strictly speaking. Minds *perceive* ideas, they *are not* themselves ideas; they are utterly unlike the ideas they perceive. "Hence there can be no *idea* formed of a soul or spirit; for all ideas whatever, being passive and inert, they cannot represent unto us, by way of image or likeness, that which acts. . . . Such is the nature of Spirit, or that which acts, that it cannot be of itself perceived, but only by the effects which it produceth" (Berkeley 1962: 284).

Does this mean that Berkeley's alternative is exploded? If there are no ideas of minds, how can a theory of knowledge rest, as his does, on the phenomenon of minds perceiving ideas? If there are no ideas of spirits, how can knowledge of the laws of nature rest, as he proposes, on the faithfulness of an active Spirit?

Berkeley has an answer. There is a huge difference between using words, on the one hand, like "material substratum," that allow no idea because they rest on an *abstraction disguising an implicit contradiction* ("unperceived perception"), and using other words, on the other hand, like "mind" or "spirit," that allow no idea because the *concrete experience that the words point to is more intimate, and more active*, than mere ideas can allow. The words do have meaning. "Ideas" are inadequate for this kind of meaning. Therefore there is another kind of meaning, which Berkeley calls "notional" meaning, that words can carry when ideas fail.

> We may not, I think, strictly be said to have an *idea* of an active being, or of an action; although we may be said to have a *notion* of them. I have some knowledge or notion of *my mind*, and its acts about ideas; inasmuch as I know or understand what is meant by these words. What I know, that I have some notion of. I will not say that the terms *idea* and *notion* may not be used convertibly, if the world will have it so. But yet it conduceth to clearness and propriety, that we distinguish things very different by different names (Berkeley 1962: 142).

There is neither an idea nor a notion, if we may now use the technical distinction, of inert matter, since it is supposed different from any ideas it "supports" and is not analogous to any activities such as are directly experienced—though not imaged—through the operations of our minds. It is by directly experiencing such operations and, thanks to this living experience, understanding our language about spirits by notion rather than idea, that we can make meaningful reference to other minds, including the Divine. Thus, "as we conceive the ideas that are in the minds of other spirits by means of our own, which we suppose to be resemblances of them, so we know other spirits by means of our own soul." (Berkeley 1962: 304). This theory is fully meaningful, therefore, even though ideas, technically speaking, fall short. And since we lack both ideas and notions of "inert matter," Berkeley is convinced that his theory is left standing alone victorious.

Berkeley, in his twenties, appreciated Locke's great achievement in analyzing human knowledge through the examination of our ideas; but Berkeley's clear young eye saw a potential epistemological gap looming between the knowing mind and the supposed material world "beyond." He moved quickly to avoid the gap by eliminating, as meaningless abstraction, the whole alien domain of matter. Ideas, for Berkeley, do not *represent* sense objects; they *are* the sense objects we can confidently know. In so doing, he saw himself as fighting against both skepticism and religious unbelief. The domain of matter, if interposed between the knowing human mind and God (as was done by both Descartes and Locke), could, Berkeley feared, take over primacy from God. His alternative rested human knowledge of nature squarely on intimate interactions with God, with whom each finite spirit is in constant communion. No doubt the subtitle of his *Principles* was carefully chosen: *Wherein the Chief Causes of Error and Difficulty in the Sciences, with the Grounds of Scepticism, Atheism, and Irreligion, are Inquired Into*. His prophylaxis against the epistemological gap, however, was not to last. In some ways his polemics against the knowability of an independent domain of nature, together with his heavy reliance on metaphysical theory for the assurance of scientific and common-sense knowledge, may have made the cognitive situation still worse.

HUME AND KANT

All the foregoing is but prelude to the conclusions to be drawn in this section; but this section is the shortest of the chapter. All the previous philosophers, with the exception of Descartes, are generally considered lesser figures, compared to Hume and Kant; but I intend to treat these giants more briefly than any of the moderns except Berkeley. The reader deserves an explanation of my tactics at this point.

If this were a conventional history of philosophy, Hume and Kant would require long, detailed attention, at least a chapter each. But I am not attempting such a conventional history; instead, I am writing a narrative account focused on thinkers and theories that led to the modern appearance of the deep, unbridgeable chasm I have called the epistemological gap. In most of this journey to the gap, the hardest work was done by the trailblazers who set directions and had to work their way, stumbling sometimes, over the hardest terrain. They were not quite aware of what lay ahead, though they had intimations. When they approached something that looked impassable, they made a circling move in hopes of getting around it. They all, in one way or another, had confidence that reality as it genuinely is, can be known with certainty. Even Hobbes, who in some ways is closest to skepticism, was sure that the geometrical method, linked to the metaphysics of matter in motion, gave certain truth about the character of the universe, human nature, and even the political arrangements needed in such a universe. Descartes was a methodological skeptic only as a phase in a project that was to assure knowledge of self, God, and the aspects of nature subject to the clarities of mathematics. Locke set the bounds of genuine knowledge narrowly—at least in certain moods—but even at their narrowest, these bounds included intuitive knowledge of many general truths and the existence of self, plus deductive knowledge of God, and "nearly certain" knowledge in the sciences where extremely high probabilities could be allowed to count as knowledge. Berkeley was genuinely alarmed by the specter of skepticism—the skepticism that would be inevitable if philosophers insisted on making independent material things their impossible objects of knowledge. But he comforted himself that these cognitive aims themselves would be abandoned once his arguments, demonstrating their implicit contradictions and confusions, were properly appreciated. In their place he offered what he thought was rational certainty about the existence of an omnipresent, spiritually active God and, through this certainty, divinely grounded knowledge about the real world of ordered perceptions. Each of these great explorers caught glimpses of the gaping chasm implied by their theories, but each moved back from it, searching for another way.

From the point of view of direction-setting values and commitments, hopes and aims, the early moderns are therefore the most subtly compelling figures to observe. Hume's greatness lies in his unswerving clarity in proceeding to the edge of the gap and seeing it as uncrossable. His arguments are forceful and uncompromising, but not hard to follow once we have been led this far by his predecessors. Kant's greatness is in his capacity to take Hume and his exposure of the gap with utmost seriousness and to propose a radically new way to respond to it.

To shift metaphors, sharply, it is as though the early modern philosophers had been busily building something, for various (mostly commendable) motives—something new and exciting, but so new as not to be quite clear in function. This is why it is instructive to watch them at work: following with some care, for example, the increasingly intertwined lives and philosophies of Thomas Hobbes and René Descartes as they tinkered with their respective parts of the still-unformed project. Likewise it is worth spending some time on the practical motives behind Locke's large but loose construction and how it alarmed the intense young Berkeley, who tightened everything in his zeal against matter and atheism.

When they were done, what they had constructed was a trap. It takes a considerable time to build and set at trap, inadvertently or not; it takes very little to spring it shut. This is the story line I now follow through Hume and Kant. Hume sprang the trap; Kant locked it shut. My treatment of these otherwise endlessly interesting figures can thus afford to be comparatively snappy.

DAVID HUME

David Hume (1711–76) was conceived in the year George Berkeley published his *Treatise Concerning the Principles of Human Knowledge*. He was born in Edinburgh into a moderately well-to-do family, with a small estate at "Ninewells," near Berwick. His father died during Hume's youth, leaving him to be raised by his mother, who was from a family of lawyers. Attending Edinburgh University from ages twelve to fifteen, he studied classics, ancient philosophy, and history. After graduation, he studied the law, at his mother's urging, but found it distasteful. During his preparations for the bar, which lasted until he was twenty-one, he devoted himself also, more enthusiastically, to a self-designed course of study in philosophy that included the reading of Descartes, Hobbes, Locke, and Berkeley. It was during this time— around age eighteen—that he first came to his general philosophic point of view; but philosophy as well as law turned sour for him. He decided not to attempt the bar and put philosophizing abruptly aside in favor of an accountant's job with a merchant in Bristol, England. Since neither the life of a clerk in a countinghouse nor the town of Bristol agreed with him, he left Britain altogether for an extended visit to France.

In France he found his way to the town of La Flèche, where almost a century and a half earlier Descartes had gone for his studies with the Jesuits; and there, from 1734 until 1737, Hume lived frugally on the small income from his father's estate, writing out his radical philosophical ideas in a large first manuscript, which was to be *A Treatise of Human Nature*. Manuscript completed, Hume, now twenty-six, returned to live with his mother and brother in Scotland, where he saw to the publication, in three volumes, of his first book. Anticipating that it would cause shock and outrage, he published this first book anonymously. It appeared in 1739, but to his intense disappointment, the book "fell dead-born from the press," without causing so much as "a murmur among the zealots." Since all his life Hume craved what he called "literary fame," this was a grievous setback, but he worked to overcome it with another book, published under his own name, *Essays, Moral and Political* (1741–42). This was a success, and Hume was encouraged both to start rewriting his *Treatise*, in hopes of making it more palatable to the public, and to apply for a chair in moral philosophy at the University of Edinburgh. The attempt at an academic post was rebuffed in 1745, probably because of his growing reputation as an atheist. In his disappointment, he left Scotland again.

This time he took a position as secretary with General St. Clair, who was engaged in fighting the French in Canada. The expedition never got to Canada, dissipating, instead, in a naval raid on the Breton coast; but St. Clair retained Hume as his secretary for a diplomatic mission to Turin that lasted until 1749 and allowed Hume to experience the Continent from Holland, through Germany and Austria, to Tyrol and Italy. Hume reported later that he took no interest in the scenery or traditions of these lands, but was fascinated by politics wherever he went. In the year before his return to Scotland, his revisions of the *Treatise* were published. They appeared first under the title of *Philosophical Essays Concerning Human Understanding* (1748), but in a second edition they were given the famous title under which we know them today, *An Enquiry Concerning Human Understanding*. In the year of the new title, Hume also published his revisions of the third part of his *Treatise* as *An Enquiry Concerning the Principles of Morals* (1751). A year later, to much acclaim, he published the last philosophical work in his lifetime, *Political Discourses* (1752); and riding this wave of literary fame, he applied again for an academic position, now for the chair of logic at Glasgow University. Again he was rejected. And at this point Hume turned to publishing other things, though it was probably in this time that he wrote (and suppressed) his brilliant *Dialogues Concerning Natural Religion*, published posthumously in 1779.

After his second failure to acquire an academic post, Hume turned to practical and historical matters. His law education finally proved its value as he was appointed librarian of the Faculty of Advocates in Edinburgh, a position he held for six years, during which he wrote histories of England, shocking and displeasing readers to his heart's content. When Edinburgh became too small for him, he resigned that position and moved to London to write more history. There he developed a friendship with Edmund Burke (1729–97), and began to be recognized in the wider world. In 1763 he accepted a position with the Earl of Hertford, Ambassador to France, and moved to Paris as secretary of the British Embassy. For a time, after the Ambassador's recall in 1765, he served as *chargé d'affaires*, all the while engaging intensely with the philosophers of Diderot's *Encyclopédie* circle, more fully discussed in *Being and Value* (159–69), who gave him all the adulation he had so long craved. The circle included Voltaire, Étienne Bonnet de Condillac, Jean le Rond d'Alembert, Jean-Jacques Rousseau, and many more, such as (from time to time) Edward Gibbon, Adam Smith, Joseph Priestly, Horace Walpole, Benjamin Franklin, and Thomas Jefferson.

When Hume returned to England in 1766, he brought Jean-Jacques Rousseau with him. They quarrelled explosively, though later reconciling. Hume, then fifty-six, returned to Edinburgh, where he served as Secretary of State for Scotland from 1767 to 1769; but declining health led him to resign that final position and retire to private life, writing his autobiography and living with his sister until his peaceful death in 1776.

Like George Berkeley, whom he admired despite deep disagreements, David Hume came early in life to his views on the possibilities of knowledge.

As early as eighteen, according to a letter he wrote later from La Flèche to his physician, he had come to his basic insight. This was, in essence, that Locke and Berkeley were both right on the fundamentals, but wrong only in not taking their positions all the way to the appropriate conclusions.

Locke, most importantly, was right in his insistence that all our materials for knowing come from experience. He was right in dividing these materials into two great sources: sensation and introspection. Hume uses a different terminology, but the essential division asserted by Locke is retained. The *Treatise* opens with this division expressed in Hume's preferred language. First, Locke's most general term for the content of experience, "idea," is replaced, following Berkeley, by the word, "perception." Second, for Locke's immediate "idea of sensation or reflection" he uses a different word, "impression." Third, for what Hobbes called "decaying sense," Hume employs (in this newly restricted sense) the word "idea." Thus his first paragraph begins:

> All the perceptions of the human mind resolve themselves into two distinct kinds, which I shall call IMPRESSIONS and IDEAS. The difference betwixt these consists in the degrees of force and liveliness with which they strike upon the mind, and make their way into our thought or consciousness. Those perceptions, which enter with most force and violence, we may name *impressions*; and under this name I comprehend all our sensations, passions and emotions, as they make their first appearance in the soul. By *ideas* I mean the faint images of these in thinking and reasoning; such as, for instance, are all the perceptions excited by the present discourse, excepting only, those which arise from the sight and touch, and excepting the immediate pleasure or uneasiness it may occasion (Hume 1888: 1).

This terminological shift helps emphasize that the originals of all our perceptions are "impressed" experiences, before which the mind is passive, just as Locke maintained. Those perceptions which we can manipulate mentally are given the name, "idea," that Locke (like Descartes before him) used for all mental contents. Hume makes no apology for this change. On the contrary, in the first footnote of his *Treatise* he expresses hope that this "liberty" will be allowed, then goes on to criticize Locke: "Perhaps I rather restore the word, idea, to its original sense, from which Mr. *Locke* had perverted it, in making it stand for all our perceptions" (Hume 1888: 2).

Hume, through this shift, builds into his definition of "impressions" that they are indeed the originals of all our perceptions. In the above passage he stipulates that impressions will include, "all our sensations, passions and emotions, as they make their first appearance in the soul." Therefore it is easy work for him to draw out the implication that under his new terminology, our "ideas" will all be derived from impressions. This is not true, of course, for many of our "complex ideas" (here Hume follows Locke exactly), which may involve combinations we have never received, as such, through impressions. "I can imagine to myself such a city as the *New Jerusalem*, whose pavement is gold and walls are rubies, tho' I never saw any such" (Hume 1888: 3). But this simply requires a more careful formulation, distinguishing (as Locke did) complex from simple ideas: "After the most accurate examination, of which I am capable, I venture to affirm, that the rule here holds without any exception, and that every simple idea has a simple impression, which resembles it; and every simple impression a correspondent idea" (Hume 1888: 3).

Simple ideas and impressions correspond to one another. That simple ideas depend upon impressions and not vice versa is shown by the order of their first appearance.

> To give a child an idea of scarlet or orange, of sweet or bitter, I present the objects, or in other words, convey to him these impressions; but proceed not so absurdly, as to endeavour to produce the impressions by exciting the ideas . . . The constant conjunction of our resembling perceptions, is a convincing proof, that the one are the causes of the other; and this priority of the impressions is an equal proof, that our impressions are the causes of our ideas, not our ideas of our impressions (Hume 1888: 5).

Later, in the *Enquiry*, Hume uses the terminology of "copies" for simple ideas as they relate to their impressions. He argues that "when we analyze our thoughts or ideas, however compounded or sublime, we always find that they resolve themselves into such simple ideas as were copied from a precedent feeling or sentiment. . . . We may prosecute this enquiry to what length we please; where we shall always find, that every idea which we examine is copied from a similar impression" (Hume 1902: 19). In consequence it follows that if there is any idea present to the mind, since all ideas are copies of impressions, we should be able to identify a prior similar impression from which the idea was copied. If there is some doubt about the meaning of a word—perhaps a new or technical term—this doubt can be resolved by identifying the appropriate simple impressions that gave rise to the ideas conveyed. If this proves impossible, however, we are left to conclude that the word has no ideas to convey.

> All ideas, especially abstract ones, are naturally faint and obscure: the mind has but a slender hold of them: they are apt to be confounded with other resembling ideas; and when we have often employed any term, though without a distinct meaning, we are apt to imagine it has a

determinate idea annexed to it. On the contrary, all impressions, that is, all sensations, either outward or inward, are strong and vivid: the limits between them are more exactly determined: not is it easy to fall into any error or mistake with regard to them. When we entertain, therefore, any suspicion that a philosophical term is employed without any meaning or idea (as is but too frequent), we need but enquire, *from what impression is that supposed idea derived?* And if it be impossible to assign any, this will serve to confirm our suspicion. By bringing ideas into so clear a light we may reasonably hope to remove all dispute, which may arise, concerning their nature and reality (Hume 1902: 21–22).

With this simple application of Locke's basic principles, Hume has fashioned himself an epistemic threshing machine, one that can release the wheat and discard the chaff in human discourse. Locke could have done this, but his easygoing values did not push him to this keen pitch of either/or. Indeed, his values of accommodation and plausibility held him back. This is exactly what Hume objects to in Locke.

Berkeley did in fact anticipate the method, selectively, in his polemic against the "meaninglessness" of the doctrine of inert, unperceiving matter, but he did not have the will to treat all suspect words so harshly. And this is exactly what Hume objects to in Berkeley.

Hume, we need to remember, did not particularly care to be popular with the establishment, but he did want to be noticed. He was neither interested in fudging for the sake of plausibility (Locke), nor in finding exceptions for the sake of religious commitments (Berkeley); but he loved clarity and was eager for fame. The latter he received, abundantly, both in his time and to this day, for the single-minded way in which he drove straight ahead with his threshing machine. And by so doing, he carried modern philosophy—not sparing his predecessors or his heirs—to the very edge of the epistemological gap.

This gap appears in Locke most obviously in connection with the question of substances "existing" beyond our ideas, supporting qualities in continued existence even when not perceived. This gap was exposed by Berkeley in full measure and need not be rehearsed here. But to this exposure Hume adds reinforcement. Hume essentially supports Berkeley's definition of "existence" as being perceived or perceiving. We are given no separate impression of existence, Hume points out. "There is no impression nor idea of any kind, of which we have any consciousness or memory, that is not conceive'd as existent; and 'tis evident, that from this consciousness the most perfect idea and assurance of *being* is deriv'd" (Hume 1888: 66). The alternative would be that along with every impression there is a second impression of existence; but there is no such second impression.

The idea of existence, then, is the very same with the idea of what we conceive to be existent. To reflect on any thing simply, and to reflect on it as existent, are nothing different from each other. That idea, when conjoin'd with the idea of any object, makes no addition to it. Whatever we conceive, we conceive to be existent (Hume 1888: 66–67).

But this has the startling epistemological consequence that (contrary to Locke or Hobbes), we can have no knowledge—nor the faintest concept—of existences beyond our own perceptions. There is an absolute gap between our impressions and ideas, on the subjective side, and any "object" that may be hypothesized as "beyond" or "stimulating" these perceptions. The gap is absolute because we cannot even formulate a genuine hypothesis (as Berkeley, too, had shown) about "existences," if they must violate the necessary condition for the very idea of existence. Hume forces the point home as follows:

Now since nothing is ever present to the mind but perceptions, and since all ideas are deriv'd from something antecedently present to the mind; it follows, that 'tis impossible for us so much as to conceive or form an idea of any thing specifically different from ideas and impressions. (Hume 1888: 67–68).

Here we are reminded of Descartes, a century and a half earlier, meditating in his stove-heated room on the problem of getting beyond the private field of consciousness to some knowledge of reality outside the self. But now, with Hume, we are not simply testing, with the attitude of methodological doubt, so as to assure that our eventual absolute certainties will be placed on firm foundations. We are well and truly trapped within our perceptions. Doubt is logically insurmountable concerning the so-called "external world," continuing in existence apart from our experience. Impressions of reflection are irrelevant to this issue of external existence; therefore we are left with impressions of sensation; but idea of an external world can never arise from impressions of sensation:

To begin with the SENSES, 'tis evident these faculties are incapable of giving rise to the notion of the continue'd existence of their objects, after they no longer appear to the senses. For that is a contradiction in terms, and supposes that the sense continue to operate, even after they have cease'd all manner of operation (Hume 1888: 188).

Nor can the general opinion that there is a continuously existing natural world come from abstruse philosophical reasoning, since it is held by children and other "vulgar" folk who certainly have not reasoned their way to such a conclusion.

> Accordingly we find, that all the conclusions, which the vulgar form on this head, are directly contrary to those, which are confirm'd by philosophy. For philosophy informs us, that every thing, which appears to the mind, is nothing but a perception, and is interrupted, and dependent on the mind; whereas the vulgar confound perceptions and objects, and attribute a distinct continu'd existence to the very things they feel or see. This sentiment, then, as it is entirely unreasonable, must proceed from some other faculty than the understanding (Hume 1888: 193).

"Entirely unreasonable?" Yes, on the basis of Hume's epistemic threshing machine, there can be no genuine idea behind the language of the "vulgar" on this matter. What can be responsible for such a widespread irrationality?

Only imagination is left as the possible source of the irrational conviction that there is existence somehow beyond and behind our perceptions. It is not necessary to follow Hume's argument in detail, but we should be reminded here of Berkeley on the "coexistence" of our perceptions: some of our impressions show a coherence and constancy that we become used to, and value; and from this it is easy to imagine our way toward the perfect coherence and constancy that would be provided by a continuous existence. Hume is working here toward a "limit" concept. "Objects have a certain coherence even as they appear to our senses; but this coherence is much greater and more uniform, if we suppose the objects to have a continu'd existence; and as the mind is once in the train of observing an uniformity among objects, it naturally continues, till it renders the uniformity as compleat as possible" (Hume 1888: 198).

Still, this is a mistake if taken as something known or knowable. It is an easy mistake. "An easy transition or passage of the imagination, along the ideas of these different and interrupted perceptions, is almost the same disposition of mind with that in which we consider one constant and uninterrupted perception. 'Tis therefore very natural for us to mistake the one for the other" (Hume 1888: 204). But nevertheless it is a mistake: it is taking the merely resembling for the same. "The imagination is seduc'd into such an opinion only by means of the resemblance of certain perceptions; since we find they are only our resembling perceptions, which we have a propension to suppose the same" (Hume 1888: 209).

Hume's verdict on all efforts to know external existence is bleak, epistemologically. We all *feel* an overpowering inclination to *believe* ourselves in a common world of external things. This feeling, however, is too basic and widespread to rest on intellectual subtlety or insight. Quite the opposite.

"Carelessness and in-attention alone can afford us any remedy. For this reason I rely entirely upon them; and take it for granted, whatever may be the reader's opinion at this present moment, that an hour hence he will be persuaded there is both an external and internal world." (Hume 1888: 218).

For philosophers eager to justify knowledge, this is no comfort at all. But Hume goes further. So far he has sided with Berkeley in undermining the inadequately examined assumptions of his predecessors, especially Hobbes and Locke, on the existence of an external world of substantial objects represented by our ideas. But Berkeley is not to be spared. His positive alternative to Locke, as we saw, rests on accepting the intelligible existence of the self and God. I have dealt elsewhere with Hume's many criticisms of the existence of God (Ferré 1967b: chap. 6) and these need not detain us; but it is of some fascination to watch the epistemic threshing machine devour the idea of a substantial self.

For Locke, we recall, knowledge of our own existence is the most intuitively obvious reality we can know. And Berkeley was certain of himself as a "perceiving being . . . I call *mind, spirit, soul*, or *myself.*" Hume's approach tells a different tale:

> Unluckily all these positive assertions are contrary to that very experience, which is pleaded for them, nor have we any idea of *self*, after the manner it is here explain'd. For from what impression cou'd this idea be deriv'd? This question 'tis impossible to answer without a manifest contradiction and absurdity; and yet 'tis a question, which must necessarily be answer'd, if we cou'd have the idea of self pass for clear and intelligible. It must be some one impression, that gives rise to every real idea. But self or person is not any one impression, but that to which our several impressions and ideas are suppos'd to have a reference (Hume 1888: 251).

If there is one idea of self, that is, there must be one constant and invariable impression which it copies. "But there is no impression constant and invariable" (Hume 1888: 251). Therefore there is no idea of this supposed entity that continues throughout a lifetime of changing experiences. There are only the changing experiences. More than that is simply not to be found. Hume cannot of course rule out that others may find something mysteriously different, but he is content that most people will report the same experience that he does in the following famous passage:

> For my part, when I enter most intimately into what I call *myself*, I always stumble on some particular perception or other, of heat or cold, light or shade, love or hatred, pain or pleasure. I never can catch *myself*

at any time without a perception, and never can observe any thing but the perception (Hume 1888: 252).

In consequence, supposing the rest of humankind shares such experience, Hume concludes that "they are nothing but a bundle or collection of different perceptions, which succeed each other with an inconceivable rapidity, and are in a perpetual flux and movement" (Hume 1888: 252).

This would also invalidate any appeal Berkeley might make to having a "notion" of a self, though not an idea. The very notion of a "notion" of active selfhood—insofar as it reflects genuine impressions—would be one more set of perceptions to be fed into Hume's epistemic machinery, an experience of fluxing activities (like deciding and wishing and hoping and fearing) that do not always occur, thus offering no firm substitute for the missing impression of some constant and continuous "self."

Once again we are left with mere imagination—this time imagination of past resembling experience, or memory—to supply the supposed identity that neither experience nor reason can manage. "For from thence it evidently follows, that identity is nothing really belonging to these different perceptions, and uniting them together; but is merely a quality, which we attribute to them, because of the union of their ideas in the imagination, when we reflect upon them" (Hume 1888: 260). But if we can have no proper idea of a substantial self, then we can have no rational theory, like Berkeley's, on which selves and their perceptions constitute the world. The epistemological gap looms inward as well as outward, preventing the knowing of one's identical, continuous self as inexorably as it blocks knowing an external world.

Finally, use of Hume's epistemic machinery destroys assurance of real causal influence. Remember his challenge: *"from what impression is that supposed idea derived?"* And what can be answered? The idea of a genuine causal influence (what in the *Enquiry* he calls "necessary connection"), must copy either impressions of sensation or of reflection. Is there a distinct impression of a causal power besides the impression of various events? Hume challenges us to find one. One billiard ball strikes another and *then* the second moves, but we have no additional impression of causal requirement in this paradigm case of causality. We might imagine, without contradiction, that the second billiard ball simply refuses to budge—or that it jumps sideways, or explodes. Only actual observation of actual events tells us what happens; no additional "force" or "cosmic glue" is experienced at the same time. Therefore there is no idea of real causal influence from impressions of sensation.

Locke saw this much, but in his view the idea of cause comes most readily from experiencing the operations of our own minds. Can this rescue the idea of causal power from Hume's threshing? No. While Locke thought that the clearest case of experiencing cause was "that, barely by willing it, barely by a thought of the mind, we can move the parts of our bodies which were before at rest," Hume asks to be shown the causal *connection*. True, in most cases the motion of our bodies *follows* the act of will, but in this we observe an impression of sequence, not of causal necessitation. The absence of an impression of real causal connection is proven, Hume argues, by the fact that when we are surprised by trying and failing to move a limb (when it is paralyzed or "asleep" or amputated) it is because we have not been able to observe anything internally different in the situation. There is no impression of "power missing," as there would be if we really had impressions of "power present." Again, as in the case of sensation, we only learn after the fact, by experience, what is or is not under our control. But if so-called causality offers no impressions of sensation or of reflection, and if the only impressions are of sensation and reflection, then there is no impression at all to be had of causal connection or power.

Something, nevertheless, leads us to expect causal regularities. What is it? Hume answers: habit. Not deductive reasoning, not inductive reasoning— not reasoning at all leads to our stubborn feeling that we live in a causally constrained world. The fact merely is that we have seen similar events followed by other similar events many times, and this leads us to imagine that the similarities will be repeated in the future. But we cannot *know* this. If there is an "idea" at all behind our use of "cause"-language, it is a copy of the feeling of expectation that future events will resemble sequences of events we have regularly experienced in the past. This habit is ingrained in us. The order of events is, however, entirely contingent. Events in our world are "entirely loose and separate" (Hume 1902: 80). Nothing assures us that the future will resemble the past.

But this stabs at the heart of science, as Hume clearly saw. Even if the external world and the self are beyond the range of knowledge, events in the world of experience still press us to act, and science attempts to develop causal laws to assure us about what we can expect to happen in the future. The loss of meaning for causal connection undermines this enterprise, as well. Hume acknowledges this radical outcome:

> And what stronger instance can be produced of the surprising ignorance and weakness of the understanding than the present? For surely, if there be any relation among objects which it imports to us to know perfectly, it is that of cause and effect. On this are founded all our reasonings concerning matter of fact or existence. By meaning of it alone we attain any assurance concerning objects which are removed from the present testimony of our memory and senses. The only immediate utility of all

sciences, is to teach us, how to control and regulate future events by their causes (Hume 1902: 82–83).

Hume himself was content to leave philosophy behind, moving after a while into the writing of history and into yet more practical affairs. He revelled in the notoriety and consternation stirred by his ideas, and was not inclined to let his conclusions worry him overmuch. His temperament was such that he could be comfortable with what he called "mitigated skepticism" (Hume 1902: 179ff.), contrasted to the "excessive skepticism" of "Pyrrhonism." The latter is subverted by action. We need in daily life to assume a common world of independently existing objects, governed by relations of cause and effect. We should simply not pretend to *know* it. In this, says Hume, "Nature is always too strong for principle" (Hume 1902: 179). But mitigated skepticism is salubrious. It reminds us to keep our thinking within the narrow boundaries of human competence: viz., matters of empirical fact and logical relations between ideas. Beyond that, we should give up all pretension to know. Hume asks us to join him in bowing to the inevitable. Unless we recognize, and steer clear of, the impassable epistemological gap, we shall either make ourselves miserable from frustration or fling ourselves into the abyss.

Immanuel Kant

The life of Immanuel Kant (1724–1804) overlapped with the lives both of Berkeley and of Hume. He was born in Königsberg (the modern Kaliningrad) of former East Prussia (now in Russia), in the year that Berkeley was first appointed Dean and at the same time the teen-aged Hume was in undergraduate study at Edinburgh University. Since I have already written in *Being and Value* (197–99) about Kant's completely undramatic life and intensely dramatic thought, I shall not repeat myself here, except to reiterate that Kant's early work, until well into his middle age, was largely scientific and mathematical, not yet epistemological. It was only after Hume woke him from his "dogmatic slumbers" that he began his major philosophical labors. Hume's arguments completely convinced Kant that the purely empirical approach to knowing leaves science and mathematics rationally groundless, at least when they are supposed to tell us something important about the real world. This was intolerable for Kant. Hume's literary temperament might have allowed him to live with the suspended judgment he recommended for others, but this temperament was quite different from Kant's Teutonic earnestness. Rather than simply ignoring Hume's challenge, as most scientific thinkers tended (and still tend) to do, Kant was stimulated at age forty-five to search for a solution to Hume's doubts. He seemed trapped between two basic values. On one side, his traditional commitment to certainty as the only standard worthy of genuine knowledge prevented him from scaling back the standards for knowing, in the way Locke—in some of his moods—seemed willing to do; but, on the other side, he could not tolerate Hume's conclusion that mathematical "relations of ideas" can give us no reliable knowledge about "matters of fact." Kant believed that he (and all of us) really know we have genuine knowledge of the empirical world; but Hume had shown convincingly that we cannot acquire this knowledge through "impressions" (whether of sensation or reflection) alone. Therefore the problem, for Kant, was to determine *what must be the case* in order to *make possible* what we *know to be true*.

I have put the problem in this way to underscore the fact that Kant's method—starting from something necessary (what is "known to be true") and working back to what needs to be postulated (what "must be the case") to make possible what has been granted—characterized his philosophical thinking from an early point, that is, from the Inaugural Dissertation he prepared for the Professorship of Logic and Metaphysics at the University of Königsberg, delivered in 1770. He came to call it the "transcendental" method, and it is indeed a major trademark of his thinking; but it came along with, not after, his so-called "Critical Turn."

The "Critical" period of Kant's thinking, essentially foreshadowed by that Inaugural Dissertation, is so named because Kant's solution to Hume's clear demonstration of the epistemological gap was to rest on a "critique" of the powers of reason. This would be far from the "historical plain method" of Locke and Hume. It would, in contrast, employ the "transcendental" method in the sense just introduced. The first of these critiques, dealing with theoretical knowing, was published (after a pause of more than a decade) as the *Critique of Pure Reason*, in 1781. It was a critique that asked what the mind must be and do in order that knowledge by mathematical science can be possible.

Kant's answer was genuinely revolutionary. If we are sure we have empirical knowledge, and if Hume proved that it cannot come from impressions of experience alone, then it must be provided by the combination of impressions (to provide the contingent material content of what is known) with formal contributions of reason itself (to provide the structural necessities that certainty requires). In other words, the *forms and concepts of the mind are themselves the source of our certainties*, without which we would have no knowledge.

Indeed, Kant insisted, were it not for the built-in forms of reason, our orderly experience of a world in space and time, as we are accustomed to it, would not be possible. All our impressions of sensation (to use Hume's language) are experienced in both space and time; and all of our impressions of reflection are experienced at least in time. There are necessary quantifiable features in both space and time that make them the reliable subject of mathematical calculations. But these "forms of intuition" are not concepts that can be learned inductively. In order even to begin experiencing spatially and temporally, space and time must already be present. We could not recognize a spatial experience without already having a grid (spatial!) in which to receive it. Space, in other words, is a priori. It must be available in general before particular spatial experiences can occur. The same is true for time. For the first temporal experience to be possible, there must already be a capacity for before-and-after provided by the mind. Space and time are both a priori forms of intuition, without which experience as we are familiar with it could not get started. For these reasons, Kant makes a startling statement in the introduction to the first edition of his *Critique of Pure Reason*. He terms "experience" not the initial stuff of understanding, spreading itself onto a passive "white paper" of the mind, as Locke and Hume had assumed with their plain, historical method; instead, he calls it the "product" of our understanding. "Experience," he wrote, "is no doubt the first product of our understanding, while employed in fashioning the raw material of our sensations" (Kant 1966: 1). Sensations never reach us raw and unprocessed. The mind (or "reason" or "understanding") initially works all sensations into temporal order and all external sensations into spatial form, as well. Space and time do not belong to the world in itself (the "noumenal" world), therefore, but only to our experience of the world (the "phenomenal" world) as we inevitably process it through these basic forms of intuition.

We can be certain, as a result of this transcendental argument, that all our future experience will be spatial and temporal, and that space and time will have the properties of divisibility and extensibility that we recognize as necessarily characterizing all spatio-temporal experience. Any mathematical calculations concerning these continua will be secure and certain, since not dependent on the vagaries of sensation. We need not fear, as Hume suggested, that future experience might be radically different from what we have known. The methods of the mathematical scientist working on objects in space and events in time can be rationally justified.

The same approach, Kant believed, could rescue knowledge of the self and substantial objects and causality—and much more—from Hume's empirical threshing machine. We saw how the concept of the self gradually disintegrated from the strong idea of a "thinking thing" in Descartes to a "notion" in Berkeley and finally to a mere play of impressions with no substantial unity in Hume. But this progression toward doubting the self was due, Kant argued, to over-reliance on the merely contingent deliverances of the "stream of internal phenomena" (Kaufmann 1962: vol. 2, 454).

What is necessarily to be represented as numerically identical with itself, cannot be thought as such by means of empirical data only. It must be a condition which precedes all experience, and in fact renders it possible, for thus only could such a transcendental supposition acquire validity (Kaufmann 1962: vol. 2, 454).

In order for there to be experience such as we actually have, we must recognize a "transcendental apperception" that is "pure, original, and unchangeable consciousness" (Kaufmann 1962: vol. 2, 454). This is not an empirical self; Hume decisively won that argument, Kant thought. There is no empirical impression of a "self" that lasts throughout a lifetime. But Kant's is a transcendentally required self, the necessary condition for our actual experience of a world of objects relating in causally dependable ways (Kaufmann 1962: vol. 2, 458). The need for this self can be known with certainty, that is, can be *known*, even though the various specific elements of the empirical self can never be learned with similar assurance. For that we need empirical psychology to tell us, in particular terms, what kind of a self we are. But that we are an identical, synthesizing self is assured knowledge and, on reflection, cannot be doubted at all.

In a similar manner, Kant came to the defense of objects and causes. Objects in their particularity cannot be known in advance of experience, but we can know with certainty that the world will be filled with objects. Locke was wrong, as Berkeley and Hume agreed, to look to the foundation of this confidence in some "I know not what" substance behind or below experience. If we adopt Kant's "Copernican Revolution," making mind central, our certainty that there are—and always will be—discrete objects can be securely grounded in the necessities of the understanding itself. We know there will always be substantial objects in any possible world because it is a requirement of experiencing any world *as a world* (and not just a chaos). We find the a priori contribution of mind is a necessary condition for the possibility of what is (the world experienced as world); therefore we are entitled to accept this Copernican Revolution and with it the assurance that our experience will always be characterized by objects.

To be objects in a world, moreover, entails that these objects will be ordered in their mutual relationships. There will be reliable causal relations in any world that is to be experienced as a world. Kant agrees with Hume that we have no impression of causality or necessary connection, but to look for such impressions is a mistake. Causality is guaranteed by the necessities of reason. It is a contribution of the understanding, not a deliverance of "sensation" or "reflection" to be found, somehow, by more careful application of the "plain, historical method." The appropriate method is transcendental. Once causality is seen as something necessarily contributed by the requirements of reason itself, we can confidently busy ourselves about the task of finding specifically what causal regularities hold in the world we experience. This is the job of the scientist, in finding the laws regulating the phenomena that make up our world of possible experience. Laws, however, there will be. We shall—and must—find them wherever we look since they are guaranteed by the character of the minds through which we experience everything that can be experienced and think everything that can be thought. As Kant put it succinctly:

> It is we therefore who carry into the phenomena which we call nature, order and regularity, nay, we should never find them in nature, if we ourselves, or the nature of our mind, had not originally placed them there. For the unity of nature is meant to be a necessary and *a priori* certain unity in the connection of all phenomena (Kaufmann 1962: vol. 2, 462).

In all this, Kant thought of himself as rescuing science from the abyss of Hume's skepticism. In many ways it was a brilliant success, worthy of being ranked with the greatest achievements of philosophy. But the rescue of scientific confidence in the rationality of its commitment to searching for laws of nature came at an immense cost. Rather than bridging the epistemological gap, shown in all its clarity by Hume, Kant internalized and absolutized it. The price of Kant's certainties about the realm of possible experience was nothing short of the total inaccessibility, to either experience or knowledge, of reality as it is in itself. Why?

> [B]ecause our knowledge has to deal with nothing but phenomena, the possibility of which depends on ourselves, and the connection and unity of which (in the representation of an object) can be found in ourselves only, as antecedent to all experience, nay, as first rendering all experience possible, so far as its form is concerned (Kaufmann 1962: vol. 2, 463–64).

Kant, by so saying, rules out the very possibility of knowing things as they are in themselves. As we saw, he coined the word "noumena" for such things conceived apart from, and totally independent of, any of the a priori forms either of immediate intuition (space and time) or of understanding (object, cause, etc.). Or, rather, *not* conceived, since our minds are incapable of thinking or imagining any such independent things in themselves. This failure is guaranteed by the fact that our minds turn whatever they consider into phenomena, by processing the noumena with the a priori forms and categories of mentality. This epistemological Midas touch turns unthinkable mystery into the ready glitter of potential knowledge. Unlike the Midas tale, and even more radical, the touch extends even to looking at things and prevents us from peeking, even briefly, at what has not already been transformed by our attention. What started as happy magic becomes deeply troubling.

Kant recognizes the complete isolation, on his theory, of the knowable domain from reality as it is apart from our conceptual apparatus. At one climactic moment in his first *Critique*, he reflects on his achievement:

> We have now not only traversed the whole domain of the pure under-standing and carefully examined each part of it, but we have also measured its extent, and assigned to everything its proper place. This domain, however, is an island and enclosed by nature itself within limits that can never be changed. It is a country of truth (a very attrac-tive name), but surrounded by a wide and stormy ocean, the true home of illusion, where many a fog bank and ice that soon melts away tempt us to believe in new lands, while constantly deceiving the adventurous mariner with vain hopes, and involving him in adventures which he can never leave, and yet can never bring to an end (Kant 1966: 187).

Here the modern epistemic trap—built by Descartes and Hobbes, baited by Locke and Berkeley, and sprung by Hume—is definitively sealed shut. Kant, wakened by Hume's skepticism to defend the possibility of knowledge, has (contrary to his initial will) absolutized doubt of the human cognitive ability to cross the gap between our best possible mental representations and reality as it is. Our knowledge of phenomena will never give us a positive understanding of noumena. Things as they are in themselves will always lie across the "wide and stormy ocean" from the secure but insular cognitions of phenomena.

With this outcome, we have reached the end of a tale that began with ancient knowers and wound through medieval believers before arriving at modern doubt. It has been steeped throughout with Plato's values: above all, with his demand that "knowing" be reserved for what is conceptually clear and certain. Between Plato and Kant there have been some dissenters, but even those who attempted to put more confidence in the senses than Plato had allowed were generally committed to the same absolute standards for success in the "knowing game." Kant certainly did not depart from Plato in this respect. As he sets his goals in the preface of his first edition, Kant puts himself under the same strict requirements for success that Plato, thousands of years earlier, would have approved:

First, with regard to certainty, I have pronounced judgment against myself by saying that in this kind of enquiry it is in no way permissible to propound mere opinions, and that everything looking like a hypothesis is counterband, that must not be offered for sale at however low a price, but must, as soon as it has been discovered, be confiscated (Kant 1966: xxv).

Many cures for modern doubt have been offered in the years since Kant's climactic internalizing of the epistemological gap. In Part Two, I shall survey the principal ones, and why they disappoint us. Finally, in Part Three, I shall offer my own reflections on where I hope the human thirst for knowing may draw us constructively for a postmodern era.

Part Two

Coping with the
Epistemological Gap

5

REDUCING THE GAP

There have been three main modern strategies for coping with the epistemological gap. These will occupy us in this and the two following chapters. The
first strategy is to *reduce* the gap to a fiction by claiming that what lies on
this side of the (alleged) gap is all that can meaningfully be required. If
successful, this would rescue the cognitive task by turning all attention to
what we can encounter directly: sense experiences. The second strategy is to
web the gap so thoroughly by strands of thought that passage to truth is
assured by something to which we have intimate access: theoretic powers.
The third strategy is to *leap* the gap, by effort of will and activity, toward
what really matters: satisfactory lives.

All three have something to offer, but none alone is satisfactory. The
three cannot be combined, since together they are mutually incompatible; but
in sorting out what can be kept and what discarded, we find clues to where
we need to go from here, from the modern impasse to something constructively postmodern.

INTUITIONS OF A WORLD

For those intent on the first strategy, which involves rendering the gap a
fiction by reducing the so-called world of independent substantial objects to
constructs made up entirely of sense experiences, an obvious obstacle would
seem to be the nearly universal intuition reported to the contrary. None of this
kills the project, of course, since someone else's intuition is no coercive

evidence—perhaps not evidence at all—if one is willing to dismiss or override it. But taking a quick look at the galaxy of great thinkers whom the reducers must reject helps us appreciate their radical boldness.

Until Parmenides, at least, as we saw in *Being and Value* (20–31), all the ancient Greek philosophers seem to have taken for granted the existence of an independent *kosmos*, full of changing objects which persisted and interacted quite apart from human perceptions. Plato's post-Parmenidean views on the subject are open to dispute, but Aristotle leaves little doubt that he conceived a knowable world of finite substances, informed by qualities and individuated from one another by their matter. Aristotle's depiction of the cognitive situation, in fact, became the standard model for Western philosophy until modern times. As Aristotle outlined it, physical objects, existing in their own right, act causally on our physical organisms to impress qualitative forms on our sense organs. The sense organs, receptive to specific sets of qualities (the eyes to colors, the ears to sounds, etc.), in turn impress their contents on the passive intellect, which Aristotle carefully defined as completely character-free, just right to guarantee perfect receptivity to all incoming qualities.

This general model (without the Aristotelian detail), in which external objects bring about percepts in essentially passive receptors, was basically agreed to by both the Epicureans and the Stoics, quarrel though they did about other issues. The Epicureans had their *eidōla*, the particular appearances of things, just as the Stoics had their sense impressions, received as into an "open hand." In both cases the world of objects was held to be different from, but cognitively accessible through, the phantasms that are present in our awareness. Both recognized the possibility (and actuality) of errors, but neither countenanced general cognitive despair. Even the Skeptics, who urged suspended judgment about the qualities of the world around us, did not seem to doubt that an independent world of objects exists beyond its various seemings.

The Aristotelian strand of medieval thought, though relatively late in emerging, was enormously powerful in the high Middle Ages. For Albert the Great or Thomas Aquinas or their many followers, there is no ambiguity about the objective independence of the created world beyond human perceptions. The main problem, it seemed to them, was how such a world could be perceived in an afterlife of disembodied existence, supposing (as they did) that the body's sense organs are essential and normative for the human perceptive process. The scourge of Thomism, John Duns Scotus, was if anything even more emphatic in his affirmation of the independence of a world of unique objects, existing apart from the various "whatnesses" we use to characterize them. It was Duns who boldly challenged a millennium and a half of received opinion by insisting that our experience is not limited to abstract "whatness" ("quidditas") but also includes direct awareness of the "thisness" ("haecceitas") of real objects. His intuition, we remember, was that in the experience of *love* we find especially clearly the sense of the unique, objective, being-*this*-reality, in addition to all the loose-fitting general qualities that we may attribute to the beloved. Those qualities, as universals, can all be shared with an indefinite number of others; the *thisness* of one's "one and only" is not available for loan or rent. Duns admits that this is not a clear intuition (he blames our "fallen" condition for that), but it is for him nonetheless a powerful one.

William of Ockham, Duns' nemesis, agreed that we *seem* to intuit a world objectively behind and causally active in our perceptions. This far he supports the general philosophical consensus I am tracing. He even went so far as to claim that genuinely intuitive knowledge must guarantee the real existence of what causes it. But Ockham, unlike his predecessors, inserted one enormous loophole into his epistemological contract with the world of objects. He was enthralled with the absolute omnipotence of God and the logical consequences of taking such omnipotence absolutely seriously. God can do anything that a lesser (created) cause can do. This follows from the very concept of omnipotence. Only logically impossible (unthinkable or vacuous) "feats" are outside the scope of omnipotence, but if a finite cause can accomplish something, then, *a fortiori*, it is not logically impossible. Since finite objects can cause intuitive percepts in human perceivers, God can accomplish the same thing directly, without the intervention of objects. Ockham does not argue that God actually does this. He simply adds his proviso in pious recognition of the logically possible role of the Almighty in human cognition. Little wonder that Ockham is often classed with the moderns! It was exactly this loophole that Berkeley was to use and make central to his view of normal human-(God)-world cognitive relations.

Apart from Berkeley, however, other earlier modern philosophers affirmed, implicitly or explicitly, the intuition of a world of independent objects. Certainly Hobbes' epistemology reflected the intuition of a world of objects—matter in motion—impinging on the peculiar sorts of objects that are our bodies and especially our sense organs. In this he returned, with the encouragement of Gassendi and Galileo, to an Epicurean epistemology appropriate to his nominalistic materialism. That there is a world out beyond our phantasms is a given, on this view, no matter how limited or faulty our characterizations of it may be. Descartes was more nuanced in his affirmation of the intuition of objective reality lying beyond the field of consciousness that is, for him, the "thinking thing" we find we are unable to doubt. This natural intuition is there and is strong, but not beyond doubt—vulnerable, at least, to systematic doubt of the initial, diagnostic variety he employed in his stove-heated room, clearing the decks of the dubious. Once his self-induced worry about a malevolent deceiving demon could be exorcised, however, Descartes returned strongly to the affirmation of the intuition of an independent world of objects. This intuition is so deep, he argued, that a good God would never allow it unless the world it points to actually exists, and he brushed off Hobbes' further probing into the possible moral justification of such deception without even bothering to justify his sense of its deep inappropriateness.

Locke and Kant, finally, showed—in their very struggles with the cognitive inaccessibility of the independent world of objects, apart from the knower—how strong the intuition of substantial objects "out there" remained for them, too. Locke gave all the arguments, picked up later by Berkeley and Hume, for the utter unknowability of "substance," if this is considered a traditional substratum within which qualities and powers somehow inhere. Still, he was unwilling to deny his intuition of "something there," a something "he knows not what," something that must be beyond cognitive reach on his theory of ideas, but still something deserving acknowledgment and affirmation, even if this creates difficulties of consistency. Kant, in just the same spirit, insisted on the concept of the "noumenal realm," even though he admitted it could never qualify as a positive concept but must remain forever something negative and "problematic" for thought. It would have been much easier for both Locke and Kant to have abandoned discussions of what their theories, respectively, told them was in principle off the map. It seems that the intuition of an objective, substantial world got the better of them both. In this I do not find fault. Instead, I believe that by being willing to allow coherence among fundamental elements within their valued theories to be trumped by these intuitions, they were courageous defenders of adequacy, the call to do justice to all aspects of experience. But there is no doubt that in so doing they made the modern problem of the epistemological gap central and unavoidable.

FICHTE AND HEGEL

Two distinct gap-denying lines of response can be distinguished. The first was for the most part a development within German philosophy; the second was mainly of French and British ancestry.

The German response rose directly out of the enormous impact made by Kant's proposed Copernican Revolution. The centrality of the mind and its necessities constituted the heart of the Revolution, and its fresh promise won many followers. One of its unfortunate consequences, as we have seen, was the radical isolation of the knower from things in themselves—but this followed only as long as "things in themselves" were acknowledged (with Kant himself) as indispensably important. Later German Idealists, though raising Kant's banner in many other respects, were not prepared to make this value judgment.

Johann Gottlieb Fichte (1762–1814) was the first in a series of Kantians who boldly resolved to let go of the so-called "noumenal" world. Fichte, in any case, was primarily interested in the ethical and religious sides of Kant's thought. He made his academic fortune by writing a highly Kantian defense of revealed religion in his *Essay Towards a Critique of All Revelations* (1792), written in a four-week burst of energy to win the favorable attention of Kant, who had given him a cool welcome on his first visit to Königsberg. The effort succeeded. Kant, delighted by the work, now received Fichte warmly and helped him with publication. Somehow in the process, however, the author's name was mislaid and the book appeared anonymously. An immediate hit, the work was widely mistaken for Kant's own, an apparent "Fourth Critique"; thus, when Kant praisingly revealed the actual author's identity, Fichte became an instant celebrity. At only thirty-two, and having also attracted the favorable attention of Johann Wolfgang von Goethe (1749–1832), he was appointed Professor of Philosophy at the University of Jena. Soon, however, opposition to his political radicalism and charges of atheism, together with his stubborn streak, forced his departure from Jena. The same readiness to accept radical solutions, and the spirit of resolution to stay with a position whatever the cost, led Fichte to declare that the "real" Kantian revolution required abandonment of the noumenal realm. Kant himself vigorously disagreed and even broke off personal relations with this former protege, but Fichte was not dissuaded. What did the "things in themselves" add, except problems? "They" were doomed to be unknowable, inconceivable, unobservable—outside the scope of either experience or theory. Let them go, and good riddance!

The attitude of Georg Wilhelm Friedrich Hegel (1770–1831) was similar. Fichte, together with Hegel's good friend, Friedrich Wilhelm Joseph von Schelling (1775–1854), had opened the way wide to discounting the intuition of an independent world of objects beyond mentality. There was among them a consensus that phenomena are not only all we *can* have but also all we *need*—and all there *is*. Hegel's first great work, *The Phenomenology of Mind* (1807), tells the story of Spirit's gradual journey toward self-awareness: phenomena as reality discovering itself. Having recounted this story in *Being and Value* (208–10), I shall refrain from repeating myself here. My present point is that the epistemological gap, inherited from Kant, could be, and was, strongly denied. Nothing important—nothing at all—can be on the other side from phenomena themselves. Even to define a "gap" is already to have digested it, having swallowed it whole in thought.

COMTE AND MILL

An entirely different approach, leading from Positivism to Logical Positivism, took its inspiration from the British Empiricist and modern scientific traditions. Auguste Comte (1798–1857), whose stormy life I described in *Being and Value* (169–74), was above all indebted to Isaac Newton (1642–1727) for what he took to be the definitive expression of scientific modes of knowing. Comte saw in Newton's public refusal to "make hypotheses" invoking occult agencies, somehow behind and explanatory of the positive phenomena of gravitational regularities, the maturity of mind that was the culmination of ages-long developments.

Comte, influenced also by the French social thinker, Claude Henri Saint-Simon (1760–1825), whom he once served as secretary, believed in the Law of the Three Stages of human thinking. The first stage is that of "theological" thinking, in which phenomena are accounted for by reference to personal agents, whether forest nymphs, water sprites, or angels—or (when these are unified by the mind's own drive to coherence) one omnipotent God. This is primitive, recapitulated in every human in childhood. It is the paradigmatically infantile way of thinking. When we blame a chair for tripping us in the dark, or implore our car to keep running at least until the next service station, we are engaging in such immature thinking. It is natural, even inevitable, but we need to grow out of it.

The second stage is that of what Comte called "metaphysical" thinking. This names the tendency that he believed everyone has, as they move up from the theological stage, to try accounting for the observable facts in our changing world by appeal to some impersonal, usually unchanging, "forces" or "substances" behind the world of phenomena. No longer forest nymphs, but "essences" or "generative forces," supply the explanatory frameworks for metaphysical thinkers. Anything in principle unperceivable, on this view, is metaphysical. Metaphysical thinking like this is a step up from the childishness of theological anthropomorphism, Comte acknowledges; but it is still immature. It represents the transitional thinking of youth, which has renounced the silliness of attributing personal traits to causal entities behind positively perceivable events, but which still clings to the supposition that there is a place for explanation by reference to "hidden" entities and energies. The ancient Greek philosophers were still at this youthful stage when they hypothesized about the "Logos," the "*eidōla*," and the rest. More shameful (if only because so much later) were the metaphysical excesses—the "crystalline spheres," the "forces" of "levity," etc.—of the Middle Ages, when, indeed, even more shameful theologizing ("nature abhors a vacuum," etc.) could be occasionally transcended.

The third stage, which abandons all references to "occult" ("hidden") causes, personal or impersonal, Comte names the Positive. It recognizes no explanation that departs from the realm of actual or possible perception. It is satisfied with discovering constant covariations among phenomena. It "makes no hypotheses." This is the Positive manner of thinking that is at last "up to the age." The maturity of human knowing finally arrived with the mathematical physics of Galileo and Newton. Now, living in the age of positive science, it is incumbent on all who would be "up to the age" to define knowing in such terms.

Comte does not outright deny the existence of causes behind positive experience, but his positivism rejects their importance. Knowing is for the sake of predicting. In this, the intermediary functions of any such "causes" as may somehow lurk in the background of the perceptible world simply fall out of relevance. Once we know the laws of covariation among variables, we are able to anticipate, predict and retrodict at will. *Savoir, pour prévoir* ("Know, in order to predict") is the goal. Once our cognitive interests in foreseeing events, based on constant rules of conjunction, are satisfied, it would show a morally reprehensible lack of maturity to seek more. Thus, this is not merely an epistemology that reduces the epistemological gap to an immature fear. Positivism is offered as an encouragement to mental health and virtue as well.

One of Comte's principal supporters—in intellectual as well as practical ways—was John Stuart Mill (1806–73). Mill was the precocious son of James Mill (1773–1836), whose force-fed curriculum of studies, demanded of his eldest son, remains a matter of controversy. John Stuart Mill himself later wondered whether it had harmed his powers of aesthetic appreciation; but there is no doubt that it provided him with early access to the best in classical languages and literature, to Aristotelian and Scholastic logic, and to up-to-date thinking in political economics. Mill, having "graduated" from his father's teaching by age fourteen, spent over a year (May 1820–July 1821) in France with the family of the brother of Utilitarian philosopher Jeremy Bentham (1748–1832), becoming fluent in the French language and appreciative of the culture. He felt at home in France. After two decades of active public life in England, serving in high positions with the British East India Company, Mill retired to a villa near Avignon, where his intensely beloved wife had lived before her death in 1858. His most important philosophical works, excepting his *System of Logic* (1843), were written in France during this period. He died there himself in May 1873.

Mill's preoccupations were primarily ethical, political, logical, and epistemological. He was not much interested in metaphysical speculations, though he did reflect thoughtfully on the rational case for the existence of

God (which he did not rule out, if taken as a tentative, modest claim). Still, the question of the "thing in itself" did attract him. His temperament inclined him to sympathize with Comte's anti-metaphysical positivism, but the question of the status in reality of the object of our empirical knowledge is one point at which epistemology engages unavoidably with metaphysics, if only in a negative way.

In his book on Comte, Mill held that Comte was simply voicing the general insight of the modern age.

> The foundation of M. Comte's philosophy is . . . in no way peculiar to him, but the general property of the age, however far as yet from being universally accepted even by thoughtful minds. The philosophy called Positive is not a recent invention of M. Comte, but a simple adherence to the traditions of all the great scientific minds whose discoveries have made the human race what it is (Mill 1873: 10).

Mill would have used other words than "theological" and "metaphysical" for the objectionably immature phases of thought; especially would he have chosen another word than "positive" for the properly mature mode of modern thinking. Mill has a different feel for the language involved.

> In all languages, but especially in English, they excite ideas other than those intended. The words Positive and Positivism, in the meaning assigned to them, are ill fitted to take root in English soil; while Metaphysical suggests, and suggested even to M. Comte, much that in no way deserves to be included in his denunciation. The term Theological is less wide of the mark, though the use of it as a term of condemnation implies, as we shall see, a greater reach of negation than need be included in the Positive creed (Mill 1873: 11).

Nevertheless, Mill heartily approved Comte's central determination to stay firmly fixed on the phenomena. On this point Comte was in the heroic line of British thinkers.

> The true doctrine was not seen in its full clearness even by Bacon, though it is the result to which all his speculations tend: still less by Descartes. It was, however, correctly apprehended by Newton. But it was probably first conceived in its entire generality by Hume, who carries it a step further than Comte, maintaining not merely that the only causes of phenomena which can be known to us are other phenomena, their invariable antecedents, but that there is no other kind of causes: cause, as he interprets it, *means* the invariable antecedent. This

is the only part of Hume's doctrine which was contested by his great adversary, Kant; who maintaining as strenuously as Comte that we know nothing of things in themselves, of Noumena, of real Substances and real Causes, yet peremptorily asserted their existence. But neither does Comte question this: on the contrary, all his language implies it (Mill 1873: 9).

Here Mill decided to forge a position somewhere between Hume and Kant, not far from Comte, but one making more concession to powerful intuitions of important permanences behind our changing experiences of the phenomena. It is absolutely impossible to perceive what is by definition "behind" perception, Mill agrees. We have nothing but phenomena available for knowing. Positivism is right in demanding that we remain maturely content with what modern science has discovered to be enough: that is, the empirical discovery of laws (preferably mathematical laws) describing the regularities holding among phenomenal data. Yet, Hume's still-unanswered questions as to what accounts for the relative stability of our experience— why the feeling of "continu'd existence" of the "things" around us, and why the consequent expectation that what we leave undisturbed in the morning will remain there to greet us in the evening—deserve respectful attention. If Berkeley's theological metaphysics and Kant's radical subjectivizing revolution are to be rejected, then what can suffice?

Mill offered a compromise solution. No mind can penetrate behind the veil of phenomena. That way is blocked by an uncrossable gap. Perhaps, indeed, Hume is victorious in holding that the very *meaning* of "causes" and "substances" must now be defined in terms of actual or possible experiences. But if so, then at least the hitherto under-utilized concept of "possible" experiences remains to be fully exploited.

Matter, then, may be defined, a Permanent Possibility of Sensation. If I am asked whether I believe in matter, I ask whether the questioner accepts this definition of it. If he does, I believe in matter; and so do all Berkeleians. In any other sense than this, I do not. But I affirm with confidence, that this conception of Matter includes the whole meaning attached to it by the common world, apart from philosophical and sometimes from theological, theories (Mill 1868: vol. 1, 213).

When not actually sensed, things in the material world remain available as possibilities for future sensing. This way of speaking does not violate the ban on knowing anything apart from phenomena. In the end, whether a thing is real or not will come down to whether actual sensations do occur when possible sensations are expected. But it has the advantage of going beyond the sheer negatives of Hume's skepticism and Comte's positivism. It positively addresses and accounts for our intuitions of an abiding world made up of more than actual phenomena. It is not, Mill hopes, "metaphysical" in the objectionable sense to offer this much acknowledgment of the question that, wrongly handled, leads to cognitive paralysis before the epistemological gap. It has the advantage, from an empiricist point of view, of referring to nothing but experience. We shall shortly see how well—or poorly—this compromise worked to satisfy Mill's hopes.

MACH AND AYER

Ernst Mach (1838–1916)—the Austrian physicist for whom the "Mach" number (indicating speed relative to the local velocity of sound) was named—was a person of major influence in a number of directions. In physics, his philosophical challenge to the unobservable "luminiferous ether" helped convince Albert Einstein (1879–1955) to abandon theoretical reliance on it, probably before he had even heard the results of the Michaelson-Morley experiment (1887) confirming its empirical irrelevance. Mach influenced Einstein in other ways as well, exposing conceptual problems in Newton's "absolute" space and time, and offering a relativistic substitute based on arbitrary reference points to be taken as "fixed." In philosophy, his prestige as Professor of the History and Theory of Inductive Science at the University of Vienna (1895–1901) led to the creation of a discussion group which later developed into the Vienna Circle, whose publications between 1928 and 1934 were issued officially as *Veröffentlichungen des Vereines Ernst Mach* ("Publications of the Ernst Mach Society"). In 1901 Mach resigned his professorship when he was named to the upper house of the Austrian parliament, from which heights he continued to support empirical, antimetaphysical causes until his death in 1916.

Mach was a strong Anglophile, whose adopted philosophical ancestors were primarily Berkeley and Hume. As he read them, science itself was—and had to be—nothing other than the description of "ideas" and "impressions," or (as Mach preferred) "sensations." Berkeley himself had come to the same conclusion, but had entangled his analysis of science with theology. For Mach, sensations alone suffice. Whatever their regularity, this must be allowed to be a purely empirical matter for noting and reporting. That is the careful scientist's job, as Mach analyzed it in 1886 in his *Beiträge zur Analyse der Empfingungen* (translated as *The Analysis of Sensations*, 1914).

There are several important scientific consequences that flow from Mach's philosophical commitment to the sole importance of sensations. One is the essential unity of all the sciences. Every science, whatever its specialization, is ultimately a science of the same basic things—namely, sensations.

Whether mechanics or mineralogy, optics or ornithology, the only thing scientists properly do is to collect and organize sensations. Mach himself dealt with a great number of fields. He wrote on what today would be called biochemistry as well as the areas of physics now associated with his name. William James, to whom in later years Mach was to dedicate a book, visited him for the first time in 1882, while Mach was Professor of Physics at the University of Prague. James was deeply impressed with Mach's brilliance and universality of interests. In a letter to his wife, James wrote:

> As for Prague, *veni, vidi, vici*. I went there with much trepidation to do my social-scientific duty. . . . I heard Hering give a very poor physiology lecture, and Mach a beautiful physical one. . . . Mach came to my hotel and I spent four hours talking and supping with him at his club, an unforgettable conversation. I don't think anyone ever gave me so strong an impression of pure intellectual genius. He apparently has read everything and thought about everything, and has an absolute simplicity of manner and winningness of smile (James 1920: vol. 1, 211–12).

Decisively clearing away the rubbish of supposedly different orders of being—physical, biological, psychological, etc.—"behind" the sensations of immediate experience, made it possible, Mach believed, to transcend the artificial barriers between scientific specialties. The only justification for maintaining different sciences, given Mach's epistemological convictions, would be purely practical convenience. Later, members of the Vienna Circle would make a primary project of realizing Mach's ideals in the ambitious *International Encyclopedia of Unified Science*, containing several important volumes.

A second consequence of Mach's epistemological reduction of all scientific work to the analysis and description of sensations was an increased emphasis on verification by experience rather than proof by theory, mathematical or otherwise. No mathematical proof could be more secure than the sensations on which it was based and from which it took any force it might have. Mach's Viennese professorship, in Inductive Science, was well-named. Deductive certainties were beside the point. Mathematical physicists, he warned, courted the fallacy of "misplaced rigor." Certainty, however, was still available to science, Mach believed. It was the certainty of sense perception. The high standards of Plato or Descartes for "genuine knowing" could be retained, he insisted, but only when cleansed of the apriorism of such rationalists. Certainty should be sought, but in the assurance that what one experiences in a sensation cannot be wrong, at least insofar as it is simply experienced as a sensation. One may be wrong, of course, if one's sensation is interpreted so as to make further claims, such as, about existence or (essentially the same thing) about future experiences. But the job of the empirical scientist is to build carefully from the foundation of private certainty to the confirmed inductive lawfulness of a shared world.

A third, related, consequence of Mach's reduction of the scientific enterprise to the description of phenomena is the heightened status of prediction, relative to the aim of "explanation." Theories and models, Mach held, are useful only to the degree that they can assist the real work of science: that is, to anticipate the future in verifiable ways. Concepts themselves, from which theories are formed, are likened to engineers, the managerial by-products of sensations.

> From sensations and their conjunctions arise concepts, whose aim is to lead us by the shortest and easiest way to sensible ideas that agree best with the sensations. Thus all intellection starts from sense perceptions and returns to them. Our genuine mental workers are these sensible pictures or ideas, while concepts are the organizers and overseers that tell the masses of the former where to go and what to do. In simple tasks, the intellect is in direct touch with the workers, but for larger undertakings it deals with the directing engineers, who would however be useless if they had not seen to the engagement of reliable workers (Mach 1976: 105).

Theoretical mappings of how "things" stand are therefore useful only (a) as shorthand summaries of past regularities in sensation and (b) as heuristic helps to finding new regularities in the future. There are serious drawbacks, of course, to such radical downgrading of theory. As Irwin W. Hiebert, editor of Mach's English translation put it, "It has been said that Mach's philosophy seemingly required no theories, and accordingly yielded no insights" (Mach 1976: xxiv). Mach would have replied, however, that "insights" of the sort obtained by theory are exactly the problem his method is designed to avoid.

Theoretical "entities" are, strictly speaking, only names for clusters of actual or possible experiences, and such names should be used with care, to prevent falling into the trap of reification and metaphysics. For this reason, Mach resisted crediting the popular language of "atoms" and "molecules." Far from a Hobbesian atomist, Mach refused to acknowledge the reality of atoms, or even of molecules, until the physicist Jean Baptiste Perrin (1870–1942) provided the latter with an empirical anchorage in observed Brownian motions, when he showed that the suspended colloidal particles in motion (discovered in 1827 by the botanist Robert Brown) could be considered huge molecules in their own right. It is noteworthy that Mach was more impressed by Perrin's more empirically relevant work, begun only in 1908, than in Einstein's earlier mathematical proofs of 1905, which provided Brownian motion a long-needed theoretical framework within a kinetic theory of matter. Einstein, especially early in his career, strove constantly to satisfy Mach's epistemological criteria, even though Mach was not much impressed by the mathematical achievements of young Einstein.

When, in 1907, three nonphilosophers in Vienna (a mathematician, Hans Hahn, an economist, Otto Neurath, and a physicist, Philipp Frank)—all deeply influenced by Mach—decided to meet regularly to discuss the character of science in general, their motivation was largely to repair the breach between Mach's conception of science and their sense of the importance of theory, especially mathematical theory. They were acutely aware of the contributions being made by Einstein and, in France, by Jules Henri Poincaré (1854–1912). This "Vienna group" hoped to find a way of retaining Mach's doughty empiricism without sacrificing the most exciting developments in early twentieth-century science.

When Mach's former chair in History and Theory of Inductive Science fell vacant in 1922, these discussants were well-positioned to recruit Moritz Schlick (1882–1936) for the opening. In 1918 Schlick had published his *Allgemeine Erkenntnislehre* (General Theory of Knowledge), carefully taking up standard philosophical issues in relation to knowledge in the sciences. Like most in the Vienna group, he was not burdened with traditional philosophical credentials. He was a trained physicist, having studied at Berlin with Max Planck (1858–1947), obtaining his Ph.D. in problems of light-reflection. He was, however, intensely interested, as Mach had not been, in the technical issues of philosophy. And when he arrived as Professor in Vienna, Schlick gave new vitality to the discussion group that had instigated his "call," formalizing and nurturing what came to be called the Vienna Circle during its most active years, from 1922 until Schlick's death at the hands of a demented student in 1936.

In his *Allgemeine Erkenntnislehre*, Schlick had examined all the purported "synthetic a priori" propositions that Kant and his followers had claimed were part of Newtonian science. If correct, Kant's claims would have had the effect of locking Newtonian conceptions of space and time into logical necessities, apart from which no one could think a world. Kant was, indeed, confident of the absoluteness of Newton's framework; but in the era of Einstein and Poincaré, as the Newtonian scheme was visibly unravelling and alternative understandings were clamoring for attention, Schlick systematically examined each purported necessary-but-informative proposition and found each one to reflect either a simple necessity of language (a tautology), or to offer merely an inductively probable empirical generalization, not necessary at all. Schlick's general liberation of science from the apriorism of German philosophy was welcomed as fresh air in the Vienna Circle, and his bifurcation became one of its mainstay principles: that the language of science could be analyzed into either an analytically necessary part, including logic and mathematics, or an empirically informative part—but that these two parts are and must be quite distinct.

In 1921, just before the official formation of the Vienna Circle, a difficult monograph, *Logisch-philosophische Abhandlung*, was published (thanks to the efforts of the author's distinguished English mentor) in the *Annalen der Naturphilosophie*. The work, which had been abandoned by its author after one publisher rejected it, was by an eccentric Austrian then teaching in an elementary school in a small village of Lower Austria. This teacher, self-isolated from the intellectual currents swirling in Vienna, was Ludwig Wittgenstein (1889–1951). Wittgenstein was the scion of a prominent Viennese family, a former Cambridge University student, and a protege of Bertrand Russell (1872–1970). While serving in the Austrian army during the First World War, he had written the book, attempting solutions of problems on which he and Russell had been working before the war. He was carrying the manuscript (and several notebooks of his thoughts) when captured by Italian forces in 1918. In diplomatic pouches (thanks to the active intervention of the economist John Maynard Keynes [1883–1946]), the manuscript was conveyed to Russell, who was awe-struck by its brilliance and penetration. Wittgenstein suspected, however, that Russell did not correctly grasp his meaning, and after failing (on his release from prison camp) to find an interested publisher, and fearing that no one would ever understand it, he gave the manuscript to Russell to handle as he pleased. Russell wrote an introduction to an English translation, which (with facing German text) was published as the *Tractatus Logico-Philosophicus* in 1922, the year Moritz Schlick moved to Vienna.

Schlick soon discovered the *Tractatus*, which he made a major focus for reading and discussion at meetings of the Vienna Circle in two successive years. Wittgenstein had set out a theory of the fundamental character of meaning and the relationship between language and the world. This theory, though abstract and difficult, clearly was relevant to the interests of the Vienna Circle. In it Wittgenstein had presented a "truth-functional" view of language, in which every proposition must be analyzed finally into atomic elements of meaning, each of which stands for an elementary state of affairs or "atomic fact" (Wittgenstein 1922: 31). As Wittgenstein put it, "The world is everything that is the case"; and "What is the case, the fact, is the existence of atomic facts" (Wittgenstein 1922: 31). It is the character of atomic facts that they can either be or not, quite apart from all other facts. "Any one can either be the case or not be the case, and everything else remain the same" (Wittgenstein 1922: 31). Since atomic statements are independently true or false, the overall truth or falsity of higher-level propositions becomes a complex function of the individual truth or falsity of atomic facts combined, by conjunction or disjunction, in the "molecular" proposition they compose.

This is what is meant by the "truth-functionality" of meaningful propositions. In the absence of atomic facts, language has no claim to truth or falsity and thought has no significant content, though there remains the empty form of the proposition. Logical form ultimately reduces to tautology, the source of necessity. As Wittgenstein remarks, "Proof in logic is only a mechanical expedient to facilitate the recognition of tautology, where it is complicated" (Wittgenstein 1922: 167). A tautology, unlike a significant proposition soundly based on atomic facts, cannot be further asserted; it simply "shows itself" (Wittgenstein 1922: 167).

It is important to observe that Wittgenstein himself never explicitly identified atomic facts with anything so concrete and limited as Mach's "sensations" or Berkeley's "ideas" or Hume's "impressions." They remained undefined foundation stones for his rigorously simple theory. The members of the Vienna Circle, however, read the *Tractatus* with such traditional empiricist contexts very much in mind. Wittgenstein's infrequent visits to the group in Vienna, responding reluctantly the implorings of Schlick, did not result in his becoming a member of the Circle. It was easy for those who chose to publish in the name of the Mach Society to interpret atomic facts as what would soon be called "sense data."

A brilliant young philosopher, Alfred Jules Ayer, only twenty-two, fresh from Eton and Oxford, visited the University of Vienna from 1932 until 1933. At Oxford, Ayer had studied Hume and Berkeley under H. H. Price (1899–1984) and had drawn Gilbert Ryle (1900–1976) as his first tutor. During his year in Vienna, he worked intensely with members of the Vienna Circle, particularly with Rudolf Carnap (1891–1970). On his return to England in 1933, he was appointed Lecturer at Christ Church College, where he had done his undergraduate work; two years later he became a Research Fellow. In those years, after his return from Vienna and before the outbreak of the Second World War, Ayer wrote the book, Language, Truth and Logic (1936), that was to detonate like a bomb among English-speaking philosophers. Before the book, not much was known in England or America of what Ayer called the "Viennese school" (Ayer 1946: 26). After the book, and after the dust of war had settled, English-language philosophy was profoundly transformed.

Ayer's approach was confrontational and revolutionary. Like Mach, he was strongly drawn to Berkeley and Hume; like the philosophers of the Vienna Circle, he acknowledged a special debt to Wittgenstein and to Wittgenstein's mentor, Bertrand Russell. The heady lacing of these positions with a young man's missionary zeal was distinctly Ayer's.

A whole new plateau needed to be scaled. Classical Positivism, such as we have seen advocated by both Comte and Mill, and (largely) by Mach, denied the legitimacy of pursuing knowledge beyond or behind the phenomena of positive experience. Both Comte and Mill had used an argument *ad eram*, that is, the argument that history has outmoded theology and metaphysics, and that to be "up to the age" requires that efforts at knowing be cleansed of old-fashioned methods. Their argument was essentially a developmental one. "Maturity" of mind, they said, demanded limitation to experience alone. Those who failed to move with the times to positivism would be exposed as infantile or at least not fully "grown up" in their manner of thinking. But this is a relatively weak argument, especially against those who might see nothing especially compelling about the goal of keeping up with "modern times." And it allows metaphysical opponents a field day, pointing out the evident mental maturity of great thinkers, such as Aristotle or Thomas Aquinas, whose minds certainly do not *seem* "infantile" or "youthfully undeveloped." A way to still higher ground against the metaphysicians was needed.

Ayer, inspired by the Vienna Circle, believed that the scaling ladder to the new plateau would be logic. Metaphysics and theology, given the Circle's understanding of Wittgenstein's new analysis, could now be more than merely "outgrown"; it could be radically eliminated. Ayer's first chapter is entitled, "The Elimination of Metaphysics." Its first sentence reads: "The traditional disputes of philosophers are, for the most part, as unwarranted as they are unfruitful" (Ayer 1946: 33).

The "unfruitfulness" of traditional metaphysical disputes, Ayer thought, had been amply shown by the classical Positivists. But to be "unwarranted" is something much more absolute. People may differ about what "fruit" they care about. What is unfruitful for one may be considered highly fruitful by another, depending on judgments of importance. But a dispute is *unwarranted* when it can be shown that there is really nothing to dispute about. The power of logical analysis, given Wittgenstein's advances, can be harnessed to show exactly that. Therefore the new plateau beyond Classical Positivism is Logical Positivism. Positivism was right, but could not compel its vision; Logical Positivism, in contrast, can at last fulfill the dream of Hobbes—to force assent, no matter how reluctant, from all who would be rational.

The sword of logical compulsion, for Ayer, was the verification principle, also known as the criterion of verifiability. This principle was attributed by members of the Vienna Circle to Wittgenstein, though it seems unlikely that Wittgenstein actually held the principle, at least as it was brandished by Logical Positivism. Its function, given both a sensationalist interpretation of atomic facts and a truth-functional analysis of informative propositions, was to make sure that any proposition claiming significance can be translated into at least a selection of the simple atomic propositions referring to sense experiences that, in combination, will determine the truth or falsity of the original complex proposition. To make these translations—from ordinary speech into what were sometimes called "protocol sentences" (so-named for the immediate reports, or "protocols," taken down by stenographers at court proceedings)—is to provide "definitions in use" of empirically significant utterances. If I say, "An apple is on the table," it will be relevant to the truth of my statement if I can make an indefinitely large set of true assertions, for example, "Red there!" and "Round there!" Indeed, the whole factual content of my assertion can be equated with the statements of atomic facts I obtain (or look for) when I try to find out whether the assertion is true. My method of verifying "An apple is on the table" is simply to obtain, or try to obtain, all the sights and smells and tastes and feelings that constitute, in atomic facts, the analysis of my claim about the apple. In the end, what I *mean* by my claim turns out to be logically equivalent to the experiences I have or could have in finding out that it is true. Thus *the meaning of a proposition is equivalent to the method of its verification.*

This is a logical doctrine about language and meaning, not a claim about "fruitfulness" or "maturity of thought." Given this sword, the Logical Positivists could swing it at anyone who advocated moving beyond phenomena. Such a person seems ready to indulge in metaphysics; but leaving the domain of phenomena will result in falling into literally empty verbiage. Key sentences uttered will fail to conform to the conditions under which alone they can be literally significant. Those conditions are laid down by the criterion of verifiability.

> We say that a sentence is factually significant to any given person, if, and only if, he knows how to verify the proposition which it purports to express—that is, if he knows what observations would lead him, under certain conditions, to accept the proposition as being true, or reject it as being false (Ayer 1946: 35).

If there are no such verifying or falsifying conditions for such a proposition, then "the sentence expressing it may be emotionally significant to him; but it is not literally significant (Ayer 1946: 35).

The verification principle, we now can see, would make the epistemological gap a fiction. Only sentences conveying propositions about actual or possible sense experiences are, on this view, "significant" in an informative or nontautological way. Thus there can be no "gap," or even cognitively grounded worry about a "gap," since the only things we can talk about meaningfully are the matters that present themselves on *this* side of the alleged divide between experience and what is supposed "behind" experience. Consider: how could we, in principle, verify exclusively *by sense experience* that there *is* a domain of things-in-themselves that are by definition *never present in sense experience*? The very question collapses in contradiction. No set of possible sensations could render even probable, on this criterion of meaning, that something mysterious, completely out of the range of experience, either "exists" or "functions" or "accounts for" anything whatever, most especially for experience itself. If all we can talk about significantly is what is, in principle, verifiable by sense experience, the so-called "epistemological gap" is reduced to literal nonsense.

There may be powerful emotions stowed away on the imagery of something "deeper" than actual or possible experience. Ayer is quite willing to acknowledge that language conveys and stirs feelings, independent of its powers to communicate factual significance. Perhaps the suggestion of a "gap" sets up affective reverberations in those who feel that science leaves them "flat." They may be haunted by the jaded question, "Is that all there is?" Any proffered answer to it (necessarily) will to be in terms of "more of the same," that is, observation language. This may not satisfy all temperaments. But this, if true, is an interesting psychological fact about some people; it is not the legitimation of an unwarranted philosophical question (really more the expression of nameless dread than a real question) that carries no literal meaning.

Other emotionally charged domains of speech are handled similarly. The question of "God," for example, is either reducible to what can be verified in experience or is factually empty. Few theists would consider it enough to speak of God as nothing more than the observable order and beauty of nature. Most insist on something more, something transcendent.

> But in that case the term "god" is a metaphysical term. And if "god" is a metaphysical term, then it cannot be even probable that a god exists. For to say that "God exists" is to make a metaphysical utterance which cannot be either true or false. And by the same criterion, no sentence which purports to describe the nature of a transcendent god can possess any literal significance (Ayer 1946: 115).

Indeed, the crucial adjective "transcendent" gives away the unverifiability of whatever it modifies, whether it attaches to the word "God" or to the phrase "things in themselves." "Transcendent" is the logical antonym of "verifiable."

Religious people enamored of "transcendence"-language, therefore, should give up pretensions not only of *knowing*, but even of *believing*. "Belief," no matter how plausible or implausible, requires something meaningful as its subject matter. But on the criterion of verifiability, language that attempts to refer to something in principle beyond sense verification *has no subject matter*. It fails to refer. Its expressions are cognitively deficient— literally empty. This does not mean that the language is not precious to those who use it. Emotions may be expressed through cognitively empty phrases: for example, "the Good Shepherd" may provide its users a sense of warm security, and "Maker of Heaven and Earth" may offer a vehicle for venting feelings (of awe, of wonder, etc.) unsatisfied by scientific prose. If "issues" all reduce to emotion, there is nothing to prove or disprove. Even more disconcertingly, for the religious person, there is no way around this cognitive roadblock by way of "faith" (as Kant had proposed [Ferré 1967b: chap. 8]), since religious language fails to supply anything logically possible to have "faith" in. Even skeptical philosophers often have referred to religious persons as "believers," but, if Logical Positivism is correct, even the honorable title of "believer" needs to be withdrawn. Instead, we are left with religious "emoters."

A similar analysis awaits values-talk in general, whether ethical or aesthetic. Socrates, we remember, founded his philosophical quest on the search for ethical knowledge. Plato continued the effort; and, even though Aristotle shifted the ground, the method, and the degree of certainty, he too concluded that important ethical knowledge is within reach. But the verification principle, even as it reduces the epistemological gap to a fiction, also bars the possibility of nonempirical knowledge (or probable beliefs) about the "good" or the "beautiful." Which sense experiences could in principle confirm that something is "good"? Of course if one defines "good" as "what is approved in a given society," then there are indeed empirical methods of determining whether in fact some act or personal trait is approved. But just as religious persons resist defining "God" in reductive ways, referring simply to what is observable, so ethical thinkers tend to reject defining "good" exhaustively in terms of such verifiable matters of fact. They point out that we need to be able to survey various societies and ask whether the fact of general approval in this society or that is itself "good." Even within a given society, the logical possibility of reformers criticizing present public preferences as "not good" remains important. But this requires a definition of "good" independent of ("transcending") general approval. The most important features of "good" seem to evade any exhaustive definition into observable fact. It is empirically verifiable (let us say) that I am happy; but is it really "good" under present circumstances that I should be happy? Perhaps I have just swindled a widow of her life savings. Then it may be "bad" that I am happy. "Good" cannot be allowed to be defined *simply* in terms of happiness, or in terms of any other similarly empirically observable state of affairs, for example, personal or group preference. There always seems something "more"—something elusive, "transcendent"—about value terms like this. When we attempt to pin them down, they always escape from what is "merely" observable.

If this is so, then this distinctive character of ethical terms, like all value-terms of this sort, must be functioning in some noncognitive way, since, on the verifiability criterion, cognition is dependent on—is equivalent to—the possibility of identifying atomic facts that will tend to confirm or disconfirm the meaningful propositions they undergird. Whatever is systematically transcendent is unverifiable; whatever is unverifiable is literally meaningless. Ayer suggests that the systematically elusive character of value-terms, like "good," lies in our feelings, not our thoughts. When we say that it is "not good" (or "bad" or even "wicked") to bilk a widow of her life savings, we are expressing our disgust at an empirical situation, not further describing it. Assume we have fully described the facts of the situation. Once all the facts are in, it points to no new observable fact to characterize the situation as "bad." Nothing *observable* would be different if we were to call the same situation "good," instead. By hypothesis, all the describable features have been laid out fully. But on the verification principle, when no further observations can count for or against an utterance, it is not functioning informatively.

The primary interests of the Logical Positivists were not, of course, in theology, aesthetics, or ethics. They were, rather, in the assertions of empirical science and daily life. Positivism in all its modes, from Comte through Mach and Ayer, was always especially close to science. The nature of scientific knowing, its warrants and its security, had a privileged spot in the hierarchy of these philosophers' concerns. Science was taken as the paradigm for good thinking and successful cognition, thus providing an implicit epistemic norm; it was also taken as in need of defense against aggressive metaphysics, which might attempt to impose categories and dictate results.

Since scientists deal with and attempt to know about material things, one of the essential steps to a positivist theory of knowing is an analysis of the meaning of material-thing statements. I put this in terms of "statements," since asking the traditional question, "What is a material thing?" sounds too metaphysical. A table, for example, is on Logic Positivist principles a logical construction. But a better way of putting the matter is that our symbol, "table," is a convenient way of organizing many other statements about actual and possible sense perceptions. Thus philosophers are not making factual claims (though they may sound alarmingly metaphysical) when they state that material objects, like tables, "are" logical constructions. Properly understood,

> the assertion that tables are logical constructions out of sense-contents is not a factual assertion at all, in the sense in which the assertion that tables were fictitious objects would be a factual assertion, albeit a false one. It is, as our explanation of the notion of logical construction should have made clear, a linguistic assertion, to the effect that the symbol "table" is definable in terms of certain symbols which stand for sense-contents, not explicitly, but in use (Ayer 1946: 63).

Therefore analyzing material things, whether in connection with scientific research or simply with the activities of daily life, is (as Ayer puts it) "the problem of the 'reduction' of material things to sense-contents." (Ayer 1946: 64). This can be achieved by making more precise what Locke and Berkeley referred to as the "coexistence" of ideas, and what Hume spoke of as the "coherence" of our impressions of sense. Ayer puts it in terms of the resemblance and continuity between sense contents, which he carefully defines (Ayer 1946: 65–66). Then, (1) when sense contents in a given area of the visual field are linked to one another by unbroken transitions and qualitative similarities, and (2) when other appropriate sense contents in an analogous area of the tactual field are similarly linked, then one can say that one is dealing with a "material thing."

The main point of this elaborate exercise in reduction is to free the scientist (and all of us) from the confusions of metaphysics, which alone persuade the unwary that there are "unknowables" on the other side of the epistemological gap—unknowables that will forever stump the best efforts of scientists. The philosophical analysis in terms of logical constructions and definitions in use may make for unaccustomed complexity, Ayer admits, but "It serves to increase our understanding of the sentences in which we refer to material things" (Ayer 1946: 68). Logically, they simply *are* more complex than the convenient simplicities of ordinary practical speech suggest. "Understanding" an unanalyzed sentence may be good enough for practical purposes, but it leaves one vulnerable to metaphysical confusion and its attendant epistemological despair. English speakers unaware of the hidden complexity of language "may be led to adopt some metaphysical belief, such as the belief in the existence of material substances or invisible substrata, which is a source of confusion in all their speculative thought" (Ayer 1946: 68). We shall see later that avoiding this metaphysical entrapment is Ayer's principal justification for his approach.

A similar analysis can be given of the long-controversial concept of the "self." Human bodies, of course, are material things, and fall under the analysis just given. But there is a persistent sense that selves are not fully analyzed in terms of bodies. Selves are minds, as well. How does Logical Positivism deal with this issue, of relating body and mind, which I identified in *Being and Value* as central to the "modern agenda"?

First, Ayer makes clear that although every meaningful object of discourse is a either a sense content or a logical construction out of sense contents, there is a vital difference between the two levels involved. Material things, like bodies, can be said to exist when a sufficient number of sense contents, with the proper character of resemblance and continuity, occur. But sense contents themselves are not logical constructions; they do not "exist" like material things; they simply occur (or not) on a logical plane prior to the level of "thinghood." Their foundational status means that they are neither material things nor mental things. Both types are constructed as appropriate. This has the important consequence that there is no really fundamental difference between the whole class of physical objects and the whole class of mental objects. As Mach had earlier believed, everything can be unified by being recognized as reducing to sensations.

This allows an analysis of self that is freed from metaphysical notions of substances—especially "spiritual substances"—and is parallel with the analysis of things. The self turns out to be a logical construction out of its history of sense-experiences (Ayer 1946: 125). This reduces, in principle, to memory. If we are interested in tracing the history of sensory contents across time, memory images alone provide the link. Expanding the notion of "sense-experiences," Ayer places "memory images" into this class (Ayer 1946: 126).

Each self, then, gains its identity as a single "thing" through the continuity of its bodily sense contents, across time, and gains its personal identity as an intelligent, purposing, loving, appreciating entity through direct awareness of its introspective states, including the memory images that tie them together. Of course one's introspective states are private, but one can experience the correlation between those states of awareness and one's own bodily movements (including speech), and when one sees or hears "a high degree of qualitative similarity" in other similar organisms—other humans—one observes, Ayer concludes, that they are intelligent persons, too.

A serious—perhaps fatal—problem arises here for Logical Positivism, however. Literally speaking, the distinction between the *meaning* of my "self" and all *other* "selves" introduces a systematic ambiguity—or worse—into reductionist language dealing with persons. What I must mean by "self" in connection to *myself* derives its significance in largest part from what Ayer calls "introspective sense contents," that is, my directly experienced feelings, thoughts, memories, plans, preferences, and the like. But what I am entitled to mean by "self" *in all other cases* draws entirely on sense contents of bodily actions, including sounds emitted, that are entirely lacking in introspective character. The sort of thing I mean by "*my* self" is unique in my universe of discourse. No *other* "self" can have introspective experience as part of its meaning for me. The meaning of "other selves," instead, reduces to protocol statements that can give "definitions in use" only for bodies in various modes of behavior. And this systematic ambiguity must hold, but with different specific references, for every person. No one can come even close to meaning the same thing by the word "self" when he or she is the referent in contrast to when someone else is the referent of the word.

This ambiguity created a serious problem for Logical Positivism and called for some of the most creative efforts of analytical philosophers in the postwar years (e.g., Ryle 1984). The key challenge was to maintain the analytical reduction of "self"-language into available sense contents without falling, thanks to the verification principle of meaning, into a form of linguistic solipsism in which one's own self is the only one of its kind, alone in a universe devoid of consciousness. But by taking notice of this problem, I have begun a needed critical reflection. To continue, I must step back to take a running start from before the origins of Logical Positivism itself.

PROBLEMS WITH REDUCTION

The various reductionist strategies followed in this chapter could be powerful antidotes against fears of the epistemological gap. Rooted in the eighteenth century, they have enjoyed much prestige in the twentieth. I earlier signalled my belief, however, that they suffer fatal flaws. What is wrong with coping in some such way with the challenges of modern doubt?

Trying to assess the reductionist strategy, one should keep in mind where the general burden of proof must lie. I began this chapter with a quick survey of the breadth and depth of the "realist intuition" just in order to emphasize the boldness of those who would escape the epistemology gap by discounting the importance of this intuition of a world behind all our observations.

Counter-intuitive theories, of course, need not be false. Human beings standing on the surface of the great earth, looking at the stars and planets, have long experienced their world as stationary and the heavenly objects as circling overhead. It is still downright counter-intuitive on many occasions, even today, to *feel* the planet *as* a planet—spinning in space—a tiny speck within unimaginably large vistas of dark gasses and raging celestial fires. Still, we must adjust our intuitions to what the evidence—based on instrument-assisted observations, tempered by thorough theoretical examination, and burnished by confirmation after confirmation (including many human flights into space)—requires us to accept. The burden of proof may once have lain heavily on the counter-intuitive suggestions of Copernicus and Galileo, but that burden has been more than amply met.

One can hardly say anything similarly supportive, however, about the proponents of the phenomenalist rejection of the epistemological gap. Oddly, they seem to make their proposals as though there were no heavy presumption against them. The notoriously stubborn Fichte, for example, followed by Schelling and Hegel, simply decided to rid himself of the noumenal burden Kant had accepted. Perhaps the intuition of an independent world behind experience did not strongly claim his own attention. He was, in any case, more interested in ethical and religious topics than in speculative metaphysics or epistemology. But thinkers need to remember that they are not beginning "from scratch" on matters of such general import. Kant retained the quasi-concept of the thing-in-itself, negative though it must be, because he considered himself duty-bound to find room on his conceptual map for what generations of thinkers had reported, and for what he himself recognized as essential though problematic. The interface between intuition and theory is never clear and simple. Intuitions themselves are seldom at all "clear"; the "simplifications" of theory may fit only awkwardly onto awarenesses that are complicated and murky. Still, to the extent that thinkers are attempting to be adequate to their own data, they will be reluctant (like Kant, and Locke before him) to paper over whole domains by thrusting upon them abstractions that clarify and simplify only by ignoring vital parts of experience. Likewise, to the extent that thinkers are attempting to think on behalf of more than their own solitary selves, they will hesitate before dismissing funded experience, widely reported by those who talk about such things, and sometimes even presupposed in the structure of natural languages.

Required to lift such a heavy burden of proof against cumulative intuitions, what do the philosophers of reduction offer in support of their proposals? Do they provide anything even approaching the strength of evidence and arguments that oblige us to accept the counter-intuitive idea of the earth as a planet in motion? Clearly not.

August Comte rests much of his case for Positivism on his so-called Law of the Stages. This presumptive "law" is immensely important for his position. Only if there is such a law, can one criticize a thinker for failing to be "up to the age"—a phrase used frequently both by Comte and Mill. A *law* of development, if it is genuine, can provide a standard, a vector, a *telos* for its domain. If all children are *supposed* to be animistic, all youths to think in terms of unseen entities and forces, and all adults to be "maturely" positivistic, then one has a basis in this law for saying "Grow up!" to grownups who refuse to act their age. If, likewise, the thought of ancient peoples is inevitably theological; if the thought of intermediate ages is fated to be self-indulgently metaphysical; and if the thought of modern times is to be parsimoniously positivist—then (but only then) is there a firm norm against which contemporary thinkers can be measured. Without the Law, Comte's position would appear to lack its main ground and its primary polemical weapon.

Mill recognized the importance of the Law of the Stages for Comte. While Mill discounts Comte's originality on the main principles of Positivism, as I noted earlier, calling them "a simple adherence to the traditions of all the great scientific minds whose discoveries have made the human race what it is" (Mill 1873: 10), he strongly credits Comte's pronouncement of the Law of the Stages as a great personal contribution to the battle for the modern mind.

The generalization which belongs to himself, and in which he had not, to the best of our knowledge, been at all anticipated, is, that every distinct class of human conceptions passes necessarily through all these stages, beginning with the theological, and proceeding through the metaphysical to the positive; the metaphysical being a mere state of transition, but an indispensable one, from the theological mode of thought to the positive, which is destined finally to prevail, by the universal recognition that all phenomena without exception are governed by invariable laws, with which no volitions, either natural or supernatural, interfere (Mill 1873: 13–14).

Mill, in giving credit to Comte for nothing but the Law of the Stages, is perhaps too stingy in his praises; but in giving him complete credit for the Law, he is too generous. Though Mill was evidently not aware of it, the Law had been fully stated by the social critic, Claude Henri Saint-Simon (often credited with being the first also to propound Socialism), whom Comte had served as secretary for some years. As Saint-Simon propounded it, it was a grand speculative hypothesis, a sweeping qualitative perspective on the history of thought. It was far from a "positive" *law*, which would need to rise from exhaustive empirical study of the covariation of observed variables. It was instead an interesting *aperçu*, not the formulation of what Comte and Mill could recognize, on good positivist methodology, as an "invariable law" or, as Mill put it, as a description of how "every distinct class of human conceptions passes necessarily through all these stages."

Comte's "Law" was no more a genuine law than Saint-Simon's, whether evaluated on his own positivist principles, or, indeed, on any other. Comte himself simply declares it. Little space (two or three pages in all) out of his enormous *Cours* is spent grounding or explicating the crucial Law of the Stages. It is taken as given, as obviously authoritative. Mill recognizes the importance, however, of defending it.

As this theory is the key to M. Comte's other generalizations, all of which are more or less dependent on it; as it forms the backbone, if we may so speak, of his philosophy, and, unless it be true, he has accomplished little; we cannot better employ part of our space than in clearing it from misconception, and giving the explanations necessary to remove the obstacles which prevent many competent persons from assenting to it (Mill 1873: 14).

To this task Mill devotes fifteen pages, mainly showing how the Law of the Stages does not require absolute abandonment of ideas of God or of all theoretical conceptions. But this middle-of-the-road Positivism is not, when

Mill is finished, the result of "invariable necessities" in human development. Mill's openness to empirical and historical fact drives him to acknowledge that there have always been mixtures of the three different ways of thinking, from the earliest times until the present (Mill 1873: 30–31). The mix is subject to constant change. There were times when far more people thought theologically than tends to be the case today; there are people in all times who are more inclined toward abstract theory than others.

Mill's defense of Comte is moderate and persuasive, but he is so ready to compromise that he ends without the benefit of the Law with which he began. In his efforts to appease common sense, Comte's rigid yardstick has been exchanged for a flexible tape measure. It is clearly true that weighing, measuring, timing, are methods vastly more widespread and powerful today than in earlier days; but does this mean that all issues can be handled adequately by these methods? A "necessary law" might provide a positive answer, but a generalization on current fashions of thinking will not.

Comte, despite Mill's efforts, is thus left without any powerful argument for giving up the intuition that behind the phenomena there looms a world, one actively engaged within itself, quite apart from human experience or thought—a world with which human knowers can engage, too, as fellow participants in the ongoing processes of nature. Comte is reduced simply to pouring disdain on those who disagree. His intense admiration for modern science and the ways of modern scientists is evident—but that is all he offers. "Look!" one might paraphrase Comte's values-based critique, "They are not thinking *à la mode*! They are not using methods and assumptions that are 'up to the age'! They are not on board with Galileo and Newton!"

To these observations, those thus accused by Comte may cheerfully plead guilty. Their admiration for the methods of seventeenth- and eighteenth-century science may be more limited. These methods may have been impressive, the achievements stupendous, but are they worth any possible price? Specifically, are they worth reducing one's entire range of cognitive interests to phenomena alone? The answer to this question will not be given by simply repeating the call to "get modern." Perhaps the "modern" is itself part of the problem.

John Stuart Mill offered not only a mediating interpretation of Comte's Law of the Stages, he proposed also, as we saw, a compromise on the vexed question of whether—and, if so, how—to think about the material objects which seem to exist objectively around us in the great world of nature. His compromise, if acceptable, would not, after all, require one to give up cognitive interest in everything not *actually* sensed (the phenomena as directly presented); one could also retain a lively concern about *possibly* sensed phenomena (the phenomena as potentially presented) if one simply defines "material things," as *Permanent Possibilities of Sensation.*

This may at first seem a useful half-way point between the sheerest phenomenalism of present-moment-sensing and the admission of murky things-in-themselves. Berkeley sought that point in the "notion" of God, of whom we can have no *idea*, strictly speaking, but whose dynamic causal role (hypothesized on analogy with one's immediate awareness of one's own active spirit) can make sense of the regularities and stabilities actually found in perceiving, both in the present moment and across time. Mill, following virtually all phenomenalists since Hume, rejected the appeal to God; but he admitted that the question of the source of nature's experienced continuities and stabilities made important sense. To fill the explanatory void he offered his definition of material objects as "Permanent Possibilities of Sensation."

But can this compromise succeed? One question immediately rises: How shall we conceive of nonactual possibilities during their periods of nonactuality? If a possibility is "permanent," then does it have an actual space-time location of its own? If not, if it disappears from space and time altogether, how can it be conceived as "waiting there" for actualization during the time no perceiver is sensing it? It seems that the "permanence" of a "permanent possibility" necessarily demands some definite location in space and time. But if so, how can mere possibilities claim actual locations without also being somehow actual, or depending on something actual, during the time no one is actually sensing them?

Again, we know that during our absence, things change in regular ways. We do not always come back to exactly the same unaltered "permanent possibilities." If we leave a fire burning in the fireplace, for example, we may return to find what were logs changed to glowing coals. "Permanent" possibilities are hardly that. The log as a "permanent" possibility of our sensation must be allowed to be changed in our absence. By what? Mill's answer must invoke other interacting permanent possibilities. The fire, a process of rapid combustion, is something we sense. If we leave the room, it, like the log, the hearth, the room itself, becomes a mere "permanent possibility of sensation," and if we return right away, we can expect to sense it, once more, crackling and glowing as before. But how does one permanent possibility of sensation (fire) actually *act* on another permanent possibility of sensation (log) while these, on this theory, can be nothing but possibilities of our sensation and not objective actualities in interaction with each other? Must we conclude that nonactual possibilities can *work* and *suffer* changes? If not, there is no explanation for the regular transformation of logs to ashes, even while unobserved. But if so, what is it that actually works? What is it that actually undergoes changes?

It may be dangerous to invoke the name of Aristotle in the context of moderns self-consciously in rebellion against the heritage of ancient philosophy, but at least Aristotle squarely faced the problem of possibilities. He argued, as we saw in *Being and Value* (61), that only actualities can provide the basis for possibilities. Possibility depends on actuality. If one asks why something is possible, or what makes something possible, the answer must always be given in terms of some prior actuality. This fundamental insight is also behind Whitehead's Ontological Principle (Whitehead 1978:19). If there is the possibility of bread, for example, this is so only because somewhere there is actual dough—or dough ingredients—and the actual makings of a bake fire. Possibilities rest in, live on, are determined by, actualities. The attempt to think about a possibility that floats free, undefined by any reference to actuality, is at least as futile as the attempt to think about a sensation undefined by any reference to actual perception. Nonsense for nonsense, the former is even more outrageous nonsense, since the latter is only one of its specific instances.

How, then, does Mill's compromise proposal fare? If Permanent Possibilities of Sensation must be granted a definite space-time location, where "they" must be conceived as acting and interacting upon one another in regular, predictable ways; and if "they" can only be understood as possibilities at all because "they" are parasitical on some prior actuality that makes "them" possible and dependable; then the natural human yearning to know turns from the phenomena to the actualities themselves, behind and responsible for these possibilities of sensation. To speak as Mill does about Permanent Possibilities takes away—at least on first hearing—the implausible sound of phenomenalism (of the Humean sort). But it does so only at the cost of reintroducing the epistemological gap. Now the gap looms between the Actual and the Possible. How can we know what is really "possible" (and what really "impossible") for these Permanent Possibilities of Sensation? What constrains such Permanent Possibilities as they change in regular—Mill allows himself the word "necessary"—order across time? How shall we conceive of their interactions "behind the scenes," while we are not looking? And how, in principle, can we think and wonder where, by definition, sensation is absent? Mill has reopened all these questions with his willingness to speak of Permanent Possibilities. The compromise, it seems, has failed.

Perhaps Ernst Mach was wise when he rejected—forbade—compromise with trans-phenomenal entities like possibilities. In consequence, his position was purer and more forceful. Unfortunately, purity has its price. The price for a scientist, like Mach, was giving up his license to theorize beyond the given. Mach did it anyway, to a significant degree. He wrote extensively about the physiology of perception, for example, making generalizations about natural kinds of things, including frogs and birds and people.

A bird is organized for life in air, and a fish for life in water, but not the other way round. A frog snatches at flying insects that are his food but falls victim to this habit if he gets hold of a piece of moving cloth and is caught on the hook attached to it. Moths that fly toward light and color for the sake of self-preservation, may in the course of this generally appropriate behaviour finish up on the painted flowers on wallpaper, which do not nourish; or in a flame, which kills (Mach 1976: 79).

Strictly speaking, however, if particular sensations are all we can know, all such talk of natural kinds is illicitly theoretical. Sheer description of sensations needs to be supplemented with theory to get from a large collection of feathery sensations to the concept of a particular bird, and even more heavily supplemented to get from particular birds to "a bird" in general, organized for an identifiable sort of life and differing in significant, stable ways from "a fish." The implicit theory is that living organisms tend to act for self-preservation; the inductive theory is that wallpaper flowers do not nourish and that flame kills—these theories are many logical steps removed from sheer sensations. Mach, to do science at all, needed to make constant use of such theory. Not just scientists, but all of us in daily life also need to think and act in terms of theoretical natural-kind entities and common-sense inductive rules like these. But on Mach's positivist principles this amounts to engaging in theorizing without a license. They go beyond the given. They postulate more than can be sensed. They assume a deep structure to which experience will regularly conform. Without thinking in terms of such theoretical entities and without extending inductive confidence to what they will do—in other words, without going beyond description of phenomena—it would be impossible to find our way about in the world, either in act or in thought. There would be no "world" in the sense of an ordered *kosmos*, and neither science nor daily life could proceed.

Of course, therefore, Mach proceeded to theorize in these and other respects, though without acknowledging what he was doing and without receiving the blessing of his rigorous epistemological rules. These, however, were the same rules that required him to be highly skeptical of more obviously "theoretical" entities, like molecules and atoms. Mach went to considerable pains defending his refusal to credit such concepts as anything more than useful fictions, rather like spindles on which a wide array of otherwise unrelated sensations could be impaled and clustered. In so refusing, he was willing to accept the cost of minimizing theory, but most scientists were not. "Insight" into the inner workings of things is one of the prime interests of many scientists. While this need not legislate for all—it remains a value judgment whether it should or should not be considered an important goal to seek—Mach's principles could not (by the same token) be legislated for the rest of the scientific community. The young Einstein was at first eager to remain within the narrow limits prescribed by Mach, but in the end he opted for the still greater importance of theoretical insight. Even Mach, as we saw earlier, was gradually forced into increasingly unsuccessful rear-guard action as more and more of the "theoretical entities" of an earlier day became, even in his lifetime, the "invisibly submicroscopic realities" of the next. Had he lived into the Atomic Age, one wonders what the doughty Positivist would have said now. Would he have surrendered (as eventually he was forced to do regarding ultra-large molecules in Brownian motion) and finally have admitted atoms—capable of fission and fusion in hideously public ways—as, after all, invisible realities? Would he have revised his theoretical commitments in view of the premier weaponry of a postpositivist age? Or would he have preferred to stand by his epistemic norms (even though he could not in practice live up to them himself) rather than admit that there is anything we can legitimately contemplate that cannot in principle be equated to sensations? The answers to these questions about Mach's own personal responses are undiscoverable, hidden beneath considerations of temperament, commitment, and values.

Logical Positivism, in the paradigmatic form stated by A. J. Ayer, would not have hesitated over what the answer to the above questions *should*, at least, have been. The issue, Ayer insisted, is not a question of preference but of logic. If one is hoping to think about matters of fact, beyond empty tautologies, one *cannot* think about what cannot be given a "definition in use," that is, a translation into protocol statements referring to actual or possible sense experiences. That is all that putative factual statements *can* mean. Under the rules of significant language, there is no choice.

But there does remain a choice. There remains the prior choice of the logical rules themselves. The manifesto of the Vienna Circle and the missionary zeal of Ayer rested on a Machian (sensationalist) interpretation of Ludwig Wittgenstein's truth-functional analysis of significant language into either tautologies or atomic statements referring to atomic facts. The Logical Positivist interpretation, equating atomic facts with sense impressions, was itself never fully agreed to by Wittgenstein. And the earnest, solitary Wittgenstein, a reluctant captive for some years of his admirers, gradually grew away from his earlier puritanical attitudes towards meaning in language. In his notebooks, and in the series of thoughts he recorded but never published in his lifetime, Wittgenstein expressed his disillusionment with his naive earlier belief that a single exact statement of the essence of meaningful language could be made. For one thing, there is no single agreed understanding of "exactness."

"Inexact" is really a reproach, and "exact" is praise. And that is to say that what is inexact attains its goal less perfectly than what is more exact. Thus the point here is what we call "the goal". Am I inexact when I do not give our distance from the sun to the nearest foot, or tell a joiner the width of a table to the nearest thousandth of an inch?

No *single* ideal of exactness has been laid down; we do not know what we should be supposed to imagine under this head—unless you yourself lay down what is to be so called. But you will find it difficult to hit upon such a convention; at least any that satisfies you (Wittgenstein 1953: §88, 42ᵉ).

It is up to us to lay down our own norms of exactness, the later Wittgenstein muses, and to decide on our own goals for language and thought. Some of these goals will doubtless be the offering of predictions—what sense experiences to expect—and other goals will be reports on sense experiences received. But these goals, while frequent in daily life and crucial in the sciences, are only a few of the goals we may have with language. Wittgenstein invites consideration of the enormous varieties of meaning:

> But how many kinds of sentence are there? Say assertion, question, and command?—There are *countless* kinds: countless different kinds of use of what we call "symbols", "words", "sentences". And this multiplicity is not something fixed, given once for all; but new types of language, new language-games, as we may say, come into existence, and others become obsolete and get forgotten. (We can get a *rough picture* of this from the changes in mathematics.)
>   Here the term "language-*game*" is meant to bring into prominence the fact that the *speaking* of language is part of an activity, or a form of life.
>   Review the multiplicity of language-games in the following examples, and in others:
>   Giving orders, and obeying them—
>   Describing the appearance of an object, or giving its measurements—
>   Constructing an object from a description (a drawing)—
>   Reporting an event—
>   Speculating about an event—
>   Forming and testing a hypothesis—
>   Presenting the results of an experiment in tables and diagrams—
>   Making up a story; and reading it—
>   Play-acting—
>   Singing catches—
>   Guessing riddles—

Making a joke; telling it—
Solving a problem in practical arithmetic—
Translating from one language into another—
Asking, thanking, cursing, greeting, praying.

—It is interesting to compare the multiplicity of the tools in language and of the ways they are used, the multiplicity of kinds of word and sentence, with what logicians have said about the structure of language. (Including the author of the *Tractatus Logico-Philosophicus.*) (Wittgenstein 1953: §23, 12ᵉ).

Here, in his wry parenthetical conclusion, Wittgenstein disassociated himself from his own great contribution to the Logical Positivist arsenal against what Ayer called "unwarranted" philosophical issues. The goals we choose for language, the standards of exactness we demand, are our own decisions, based on our own interests and values. Not only is there a choice—our choice is the principal thing.

Since one must choose the logical standard to be applied— amounting to whether approbation will be withheld from any nontautological discourse not logically translatable into a set of sentences referring to sense contents— what might be some of the considerations that could incline us toward or against the Logical Positivist reduction of the epistemological gap? One important concern (for philosophers, at least) is the status of philosophical language itself, including the logical status of discussions of such important matters as theories of meaning and of crucial principles like the Logical Positivists' own principle of verifiability. Does the verification principle, once accepted, adequately allow for its own significance? It seems to assert something important: that the meaning of factual statements is equivalent to the methods one might use to verify them in sense perception. But how would one, in principle, verify such a claim in sense perception? One could not verify the verification principle by sight or touch or taste, or the like. The principle stands at a logical remove from such activities, talking *about* them and their relations to cognitive content, rather than translating into more *of* them. But if this is so, then (if we were to choose to adopt this logical theory) we would have to conclude that the crucial principle undergirding Logical Positivism is literally empty of significant content. The principle, if taken as informative, devours itself.

Interpreting the principle as the statement of a tautology remains the only significant alternative; and this was indeed the option adopted by Ayer when confronted by this anomaly. The difficulty is that if the principle is taken simply as a proposed definition, the stipulative and arbitrary character of such a definition of "meaning" becomes apparent. Ayer had said of logical truth in the first edition of *Language, Truth and Logic*, "The principles of logic and mathematics are true universally simply because we never allow them to be anything else" (Ayer 1946: 77). Thus the logic behind Logical Positivism, instead of lending itself to Hobbes' ideal of coercion, is exposed as a matter of judgment and will. In the introduction to the 1946 edition of his book, Ayer admits this inevitable consequence:

> It is indeed open to anyone to adopt a different criterion of meaning and so to produce an alternative definition which may very well correspond to one of the ways in which the word "meaning" is commonly used. And if a statement satisfied such a criterion, there is, no doubt, some proper use of the word "understanding" in which it would be capable of being understood (Ayer 1946: 16).

Coercion gone, then, judgment remains. Does it make for a good bargain to reduce the epistemological gap at the cost of everything else that would be eliminated by the principle of verification? As we saw, reasonable discussion in the language of ethics and aesthetics—value language generally—is a casualty of verificational analysis (Ferré 1961b: chap. 4). Such speech, if this logic is adopted, can be nothing more than expressions of emotion: more "utterance" than "discourse," more "ejaculation" than "conversation." I must not try to deal in any depth with the wisdom of this choice here. That may be left to the final volume of this trilogy, *Living and Value*, where ethics and other domains of value will take center stage. But it can at least be reckoned as a cost of the verification principle that value questions *qua* value questions (distinct from any factual component that may be involved) must be removed from the list of topics that can be rationally examined. In the absence of rational discussion, what remains in settling our disputes except conflict and coercion? And "coercion" now would not be exclusively of the polite logical kind. It would often come, rather, wearing the brutish face of which Hobbes was rightly so afraid.

Another consequence of adopting the logic of verificationism is extreme phenomenalism regarding the character of things in the world around us. Ayer's analysis of our language about material objects results in an impossibly complex translation, one that could never in fact be given, both for practical and for theoretical reasons. The practical difficulties of translating normal talk about tables and chairs and apples into long lists of atomic propositions referring to sense contents is obvious. Asking for an apple, we would hardly be able to utter our huge set of logically equivalent assertions—"Red here," "Round there," "Cool there," "Sweet here," etc.—before the fruit rotted! But this is "only" a practical difficulty, and one that no Logical Positivist would deny. All acknowledge that we must in practice be given license to use the "shorthand" discourse of unified physical objects, even though the logical gap between ordinary discourse and "logically exact" discourse is made huge to the point of inapplicability.

The theoretical difficulties are no less daunting. One rests on the problem—in principle—of ever completely referring to any material thing. The set of atomic propositions into which physical-object talk needs to be analyzed, on this logic, is literally infinite. There is no obvious limit to the sorts of experiences that might be obtained from just one sense organ, given slight changes in perspective or modification of bodily position or circumstances. Multiplying atomic facts gained from other sense organs, as well, merely compounds infinities. Far from offering an "exact" analysis, this logic results in inevitably incomplete analysis and thus imperfect reference. As Wittgenstein noted, the specification of "exact" itself needs assessment. So it is with goals, as well. Perhaps, if the goal is clarity of reference, it is more harmed than helped by such infinite and elusive approximations.

Ayer's defense of the complexity of his purportedly "exact" analysis, despite the availability of serviceably clear ordinary language about material objects, finally comes down to what he considers the one virtue that trumps all other difficulties: adopting this style of logical analysis, he declares, is prophylaxis against the hidden dangers of metaphysics. As noted above, Ayer acknowledges that those who use the English language "have no difficulty, in practice, in identifying the situations which determine the truth or falsehood of such simple statements as 'This is a table,' or 'Pennies are round' " (Ayer 1946: 68). But he worries lest people, "unaware of the hidden logical complexity of such statements," may consequently, "be led to adopt some metaphysical belief, such as the belief in the existence of material substances or invisible substrata." (Ayer 1946: 68). In other words, Ayer's basic value judgment, which he offers as his bottom line justification for adopting even a cumbersome and flawed logical approach that would, if adopted, eliminate the possibility of metaphysics is . . . that it would be *good* to eliminate the possibility of metaphysics! As he sees it, "the utility of the philosophical definition which dispels such confusions is not to be measured by the apparent triviality of the sentences which it translates" (Ayer 1946: 68). Rather, its "utility" will be found in its achieving—he hopes—the goal which to him is evidently more important than clarity or simplicity: namely, the elimination of the gap between independently existing "material substances" and what we can possibly know. "Justifying" a problematic goal by simply reiterating it, however, leaves the unpersuaded unmoved.

There is yet more reason for caution in opting for Ayer's logic, even if the avoidance of metaphysics is an unquestioned goal. Ayer has not, despite all, managed to avoid the metaphysical problems posed by the concept of "permanent possibilities." We first noticed these in connection with Mill's efforts at a compromise between "things in themselves" and pure phenom-enalism-of-the-moment. Ayer's analysis of all statements about objects into reports of "actual or *possible* sense contents," however, leads him directly into Mill's briar patch of metaphysical puzzles. He is explicit about his embrace of Mill's formula: "An outline of what I take to be the correct view of these matters was given by John Stuart Mill when he spoke of physical bodies as "permanent possibilities of sensation" (Ayer 1940: 244). Accepting Mill's general account, Ayer simply wants to provide a better description of the origins of our expectations that clusters of these perma-nent possibilities will continue to be experienced in mutual association with one another. In the course of this description, he compounds his metaphysi-cal difficulties by speaking repeatedly, without explanation (or apparent embarrassment), about the way in which sense data constantly come sud-denly and fleetingly into existence and others suddenly cease to exist. Here is an example:

At the present moment I am aware of a visual sense-field the contents of which I may describe by saying that I am perceiving, among other things, a table covered with papers, and beyond the table a chair, and beyond the chair a section of a book-case fastened to a wall. If I now turn aside to look out of the window on my right, these particular sense-data cease to exist, and in their place I obtain a new set of visual sense-data which I may describe by saying that I am perceiving a garden fringed with trees, and beyond the trees the roof of a cottage, and in the distance a thickly wooded hill. And if I execute a further movement, I shall find that these sense-data too will cease to exist, and that others will take their place. But suppose that at some stage in a process of this kind I reverse the direction of my movements. In that case I shall find that this fragment of my sense-history repeats itself, but in a reverse order. I do not mean by this that I shall sense numerically the same sense-data as I sensed before; for that is excluded by the conventions of the sense-datum language. But there will be a general resemblance between these two sections of my experience; so that I shall find not merely that individual sense-data are closely similar to ones that I sensed before, but that they occur in similar contexts. In the end I shall have a sense-field whose similarity to the first will make it proper for me to describe it by saying that I am again perceiving a table, a chair and a book-case, related as before; but whereas, in the previous case, the sense-field which I described in this way preceded the sense-field which I described by referring to a garden fringed with trees, in the case of their counterparts this order will be reversed (Ayer 1940: 247–48).

The question *why* these stabilities and regularities occur, and can be counted on to occur, is addressed only in Mill's way: by referring vaguely to stable "possibilities" again. Suppose a physical object has been moved while unobserved. Is it, Ayer asks, the "same" object? He answers in the affirmative on the "assumption that one could have 'traced its path' through a series of partially overlapping sense-fields, of which any two adjacent members would have been directly resemblant" (Ayer 1940: 251–52). But why do we allow ourselves to make such an assumption? "[This] assumption is grounded on the fact that in many cases this 'possibility of sensation' is actually realized" (Ayer 1940: 252). Yes, in many cases the possibilities we expect are realized—but when they are, *why* is this the case? And when they are not realized, *why* not? Were they really possibilities if they were not realized? Did something change "them" while "they" were still unrealized? What was that something? It turns out that as soon as Ayer tries to get beyond extreme phenomenalism, by invoking "permanent possibilities," the dreaded Thing in Itself, and with it the epistemological gap, threaten to invade even the inner sanctum where Ayer's logical weapons are being forged.

In the end, Ayer found it necessary to abandon his earlier phenomenalist position. Decades later, after extended discussion, he finally surrendered it:

We must conclude, then, if my reasoning is correct, that the phenomenalist's programme cannot be carried through. Statements about physical objects are not formally translatable into statements about sense-data. . . . That phenomenalism has commanded so strong an allegiance has been due not to its being intrinsically plausible but rather to the fact that the introduction of sense-data appeared to leave no other alternative open. It has been assumed that since statements about physical objects can be verified or falsified only through the occurrence of sense-data, they must somehow be reducible to statements about sense-data. This is a natural assumption to make, but the result of our examining it has been to show that it is false (Ayer 1956: 129).

In place of phenomenalism, a more chastened Ayer recommended, on the prestigious model of science, that we consider the world of objects to be theoretical entities. "One way of expressing this conclusion would be to say that in referring as we do to physical objects we are elaborating a theory with respect to the evidence of our senses. The statements which belong to the theory transcend their evidence in the sense that they are not merely re-descriptions of it. The theory is richer than anything that could be yielded by an attempt to reformulate it at the sensory level" (Ayer 1956: 132). But this assumes a model of science freed from the very prohibitions against speculation "transcending" sensation—"transcendence" that Mach and the

Positivists would have most fiercely opposed. Theory has been returned to its place of honor. Perhaps only experience can *verify* theories, but theories are again allowed to *mean* more than can be translated into reports of sense experiences.

The reductionist strategy for coping with the epistemological gap proved a failure. It simply did not work to pretend that all that is interesting to know is what we can touch and see and hear. There are depths—strongly and widely intuited—behind our powers of perception. These depths, too, call for cognition. This does not mean that experience, properly understood, is unimportant. The great value of the extreme empiricist efforts in recent times has been to refocus attention on the utter importance of bringing all knowledge claims to accountability in experience. To this theme I shall return in Chapter 8, below. But reductionism is not a viable epistemological strategy. In the end, sense experience is too tightly bound to theory—and both are too intimately involved with the intuitions and urgencies of daily life—to win by itself the prize of knowing.

6

WEBBING THE GAP

A central effort of the main, Positivist, line of reductionists, as we saw, was to describe knowable objects as nothing but logical constructions from sense contents. Assertions about things, other persons, and one's own self were to be completely exhausted by "definitions in use" reporting on sense data. This would be done by protocol sentences directly denoting the clear, mutually independent atomic facts, for example, "Red there," "Round here," that are supposed to make up basic perceptual awareness. Such awareness, reductionists assumed throughout, must be *completely nontheoretical.* This is necessary if it is to serve as the neutral foundation for theory, that is, if it is to qualify for the material of construction.

The coherentist epistemological tradition takes rejection of this basic assumption as its point of departure. According to the coherentists, perceiving is itself a variety of thinking, always somewhere on the spectrum of knowing. It is not nontheoretical. And since it is immersed in thought—thus highly subject to error—sense experience is not properly described as coming in the individually clear, free-standing building blocks required for atomic facts.

More will be said about this later, but an initial overview would show that this alternative epistemological tradition stresses the vagueness of primitive, ground-level experience. Gradually waking from a deep sleep, for example, or coming out from under anaesthesia, are experiences that give adults the chance to relive what infant perception of the world must be like: a blur of undiscriminated feelings, in which sensations internal to the body are not yet sorted out from sensations externally caused—the cramp in the leg not clearly untangled from the pressure of sheets and blankets, the dull headache not separated from sounds pulsing through the room (or is it the skull?), residue of dream not differentiated from images formed by half-opened eyes. Here, where consciousness first starts to flicker up from the depths of unconsciousness, we find nothing like Aristotle's neatly discriminated "special sensibles" or Hume's clearly distinguished "impressions of sensation" and "impressions of reflection." Indeed, there seems nothing to correspond even to the still more basic Humean distinction between "ideas" and "impressions." All these classifications—so valued within most of the epistemic tradition—are added later, in full light of day, after a bracing cup of tea or other stimulant to wakeful consciousness. Even my description of the groggy waker's situation required importing concepts and theories, based on learned language ("leg," "sheets," "skull," "sounds," "room," "eyes," etc.) and parasitically, therefore, on presupposing wide-awake adult analysis of discriminated experience. But to the groggy waker in this example, and to infants, these fine distinctions and neat categorizations are not available. They only become available when the waker wakes enough to take thought, or when the infant gradually learns to sort out arms and legs and lips from bedding and milk and nipples, and above all learns concepts that empower discrimination. The "elements" of experience therefore seem more products of a learned process than true starting points.

This, for the coherentist epistemological tradition, is not necessarily to deny that perception provides vital input to reality. But this will be an input so entangled with theoretical elements, learned distinctions, memory, and imagination, that the so-called epistemological "gap" is nothing to be feared. The input can never be sundered from its meaning. There is no need to fear an abyss between human thinking and what it purports to be about. Indefinitely many strands of thought will firmly bridge the distance between the known and the real. What the "real" means, of course, and how "knowing" should be described, will be a matter of debate, even within the tradition.

THE COHERENTIST PEDIGREE

If Aristotle is the ancient empiricist patron of the tradition that lies behind sense-datum analysis of knowing, Plato is the fountainhead of the coherentist alternative. Plato's depiction of experience would never lend itself—as Aristotle's, for better or for worse, eventually did—to taking raw sensory data as clear, distinct, atomic facts for the logical construction of knowledge.

Sensory images, as we saw in Chapter 2, are for Plato at the very bottom of his divided line. The flickering, deceptive shadows are at the very edge of total unintelligibility. Not vivacious and forceful "impressions" undergirding subsequent "ideas" (in Hume's way), they gain for Plato, rather, whatever cognitive strength they may acquire from being bound together in regular ways as aspects of supposed entities, the "things" of belief. The wretched prisoners in the Parable of the Cave gradually develop these beliefs as unifying hypotheses, after mental effort, in order to make sense of the repeated patterns in the shadow play they are forced to watch on the walls of their great cage. Theory is all that gives sensory images any intelligibility whatever. One might say that the first task of mind is to sort the blurry welter of mere images into types and kinds, then to construct their preliminary meanings by coherently unifying them.

These preliminary meanings by themselves remain exceedingly unsatisfactory, since the "things" we may believe in, once we have reached this stage of coherence, are individually quite unintelligible—they are just brute facts—until they are further related to one another under general unifying rules of empirical regularity. These empirical rules, which themselves need further interpretation through formal laws, especially mathematical formulations, give (and in turn receive) intelligibility through unification in a hierarchy of ever more-inclusive patterns of coherence. At the very top, Plato's ideal of perfect knowing is expressed as the Form of Forms, the Form of the Good, that brings everything into perfect (though ineffable) coherence.

There is no need for me here to repeat, even briefly, the narrative of Chapter 3 in which I traced the powerful play of Platonic tradition in the centuries between ancient and modern times. Aristotle-based empirical views became stronger late in the period, but we should not forget that for Western thought, roughly four-fifths of the time between Plato's death and Hobbes' birth was dominantly Platonic in inspiration.

Many Moderns, especially the English founders, tended to continue and amplify the late-medieval Aristotelian tradition, at least regarding trust in the senses as foundational, but this was not the case for equally well-pedigreed founders on the Continent, especially Descartes and Spinoza.

Descartes mistrusted raw sense data. He would have scoffed at the notion that sense contents could be taken as atomic facts. Nothing, he argued, was less clear and distinct. Only the clarities of the mathematical characters woven through experience could qualify for knowing. Only they are worthy of being affirmed. To believe anything else about experience is to misuse our free will.

Benedict Spinoza, a tough-minded modern whose life and metaphysics were outlined in *Being and Value* (145–46), saw in the *passivity* shown in the process of merely receiving sensation *weakness* rather than a strong foundation. Primitive experience, Spinoza held, is confused. It rises through physiological changes in our bodies which are ultimately correlated with mental events. As long as our sensory images are related merely by the local happenings of mechanical causes, they will be confused and meaningless. We develop empirical concepts (rather as Hobbes thought) by the repetition of similar physical events, which we remember and name. But all this is highly contingent, simply a matter of what happens to happen to our bodies.

Whereas Hobbes and the tradition following him stopped there, Spinoza continued to describe what makes real knowing possible. There are universal characters of things, geometrical necessities of space and time that all bodies are subject to. Inasmuch as they are necessary and universal, all intelligent bodies will have these concepts in common. And to the degree that we organize our thoughts in terms of such necessary and universal concepts, to that degree our thoughts will approximate necessary truth. Since everything that happens in this universe is necessary, according to Spinoza, there must be at least a tiny degree of truth in every thought, however generally inadequate. The more central to our thinking we make the great necessities, the more unified and coherent our ideas will become. The one and only perfectly coherent system of thought would be God's. Thus the closer to coherence we approach, that is, the more genuinely active our minds become in organizing our beliefs under the necessities that determine the universe, the closer we come to thinking God's thoughts. This is an impossible goal, since our bodies and minds are finite, but it sets a standard: the more coherent our thoughts, the more adequate they will be; the more primitive, "raw," and "given," the more incoherent ("confused") they will be. Uninterpreted sense data, on this account, rank as least of all cognitive authorities, not as the greatest.

Immanuel Kant's enormous influence is too large to be confined to any single tradition. He can be claimed by the Positivists, because of his stinging rebuke to those metaphysicians who would try to gain knowledge of ultimate reality beyond, or independent of, the possible reach of experience. Indeed, as we saw in Chapter 4, he was the one to seal shut the epistemological trap sprung by Hume. Viewed from this angle, Kant is a step on the way to A. J. Ayer. But in the context of this chapter, there is no doubt that his influence is huge within the coherentist tradition as well.

The key to Kant's "Copernican Revolution," after all, is the centrality of mind in the knowing process. Sensation itself is not prior to the categories of mind but is inescapably the joint product of contingent content and necessary formal character. As we saw earlier, space and time are themselves the universally necessary forms of all intuitions of particular sense contents. Without particular sense contents, on the one hand, we would be left with a mere "manifold," impossible to imagine without any definite characters. Without the a priori forms of intuition, our necessary modes of reception, on the other hand, we could receive nothing at all. Actual sense experience, therefore, is completely shot through with mentality, even at the lowest level of reception. Above this level, the a priori categories of understanding are ingredient, as well, giving us causality, unity, substantiality, and all the rest of what must be presupposed for the possibility of experiencing a world.

Thus Kant, viewed in this context, is one of the principal founders of the modern tradition insisting that sense data do not come in theory-neutral atomic facts. Experience, he proclaimed, is the first *product* of understanding. It is not raw material but already partially finished goods.

In the context of this tradition, we can understand more easily the thought of Francis Herbert Bradley on knowledge, truth, and reality.

F. H. BRADLEY

To enter Bradley's epistemological arena with a minimum of metaphysical preparation, I shall start at the end of his large book, *Appearance and Reality* (1893), where he discusses his "infallible criterion." In taking a strong infallibilist position he does not think himself alone or even exceptional. Everyone who judges at all must assume, wittingly or not, a similar infallibility.

> Even the extreme of theoretical scepticism is based on some accepted idea about truth and fact. It is because you are sure as to some main feature of truth or reality, that you are compelled to doubt or to reject special truths which are offered you. But, if so, you stand on an absolute principle, and, with regard to this, you claim, tacitly or openly, to be infallible (Bradley 1893: 454).

The difference between Bradley and his opponents, however, is that his assumption of the infallible posture is, he firmly believed, appropriately grounded in a principle that is really infallible: namely, the principle that logical contradictions make no sense, cannot be thought, and therefore cannot be believed or tolerated. In this he is more impatient with contradiction than was G. W. F. Hegel (*Being and Value*, 205–12), who saw opportunity for dialectical growth in conflict. Bradley accepted (insisted) that clashing elements within a system would give way to harmonization in higher synthesis, as Hegel did, but his attitude toward finding contradiction was less welcoming than Hegel's.

Taking firm hold of this absolute, infallible principle, Bradley used it as a scythe to mow down all the ordinary elements of human thought and experience as unthinkable for a fully rigorous theory of reality. I showed in *Being and Value* (215–17) how he found contradictions in such would-be concepts as quality, relation, space, time, motion, change, and cause. This makes all such putative concepts unknowable—unthinkable—and thus rules out a fortiori thinking that they are part of reality.

Such epistemological negations make it possible, therefore, to assert confidently of reality that it is *not* characterized (as such) by these appearances.

You can hardly take the position of admitting any and every nonsense to be truth, truth absolute and entire, at least so far as you know. For, if you think at all so as to discriminate between truth and falsehood, you will find that you cannot accept open self-contradiction. Hence to think is to judge, and to judge is to criticize, and to criticize is to use a criterion of reality. And surely to doubt this would be mere blindness or confused self-deception. But, if so, it is clear that, in rejecting the inconsistent as appearance, we are applying a positive knowledge of the ultimate nature of things. Ultimate reality is such that it does not contradict itself; here is an absolute criterion. And it is proved absolute by the fact that, either in endeavouring to deny it, or even in attempting to doubt it, we tacitly assume its validity (Bradley 1893: 120).

From this forced conclusion about reality, it is a short step to a more positive statement of the same result. As Bradley puts it, "[The] real is individual. It is one in the sense that its positive character embraces all differences in an inclusive harmony" (Bradley 1893: 123).

It is clear why something excluding contradictions must be internally *harmonious*, and why something completely harmonious must be integral or *individual*. But why should there be any *"differences"* at all in the one inclusive individual that makes up reality? Bradley's answer is, in short, "Where else *could* experienced differences *be*, except somehow in reality?" No matter how defective, appearances, after all, really do appear. There is nowhere they could appear except within reality. For this reason, the unified, noncontradictory reality we infallibly know to exist must be the repository and harmonizer of whatever, seen out of ultimate context, clashes and contradicts.

Reality is one in this sense that it has a positive nature exclusive of discord, a nature which must hold throughout everything that is to be real. Its diversity can be diverse only so far as not to clash, and what seems otherwise anywhere cannot be real. And, for the other side, everything which appears must be real. Appearance must belong to reality, and it must therefore be concordant and other than it seems. The bewildering mass of phenomenal diversity must hence somehow be at unity and self-consistent; for it cannot be elsewhere than in reality, and reality excludes discord (Bradley 1893: 123).

One last enormously important positive thing can be said about reality. It not only must be able to *contain all* appearance, but also it can be *nothing apart from* appearance. Here we recognize a Berkeleian theme that becomes dominant in Bradley. With Berkeley he argues that to be is to be perceived or to perceive. We can never think or imagine anything apart from or besides experience of a sort like ours. All the experience we have is appearance, since it is spatio-temporal, qualified, etc.; all those features, as we saw, are thoroughly shot through with contradiction. Therefore reality cannot be thought or imagined to be other than a harmonization of contradictory appearance.

> We perceive, on reflection, that to be real, or even barely to exist, must be to fall within sentience. Sentient experience, in short, is realty, and what is not this is not real. We may say, in other words, that there is no being or fact outside of that which is commonly called psychical existence. Feeling, thought, and volition . . . are all the material of existence, and there is no other material, actual or even possible (Bradley 1893: 127).

The value of unity has played an enormously powerful role, so far, in my exposition of Bradley's views. We moved from epistemological integrity, guarded by the infallible Law of Contradiction, in which division or conflict guarantees unthinkability, to metaphysical oneness, in which all apparent conflicts ultimately must be harmonized by the great sentient, all-encompassing Individual that Bradley called the Absolute. Given the necessary ground in metaphysics, we may now move back again to epistemology, where we find that, for Bradley, degrees of wholeness in thought vary with degrees of reality, and degrees of truth will be marked by degrees of comprehensive coherence.

Thought, Bradley notes, is essentially ideal, that is, a matter of ideas which reflect but are different from the realities to which they refer. For all things, he points out, substantial existence ("thatness") and qualitative characterization ("whatness") are inseparably intertwined.

> That anything should be, and should yet be nothing in particular, or that a quality should not qualify and give a character to anything, is obviously impossible. If we try to get the 'that' by itself, we do not get it, for either we have it qualified, or else we fail utterly. If we try to get the 'what' by itself, we find at once that it is not all. It points to something beyond, and cannot exist by itself and as a bare adjective. Neither of these aspects, if you isolate it, can be taken as real, or indeed in that case is itself any longer. They are distinguishable only and are not divisible (Bradley 1893: 143).

But the nature of thinking is to separate the two. "Without an idea there is no thinking, and an idea implies the separation of content from existence"

(Bradley 1893: 143). In judgments, when we say of a subject that it is characterized by a predicate ("S is P"), the "whatness" is intended to be reunited with the "thatness" of the subject. "Judgement is essentially the re-union of two sides, 'what' and 'that', provisionally estranged. But it is the alienation of these aspects in which thought's ideality consists" (Bradley 1893: 145).

A true judgment is one in which there are no contradictions, in which everything harmonizes, and in which mind can finally come to rest, not driven on by conflicts. As Bradley puts it:

> Truth is the object of thinking, and the aim of truth is to qualify existence ideally. Its end, that is, is to give a character to reality in which it can rest. Truth is the predication of such content as, when predicated, is harmonious, and removes inconsistency and with it unrest (Bradley 1893: 145).

This means that there can be—must be—degrees of truth, since there are more or less harmonious judgments, wider and narrower ideal qualifications of existence. A system of thought that interprets coherently a vast number of particulars offers a wider harmony and much more opportunity for "rest" than a low order particular judgment that presents itself as unconnected to anything else. The low order judgment may be partially true, so far as it goes, but by itself it provides very little intellectual rest. It is less true than the wider system that offers more harmony, more integration.

This principle allows Bradley to state why sense experience, for all its submersion in appearance, is more true than fleeting daydreams. Bradley wants to avoid two extremes, both errors.

> There is a view which takes, or attempts to take, sense-perceptions as the one known reality. And there is a view which endeavours, on the other side, to consider appearance in time as something indifferent. It tries to find reality in the world of insensible thought. Both mistakes lead, in the end, to a like false result, and both imply, and are rooted in, the same principle of error (Bradley 1893: 334).

The common error is the supposition that "thatness" (existence) and "whatness" (idea) can be separated. The first, empiricist, error takes sense experience as though it were a reliable guide to the existence of the Real, apart from or prior to theory; the second, rationalist, error supposes that the Real has nothing to do with Appearance. But if the Absolute is made up of nothing but appearance, harmonized by whatever modifications are required to achieve consistency, then neither the empiricist's naive acceptance of sense perception nor the rationalist's disdain of it will do. Therefore, even though temporal existence, totally laced with appearance as it is, cannot *be* reality, it is nevertheless an essential factor *in* reality.

> And to suppose that mere thought without facts could either be real, or could reach to truth, is evidently absurd. The series of events is, without doubt, necessary for our knowledge, since this series applies the one source of all ideal content. We may say, roughly and with sufficient accuracy, that there is nothing in thought, whether it be matter or relations, except that which is derived from perception (Bradley 1893: 336).

Everything in thought is derived from perception! Perhaps there is no need to be astonished by this echo of Aristotle and the empiricist creed in Bradley, since all experience is essential to the Absolute. Yet it is surprising to find such a statement in this coherentist context.

"Raw" sense contents, of course, despite offering limited truths, are relatively low in the epistemic hierarchy. They are not lowest. Lower yet is the "mere thought" of something, like the mere thought of an imaginary dollar. The perception of a real dollar is a limited truth, but it is far more comprehensive in its epistemic status than the flitting thought of an imaginary one. Why?

> The dollar, merely thought of or imagined, is comparatively abstract and void of properties. But the dollar, verified in space, has got its place in, and is determined by, an enormous construction of things. And to suppose that the concrete context of these relations in no sense qualifies its inner content, or that this qualification is a matter of indifference to thought, is quite indefensible (Bradley 1893: 337).

The sensed world, despite its immersion in appearance, is a tightly networked world. This is why science is possible. Science works within the connections, and discovers more connections as it integrates individual verified perceptions into wider and wider empirically relevant laws and theories that provide coherence—and thereby truth—to our understanding of reality.

This result is important for a coherentist position, since it makes a positive (coherent) connection with scientific observation. But it should not be overstated. The idle imagination is epistemically lower than verified perception, for the reasons stated, but not all imaginations are idle. Bradley adds quickly: "There is imagination which is higher, and more true, and most emphatically more real, than any single fact of sense" (Bradley 1893: 338). This is the disciplined speculative imagination that provides the basis for comprehensive, wholeness-making theory in which single facts take on new (and transformed) significance. These wider truths must also appear, since the

Absolute is nothing but appearance unified consistently, but they need not appear under the gross limitations of sense perception.

> To be nearer the central heart of things is to dominate the extremities more widely; but it is not to appear there except incompletely and partially through a sign, an unsubstantial and a fugitive mode of expression. Nothing anywhere, not even the realized and solid moral will, can either be quite real, as it exists in time, or can quite appear in its own essential character (Bradley 1893: 338).

With this warning, however, we are brought back sharply to earth. Bradley has shown how on his approach there can be degrees of truth, including sense perception, depending on wider and more unified modes of ideation; but, as he has built his case, the vector toward complete unification cannot in principle point to ultimate truth or perfect knowing. There is something internal to his doctrine of thought that makes the drive to knowledge and truth ultimately self-destructive.

Thinking, as Bradley earlier declared, is essentially ideation. And ideas, no matter how comprehensive and systematic, are different from the existences to which they refer. Were they not different, they would no longer be ideas *of* something, they would *be* the something itself. Thought has a literally (logically) impossible dream: namely, to unite everything, beyond the goadings of contradiction, in a degree of truth that is completely harmonious and worthy of final rest. But this can be done only by following the vector of inclusiveness all the way to the limit condition. By definition thought is finite, since ideas are only part of the ultimate whole, but thought moves toward greater truth by transcending whatever finite state it has reached in an act of self-transcendence.

> And by pushing this self-transcendence to the uttermost point, thought attempts to find there consummation and rest. The subject, on the one hand, is expanded until it is no longer what is given. It becomes the whole universe, which presents itself and which appears in each given moment with but part of its reality. It grows into an all-inclusive whole, existing somewhere and somehow, if we only could perceive it. But on the other hand, in qualifying this reality, thought consents to a partial abnegation. It has to recognize the division of the 'what' from the 'that', and it cannot so join these aspects as to get rid of mere ideas and arrive at actual reality. For it is in and by ideas only that thought moves and has life (Bradley 1893: 147).

Thought, knowledge, truth, are all confined within the domain of ideation; but ideas cannot be identified with reality. Suppose, just as an ultimate thought experiment, that thought attained final truth, a complete harmonization of all lesser truths in a perfect ideal synthesis. This would still be inadequate to its dream, since the one remaining synthesis between idea and existence would not—and, as long as truth remains moored to thought, *could not*—have been achieved. Truth does remain always moored to thought, however. It is a property of ideas, and if it ceases to be ideational, it loses its character as truth and is transformed into reality.

Bradley himself pronounces the fatal sentence on truth and thought as it struggles toward its inherent goal.

> Thought, in its actual processes and results, cannot transcend the dualism of the 'that' and the 'what'. . . . I mean that in no judgement are the subject and predicate the same. In every judgement the genuine subject is reality, which goes beyond the predicate and of which the predicate is an adjective. And I would urge first that, in desiring to transcend this distinction, thought is aiming at suicide (Bradley 1893: 148).

The desire to transcend all distinctions, differences, and otherness is essential to thought; but the status of thought as distinct from, different from, other than existence is essential, too. There is thus a drive to self-destruction within the heart of thinking, truth, and knowing as such.

The problem comes down, finally, to the poisoning of truth and thought by relations. Thought is essentially relational. It tries to relate the subject and the predicate of judgments, and to relate them in as complex and complete a way as will do the subject matter justice. Success in this effort is truth. But truth, in consequence, can never get beyond the relational mode in which it is set. "The relational form is a compromise on which thought stands, and which it develops. It is an attempt to unite differences which have broken out of the felt totality" (Bradley 1893: 159). Relations are incompatible with unity. The opposite of "absolute" is "relative." Just so, the Absolute excludes, by its very nature, relations. There is diversity in the Absolute, since there is diversity in appearance, but this must be diversity beyond the level of relativity, through which all unities fall apart.

Only deep feeling can give us finite persons a taste of such diversity—without the clarity that can support relations—might be like. Recall again the example of someone coming up out of anaesthesia. In such feeling-states there may be great diversity but nothing distinct enough even to relate. As Bradley acknowledges, "It may be said truly that in feeling, if you take it low enough down, there is plurality with unity and without contradiction. There being no relations and no terms, and yet, on the other side, more than bare simplicity, we experience a concrete whole as actual fact" (Bradley 1893: 90). It is this, on a much higher level, that the Absolute's experience must resemble, if such experience is to contain and harmonize all the diversity of the universe without the introduction of relations and qualities, as such.

But the consequences for knowing, if this is accepted, are bleak. Even the Absolute would not have knowledge, since knowing entails separation of ideas from existence. The Absolute would "transcend" knowing and truth, because knowing and truth are ultimately on a suicide mission. And if relations are inherently poisonous to truth or knowing, it is hard to know what "coherence" can mean, since traditionally, on theories of coherence, harmonies are built by *relating* elements of a system to each other. Literally to leave relations behind spells the death not only of truth and knowledge but evidently of coherence as well.

BRAND BLANSHARD

A more down-to-earth interpretation of coherentism was offered by the redoubtable Yale professor, Brand Blanshard (1892–1987), whose thought I have long respected—and the memory of whose friendship I warmly treasure. His two-volume masterpiece, *The Nature of Thought* (1939), was one of the first major pieces of philosophy by a living contemporary I was required as an undergraduate to study. For years after entering the profession, I had the pleasure of engaging him in philosophical dialogue (Ferré 1971: 95–100; Ferré 1980: 908–29; Ferré 1990: 122–39).

Blanshard agreed with Bradley in central respects. Metaphysically, he accepted idealism. Epistemologically, he agreed that truth comes in degrees, and that its maximum is to be found in a unique, perfectly inclusive system, "namely the system in which everything real and possible is coherently included" (Blanshard 1939: vol. 2, 276). But quite unlike Bradley, Blanshard had no problem accepting relations. As he wrote toward the end of his life, "I cannot follow Bradley into his final mysticism, in which all relations including that between thought and its object are transcended, a position in which coherence itself becomes meaningless" (Blanshard 1980b: 599–600). Without relations there are no distinctions, without distinctions no propositions, without propositions no inferential connections, and without inferential connections no system of coherently related, mutually necessitating elements.

Blanshard defined coherence in terms of such elements. "Fully coherent knowledge would be knowledge in which every judgement entailed, and was entailed by, the rest of the system" (Blanshard 1939: vol. 2, 264). This is, of course an ideal, doubtless an impossible ideal for human knowers. The closest we come to achieving it is in geometry, and that is far from perfect (Blanshard 1939: vol. 2, 265). In a fully ideal system, everything (including sensory properties) would be included in the whole, and that not only would the whole entail every part but also every part would entail the whole as well.

This most stringent requirement, that each part, taken alone, would imply the whole system, rested for the early Blanshard on the view that internal relations would be so rich in every element that each flower in any crannied wall—if it could be known completely—would allow unpacking the universe-system in its entirety. But coherence can be genuine even without this extra tightness of part-to-whole entailment. We certainly would never expect to deduce all the other propositions in a mathematical system from any single proposition in isolation (Blanshard 1939: vol. 2, 265, n. 1).

I think I can see why [some early coherentists] should have gone further in their thought of the ideal. They conceived of the universe as organic and even superorganic, a system in which the influence of the whole so permeated every part that the integration was complete. One could see any part as it really was only as one saw its unique part in the whole, which involved, of course, that the grasp of the whole was implicated in the grasp of the part. The process was somewhat like that of the modern comparative anatomist who, given a piece from the jawbone of a brontosaurus, will reconstruct the skeleton as a whole. I cannot, now at any rate, go this far myself, since I do not think the internal relations theory can be carried all the way through (Blanshard 1980b: 598).

It is enough, for Blanshard, that A. C. Ewing's statement of a more limited ideal be adopted instead: viz, "a coherent system is 'a set of propositions in which each one stands in such a relation to the rest that it is logically necessary that it should be true if all the rest are true, and such that no set of propositions within the whole set is logically independent of all propositions in the remainder of the set'" (Ewing 1934: 229–30). This is more than demanding enough. If we remember that this ideal is ultimately to be applied to an all-inclusive system—one that integrates everything "real or possible"—then logical necessity of this sort is doubtless forever out of reach for us. But at least it is a worthy goal, against which lesser systems can be tested.

On the question of how we can test for truth, Blanshard is quite uncompromising. In the last resort, coherence is the only test we have. It may appear at first that there are other candidates for testing truth: (1) authority, (2) mystical revelation, (3) self-evidence, and (4) correspondence; but on closer examination, Blanshard argues, all these turn out either to be no tests at all or to depend finally on coherence. I shall summarize his arguments as follows:

(1) The appeal to authority as test of truth is easy to explode. Does one defer to one's authority *for* reasons or *without* reasons? If the former, then it

is those *reasons* that are really functioning as the test of truth, and the appeal is not, after all, to authority. If the latter, then in consistency one must allow anyone else to embrace any other authority without reasons, even authorities that contradict one's own. But this is completely self-destructive of every authority's claim to truth. Why accept such consistency if it leads to these self-destructive consequences? Blanshard's answer is that refusal to accept consistency is no less self-destructive since it would mean that one's claim for the special status of one's authority would be compatible with the denial of that claim. Authority is no test for truth.

(2) What of mystical insight? Blanshard sets up another fork: is this "insight" *inexpressible* or *expressible*? If the former, then (quite literally) there is nothing more to be said. The so-called insight does not venture any claim at all and is thereby "condemned to inadequacy" (Blanshard 1939: vol. 2, 222). But if the latter, then this alleged test of truth frequently has given backing to diametrically opposed claims. Plotinus, as we saw in *Being and Value* (82–84), a pagan philosopher, was assured by mystical insight that the Ultimate must be One, without the slightest hint of diversity; but Christian mystics (Blanshard cites Richard of St. Victor) have received equally firm assurance by the same test that God is a Trinity. A test of truth that supports mutually contradictory claims is no test at all. If we are to sort out which mystic insights are the more reliable or the more likely to be true, we need to apply further tests. What might these involve?

(3) Might self-evidence offer such a further independent test? This seems more plausible, though surely not in the case of contradictory mystic revelations which glory in their status as "beyond reason." Instead, the home territory of self-evidence as test of truth is in axiomatic systems, like mathematics or geometry, and in the principles of logic. But here again the test seems not to function as it should. It might have seemed otherwise in the days before alternative geometries and arithmetics. Between Euclidean and non-Euclidean geometries there lies freedom of choice, depending on convenience, or depending on the observational results stimulated by physical theory. Einstein's model of the universe works better with non-Euclidean axioms. NASA's engineers still find the Euclidean axioms more useful for their purposes. If there were something self-evident about these axioms, this domain of choice would be ruled out. What commends a set of axioms is not their self-evidence but their coherence and their capacity to ground a coherent system of a certain level of inclusiveness. Lobachevsky's (or perhaps Riemann's) geometry has a greater degree of truth than Euclid's to the same proportion that Einstein's physical theories have a greater degree of truth than Newton's. And this is to be determined not by self-evidence but by the scope and quality of coherence in the systems supported.

Even the laws of logic—including the Law of Contradiction—are not tested by self-evidence, Blanshard continues. Clearly they cannot be demonstrated in any normal way, since they constitute the rules of demonstration and would need to be assumed for any such demonstration. Moreover, there are different logics. There is the familiar two-valued logic of *Principia Mathematica* (Russell & Whitehead 1927), in which all well-formed formulae must have a truth value of either "true" or "false," but there is also Tarski's three-valued logic, in which a proposition may be "true" or "false" or "doubtful" (Blanshard 1939: vol. 2, 251). Which logic to use is determined by purposes, not self-evidence.

The Law of Contradiction is inescapable, Blanshard argues, not because it is *self-evident*, but because of the *incoherence* implied by its denial. To be denied, it must be affirmed (implicitly) if one's denial is to make any sense. This is a self-contradictory. This defense of the inescapability of the Law of Contradiction may *feel* like self-evidence, but that is a mistake. The defense rests on the demonstration of systematic incoherence, at the very deepest level of theory, rising from any attempted denial of the law. "To perceive self-evidence is one thing; to perceive that a judgement is true because of what is implied in its denial is something else" (Blanshard 1939: vol. 2, 252). The Law of Contradiction does not rest on self-evidence. Rather, just the opposite, the sense of self-evidence rests on the radical incoherence of the law's denial.

(4) So far Blanshard's strategy has been to show that where there is a test of truth at all, it turns out to be the test of coherence. Can this hold even in the stronghold of the correspondence theory of truth, in matters of empirical fact?

It is easily seen to hold in issues of fact that are indirect, such as historical claims. If it is claimed that Caesar crossed the Rubicon, there is now no state of affairs that corresponds to the famous act of yore. That is long gone, and what tests we have for it (and like claims) are simply the tests that show all the different lines of evidence pointing in the same direction, mutually supporting the judgment that, indeed, the claim is true. But this is coherence. Questions of fact and coherence are not strangers, after all.

Still, these are indirect matters. What about the immediate evidence itself, what is seen and heard and touched and smelled? When a factual claim is in the present tense and in close proximity, is it not correspondence between a claim and what we simply experience that warrants our saying that the claim is true? Blanshard denies that it is. Suppose we are bird watching and someone says, "That bird is a cardinal." Confirming the truth or falsity of that assertion is not a simple matter of looking and registering an atomic fact that confirms or disconfirms it. Before verification can occur many other things must happen: there must be recognition, which depends on classification, the understanding of public language, adeptness at the use of concepts. Just recognizing a particular bird as a cardinal, for example, requires all sorts of concepts: "living organism," "flight," etc., that provide determinateness to any sighting (Blanshard 1939: vol. 2, 228–29).

Verification at this level is not simply a matter of correspondence between claim and world, or claim and naked sense content. Testing for the truth of such facts will be immersed in concepts and theories and will require judgments of many kinds. The importance of this is enhanced by the fact that even simple perceptions are notoriously subject to error. Illusions and hallucinations teach us that the veridical character of any perception depends on its cohering with its context. We can never get beyond the need to certify the perception, but this means that correspondence, so called, is a derivative from coherence, which turns out to be the real test at work, though we may not notice how dependent we are on its presumption.

Can this dependence on coherence not be broken at the level of immediate reports of pains, or the like? Is the truth of "I have a headache" not tested by my determining, straight off, that my present achy experience corresponds to my claim? Even here, at the bottom of the hierarchy of empirical claims, Blanshard finds correspondence giving way to coherence. First, it is necessary to strip the claim of all the conceptual baggage that even such a simple remark carries. "I" presupposes the concept of a self; "have" presupposes relations of ownership and terms to be owned, while its present tense presupposes a theory of time and present-momentness; "a headache" presupposes knowledge of anatomy, spatial locations, and the like. But this further stripping can be attempted, perhaps by employing one of the positivist protocol sentences like "Pain here!" Even this, however, tests for truth, if it does so, by coherence. The concept of pain is a loose-fitting universal, underdetermining its reference and thereby admitting many possible particulars that would satisfy it. We can be wrong even about our pains. Blanshard reminds us of George Eliot's heroine, who could not distinguish her feeling of love from a state of extreme suffering—except by the reflection that she would not part with it (Blanshard 1939: vol. 2, 231–32). Classification—which always involves connection, comparison, inference, adjustment, the risk of possible error, and the use of one's best judgment, all things considered—lies in the domain of coherence. Correspondence, even in the apparently simplest cases, never works by itself. It always depends on coherence.

To summarize: Blanshard finds that in the realm of fact, we may at first say that what makes empirical propositions true is their "correspondence" to what we find to be the case, but on closer reflection we see that such "correspondence" rests on presupposed or assumed coherences. In the realm of logic and mathematics, similarly, we may begin by saying that axioms or principles are tested for their truth by "self-evidence," but on deeper analysis we find that such "self-evidence" itself depends on coherence. Since at bottom there is at work no other test of truth, across the entire spectrum of claims, coherence stands alone, victorious.

The *test* of truth is one thing; its *definition* another. To this point Blanshard's argument has been limited to the question of justification: that is, by what *test* are we *justified* in believing that some proposition is true? His answer is always the same, that we are justified to the degree that on testing we can find systematic coherence in which the belief in question is nested. No proposition is ever simply true by itself. Every belief is justified, if it is, by its larger context. In principle, the truest beliefs would be those implicated in a logically necessary web of propositions systematically relating everything real or possible.

But this finding provides a decisive way, Blanshard holds, also of *defining* truth. What does it mean for a belief to be "true"? The word, "true," is an adjective that links a belief to something else, an object of that belief. That the epistemological gap can be tightly webbed does not mean that there is no distinction between a belief and its referent. Coherence is not that sort of reductionist position. Blanshard quotes approvingly from Bradley, the stout defender of coherence, "'[T]ruth, to be true, must be true of something, and this something itself is not truth. This obvious view I endorse'" (Bradley 1914: 325). Bradley even uses the potentially dangerous concept of "representation" concerning our beliefs and judgments. "They are [the Real's] representatives, worse or better, in proposition as they present us with truth affected by greater or less derangement. Our judgements hold good, in short, just so far as they agree with, and do not diverge from, the real standard" (Bradley 1893: 321).

Does this imply a definition of truth as "correspondence" between our true beliefs and reality "out there"? No, the sense in which Bradley and Blanshard might use the language of "representative" does not imply the familiar "mirroring" imagery of correspondence theories of truth. The actual sense of representation is more akin to how a child represents the adult she or he is going to become. The child is not yet the adult; the promise is not the fulfillment; there is a gap; but the gap is a matter of incompleteness to be filled, enriched, and satisfied.

Indeed, if the meaning of truth should unwisely be defined in terms of correspondence between a coherent set of propositions (and concept-laden experience including colors, odors, sounds, and the like) and something over against the set, a reality that it must somehow resemble, then the test of coherence can never prove such a relation. Blanshard does not merely admit this point, he insists upon it: "Would the mere fact that such elements as these are coherently arranged prove that anything precisely corresponding to them exists 'out there'? I cannot see that it would, even if we knew that the two arrangements had closely corresponding patterns" (Blanshard 1939: vol. 2, 268).

Here, in all its abyssal character, we are once again placed before the epistemological gap. The danger rises from attempting to define truth as correspondence.

But for coherentists such a definition is not necessary. It is not even coherent. The universal and sole *test* of truth demands coherence in all propositions, including our statements about the nature of truth. If our theory of truth is such that its *meaning* is in principle cut off from its *test*, we thereby introduce a systematic disconnection between the two. But systematic disconnections are the bane of coherence. Therefore, the theory of truth that would define it in such a disconnected way must be false.

A connected, harmonious theory, however, is available. It is the theory of truth on which not only the *test* but also the *nature* of truth is identified as coherence. On this view, truth is not simply *indicated* when a set of propositions is found to be coherent; rather, that propositional system, to the extent it is coherent, *is* truth.

Problems with Coherentism

The theory of coherentism is hard to resist. As Blanshard quips, "Coherence is a pertinacious concept and, like the well-known camel, if one lets it get its nose under the edge of the tent, it will shortly walk off with the whole" (Blanshard 1939: vol. 2, 267). But at the point of application, where the tentpegs of theory meet the earth of practice, we find serious problems. These problems are so serious, in my view, that we are required to conclude that modern coherentism, taken as the sole standard (and coherentism insists, as we have seen, on being the sole standard), is fatally flawed in its attempt to web over the epistemological gap.

A key problem for coherentist theory, in application, is the sinking realization that if truth must be equated with a final, complete synthesis of all-inclusive, mutually entailing, propositions (and with that alone), we do not have—and will almost certainly never have—such truth. It is far beyond human cognitive powers to achieve such an ideal. The ideal by definition lives or dies on its wholeness. Tears or gaps in its webwork are not simply unfortunate; they are fatal to its integrity. Approximations, by the nature of this case, do not count.

Blanshard forces his position to this limit by responding to a possible critic's question, whether on a coherentist definition the truth can change with changing systems. Committed to Plato's values, he forcefully denies that truth can possibly be alterable, but he admits that our human epistemic systems change all the time. "What we have said is that while truth as measured by the ultimate standard is unchanging, our knowledge of that truth does change—which is a very different thing" (Blanshard 1939: vol. 2, 272). Yes, most certainly these are very different! But acknowledging this is extremely costly for the coherentist position. Truth itself, unknown but secure from change, stands on one side, while, on the other, metamorphose the constantly altering systems of present knowledge as apprehended by particular minds. In making this vital distinction, Blanshard has welcomed the nose of another extremely pertinacious camel under the tent of his coherentism: it is the camel carrying us to the epistemological gap between "truth" and "our knowledge." His ideal has been skewed so far toward perfection that it is impossible to judge whether our imperfect, fragmentary stabs at coherence are even coming close to it, the ideal that can never, in practice, be applied.

Is this unfair? After all, the coherence theory has been presented, by both Bradley and Blanshard, as a domain not of either/or but of degrees. Truth and reality both come in lesser and more. Blanshard himself attempts to deal with the problem he acknowledges might seem to flow from taking truth as identical solely with the ultimate, ideal coherence of all things and all thoughts.

He begins with an admission. "The admission is that the theory does involve a degree of scepticism regarding our present knowledge and probably all future knowledge" (Blanshard 1939: vol. 2, 269). But this does not prove, he continues, that the theory is wrong. "Such a conclusion may bring disappointment, but disappointment is not discredit" (Blanshard 1939: vol. 2, 270). On the contrary, a dash of healthy skepticism may be just the right prescription for human knowing. The dash of skepticism present in coherence theory harmonizes well, he avers, with the story of scientific investigation, constantly short of absolute truth as it has repeatedly proven to be.

In addition to his admission, Blanshard offers an explanation and a plea. "[The] coherence theory, like other theories, needs to be applied with some common sense" (Blanshard 1939: vol. 2, 270). Common sense reminds us that, *in practice*, "While the truth of a judgement does consist in the last resort in its relations to a completed system, no sensible person would claim to know these in detail, or deny the judgement *any* truth till he did know them" (Blanshard 1939: vol. 2, 270). It does seem odd, however, suddenly to hear these appeals to practice, these pleas to use common sense, when to this point Blanshard's whole orientation and commitment has been to the purest of theory. Practice seems contented with the degree of theoretical fit we can actually achieve at any given time, which is fine as a measure of *justification* for approving a system of limited scope, despite its limits. Theory, in direct opposition, holds that no fragment, no matter how true-seeming, can be trusted to be true until its complete context is given.

In one tone of voice Blanshard urges us to be exact; in another he pleads with us to be sensible. The two "fall apart" to use a coherentist's phrase. They pull in opposite directions. They are, in a word, incoherent. Or, at least, they would certainly be so unless there could be provided some independent principle on which we could be assured that our practice, in science or in culture generally, is gradually approaching the ideal goal. If *change* could be viewed as *progress*, then instead of mere incoherence between cognitive practice and the theoretical ideal, we might confidently expect a convergence of practice on the ideal goal, even if (like a mathematical asymptote) our gradually improving finite coherences never actually reach the limit of perfection.

Blanshard clearly assumes such a principle of steady progress, to ground his confident rationalistic triumphalism. He admits the presence of an element of skepticism in his theory of truth, as we saw; but there is no need to fear, he says, since the gap between our knowledge and ideal truth can be counted on to narrow as this "healthy" skepticism drives steadily forward, in a gap-closing progression that refuses to take any level of scientific achievement as final. Moreover, this progress is not only to be found among individual scientific thinkers, trading in their previous personal beliefs for ever-more-coherent theories, it is also found in the "intellectual climate" (Blanshard 1939: vol. 2, 281). Belief in witchcraft, for example, faded away not because of specific refutations but because of its failure to cohere with the modern worldview in which there cannot possibly be witches. All educated people today reject witchcraft out of hand, he asserts. "We do so because it is incoherent with our intellectual world. That world is one whose outlines have been fixed by science" (Blanshard 1939: vol. 2, 282). This shows the steady march of reason, Blanshard says. Detours and blockages are not ruled out, but they are bound to be temporary. He admits that it is simply sophistical to suppose that the reasonable position is always the winning one. At the same time, "there is a continual pressure and tendency in this direction; to deny it would seem to me merely perverse; introspection and history testify to it alike" (Blanshard 1939: vol. 2, 283).

The same steady "pressure and tendency" toward the more inclusively coherent is also discoverable through a review of the history of thought. There is no need to make predictions or to suppose that Hegel's dialectic or Comte's three stages can be historically verified, but when we consider a series of worldviews extending over long periods of time, "such a series shows a constant nisus toward an ordering of the world which, as coherently comprehensive, may be taken also as true (Blanshard 1939: vol. 2, 283).

This "nisus" (from the Latin word "to strive") invokes the concept of an effort in a given direction. That direction, Blanshard believes, is rational unity. Despite his disclaimers in the previous quotation, he allows himself to conclude that "the issue tends *always* to be settled by acceptance of the view that, in the sense defined, is more coherent" (Blanshard 1939: vol. 2, 284, emphasis supplied). Blanshard's "always" (itself resting on the "pressure and tendency" claim embodied in his "nisus") gives this characteristically modern coherentism whatever warrant it has to assurance that our finite cognitive practice (our still-fragmentary "knowing") is steadily converging on the ultimate, unalterable truth, fixed, though it is, forever beyond our grasp. Without the "always" or the "nisus," we would have plain divergence, incoherence between human knowing and eternal truth. We would encounter the epistemological gap in its pure rationalist form. But with the "pressure and tendency" of the "nisus" toward reason, we can count instead on progress. With progress we receive comforting assurance that the gap is not fearful, since it is steadily being bridged over by the webwork of increasingly coherent systems.

But is this really the case? Is cognitive progress—even in the sciences—a fact or an illusion? One of the most important challenges to modern habits of thought, particularly to the assumption of smooth progress from triumph to triumph in science, was laid down in the decades after *The Nature of Thought* was published. As we have seen, one of the most important sources of Blanshard's imperturbable confidence in the adequacy of his view of reason—a proof he often drew upon to serve as the final clincher of his arguments—was a view of the nature and achievements of science. Blanshard's vision of science continued, despite the turmoil of mid-twentieth-century rethinking on this subject, to be that of a universal, culture-free enterprise. "There is simply physics or chemistry, with one universal standard of truth, to which place, time, and nationality are irrelevant" (Blanshard 1975: 559–60), Blanshard continued calmly to assert as late as 1975, never acknowledging that his modern ideal of the scientific enterprise had been profoundly challenged in the twenty years that had elapsed between the original preparation of his 1955 Gifford Lectures and their publication. Despite the storms of controversy in the decade following the appearance in 1962 of Thomas S. Kuhn's *The Structure of Scientific Revolutions* ([1962] 1970), Blanshard apparently felt no need to defend his firm convictions about science against the historical, sociological, epistemological, and psychological arguments put forward by Kuhn or by Hanson (1953), Toulmin (1961, 1972), Lakatos (1977), or Feyerabend (1975). My own perspective is quite different from Blanshard's on this, perhaps because I spent a sabbatical year, 1969–70, working closely with Kuhn at the Princeton Center for the History and Philosophy of Science. To me, Blanshard's assurance that science is steadily closing in on absolute truth does not seem well-grounded.

It would be impossible, and I judge unnecessary, to rehearse the whole range of arguments on such issues. They have been the common staple of discussion in philosophy of science for nearly twenty years. I shall content myself with three large observations.

First, the asymptotic model of scientific advance—steadily filling in more and more coherent details on a basically established framework of partial but insufficiently determinate truth—seems not to describe at all well the largest, most important advances. This model may well apply *within* a framework of beliefs, methods, instruments, and values (what Kuhn called a "paradigm"), since the normal work of scientists is not to overthrow or replace basic presumptions but to add detail and draw consequences from them (Kuhn 1970: 10–50). The continuous-progress model might even seem (it did in fact seem to most until mid-twentieth century) to apply *between* such major frameworks because revolutionary changes often are disguised by victorious revolutionaries in the mock-modest language of mere accretion. But in historic fact, scientific advances of the profoundest type are characterized by stressful, wrenching changes in basic point of view, concept, and practice. As we saw in *Being and Value* (109–14), the advance from Ptolemaic astronomy to Copernican was not a step, even a wide one, made on a continuous path. It was a leap from one universe to another. Of course, as Blanshard would point out, the mathematical coherences were greater, while the range of data was at least as great. Copernicus was offended by the ugliness of the incoherent mathematics allowed by the Ptolemaic astronomers. He called it "monstrous," and compared it to a dismembered organism, "hands, feet, head and other members . . . each part excellently drawn, but not related to a single body" (Kuhn 1957: 139). This greater coherence, however, was purchased at the cost of huge destruction: the shattering of the great framework of belief and value in which the earth was assumed central in the universe. Some expressions from that earlier framework remain to this day, as in "sunset" and "sunrise," but the Ptolemaic picture of the universe had to be smashed, and with it a worldview with huge valuational resonances, so that Copernicus' new coherences could be fitted together. Similarly, the enormous revolution involved in the shift from Newton's to Einstein's physics required Newton's key concepts—mass, space, time—to be drained of their former meaning and redefined. The extent of the changes involved have still not been generally recognized by ordinary people, since familiar words employed give the comfortable feel of continuity; but behind the seeming smooth progress, Newton's picture of the universe (though still approximately applicable to many practical contexts) has been set aside as false for the sake of the wider inclusiveness of quantum and relativity theory.

The history of science, then, should not give comfort to coherentists like Blanshard, who suppose that the "falling apart" between finite, fallible human cognitive practice and unalterable absolute truth can be mitigated by an appeal to progress. Certain things are guaranteed. The steps *within* a paradigm are guaranteed to be continuous, since that is what a paradigm provides: a context for continuity. Furthermore, a successor paradigm *replacing* former frameworks is guaranteed to offer increased coherence over its predecessor—at least within the problem areas accepted by the new paradigm as "important," and regarding evidence which on the new paradigm is deemed "relevant"—because this increased coherence, and the attractive promise of still more coherence, is what persuades its advocates to adopt, defend, and explore it. But what is not guaranteed is that the successor paradigm will represent a linear step "closer to the truth." On the contrary, what is suggested instead, is that the very *organizing principles* of coherences we prize today will be replaced *in basic ways* by future revolutions. The comforting thought of a "nisus" drawing us steadily toward a single, incrementally growing truth, resembling ultimate truth in all but detail, is based on illusion.

My second general observation is that the issue of confirming and disconfirming beliefs, even scientific beliefs, is far more complex and value-dependent than Blanshard (in some moods, at least) will allow. He allows things in other moods, however, that should give anyone pause who thinks that science threshes wheat from chaff according to some mechanical set of rules.

At what turned out to be the final point in our extended dialogue, I urged Blanshard that he acknowledge the extent to which variable human judgment is involved in deciding what new beliefs should be accepted into the scientific system at any given time. Instead, he declared: "The applicable principles of logic and scientific method have been worked out with high precision; nor is it very difficult to test whether a claimant to new truth has conformed to them" (Blanshard 1980a: 933). I still beg to differ. It is sometimes very difficult indeed to test for new truth—the more important the claimant, the more difficult, since more is at stake. At the level of "normal science," securely within a well-accepted paradigm, it may indeed be relatively easy to decide on whether a novel claim fits the standard criteria well enough to be accepted or not. But what Blanshard leaves out of account is that this "normal" activity (though doubtless the most frequent) is not the most important activity of science. More important are the struggles over whether an "anomaly," a phenomenon that is irritating because it does *not* fit comfortably into the expectations raised by the dominant framework, should be accepted, rejected, or set on the shelf for later pondering. The phenomenon of "ball lightning," for example, was widely rejected as simply a matter of misreporting before a way of interpreting it, by extending the mathematics of current electrical theory, was found. Electrical communication between parts of plants, functionally substituting for absent neural networks, is another anomaly that is only grudgingly being accorded serious attention (Ferré 1996: 332). Research in telepathy is scorned by virtually all modern-minded scientists and is left to parapsychology to be studied, if it is studied at all (Ferré 1994: 147–66). How does one decide what confirms, what disconfirms anomalous claimants for new truth?

Blanshard makes a point of noting that mere observation will not suffice. He cites a famous case from 1874, in which a leading chemist, Sir William Crookes, published a series of rigorous observations of a spiritualist medium. They were conducted in front of witnesses and in the "full blaze of the electric light," and photographs were taken. But Crookes, despite his fame and reputation for integrity, was not heeded. (Blanshard 1939: vol. 2, 235–36). Blanshard approves of this scientific incredulity, despite all the care with which Crookes enveloped his research. This anecdote, he remarks, is quite typical in science toward merely perceived facts. "If these facts may be read as cohering with the body of established science, in the way of supporting it or extending it, well and good; if they conflict with it, then . . . [their] plain message is disbelieved" (Blanshard 1939: vol. 2, 236).

But by now, Blanshard has acknowledged, despite himself, serious complications in "testing" a claimant to new truth. An alleged new truth needs to pass muster with more than batteries of tests, more than numerous credible witnesses, and more than the "full blaze of the electric light"; it needs to fit a whole metaphysical worldview. It will be accepted only if rejecting it would be intellectually even more disastrous than accepting it. And of course measuring the meaning of "disastrous" in given circumstances, like this one, is neither a matter of "high precision" nor of algorithmic calculation. It requires human judgment, preferably not alone but in concert and mutual support. It requires a community.

My third observation has to do with community in cognition, especially with scientific communities in all their genuine humanity. I attempted to make this point in my 1980 critique:

> Blanshard writes . . . as though "reason" were an individual's possession quite apart from the social context in which that individual has been provided his language, his standards, his general goals, his admired paradigms, and (to some degree) his particular projects. But this intellectual privatism is not the case even in the sciences, to which Blanshard appeals as his own paradigms of good thinking. What constitutes acceptable scientific method, logically relevant evidence, a scientifically convincing solution—even what counts as a legitimate scientific problem—all these are deeply dependent upon the shared convictions of the scientific community, including the interlocking and overlapping groups of persons who are editors of technical journals, judges on applications for grant support, graduate degree committee members, as well as researchers, experimentalists,

and theoreticians. Recognition of this fact does not in any way de-
mean science or its rationality; it simply requires a broadening, a
humanizing, and a socializing of what "rationality" really entails (Ferré
1980: 924–25).

My attempt, however, did not win Blanshard's favor. His summary reply:
"The answer here is (1) that I recognize the role of the community in determining how people do think, but (2) that I do not consider that this role
counts for much in determining how they ought to think" (Blanshard 1980a:
939). His principal displeasure was expressed against the idea that communities might have a legitimate say in fashioning norms of meaning and thus
the standards of relevance for evidence. When it came to science, his response was flat denial.

Since the sixteenth century the understanding of the world has moved
forward at a precipitate and accelerating pace. The knowledge that this
has been attained is not opinion merely; in large part at least it is
verified, exact, and securely established. The rules of logic and scientific
method by which it was attained and tested have been codified in detail.
They are not arbitrary rules, for not only has their reliability been tested
times without number but they are in truth formulations of the way a
rational mind works when it is at its best and clearest. Since they wear
this fundamental character, they are not the products of any group
resembling a religious community. They are the rules that are followed,
consciously or not, by everyone who is conducting a responsible inquiry into fact (Blanshard 1980a: 940–41).

It may be granted that some of the extreme talk, about the "incommen-
surability" of theories defended by groups of scientists in the thrall of different paradigms to which they had been "converted" during sudden "revolutions" and thereafter lived and worked in "different worlds," has been toned
down in the years since Kuhn's explosive book shook the orthodox view
expressed above by Blanshard. Science does not develop quite so discontinu-
ously as that rhetoric suggested, and Kuhn himself was willing to add, to his
images of political revolution, gestalt switch, and conversion, the more moderate analogies of language and culture acquisition (Kuhn 1970: 198–207).
Languages, no matter how foreign, admit of translation (even if translations
are often imperfect); and cultures, however alien, allow of diplomatic mediation. These metaphors carry a less absolutistic ring to them, opening the door
again to civilized discussion of differences, to feeling the way, despite
difficulties, toward larger understandings.

But the difficulties are real and much more important than Blanshard ever acknowledged. One much discussed difficulty is found in the inherent conservatism of the scientific enterprise—at least in "normal science" (Kuhn 1970: sections 2, 3, and 4)—and the consequent reluctance of real life scientists to allow major research programs to be falsified by contrary evidence. Blanshard, in the Sir William Crookes example, makes a point of this conservatism. But conservatism, whether negative (as in the Crookes instance) or positive (soldiering on despite setbacks) is a community standard. The scientific community persists, despite sometimes glaring incoherences, when a promising research program still is judged to have more promise than any other available line of work. That "judgment" is not a simple one for which an algorithm might in principle be developed. It involves the personal investment of many careers and past publications; it involves shared, and mutually reinforcing, hunches about how the world ought to be, including aesthetic preferences; it involves respect for admired leadership and Nobel Prize achievements; it involves the quiet, anonymous decisions of peer reviewers on publications or on grant proposals. This is the stuff of which real life is made. It is not mechanical or abstract rationality, but it is reason set within the passions and frailties to which human political animals are subject. It is reason that knows what it is like to take "leaps of faith," and to hope against hope. It shows that reason and commitment, as long as commitment is not blind, can go together. And in many ways it shows that there are more continuities between reason's operation in dedicated scientific communities and in other communities, including some religious communities, than Blanshard wanted to admit.

Another influence of human community on scientific theory can be found in the very definition of what counts as a scientific "problem." For Galileo, for example, it was not a "problem" that objects on the surface of the earth cling to the earth rather than go shooting off on a tangent into space; he had inherited (from Plato, Aristotle, Ptolemy, even Copernicus) the ideal of the natural order (Toulmin 1961: chapters 3 and 4) that closed circular motion around the earth "stood to reason" and needed no further explanation. Newton, on the other hand, considered it a "problem" for which his theory of gravitation was the answer. After Newton, with a different ideal of natural motion (straight-line, infinite, unaccelerated), the scientific community saw different problems from those it had recognized before. Again, for Descartes and virtually all the scientific community before Newton, the possibility of action at a distance, as assumed by the theory of gravitation, would have been a terrible problem; but after Newton's triumph, and his public rejection of seeking "hypotheses," or physical mechanisms, to account for gravitational effects, the scientific community found no "problem" in such unexplained influences. That is, the scientific community found no "problem" until

Einstein's Theory of General Relativity appeared, after which gravitational action at a distance was again a "problem," but now with a new candidate solution. Today other research programs seek "gravitons" or "gravity waves," and the "problem" is back in good standing. There is nothing absolute about what is or is not a scientific problem and, therefore, what needs a scientific answer at all.

Similarly, there is nothing absolute about what counts as properly scientific "evidence." As the scientific community defines its own problems, so also it defines what is logically relevant to their solution. What is evidence for something else always presupposes a theoretical network providing the connections. Those that weave the network thereby determine the rules of evidence. And in the same way, what is "satisfying" to reason is a function of the cognitive standard-makers, not of nontemporal, universal rules of logic. Before Newton, action at a distance was totally unsatisfying to reason; gravity would have been an "occult" force. After Newton, Auguste Comte, as we saw in the previous chapter, took the radical rejection of "hypotheses" as the final maturity of theoretical reason. To Positivists ever since, this has been the very model of good thinking. To Einstein, "God does not play at dice" (Einstein 1949: 176) meant that Quantum Theory could never finally be "satisfying to reason"; but to Heisenberg (1958), against others, like Bohm (1980), the statistical laws of Quantum Mechanics are quite sufficient without "hidden variables." In all this, basic judgments of value and reality are made and followed in the context of a living community which organizes itself and its activities around these fundamental, unproven judgments. Blanshard insisted in his "Reply" to me that "the rules of logic and scientific method . . . have been codified in detail . . . , [and] are not the products of any group resembling a religious community" (Blanshard 1980a: 940–41).

I hope I have sufficiently shown the basis for my wish to differ. The key here is not "religious" but "community." I do not wish to be distracted into a discussion of "religion," which will need to await *Living and Value*. There are many obvious differences between scientific and religious communities; Blanshard is obviously right, if that is all he meant. But any community is based—to the extent it is a community at all—on some shared values. What distinguishes religious communities from secular ones is simply the maximal intensity and comprehensiveness of the undergirding values involved (Ferré 1967b: chapters 2 and 3). Religious communities are, above all, communities of worship, in which ultimate valuations are manifest. Other, less dedicated, communities may not take their constituent values so seriously or centrally. But scientific communities, on this spectrum, are not far from religious communities if one measures by the comprehensive relevance of their constitutive values and the intensity of members' commitment to them. Nothing mystical, supernaturalist, or irrational is implied by this comparison. The point is the working of community values in shaping and retaining patterns of thought. From mundane politics to noblest ideals, values are at work in every human community, emphatically including science.

What does this stress on community have to say to coherentism? It is fully compatible with much of what Blanshard had to say about the crucial importance of local domains of systematic coherence in the comparative justification of human efforts at knowing. The relative breadth and integrity of these limited domains are important gauges of their rationality. There need be no quarrel there. It also supports coherentists' insistence on the richness and complexity of experience. Perception is shot through not only with universal concepts, as Blanshard showed, but also with preferences and aversions—values shaped in many cases by living in community with others.

But it does not support the crucial subtheme in Blanshard's version of coherentism: that impersonal reason provides a driving "nisus" within human knowing toward the single, unalterable, all-inclusive system of coherent propositions that defines the ultimate truth. To this extent it throws into sharp contrast the theoretical ideal of perfect coherence, forever unrealizable, and the practical fact of value-laden local systems: finite, changing, more or less comprehensive, more or less coherent. All are indeterminably far distant from the ultimately unreachable truth. And to that extent it exposes as wishful thinking any confidence that the epistemological gap—between what we think we know and what is finally true—allows successful webbing over by human systems of thought.

In place of a steady progression of wider and wider coherences, we may find ourselves left with a number of island universes of the mind, some larger and some smaller, organized in different ways, each with its own beauty and structure, each with its own key problems and its own standards of evidential relevance. What then? Blanshard has advice for those who may be weighing incompatible finite systems with no clear comparative advantage in comprehensiveness or coherence: suspend judgment. Wait for a crucial experiment that will break the impasse.

And if, in the nature of the case, there can be no crucial experiment that can distinguish the more coherent from the less? Then, Blanshard says, we should remain *permanently* in the state of suspended judgment (Blanshard 1939: vol. 2, 278). But is such a state of permanent suspension genuinely possible? Is it even reasonable, when life decisions need to be made that have different significance within the rival worldviews? Under such circumstances, are we not forced into choice, at least at times when "not choosing" is not one of the choices? If it results in permanent paralysis, is the "equation of truth with coherence" not "so far verified" after all, but reduced to absurdity instead?

These are questions to be taken up in the following chapter, in which leaping the epistemological gap, under carefully defined conditions, is defended as necessary and rational. But in connection with such "leaps," it is only fair to note in closing that Brand Blanshard, when sufficiently motivated, could and did leap with the best. His bold coherentist position is adopted by reasoned *choice* in the very teeth of a skepticism that offends Blanshard's deepest values. "If any one cares to doubt whether the framework of human logic has any bearing on the nature of things, he may be silenced perhaps, but he cannot be conclusively answered" (Blanshard 1939: vol. 2, 262). Such skepticism is unanswerable, perhaps, but Blanshard finds nothing in its favor. It is a mere suspicion and should be set firmly aside. Thus, although such skepticism *cannot be conclusively answered*, it may and should be met with a resolute *act of choice*, affirming the possibility of knowing. Blanshard's was, at bottom, a decision for coherence that was coherent with his deepest commitments, his profoundest preferences. In this, if the voices to be heard in the following chapter are to be trusted, he was setting a good—though incomplete—example.

7

LEAPING THE GAP

Readers will already have noticed significant differences not simply between doctrines but, more deeply, between thought-worlds, approaches, models, and fundamental value-commitments of the reductionists in Chapter 5 and the coherentists in Chapter 6. Such differences will become even more obvious in the present chapter, in which we will encounter representatives of existentialism and pragmatism.

Claiming to "know" is, as we saw (as early as Plato), claiming to have achieved something—to have achieved *success* according to adopted standards or basic epistemic norms. The reductionist empiricists take, as their central model for success in knowing, the highly specific observation report, such as we associate with carefully controlled scientific research. These statements, describing sensory experiences, are taken to be our clearest, most fundamental, incorrigible direct encounters with the world. For the Logical Positivist, these basic or atomic statements asserting sense data, when combined in "definitions in use," provide all the content there is (or can be) for what we mean by "objects" in the "world." Understanding the "world," so defined, requires analysis of relatively confused objects and events into the pellucid parts from which they are constructed. Knowing is most secure at its foundational levels in minimum sense contents. Theory is best when most tightly tethered to these most knowable minima. The more theory floats into more distant reaches, the more suspicious one should be.

Coherentists take a completely different model for their ideal of cognitive success. Their model is the completed theory in which everything has its mutually supportive place. Broad, unifying scientific theories are admired, but even these great achievements are not all-inclusive. Science itself is still fragmented. It is more accurate to speak of "the sciences" than of "science." Even if all the special sciences were one day to be unified under a single set of scientific laws and theories, it is still not clear that everything would be included. Perhaps morality and religion and the "hard core" humanities would remain outside the dream of scientific synthesis. Therefore, the highest ideal of success in knowing is even wider than the widest scientific system; it is where science and philosophy meld together in an all-encompassing system of tight inferential connections covering all that is actual or possible.

To summarize: Reductionists admire the scientific observation statement as ideal foundation, while coherentists prize the completed philosophical system as ideal aim, of knowing.

Existentialists and pragmatists, in somewhat different ways, have a different goal in knowing, and consequently a different standard for success. The goal is complete human fulfillment, in which the mind's needs play a major but not sole part. We human beings are not just intellects. We are active beings, centers of feeling and need as well as thought. Complete fulfillment will involve all aspects of our humanity, including the appropriate exercise of our capacity for making decisions. Reductionist empiricists are most confident when most passive before the inputs of perception. Coherentists are happiest when confronted with necessities of inference that allow no free play, no escape, in their systematic webwork. Existentialists and pragmatists, as we shall see, celebrate our powers of choice.

Not all existentialists or pragmatists include the language of "leaps" in their epistemologies. I adopted this metaphor for the title of this chapter to dramatize the importance of active decision-making, value-based choice, as the third major modern way of coping with the epistemological gap. One representative from each movement did, however, make this metaphor especially vivid. Søren Kierkegaard (1813–55), the "father of existentialism," is remembered for his advocacy of the "leap of faith"; and William James (1842–1910), one of the fathers of pragmatism, gave a famous epistemological illustration based on the tale of an Alpine climber confronted with the need to leap a fearful crevasse. I shall feature these two thinkers in the sections to follow.

Also featured, in a way contrasting with the previous two chapters, is what might be called the epistemology of ultimate matters. Both reductionism and coherentism deal, in their own ways, with ultimates, of course. Atomic facts are intended to be the ultimate foundations of what we can know and what is the case. The all-inclusive, necessary system is intended to be the ultimate goal of cognition and to provide a meaning for ultimate truth. But existentialists and pragmatists, especially as represented through Kierkegaard and James, are interested in ultimate fulfillment of the whole thinking, feeling, active person. Therefore, religious belief and claims of religious truth are inseparably linked to their central projects. "Eternal happiness" (Kierkegaard) and getting "upon the winning side" of the universe (James) require taking risks, making choices, launching oneself across the epistemological gap in responsible uncertainty, in fear and trembling. But, they argue, only through taking these risks do we find hope and truth. The alternative to attempting a leap is remaining forever frustrated and diminished.

SØREN KIERKEGAARD

It would be misleading to attribute a full "epistemological theory" to Søren Kierkegaard, but he has challenging things to say about epistemological issues—the possibility of knowledge, the nature of truth—that deserve to be heard. They have resonated widely, especially in the twentieth century and more especially among religious thinkers. His epistemological method, though not his substantive religious views, has also been influential among existentialist philosophers.

Kierkegaard was stung into his position by furious opposition to the great systematizer, Hegel. Therefore, we can locate his epistemological stance as most directly in conflict with the coherentists, who have sometimes returned his withering fire with great force and enthusiasm (Blanshard 1968; Blanshard 1975: 187–247). But if we look closely at some of Kierkegaard's background assumptions, we find that there is much of the coherentist tradition since Plato that has wormed its way, willy-nilly, into his outlook on the knowable.

This comes through indirectly in such ethical and religious writings as *Either/Or: A Fragment of Life* (1843) or in *Fear and Trembling: A Dialectical Lyric* (1843), where he sharply contrasts the level of the "aesthetic," on the one hand, in which feeling and sheer particularity are dominant, brooking no rules and therefore grounding no knowledge, with the level of the "ethical," on the other hand, which lies in the domain of the "universal," where concepts and regularities allow laws to be formulated and knowledge to occur. We are immediately reminded of Plato's Parable of the Cave or the Divided Line, where the mind gains in cognitive grasp as universal features—the Forms—rise in importance. For Kierkegaard, living on the aesthetic dimension is living among the bright appearances, the domain of seeming, where there can be no permanence, no basis for rational planning. Living on the ethical level is moving up to what Plato called the Intelligible World, where there can be stability, security, responsibility. In dramatic mode Kierkegaard brilliantly contrasts his "Seducer" (the aesthetic) with his "Judge" (the ethical) in the respective volumes of *Either/Or*.

But in *Fear and Trembling*, Kierkegaard (through his pseudonym, "Johannes de Silentio") offers yet another level, which he claims is higher than even the level of the universal. The level of universal laws allows understanding, but it also inevitably brings guilt in its train. When we break a law of ethics, we are condemned. The ethical thinker can understand this— that is just the trouble. There is no way beyond guilt, even with the help of most religions, as long as religion remains at the level of the universal. The "knight of infinite resignation," in Kierkegaard's terminology, has gone as high as the universal allows, seeing the inevitability of moral failure and giving up the joys of this world in an act Kierkegaard describes as heroic, admirable, but still not the highest possible. The knight of infinite resignation is still the tragic hero, stuck hopelessly in guilt and grief.

The very highest would be—and here Johannes de Silentio writes in hypotheticals—*both* giving up the world in one "infinite movement" *and*, in another "infinite movement," accepting the world back again in its particularity. This "double movement" is what Kierkegaard calls faith. It involves going all the way from the aesthetic to the ethical, and all the way to the top of the ethical, with the Tragic Hero, then (paradoxically) leaping *beyond* the ethical, thus beyond tragedy, beyond the domain of the universal where knowledge, security, understanding—and guilt—are found.

Kierkegaard insists that the best life is to be found when the tragedy that clings to the ethical is transcended. Transcending the ethical is goal-directed, oriented teleologically toward the best mode of existence, beyond justice and its inevitable shadow, guilt; and for this Kierkegaard advocates a "teleological suspension of the ethical" (Kierkegaard 1954: 69).

What this involves, however, is getting above the level of the universal, which alone makes understanding possible. This itself can hardly be understood; and though "Johannes" can make it out as a goal, he cannot understand how it could be possible, or even make sense, since all understanding resides at the level of the universal. Success in going beyond the level of universals would guarantee the impossibility of understanding or being understood. Again we are reminded of Plato and some medieval thinkers, following Plato, who interpreted the very highest level of the Divided Line as passing beyond intelligibility into ineffability. Kierkegaard gives some suggestion that he accepts this tradition when he discusses how for a "knight of faith" (for Abraham, the archetype of the faithful one) trying to explain the dynamics of faith would be a "temptation" to be drawn down again into universals. Just as the aesthetic life, seen from the ethical level, is a temptation to irresponsibility and wickedness, so the ethical life, seen from the level of faith, is a temptation to retreat to the tragic securities of intelligibility, "standards," and guilt. As Kierkegaard's "Johannes" writes: "Therefore if Abraham would express himself in terms of the universal, he must say that his situation is a temptation, for he has no higher expression for that universal, which stands above the universal which he transgresses" (Kierkegaard 1954: 70–71). Here Kierkegaard's reference to a "universal, which stands above" the level of our normal universals, suggests the Platonic Form of Forms. But this is of no use to us, who inhabit the domain of ordinary discourse and normal experience. The leap of faith is straight to unintelligibility, from our point of view, and even from the point of view of the knight of faith who has made the leap.

> Faith is precisely this paradox, that the individual as the particular is higher than the universal, is justified over against it, is not subordinate but superior—yet in such a way, be it observed, that it is the particular individual who, after he has been subordinated as the particular to the universal, now through the universal becomes the individual who as the particular is superior to the universal, for the fact that the individual as the particular stands in an absolute relation to the absolute. This position cannot be mediated, for all mediation comes about precisely by virtue of the universal; it is and remains to all eternity a paradox, inaccessible to thought (Kierkegaard 1954: 66).

The *best* life, the life of a knight of faith, is *inaccessible to thought*. Thought depends on universals, but these bring guilt and tragedy. Life in faith depends on paradox—eternally unresolvable paradox—which generates a maximum of mental tension, the tension of "impossible-yet-true," screwing to its maximum level the intensity of a thinker's subjective passion.

Kierkegaard shows ambivalence toward objectivity. In its place, analogous to the place of universals and the ethical, objective methods of thought are appropriate and worthy. But if subjectivity is more valuable, then objectivity can become an evasion, just as the ethical can become a temptation. Kierkegaard grounds his case in human need. Humanity's most vital problem, he maintains, is posed by the inescapable tension in which we finds ourselves, as a matter of experiential fact, torn between a longing for satisfaction which is insatiable and a status in existence which is finite. Human longings outstrip the human situation, because the former—being without limit—would require an eternal satisfaction, but the latter is irrevocably set in time. The infinite gap between time and eternity, then, is discovered within ourselves, who find ourselves involved in both realms. "The existing subject is eternal," says Kierkegaard epigrammatically, "but qua existing temporal" (Kierkegaard 1941a: 76). If this is the case, then logical systems and objective methods miss the point of our anguished need and may instead do greatest harm.

Kierkegaard argues in various ways against placing reliance on theoretical systems, like Hegel's (and, by implication, Bradley's or Blanshard's), which are aimed at providing objective truth about the ultimate nature of things. The ideal system, as we have seen, is final, fixed, settled; but existence is at heart temporal, fluxing, unsettled. Existence thus necessarily rejects every attempt at freezing it into system which is no system at all unless it is complete. But existence, precisely because of its temporal character, is never complete (Kierkegaard 1941a: 99). Logical systems can have no relevance to existence, therefore, and the system builder shows unseemly pretension in making the attempt. (Only if the system builder were outside existence, where alone might be found an absolute point of view, could a theoretical system be constructed that might be worth such effort.) Kierkegaard, by the way, is not denying that reality somehow might hang together if we existent mortals could only know it. On the contrary, the impossibility of a completed system is entirely due to our immersion in existence.

> An existential system cannot be formulated. Does this mean that no such system exists? By no means; nor is this implied in our assertion. Reality itself is a system—for God; but it cannot be a system for any existing spirit. System and finality correspond to one another, but existence is precisely the opposite of finality (Kierkegaard 1941a: 107).

Humans are not God; humans are subject to the conditions of existence, but God is not. Any attempt at making a systematic representation of all reality, then, is close to idolatry—it is to confuse one's own conditioned point of view with God's.

But perhaps pretension like this is better punctured by ridicule, Kierkegaard suggests, than by heavy polemic. Consider the system builder in his armchair: the perfect cartoon of "Herr Professor," including the proverbial absentmindedness. In fact, absentmindedness is his primary characteristic. It is a minor thing, comparatively, for a professor to forget to bring his notes to a class or to neglect to wear his trousers to a faculty meeting. These things make him a comical figure, to be sure; but consider how much more absentminded (and therefore even more comical) it is for Herr Professor to forget about the conditions of his own existence. And that is exactly what he must do every time he sits down to work out his logically systematic account of the ultimate nature of things. Whoever does well what nature intended, we admire; but whoever pretends to do what is plainly impossible is a fool and fit only for ridicule.

> If a dancer could leap very high, we would admire him. But if he tried to give the impression that he could fly, let laughter single him out for suitable punishment; even though it might be true that he could leap as high as any dancer ever had done. Leaping is the accomplishment of

being essentially earthly, one who respects the earth's gravitational force, since the leaping is only momentary. But flying carries a suggestion of being emancipated from telluric conditions, a privilege reserved for winged creatures, and perhaps also shared by the inhabitants of the moon—and there perhaps the System will first find its true readers (Kierkegaard 1941a: 112–13).

Not only completed systems but also limited objective methods of inquiry such as are used in the sciences come under Kierkegaard's critical eye if they claim relevance to issues of humanity's greatest concern, "eternal happiness." At any lesser level Kierkegaard doffs his hat politely (though with perhaps more than a trace of irony) to the scholarly research worker. "One sometimes hears uneducated or half educated people, or conceited geniuses, speak with contempt of the labor [of objective scholarship]; one hears them foolishly deride the learned scholar's careful scrutiny of the most insignificant detail, which is precisely the glory of the scholar, namely, that he considers nothing insignificant that bears upon his science" (Kierkegaard 1941a: 27). But Kierkegaard points insistently to one logical characteristic of all inquiry carried on in this objective mode: it is forever unfinished. In principle the concern of the objective thinker for each "insignificant detail" means that the job is never done, the results never secure. More and more evidence may pile up in favor of some conclusion, but one more "detail" may overturn the entire deposit of previous scholarship. This is the glory and the agony of the scientific method. But, on the other side of the coin, this illustrates the fact that just as long as the future remains open, objective inquiry can never more than *approximate* an answer to our questions.

Such approximation knowledge may have its usefulness; indeed, it would be absurd to deny this. Our ordinary practical purposes can make do quite well enough with hypotheses and probabilities. It would be at least as absurd, on the other hand, to suppose that *all* questions admit of treatment by methods of approximation knowledge. Specifically, Kierkegaard says, approximations, probabilities, and the like, are strictly incommensurable with one's boundless personal interest in eternal happiness. Objective inquiry, that is, simply cannot do the job needed for answering questions relevant to this dimension of life.

It is always possible to ask of the results of objective research: How likely are they? But our concern for eternal satisfaction is too pressing to permit such weighing and measuring. To illustrate, Kierkegaard argues that the area of scientific biblical research is entirely inconclusive for personal religious faith (Kierkegaard 1941a: bk. 1, chap. 1). If the texts are (at the present time, given presently known evidence) verified, this is not enough: one must still decide whether to stake his or her hopes for eternal happiness on their claim of authority. But if, contrariwise, the texts are shown ("probably") corrupted by secondary material or even worse, this cannot settle the matter for faith. One still must *decide* whether this is to be decisive or only a temporary test of faith; and one cannot shift responsibility onto any other shoulders than one's own. No approximation result of objective scholarship can remove the responsibility of decision; thus the issue of faith is outside the proper scope of objective approximation knowledge. The issues of faith are not objective issues.

Blind devotion to objective methods is not only inappropriate but also contains a terrible danger, Kierkegaard warns. When we insist on objectifying all questions, including questions relevant to our infinite concern for eternal happiness, we must accept the crucial condition of objective truth-seeking: postponement and delay. By mistakenly supposing that something hangs on the results of objective scholarship, we postpone decision until we can read just one more book, which leads us to three more articles, which involve rebuttals in five more journals, which . . . never ends. And so our life is spent, dribbled away into an endless slough of approximation knowledge, while opportunities for decisiveness are missed. In the process our capacity for feeling the infinite concern that first started us on our search is dulled.

If a method of answering a vital question only succeeds in destroying the question, Kierkegaard concludes, it is the method that is at fault. As existing beings we simply have no right to be objective about all questions. There is not enough time for endless delay; and the stakes are too high to lose them by default. Some questions, it appears, are essentially subjective, requiring concern, decision, passion in their method of being answered.

Objective theoretical reason, however, has a positive function to fulfill. It provides the background against which paradox can be recognized and passion generated. Passion is the state of being alive; without passion of the mind we are intellectually dead. But passion of the mind is created by paradox; the more paradoxical, the more passion we feel, until at last we find a paradox commensurate with our infinite, unpostponable concern about eternal happiness. Such a passion would require an "absolute" paradox of the mind. But trying to think coherently about God, we stumble on just such a paradox. What, after all, can "God" mean to beings who are existing creatures under the conditions of temporality and finitude? If humanity is the paradigm of what is knowable to humans, then the knowable turns out—as a matter of fact, discoverable by introspection—to be finally unsatisfying to human minds. Built into our intellect is a thirst that forever drives beyond the known, forever searches for the unknown. Its ultimate object would be the Object that thought cannot think; its ultimate satisfaction would be in the Unknowable. Kierkegaard is not far from Bradley here. Intellect is engaged on a paradoxical quest, since in its restless craving for the Unknowable it is in a sense struggling to get beyond itself, even to destroy itself. The Object that would accomplish this satisfaction-in-suicide needs to be given a name. "So let us call this unknown something: *God*. It is nothing more than a name we assign to it (Kierkegaard 1936: 31).

This is not so arbitrary as it sounds. God *must* be so considered by human minds if the conditions of existence do not apply to the divine, inasmuch as human minds can conceive only what is like themselves, and God in consequence becomes identifiable only negatively, as Wholly Other.

Very well, take God as Wholly Other; but concerning such an absolutely inconceivable subject, we cannot even have an idea of what being "unlike" or "like" *means*; and so the ultimate paradox would be the Wholly Unlike becoming Wholly Like while remaining Wholly Unlike; that is, the absolute passion of the intellect would be roused by the thought of *God* (infinite) becoming *human* (finite) while still remaining God. This, however, is precisely the central doctrine of Christianity, the doctrine of Incarnation.

In the face of such an objectively paradoxical doctrine the mind reels, but in this experience it has fulfilled itself by getting at last beyond objectivity. The would-be thinker is like the would-be lover. Both must be fulfilled only by "letting go" and being transcended. If a person wants to be genuinely loved, he or she must be ready to sacrifice the prime desire itself, wanting to receive love, in order to *give* genuinely to another; likewise, if a person wants to find truth in matters of religion, he or she must drive beyond the narrow securities of objective truth to the place where restless reason can be transcended in the paradox that comes from pushing its own quest up to—and beyond—the limit. "One should not think slightingly of the paradoxical," then, says Kierkegaard; "for it is the source of the thinker's passion, and the thinker without a paradox is like a lover without feeling: a paltry mediocrity" (Kierkegaard 1936: 29).

Even if passionate thinking is best for human beings concerned about their eternal happiness, as Kierkegaard maintains, does this have anything to say about *truth*? Does it help us across the epistemological gap, or does it simply change the subject? Kierkegaard's answer is to challenge as partial and inadequate the objective concept of truth itself.

Objective methods have by now been shown, Kierkegaard believes, to rest upon an arbitrary and harmful subjective requirement: neutrality or unconcern. This is a *subjective* requirement, certainly, since studied indifference or detachment is merely one among many possible subjective moods; it is not *no* mood, as its uncritical defenders sometimes seem to assume. Unconcern, further, is an *arbitrary* subjective requirement, since it is imposed by fiat rather than by intelligent response to the nature of the problem at hand, that is, the tensions of the human existential situation. And it is *harmful*, since it diverts attention from issues and answers that will not be evaded, however hard we try. They cannot be escaped because we are finite beings with infinite longings, and above all because we are faced with the inescapable fact of death which threatens all our values. Questions of this sort cannot be approached clinically; they demand a living response now. Otherwise we are dead already.

Kierkegaard proposes, therefore, that in issues of this kind, at least, we adopt a new understanding of truth as "subjectivity." He explains himself through a series of contrasts.

1. *Remembering the thinker.*   Objective truth forgets about the thinker. The individual's particular existence is of no consequence to such truth, nor does it matter whether an individual recognizes or understands this kind of truth—it is true all the same. But subjective truth remembers the thinker; it stands on the principle that what is not *appropriated* by the individual thinker is not the truth *for this thinker* at all. A solution may be splendid—in the abstract; but unless the individual makes it his or her own, it is worthless. There may be (objectively) a safe way out of a burning building that I could take, but unless I make this truth my own—appropriate it subjectively—for me it is no truth at all.

Objective truth, therefore, is not the whole story. And if the problem is one that essentially involves the thinker, the due importance of this thinking subject must be recognized by adopting a view of truth that recognizes his or her existence and his or her role in the knowing process.

2. *Focusing on the relationship.*   Again, in matters of objective truth the focus of interest is on the "content," the object of cognition. And if this is carried to its appropriate conclusion, the subjective factors of emotion or volition tend to vanish—ideally they will disappear altogether (Kierkegaard 1941a: 175–76). All that matters is that the proposition's content is true. The nature of the cognitive relation is irrelevant. But in matters of subjective truth, says Kierkegaard, the focus of interest is properly on the relation that binds the thinker to what is known. This kind of truth has its ideal limit, too; the objective content tends to vanish, and all that matters is that the manner of the relationship—that is, the subjective state of the knower—is of the right kind. Kierkegaard himself puts it (in his own italics) as follows: "*When the question of the truth is raised subjectively, reflection is directed subjectively to the nature of the individual's relationship; if only the mode of this relationship is in the truth, the individual is in the truth even if he should happen to be thus related to what is not true*" (Kierkegaard 1941a: 178).

3. *Vindicating the passionate postulation of God.*   The application of this to the question of belief in God is quite straightforward. We have already en-

countered Kierkegaard's reasons for refusing to grant the appropriateness of objective methods in dealing with an issue so deeply fraught with consequences for the possibility of the individual's eternal happiness. God simply refuses capture by objective techniques. Not a phenomenal object, God "therefore exists only for subjectivity in inwardness" (Kierkegaard 1941a: 178). And since "every moment is wasted in which he does not have God" (Kierkegaard 1941a: 178–79), the existing individual's legitimate course is to claim God subjectively, and thus short circuit the never-ending approximation process of objective approaches.

4. *Fending off the perils of subjectivity.* There are dangers in embracing subjective truth, Kierkegaard admits; but he believes that they can be met. One such danger is that of fanaticism, which is defined by Kierkegaard as the directing of one's infinite interest toward mere approximation objects (Kierkegaard 1941a: 32). But this, he believes, can be avoided by making sure that passionate commitment is given only to appropriate objects. A second danger might be: madness. Where subjectivity is truth, the situation objectively seen is an unresolvable paradox (Kierkegaard 1941a: 182–83). The paradox, as we have seen, is the source of the thinker's passion; the more paradoxical something is, therefore, the more inward passion it arouses, and the more inwardness it arouses the truer it must be held to be. But this is to let go, entirely, all objective criteria and controls. This way lies madness.

Kierkegaard agrees. Faith without risk—including the risk of madness—is not faith. "In a merely subjective determination of the truth, madness and truth become in the last analysis indistinguishable, since they may both have inwardness" (Kierkegaard 1941a: 173–74). What, though, is madness? *Lack* of inwardness is madness, too. Failure to appropriate truth can lead to mere babbling, as in the case Kierkegaard delightfully describes of the madman on a walk who tries to prove his sanity by saying, "Bang, the earth is round!" every time a ball in his back coat pocket strikes his backsides (Kierkegaard 1941a: 174). Nothing could be more "objectively true" than his statement; but nothing could be a surer proof of his insanity. Therefore, he concludes, let us prefer the madness of intense subjectivity to the madness of mere prating, especially when in apparent madness—in what objective knowledge considers paradox or absurdity—lies the most profound truth.

REFLECTING ON KIERKEGAARD

Kierkegaard is a tricky thinker to criticize. It is a thankless task, since he did not want the praises of professors and admitted in advance—flaunted—flaws ("inconsistency," "madness") that normally might be considered fatal. He is always just ahead of the would-be critic, around the corner, laughing.

But reflection is always in order, for Kierkegaard too. Therefore I shall simply reflect on a few points raised by this artful dodger on matters of method, thought, and truth. Has he indeed found a way to leap the epistemological gap between the best we can think and what is real and true?

First, does he even recognize that there is a gap? The answer is clearly affirmative, found in his absolute dualisms between finite and infinite, time and eternity, humanity and God. It is expressed as well in his curious saying, quoted above, *"if only the mode of [someone's] relationship is in the truth, the individual is in the truth even if he should happen to be thus related to what is not true."* The epistemological gap has been translated into the gap between "objective truth" and "subjective truth." By being passionately subjective enough, in the right way, by being willing to leap without the slightest safety net of shared concepts and objective evidences, one may put oneself into the truth that matters, even though this may be in relation to what is objectively false. Kierkegaard's position depends on a spectrum of judgments of importance. Scholars and objective thinkers evaluate objective truth as the only thing that matters, allowing the question of subjective truth (the thinker's passion, need, concern, "relationship") to vanish from the evaluational screen. That is a kind of objective madness that loses everything of importance to existing individuals. Kierkegaard then reverses the evaluative field. The interiority of the thinker is all that matters; thus the object beyond the thinker, to which the thinker is related with the infinite passion that constitutes the highest goal, disappears into insignificance. But the gap itself remains. "Out there," in the realm of objective truth, some finite object of thought is false; but "in here," in the realm of subjective truth, the truth value is reversed.

Kierkegaard does not shrink from drawing his conclusion even regarding God and idols.

> If one who lives in the midst of Christendom goes up to the house of God, the house of the true God, with the true conception of God in his knowledge, and prays, but prays in a false spirit; and one who lives in an idolatrous community prays with the entire passion of the infinite, although his eyes rest upon the image of an idol: where is there most truth? The one prays in truth to God though he worships an idol; the other prays falsely to the true God, and hence worships in fact an idol (Kierkegaard 1941a: 179–80).

The "bottom line" for Kierkegaard is then that one's leap of faith does not take one *across* the epistemological gap. The idol remains an idol—by definition not the true God. But for Kierkegaard this *is unimportant*. One's leap is to internal, subjective truth. One's leap *creates* this subjective truth. The leap, with all the "passion of the infinite," is the necessary and sufficient condition for finding ourself in the only truth that matters, but not in objective truth.

Thus the epistemological gap is not leaped across in this passionate process; it is instead deliberately forgotten about, made negligible. Is this something in which we might wish to join Kierkegaard? There are obvious attractions. He speaks for the importance of remembering the thinker in an age excessively, perhaps dangerously, fond of objectivity. He gives a needed reminder of the warm, embracing "Hebrew" sense of "knowledge" that in our culture has been largely overshadowed by the cool "Greek" admiration for contemplation.

Still, there are many reasons why we might prefer to decline Kierkegaard's invitation to leap to purely subjective truth as though this were all that matters. First, are we really obliged, as Kierkegaard rhetorically suggests, to choose between subjective madness and objective madness? If so, then many would doubtless choose, with him, to go down flailing in a sea of subjectivity—for the sake, at least, of feeling alive—rather than to settle for the juiceless desiccation of pure objectivity. But are these extremes our only alternatives? Must commitment, feeling, decisiveness rule out all objective criteria? Can there be no sane option between the opposite extremes of madness Kierkegaard portrays? Perhaps Kierkegaard's forced "either/or" is premature.

Second, Kierkegaard's denial of the objective pole admits no hope for the wholeness of human personality that may deserve to be craved as keenly as Kierkegaard felt the "infinite passion for eternal happiness." All the hope that Kierkegaard seems to hold out for the mind's yearning for coherence is the odd masochistic satisfaction that follows self-destruction. But this involves a pessimism toward the intellect that seems a last resort—or perhaps no resort—for those who value full human nature, including the powers of critical reasoning.

Third, the social dimension of life seems violently excluded from our most important questions if, as Kierkegaard contends, the *individual subject* is the lone focus of truth in these matters. Communication between people on these matters becomes impossible in principle if every individual's unique inwardness becomes the only important consideration. Language becomes impossible if the "objective" content tends to "vanish." The person at the pinnacle of existence must for Kierkegaard be entirely, invincibly alone. Community depends on communication, and Abraham—excluded, as we have seen, from universal concepts—cannot explain himself to others or even to himself, since the availability of universals has been abandoned (Kierkegaard 1954: 70, 82, 89, 102).

Fourth, if all objective content tends to vanish, as it must when ultimate reality is defined as Wholly Other and the road of "subjective truth" is taken, then it becomes impossible even for the subject to know what he or she is committing, with all infinite inwardness, *to*. This, together with the glorification of paradox and the elimination of objective criteria of any kind, would seem to rule out any possibility for orderly growth in faith, or for constructive maturation. Every change—if change comes—is necessarily a "revolution of inwardness"; every change, if it threatens what is held with infinite passion, becomes a defeat for faith unless there are some criteria whereby one may measure growth in cognitive maturity.

Fifth, if objective content is the vanishing factor and sheer subjectivity takes the place of all objective criteria in judging faith, Kierkegaard's proposed defense against fanaticism becomes unconvincing. He said, we recall, that fanaticism is the devoting of one's unlimited passion to a limited object. But for objective thought *every* object, including the Jesus of history (Kierkegaard 1941b), is limited; every object to which one commits oneself entails a risk. Any criterion that will distinguish faith from fanaticism—if Kierkegaard is serious in his rejection of objective criteria—is inapplicable. We must, even with regard to the criterion itself, still make a passionate and objectively uncertain leap in our decision that our commitment is not directed merely at another object of approximation knowledge but at the "appropriate" object.

Especially is this evident if, as Kierkegaard's own explicit statement makes clear, the passionate inwardness of the decision is more important than the decision's being right about its object. If the idolater may have truth *simply by virtue of his passionate relation* to the object of his worship, what barrier can stand against the fanatic? Such a one would appear justified by fanaticism itself, just as long as it is fanatical enough. How, then, does commitment to Christ differ essentially—on this purely subjective view—from commitment to Hitler? Perhaps the character of the "idol on which ones eyes rest" does matter, when it comes to behavior. Abraham, taken by Kierkegaard as the paradigm of justified faith, was prepared to slaughter his own innocent son for no visible good purpose. He lifts the knife without being able to explain his impending act to anyone, not to Isaac, not to any other knight of faith, not to himself. Kierkegaard describes this readiness to murder, from Abraham's point of view, and concludes that humanly speaking, Abraham was crazy:

> [Abraham] knows that it is beautiful to be born as the individual who has the universal as his home, his friendly abiding-place, which at once welcomes him with open arms when he would tarry in it. But he knows also that higher than this there winds a solitary path, narrow and steep; he knows that it is terrible to be born outside the universal, to walk without meeting a single traveller. He knows very well where he is and how he is related to men. Humanly speaking, he is crazy and cannot make himself intelligible to anyone (Kierkegaard 1954: 86).

Such craziness may express itself, paradoxically, in actions that are the exact opposite of what love or duty normally mean: "for example, love to God may cause the knight of faith to give his love to his neighbor the opposite expression to that which, ethically speaking, is required by duty" (Kierkegaard 1954: 80).

Commitments have consequences. Kierkegaard, by stressing subjective commitment to the point where it has nothing to do with the controls of theoretical or practical reason, has left the door wide open to subjectivists of many sorts.

Among these, for example, and supporting with passion very different views on the ultimate nature of things, is Friedrich Nietzsche. I draw attention to Nietzsche because epistemologically he shares Kierkegaard's basic disdain for theoretical intellect, shares also the readiness to "leap" with infinite passion on matters of ultimate concern, and shares Kierkegaard's willingness to praise the transvaluation of values, the reversal of good and evil, when evil acts are committed from heroic subjectivity:

> The strongest and most evil spirits have so far advanced humanity the most: they have always rekindled the drowsing passions—all ordered society puts the passions to sleep; they have always reawakened the sense of comparison, of contradiction, of joy in the new, the daring, and the untried; they force men to meet opinion with opinion, model with model. For the most part by arms, by the overthrow of boundary stones, and by offense to the pieties, but also by new religions and moralities. The same "malice" is to be found in every teacher and preacher of the new. . . . The new is always *the evil*, as that which wants to conquer, to overthrow the old boundary stones and the old pieties; and only the old is the good (Nietzsche 1954: 93).

But Nietzsche's "passionate inwardness" leads him to reject—hotly—the leap to God that Kierkegaard finds the essence of subjective truth. Quite the contrary, Nietzsche declares God dead. Only by leaping to atheism is it possible to show "integrity" and to exercise subjectivity properly, he asserts:

> That requires greatness of soul: the service of truth is the hardest service. What does it mean, after all, to have *integrity* in matters of the spirit? That one is severe against one's heart, that one despises "beautiful sentiments," that one makes of every Yes and No a matter of conscience. Faith makes blessed: consequently it lies (Nietzsche 1954: 632).

And arguing with theologians? There is no point. The final response to religious faith must be a decisive action, according to Nietzsche, not the idle flickering of wit. "One refutes a matter by laying it respectfully on ice—that is how one also refutes theologians" (Nietzsche 1954: 637).

Nietzsche's "refutation" of theologians is hardly a refutation of Kierkegaard's approach to subjective truth and paradoxical claims. It is more nearly an example of it than a refutation. Indeed, it is hard to imagine what a "refutation" of Kierkegaard's passionate call for faith "by virtue of the absurd" would be. Should we lay the call "respectfully on ice," as Nietzsche counselled? Shall we dismiss the Kierkegaardian infinite longing for God as the impossible and freedom-denying "desire to be God," with Jean-Paul Sartre (Sartre 1957: 60–67)? Kierkegaard's incandescent rhetoric illuminates much that is faulty in any epistemic norms that ignore the needs and feelings of the humans who try to do human thinking, but there is much that is febrile and exaggerated in the postures struck by this dazzling Dane. In Kierkegaard we sense a leap without a landing. American pragmatism, while acknowledging the need for leaping, is far closer to the earth.

C. S. Peirce and William James

The pragmatic philosophy of William James will be the prime topic of this section, not "pragmatism in general." But James was not—certainly not in his own estimation—the founder of pragmatism. For that honor he freely acknowledged Charles Sanders Peirce (1839–1914), his friend, colleague, and stimulus.

Peirce, son of a distinguished Harvard University astronomer and mathematician, was always drawn toward science. First he attended Harvard College, graduating in 1859, then received an additional degree in chemistry from the Lawrence Scientific School in Massachusetts with highest honors (1863). After this, he served simultaneously as assistant astronomer at the Harvard Observatory and as a physicist for the United States Coast and Geodetic Survey, working all the while privately on logic and philosophy. He never brought out a book, but the philosophical papers he published from 1866 led to his invitation in 1879 by the newly established Johns Hopkins University, in Baltimore, to a part-time teaching post in logic. He remained at Johns Hopkins only until 1884, however, when he was dismissed in the aftermath of controversies with a senior colleague and in the shadow of sexual scandal in his personal life. Since he had never relinquished his position with the Geodetic Survey, he continued with that job until 1891, when he was dismissed from it, too, never to find another regular employment. Meanwhile, from 1887, he and his second wife made their life on a small farm in Milford, Pennsylvania (not far from the New Jersey border), where,

despite increasing obscurity, ill-health, cold, and even hunger, Peirce continued refining his philosophical views. In part these refinements involved distinguishing his views from those of his continuing good friend, James—who
in the meantime had become much better known. James, always faithful,
organized a fund for the support of the Peirces and helped point favorable
public attention to Peirce for having been the real founder of pragmatism.
Peirce died, sad and impoverished, in 1914.

James and Peirce, close in age, shared many interests. James, too, had
early scientific training, though (perhaps significantly) James' sciences were
in the biological rather than in the mathematical domains. James, son of the
philosopher, Henry James, Sr., and brother of the novelist Henry James,
obtained his early education in Europe, entering Harvard College in 1861,
shortly after Peirce had graduated and gone on to the Lawrence Scientific
School. Peirce had many Harvard connections, however, and remained involved with the Harvard "Metaphysical Club," in which James became an
active member. After graduating from Harvard College in 1864, James continued at the Harvard Medical School. In 1873 he joined Peirce on Harvard's
staff, teaching anatomy and physiology, then adding lectures in psychology
in 1875. In 1879, the same year in which Peirce received his invitation to
teach at Johns Hopkins, James, remaining at Harvard, also began his formal
philosophical career, adding lectures in philosophy to his repertoire. The
two philosophers remained closely in touch, despite the new geographical
distance between them. They shared many fundamental convictions, though
differences in temperament and background interests led to noteworthy
divergences.

Peirce, with physics, chemistry, astronomy, and mathematics behind
him, was above all interested in knowing as a natural scientist. He was well
aware of the modern predicament, having begun as a devoted Kantian; but he
was not content to leave matters as Kant had, staring into the abyss of skepticism. It is outside my aims to go into the various logical strategies Peirce
attempted, patiently revising and reworking his ideas throughout his life. But
Peirce had two major insights, among many others, on which pragmatism's
hopes to leap the epistemological gap are based: one defined the character of
scientific inquiry, while the other laid down the basis for reaching new hypotheses in the sciences.

One of Peirce's earliest essays, "The Fixation of Belief," published
in *Popular Science Monthly* in November 1877, but actually prepared
years earlier and presented to the Harvard Metaphysical Club in 1872,
was a key statement on the best and most secure way to approach the goal
of human knowing. In it, Peirce contrasts various methods of "fixing
belief"—moving from the "method of tenacity" (sheer private dogmatism)
to the "method of authority" (enforced group-think) to the "a priori method"

(believing whatever feels agreeable to our minds)—with the "method of science." The first three are all vulnerable to disillusion and doubt, and tend to come crashing down on believers who have fixed their opinions by such arbitrary methods. The method of science, however, is self-correcting. It knows it is open to error, but by embracing its own falliblism, it removes its sting. Better put, it uses the stinger of doubt as a goad toward continually improved beliefs. It deliberately lays itself open to be convinced only by the facts, not by human whim or authority or a priori mental preference. "To satisfy our doubts, therefore, it is necessary that a method should be found by which our beliefs may be caused by nothing human, but by some external permanency—by something upon which our thinking has no effect" (Peirce 1995: 79). This presupposes independent reality, standing over against our human investigations, controlling and disciplining them. This is what allows Peirce to define scientific method by its ultimate outcome: namely, that "the method must be such that the ultimate conclusion of every man shall be the same. Such is the method of science" (Peirce 1995: 79).

Self-correcting convergence on unanimity, constrained by independent reality, is Peirce's prescription for those who would know. Independent reality is of course not directly known as it is in itself. There is a gap between our concepts and theories and what they attempt to explain, but this epistemological gap will gradually narrow if only we adopt the right *method* of inquiry, that is, if we *do* our cognitive work properly. The normative "properly" is significant, here, since the other methods of "fixing belief" do not allow of being done well or badly. They are just done, and when done they harvest their "unlasting success" (Peirce 1995: 81); scientific method, in contrast, is governed by standards of better and worse that allow its self-criticism and improvement.

But "being improved" by the discipline of independent reality requires having one's beliefs made vulnerable to verification or falsification in experience. To assure this, Peirce defines the meaning of our concepts in what later came to be called the "pragmatic" manner. "Consider what effects, which might conceivably have practical bearings, we conceive the object of our conception to have. Then, our conception of these effects is the whole of our conception of the object" (Fisch 1982: vol. 3, 263–64). Is this simply a restatement of the positivistic reduction of our concepts to sense data? No, Peirce insisted, since the meanings of our concepts will never be reducible to any finite set of actual verifying experiences. What we mean by the entities we conceive in science (and ideally in daily life) is equivalent to the *whole* range of practical bearings these concepts *might* have on our lives, and this range can never be exhausted by any set of particular verifying experiences, no matter how large. There will always be contrary-to-fact consequences—

the ones that *could* have happened but *did* not—that are part of our meaning but not part of our experience. The thin nominalism of the reductionists is avoided by Peirce's determination to include significant might-have-beens in the meaning of reality.

Still, where do we find the concepts and hypotheses that in scientific method need to be subjected to the constraints of verification? Peirce offered a new term, "abduction," for the process of creative leaping that brings about the new theories that later need to be subjected to our sober tests. As Peirce laid out the steps of scientific method, abduction leads the way. It is a type of inference that is continuous with perception itself. It takes us beyond what we are given in perception (just as in perception we are taken beyond the sheer sense-contents to the experience of something really there) and offers us ideas that may provide interpretation of why experience is as it is. The next step is deduction. From the hypothesis formed by the leap of creative imagination we need to deduce what further practical consequences would follow, supposing that the hypothesis holds. And finally, in what Peirce calls "induction," we observe and weigh whether our experience is disappointed or gratified by the expectations raised through deduction. If disappointed, then the time is ripe for more abduction, more creative leaping, in the never-ending attempt to converge on unanimity.

Others have seen in the abductive process of leaping the primary meaning of "induction." Nicholas Rescher offers a charming quotation from an older contemporary of Peirce to this effect:

> Long ago, William Whewell put the point nicely. "Deduction," he wrote, "descends steadily and methodically, step by step: Induction mounts by a leap which is out of the reach of method [or, at any rate, mechanical routine]. She bounds to the top of the stairs at once" (Whewell 1858: 114, in Rescher 1992: 135).

Peirce's lifelong friend, William James, shared a great deal with him in philosophical approach, but James always tended to push further. Peirce treated the pragmatic method, we saw, as one translating the *meaning* of concepts into practical consequences; James, as we shall see, treats the method as providing a theory of *truth* based on those practical consequences. Peirce, the mathematician, astronomer, chemist, physicist, was above all interested in the logic of scientific method; James, the physician, psychologist, ethicist, student of religion, was above all interested in health and fulfillment: physical, mental, and moral. Peirce contemplated the legitimacy of making abductive mental leaps; James, in a famous example of the self-involvement of belief in successful behavior, imagines himself a climber faced with a difficult situation:

Suppose, for example, that I am climbing in the Alps, and have had the ill-luck to work myself into a position from which the only escape is by a terrible leap. Being without similar experience, I have no evidence of my ability to perform it successfully; but hope and confidence in myself make me sure I shall not miss my aim, and nerve my feet to execute what without those subjective emotions would perhaps have been impossible. But suppose that, on the contrary, the emotions of fear and mistrust preponderate; or suppose that, having just read the *Ethics of Belief* [by William K. Clifford (1845–79)], I feel it would be sinful to act upon an assumption unverified by previous experience—why, then I shall hesitate so long that at last, exhausted and trembling, and launching myself in a moment of despair, I miss my foothold and roll into the abyss. In this case (and it is one of an immense class) the part of wisdom clearly is to believe what one desires; for the belief is one of the indispensable preliminary conditions of the realization of its object. *There are cases where faith creates its own verification.* Believe, and you shall be right, for you shall save yourself; doubt, and you shall again be right, for you shall perish. The only difference is that to believe is greatly to your advantage (James 1957a: 27).

James' example is meant to show that in cases where the truth is partially dependent upon our choice of belief, it is more rational to choose what we want the truth to be. But this raises the prior question, what is the proper understanding of "rationality"? Then we can return to the issue of what cases lend themselves to this "engaged" standard of rationality.

Rationality, says James, is first of all—when we are driven all the way back to essentials—something that we can identify in experience. If it had no consequences for experience, as Peirce had said, we would have no idea what it is that we are naming by the term, nor could we recognize it when present. What is this root experience of rationality (James calls it the "sentiment" of rationality) like? Basically, he answers, it is the awareness of a change in mental state from confusion or perplexity or puzzlement to a "strong feeling of ease, peace, rest" (James 1957a: 3). In fact, it is even more accurate to say that the experience of rationality is a sense of the *absence* of *ir*rationality, somewhat (to borrow an example from Epicurus) as the experience of the pleasure of a good digestion is really manifested in absence of pain from the visceral regions. The ease of intellect that constitutes rationality is distinctive, however, in that it has to do with the smooth flow of our *thoughts*, not of our stomach juices. An irrational thought is one that blocks this flow, that refuses to fit in, that irritates us into attempts to remove the obstruction.

James is sometimes bitterly criticized for this basic description of rationality, but although his terminology is somewhat novel, perhaps reflecting his professional background in medicine, it is hard to see how, at the basic level he is discussing, his account could be made much more precise. As every teacher of logic knows, when the questioning is driven back far enough, either one's student just "sees" that something is a contradiction, or an identity, or the like, or it is no use wasting words. One can draw attention, point out, repeat, plead—but one cannot do another's recognizing. This is what James is saying, too: that rationality in the last resort must be seen for itself. Just as Descartes said that one must at last simply *see* that an idea is clearly and distinctly true, so James acknowledges, right at the start, the necessity for what (with a nod to Kierkegaard) we might call "appropriation" in any discussion of rationality. At some point, to avoid infinite regress, there must be some thoughts that are acceptable simply because they commend themselves to us without further proof. For James this experience, "this feeling of the sufficiency of the present moment, of its absoluteness—this absence of all need to explain it, account for it, or justify it—is what I call the Sentiment of Rationality" (James 1957a: 4). If so, now we must ask what methods may help us to achieve this experience. In what does the rational quest, most inclusively conceived, consist?

1. *Theoretical rationality.* One of the ways in which our minds seek rational ease is through the drive to unify all our knowledge, ideally under a simple principle or within a simple system. From the earliest beginnings of philosophy, when Thales and other presocratics attempted to identify the one "worldstuff" out of which all the variety of things is formed, through such masters of synthesis as Hegel, to our own day's scientific quest for a unified field theory by which to explain all physical phenomena, the insistence on *seeing together* has over and over again been manifested as a primary desire of intellect. We may call this (with a doff of the cap to the previous chapter) the demand for coherence. What is not able to be thought in relation to everything else—what is disconnected, incoherent—is irrational.

Another, equally important drive of the intellect is for comprehending the uniqueness and particularity of thoughts and things. The fascination of a child before an individual blade of grass; the curiosity that prompts us to take things apart to see what they are made of; the thirst for clarity of mind that is satisfied only by distinguishing the distinguishable and by unraveling the tangled—these are all instances of another undeniable and primary path to rationality, which (with a salute to the Positivists of two chapters earlier) we may call the demand for analysis. Until this demand for analysis is satisfied, our minds are left without the ease and fluency of rationality.

In general, then, theoretical rationality, as James sees it, is made up out of the demand for coherence and the demand for analysis. Both are in-built requirements of mind. Either demand is ignored or violated at peril.

2. *The limits of theoretical rationality.*   Unfortunately, theoretical rationality has two very serious defects, according to James, which perhaps account for the notorious inability of philosophers to come to agreed conclusions by its use.

The first of these defects is the inevitable and unresolvable tension that must hold between the demand for coherence and the demand for analysis. Both are essential, but each is destructive of the other. The drive to see everything together forces us to think in broader and broader abstractions until, at last, the barren union of empty categories alone remains. This ghostly ballet may lift us to the heights of rational contentment of one kind, but at the same time it completely negates our equally strong urge to confront clear particularity and to explore detail. Our demand for analysis, on the other hand, if given free reign to satisfy our undoubted craving to chop great, vague abstractions into their clear component parts, leaves us with nothing but what James calls a "sand-heap world" (James 1957a: 7) in which all the grains are disconnected from all the rest and the irrationality of incoherence reappears.

Theoretical rationality, then, contains within its own structure the source of its great impasse. There is no perfect way out on the theoretical level itself. The best we can do is to compromise. No philosophical position which completely violates either of our two basic legitimate theoretic interests can hope to win our approval. But any balance between them is going to seem somewhat unsatisfactory in both directions. Further, it would seem that different people have more or less strongly developed temperamental cravings for coherence or for analysis. In terms of purely theoretical considerations, it would appear to be impossible to deal with such differences or with the resulting preferences for correspondingly different philosophic positions.

Second, even if the impasse of theoretical rationality could somehow be overcome, a further inherent limit is found by James to undermine the search for rational satisfaction through mere speculation. This limit, paradoxically, is the very limitlessness of the speculative enterprise. Suppose, *per impossibile*, that a perfectly satisfactory scheme of thought could be developed by which our minds could encompass all reality with neither the irrational sense of disconnection nor that of vagueness. Would we then be able to rest content with such a conception of the world? Would that conception, in other words, need no further explanation or justification? The answer, unfortunately, James replies, is negative. Our minds are so constructed, or so conditioned, that we can never escape the question: "Why?" Even at these outer limits, we can imagine that this supposedly coherent, intelligible world *might not have been*; we contrast it with pure nonbeing; its being actual strikes us as arbitrary; we ask in James' own words: "Why was there anything but nonentity; why just this universal datum and not another?" (James 1957a: 9). And when we ask this question, James holds, we are in the grip of "the ontological wonder-sickness" (James 1957a: 9). The question can never be answered, even in principle; we must draw the curtain of inquiry and remain theoretically unsatisfied.

Hegel, as we observed in *Being and Value* (211), attempted to find a way of transcending the blank contradiction between being and nonbeing in a higher synthesis that would cure the "ontological wonder-sickness" that James diagnoses here. "But for those who deem Hegel's heroic efforts to have failed," he says, "nought remains but to confess that when all things have been unified to the supreme degree, the notion of a possible other than the actual may still haunt our imagination and prey upon our system. The bottom of being is left logically opaque to us, as something which we simply come upon and find." (James 1957a: 10).

If this is so, then theoretical rationality necessarily ends in the frustrations of arbitrariness. Since philosophers are forced to ignore the ultimate "Why?" their conceptual labors—if judged solely from within theoretical criteria—would seem to be in vain. Why not stop much sooner, with the unphilosophic "boor" (James' term), or with the "method of tenacity" (as Peirce calls it), if speculation must end eventually anyway in arbitrary opaqueness? Or why not seek escape from irrationality in the flights of the mystic? The boor, who never reaches high enough to meet a philosophic problem, and the mystic, who soars ecstatically above all problems, represent no answer for us, however. Mysticism is uncertain, available only to a few, and sporadic, "being apt to be followed by fits of reaction and dryness," and therefore "a plaster but no cure" (James 1957a: 11). Deliberate relapse into boorish thoughtlessness is impossible; but even if it were possible, we would thereby be subjecting ourselves, as Peirce held, to an inherently less stable condition for life. The unthinking person is more vulnerable to uncertainties, confusions, and mistakes; the person whose conceptual account of things is more unified and more consistent with the evidence is in a far better position. But his or her advantage, we note, is *practical* rather than theoretical. In pure theory, a beautifully organized mode of conceiving the cosmos is in the last resort no less arbitrary. Rationality, then, here meets its theoretical limit; but here, too, we have been forced again to note that practical considerations may remain exceedingly relevant even after pure theory is driven to despair.

3. *Practical rationality.*   We shall continue to think, then, as best we can within the inherent limitations of theoretical rationality. But since we are living human beings we cannot be content merely to contemplate various conceptual accounts of our universe; we shall need to choose between them and to take the best one, putting it to work in guiding our behavior and orienting our total life—values and expectations. How shall we most

rationally make our choice? Theoretical criteria end in impasse and arbitrariness; are there any practical criteria that might give us reliable guidance?

James begins with a proviso: the criteria of practical rationality come into play *only if all other things are equal theoretically* (James 1957a: 12). Serious misunderstanding of James' pragmatism has sometimes followed from ignoring this proviso. But supposing that there is nothing to choose between two rival conceptions in terms of speculative criteria, then the more reasonable one to adopt—if one must be adopted—will be the one that better satisfies our deepest human needs, aesthetic and active. That is, if irrationality most broadly conceived is uneasiness of thought, and if the frustration of deep-seated values (as a consequence of some speculative account of things) is the source of that uneasiness, then rationality will be restored by opting for an alternative account of things (if a theoretically permissible one is available) from which such values-frustration does not follow. As James put it: "[Of] two conceptions equally fit to satisfy the logical demand, that one which awakens the active impulses, or satisfies other aesthetic demands better than the other, will be accounted the more rational conception, and will deservedly prevail. . . . If, then, there were several systems excogitated, equally satisfying to our purely logical needs, they would still have to be passed in review, and approved or rejected by our aesthetic and practical nature" (James 1957a: 12). Taking due note of James' proviso, then, and postponing for the moment the question of whether or not we are ever in a position of being really required to make a decision between alternative accounts without adequate theoretical warrant, we must ask what in particular the needs of our practical life might be, as regards philosophical alternatives.

James distinguishes two criteria which, though he does not explicitly say so, appear to be necessary and sufficient conditions, respectively, of practical rationality in a conceptual scheme. The first, the necessary condition, is that a philosophic conception must *give determinateness to our idea of the future*, at least in some general way (James 1957a: 13). To active beings, the unpredictable is the irrational. Our minds feel an inevitable disquiet before the object whose future is in doubt. This is why simply becoming familiar with something's way of behaving, without "understanding" it fully in a theoretical way, can provide an important sense of rationality. There can be no doubt of its vast importance.

For this reason, any worldview that would appeal for acceptance by rational agents must not violate entirely Comte's dictum: *Savoir pour prévoir.* The "prevision" that Comte had in mind is far more limited in scope than James' requirement will demand, but prevision there must definitely be. That is, "although we may not be able to prophesy in detail the future phenomena . . ., we may set our minds at rest in a general way, when we have [appealed to] *God, Perfection, Love,* or *Reason,* by the reflection that whatever is in store for us can never at bottom be inconsistent with the character of this term; so that our attitude even toward the unexpected is in a general sense defined" (James 1957a: 15). Some foothold for verification by future experience, however tenuous, is James' first criterion of practical rationality for a philosophy. If the future makes no difference at all to a conception, it holds no interest to living agents.

Second, although the first criterion is *necessary* for practical rationality, it is not *sufficient*. To pass the latter test a philosophy must also determine the future in a particular way: viz., *"congruously with our spontaneous powers"* (James 1957a: 16). This means that—all other things being equal—pessimism in a philosophy should be considered less rational than optimism, since any doctrine that foretells the final frustration of our hopes and efforts cannot fail to rouse that disquietude that is the subjective mark of irrationality.

But even worse than honest pessimism would be the philosophical scheme that, if true, would *explain away* or *make irrelevant* all our hopes and efforts themselves. The universe pushes in on us, if we may express it thus, and our spontaneous active need is to have something on which we can push back with zest and meaning. Our conceptual account, if it is to satisfy this requirement, must be one that can provide us with this sense of meaning and worth. Anything else, from the side of practical rationality, is a failure; and since James argues that all theory is ultimately for the sake of action (James 1957a: 18), such a failure can only be treated with the utmost seriousness.

These considerations only apply, of course, under appropriate conditions. Some kinds of propositions are outside the scope of these criteria. "The future movements of the stars or the facts of past history are determined now once for all," James acknowledges, "whether I like them or not. They are given irrespective of my wishes, and in all that concerns truths like these subjective preference should have no part; it can only obscure the judgment" (James 1957a: 27). But if there are beliefs of a radically different logical character, in which we are more essentially "involved," and concerning which subjective preference plays a vital part, it is of the utmost importance that the demands of practical rationality be properly gauged and employed.

Are there such beliefs? The example of the climber faced with his leap shows that there are. That is, one kind of belief in which subjective decision makes a great difference is in predictions concerning the outcome of enterprises in which we are actively engaged. If we believe that we shall succeed, it is far more likely that success will be ours. Gloomy forecasts actually contribute in many ways to defeat. Therefore, it is far more rational, all other things being equal, to believe optimistically if such believing will contribute toward its own verification. But this can be generalized: whatever questions require an ingredient of personal commitment—a *going in* (James 1957a: 26), as James vigorously phrases it—are subject to the logic of practical rationality.

Among these, James holds, are the interminably disputed yet profoundly insistent "ultimate" questions of religious belief. He argues that religious beliefs are not primarily theoretical but practical. It makes a difference to life *now* whether we believe that in the longest run "the best" will turn out to be "the eternal" (James 1957b: 105). The ultimate justification of deliberate leaps to such beliefs, then, will be found in the long-run experience of those who make it the governing basis of their behavior. It must be *long-run*, because the very nature of the hypothesis is so general as to defy being overturned in a year or even a lifetime. But it must be verified in *experience*, no matter how difficult and indirect the tests, or face the charge of irrelevancy.

For James the process of verification appropriate to this kind of hypothesis consists in a general sense of adequacy of the fit of conceptual picture to experience as a whole, so that "if you proceed to act upon your theory it will be reversed by nothing that later turns up as your action's fruit; it will harmonize so well with the entire drift of experience that the latter will, as it were, adopt it, or at most give it an ampler interpretation, without obliging you in any way to change the essence of its formulation" (James 1957a: 33). The process of *dis*proof, on the other hand, would be accompanied by a process of increasing conceptual clumsiness and *ad hoc* efforts to save the appearances: "the course of experience will throw ever new impediments in the way of my belief, and become more and more difficult to express in its language. Epicycle upon epicycle of subsidiary hypotheses will have to be invoked to give the discrepant terms a temporary appearance of squaring with each other; but at last even this resource will fail" (James 1957a: 33).

Ultimately, then, James concludes, the one willing to leap to belief is in the intellectually sound position of any inquirer who is proceeding by trust in a working hypothesis that gives promise of increasingly showing itself adequate both to the givenness of experience and to the requirements of thought. But, in addition, the believer in the "best as the eternal" has the advantages of gratifying his or her spontaneous human impulses, of siding with the lovers of truth rather than the mere avoiders of error, and of employing the one method—trust—best designed to succeed if a personal God can in fact be known. Nothing could be more eminently reasonable, then, than the leap we have been contemplating. The only really unreasonable course, indeed, would be to become so obsessed with measuring the gap that we hesitate to the point of starvation on its stony, inhospitable brink.

PROBLEMS WITH THE LEAP

William James, like Søren Kierkegaard, focused on ultimate reality as the appropriate locus of a passionate leap. If we should remark that they are offering desperate epistemological advice, they might reply that we are in a desperate epistemological situation. How desperate is it, really? Can the modern epistemological gap be spanned by passionate choice?

The obvious first line of attack against James is to charge him with incitement to wishful thinking, and with giving aid and comfort to credulity. It was, of course, an accusation that he was himself accustomed to encountering; consequently, he takes pains to defend himself against it. Still, the facile charge is raised again and again.

The epistemological situation is more complicated, since the indictment of wishful thinking fails to take seriously James' absolutely crucial distinction between *(a)* the logical proprieties of scientific inquiry for the vast bulk of less than ultimate decisions in ordinary life and *(b)* the appropriately rational methods of dealing with the inescapable demands for risk-filled, theoretically unprovable life decisions concerning the ultimate nature of things. James agrees that on questions of the *former* logical type it is usually most prudent to withhold belief until enough evidence is in hand to tip the theoretical balance; but such a prudential methodology, which depends on the "long run" to reward its conservative approach, is simply not applicable to the situation (as Kierkegaard would have said) of the existing individual. That finite, mortal, objectively uncertain individual is James' concern, too:

> He plays the game of life not to escape losses, for he brings nothing with him to lose; he plays it for gains; and it is now or never with him, for the long run which exists indeed for humanity, is not there for him. Let him doubt, believe, or deny, he runs his risk, and has the natural right to choose which one it shall be (James 1957a: 25).

Unlike Kierkegaard, however, James has offered a set of general criteria to judge *which* "objective uncertainties" are worthy of choice, and under *what circumstances* a "leap" is the most reasonable response. For James, even a leap is never properly taken with closed eyes, but always with a lively interest in the consequences. To reduce James' argument to a mere defense of wishful thinking, therefore, would appear at best to be based on a superficial reading.

One cannot help noticing, however, an interesting shift that has quietly occurred in James regarding the kind of status our beliefs and doubts about ultimate reality should be thought to have. This is illustrated in his repudiating talk of facts in astronomy or history as the improper context for discussing worldviews. Instead he proposes moral discourse as our appropriate model.

Does this mean that worldviews are not about "the facts" as we tend at first to use that expression? Has James subtly transposed his discussion into nonfactual categories of thought? Can a leap to belief about ultimate reality permit its key conceptions to be nonfactual, or of a radically different kind of fact from the facts of history or astronomy? Or must even these latter facts be reconceived more adequately? These are some of the issues raised by James' use of primarily *moral* models in connection with his arguments for religious belief.

Another issue for the Jamesian pragmatist is raised by the self-admitted possibility that different individuals might find satisfaction in "leaps" to different—and to what seem mutually incompatible—world-hypotheses. James is a pluralist both when dealing with demands of theory, concerning which different temperaments might require different compromises between analysis and coherence, and when discussing the needs of practical rationality, in which again differently constituted individuals might be legitimately stimulated to "go in" for different hypotheses. These consequences are startling, to say the least, for those who might have joined the conversation with the expectation that a conception, once certified as adequate for belief, must *correspond* at least in a general way to the realities it aids our minds to grasp and our actions to confront.

Since Kant, however, virtually everyone has been stymied by the epistemological gap's preventing things in themselves, as they are "by themselves" (apart from the built-in structures of mind), from being directly known. And as we have seen repeatedly in recent chapters, this raises a deep question about the correspondence ideal itself. Since it is impossible in principle ever to *compare* our ideas with their objects (as though we could climb out of our ideas to examine both the ideas and their objects in some inconceivable, idealess way), the best that we seem able to hope for is the long-run "fit," as James puts it, among our ideas, and between our ideas and the totality of experience.

This epistemological conclusion, however, if accepted, calls for considerable changes in traditional views of the logical status of ultimate beliefs. That one such structure of belief is rationally justifiable, under these circumstances, would not necessarily guarantee either *(a)* that all other conceptions are automatically exposed as inadequate or *(b)* that the ultimate nature of things needs to resemble the one that a particular person, or a particular community, finds genuinely adequate at a given time. Epistemological pluralism would rule.

Must this pluralism continue without resolution forever? James gives us no guarantee that it will not. But it is at least possible, on his position, to foresee a gradual narrowing of the choices as the cumulative experience of the human race eliminates some conceptions as no longer living options, while it establishes others ever more securely as reliable accounts of things. Suppose, then, we grant to James the possibility that the human race will one day come to general agreement on ultimate questions. (Even to state this, however, is to feel its unlikelihood.) If this great improbability occurs, it will not necessarily mean that ultimate reality is literally *like* the ideas we then shall agree upon. James' approach remains unable to provide assurance that what we leap to will resemble even our best, most widely accepted, ideas.

James makes a good deal, we have seen, of the principle that prediction, at least in general terms, is a *sine qua non* of practical rationality, and that the capacity of a conception to "determine the future" is the basis of our most essential ability to verify or falsify it. But it might be feared that James has been so permissive about the "general terms" in which he will allow a "prediction" to be formulated that he has destroyed the very possibility of verification or falsification in questions of ultimate reality.

If we call the ultimate "God," we may "set our minds at rest in a general way," as he says; but will this "rest" be based on having encountered any definite experiences validating prior predictions, or will it be only a matter of satisfying our psychological responses? James would seem logically to require the former if he is going to appeal to the cumulative judgment of humanity regarding the "fit" of experience with conception, but he appears actually to have set his requirements so loosely that only the latter can be claimed. He points out that given religious belief, "*whatever* is in store for us can never be inconsistent with the character of [e.g., God's love]; so that our *attitude* even toward the unexpected is in a general sense defined" (James 1957a: 15). But if this is *all* that a conception of the universe does—"define our attitude" towards *whatever* is in store—then anything that could possibly happen would be compatible with it, and our hope of gradually establishing some conceptions as better verified than others, singling them out of the welter of theoretical possibilities, disappears.

Even if such a hope does not disappear completely, as might be allowable if James' statement about adjusting human attitudes is not taken as *exhaustive* of his position, one may continue to wonder whether this hope for verification or falsification might not fade indefinitely far into never-ending futurity. Suppose that some definable state of affairs, however general, were to be previsioned by a religious conception of the world. This granted, the process of verification can go forward, James says, toward the happy day when, in the "final integration of things" all the evidence being "in," "it will appear without doubt" (James 1957a: 34) which conception is victorious. But will it? If, as James admits, the present human situation is such that "the facts of the world give countenance to both" sides of nearly all really significant disputes between ultimate worldviews (James 1957a: 34), why should the simple addition of more time and more experience with these indecisive facts make any crucial logical difference? Here James seems to have a major quarrel with Kant and Kierkegaard, who both insisted that questions appropriate to faith are not items even of *possible* knowledge. Neither of the latter would have agreed with James' claim that the "long run . . . exists indeed for humanity" (James 1957a: 25), in which the present day need for risk and moral courage will presumably be displaced. And in this disagreement, James seems to have the less defensible side, especially in light of his own dictum that since truth-getting is an endless process, "no bell in us tolls to let us know for certain when truth is in our grasp" (James 1957b: 108). Why people in the future should expect a different cognitive situation is hard to imagine.

Supposing, however, that verification or falsification are in principle possible for worldviews, then the question inevitably must be sharply raised: do we not have enough grounds *already* to make the leap of faith illegitimate even within James' elastic boundaries? Three possible circumstances could force even James to come down against his favored theistic worldview.

First, one might find that pragmatic theism is *not even a living option* for large numbers of modern men and women. We must at least consider the possibility that Nietzsche's proclamation of the death of God may ring subjectively true for large secular segments of the modern world in a way that had not yet happened at the time of James' writing. If so, then all questions of such people's "right to believe" are beside the point, and other issues— such as whether the conception of God ought to become living again for them, or allowed to rest in peace—become central.

A second circumstance would strip us of our right to believe: if it should be discovered that pragmatic theism has not met James' initial proviso that from the point of view of purely intellectual criteria all rival hypotheses actually are equal. It must be acknowledged that James has made it difficult for us to judge what it means for philosophic conceptions to have adequately met what he calls in one place "the logical demand" (James 1957a: 12), because it is not, for him, a matter of *the* logical demand at all but, rather, a balance or compromise between theoretical demands that counter and inherently frustrate one another. He does, however, maintain that some extreme positions—he cites Hume and Spinoza as such cases (James 1957a: 5)—can genuinely fail to effect the theoretically needed balance and so be rejected on those grounds alone.

Are we confident that the position of theism is not at least as vulnerable to such rejection as are the positions of those distinguished thinkers? Many contemporary views would attack the assumption that theoretically "all other things" *are* epistemically equal where belief in God is concerned. And if these doubts can be made good, then we are not entitled even by James to consider going beyond theoretical to practical justifications of faith.

Finally, even granting that theism is a hypothesis both living and epistemically defensible to the same partial degree, at least, as its main alternatives, we may ask whether the verification or falsification process that James pictured in the future has not already taken place in the twentieth century—with weighty results on the negative side. We recall his description of what to look for: ever new impediments to holding the belief in question, ever greater difficulties in expressing our experience in the language of that hypothesis, "epicycle upon epicycle" of qualifications to square theory with fact, and finally even the failure of these rationalizations to convince. Has this been the story of the years between James and ourselves, particularly as a consequence of the gigantic growth of twentieth-century sciences? If so, then practical rationality cannot justify us in leaping to those beliefs, however appealing they may be to our practical interests or desires. Some of these questions will engage us again in the final volume of this trilogy.

Efforts like those of Kierkegaard and James to overcome epistemological problems with acts of will have not fared well, but existentialists and pragmatists gave us something of potentially even greater value. Both philosophical movements turned fresh attention to the examination of experience as it *really is*, rather than as it must be *assumed to be* if classical commitments to clarity, distinctness, and the superiority of unchanging formal characteristics are to be honored. Closely related to existentialism, the movement known as Phenomenology scrutinized the structures of consciousness and found "intentionality"—a felt outward reference to a world beyond mental images—embedded at its core. Pragmatism, especially as practiced by William James and his younger friend and admirer, John Dewey (1859–1952), also strongly opposed the accounts of experience favored by orthodox Empiricists, calling instead for a "Radical Empiricism" in which the warm, value-laden, obscure, but profoundly important elements neglected by the main tradition could better be acknowledged. The latter demand, that experience not be "prettied up" by tendentious preferences for cool clarity, was also voiced by Alfred North Whitehead, who shared James' and Dewey's thirst for a more adequate account of human experience. In this reexamination of experience, quite apart from the issues of "leaping," the existentialists and pragmatists of modern times started the turn toward a postmodern epistemology. Further enriched by Whitehead, who himself was encouraged by James and Dewey, such a fresh epistemological start will show that we need not be intimidated by the epistemological gap.

In the next three chapters, I plan to offer such an constructive alternative viewpoint which, if successful, will deconstruct the basis for modern gaps and bifurcations. But this will require abandoning some of the most familiar of the modern epistemic norms before we find ourselves in a postmodern place, where the epistemological gap—recognized as the grand myth that it is—will have lost its power to dismay.

Part Three

Deconstructing the Epistemological Gap

8

EXPERIENCING THE WORLD

The previous two parts of this book have shown the need for something new. The first part traced the path to the edge of the epistemological gap; the second sampled primary ways in which later modern philosophers attempted to cope. These turned out in each case to be not particularly effective. Classical modern reductionism, coherentism, and pragmatism—in different ways—all leave us wondering whether we can ever get across that gap between the knower and the known.

This final part will do something else. Here I offer my suggestions for a postmodern epistemology. In the three chapters of this part, I shall work in parallel with the three topics emphasized respectively by the protagonists of the previous three chapters. The empiricist reductionists of Chapter 5 grounded their analysis on a theory of *experience*. The present chapter will rethink values and experience. The rationalist coherentists of Chapter 6 placed their confidence in the powers of *thought*. Chapter 9 will take another look at values and thinking. The pragmatists of Chapter 7 tied their hopes to the needs of *life*. Chapter 10 will return to the question of knowing and fulfillment.

My overall strategy will be deconstruction of the epistemological gap as a grand modern myth. This book has followed, in some detail, its construction. Granted, it seemed not to be a "construction" at all—much less a myth—to those who found themselves on its brink. It seemed a discovery or, once "discovered," a threat to be coped with. But my tactics in the first part of the book involved also laying bare the preferences, assumptions, and commitments behind the seeming discovery. These were quintessentially human and historical. Hence these value-based outcomes could have been otherwise. The supposed threat to knowing posed by the dreaded gap does not need, therefore, to be reduced, webbed, or leaped. It needs, instead, to be deconstructed, deflated, or dissolved (depending on the metaphor of choice). It has never really been there at all.

My specific plan is to invoke an alternative worldview offering a microaccount of what experience, thinking, and knowing involve and how they relate to the larger cosmos of which knowers are natural parts and exemplars. This will be what, in *Being and Value*, I called the "ecological worldview" (Ferré 1996: chapters 10–12). It is inspired both by ecology itself, which I take to be the bellwether postmodern science, and by the metaphysical insights of Alfred North Whitehead. It is an essentially relational ontology of continuities. It leaves no room for an epistemological gap. Mine is to be a deconstruction, then, that is achieved constructively; it involves the elimination of an oppressive epistemological myth by appeal to a liberating metaphysics. This will strike many as paradoxical, but so be it. Epistemology and metaphysics are always inextricably intertwined. Whether a postmodern epistemology—one freed from the modern impasse epitomized by Hume and Kant—can be defended on Whiteheadian-ecological grounds will need to be tested by trying.

As I proceed through these chapters, I shall therefore need to build on positions I have shaped in part three of the first volume of the present trilogy. This puts me, as expositor, in a difficult position. I want my suggestions to make sense to all my readers, whether or not they have read *Being and Value* by the time they come to this point in the present volume. Obviously I am unable to reproduce and reargue those earlier chapters here in any detail—nor should I, even if I could, out of consideration for those readers who have already digested the first volume and now have an appetite to interpret knowing within the postmodern worldview offered there.

A compromise is called for. The next section of this chapter will provide a quick synopsis of just the main points needed to continue without detouring. Veterans of the first volume may feel free to skip. Newcomers should be able to gain a general sense of where I am coming from; but those who have not yet read the last part of *Being and Value* should not assume they can gain an adequate understanding of the worldview, or even what I mean by "postmodern," from the following section alone.

The Postmodern Turn

I am not particularly enamored of the term "postmodern," especially in view of its widespread association with trendy deconstructionist movements, with which I disagree at least as much as I make common cause. But, until a serviceable positive term emerges, to capture the character of the age we are entering, I am not willing to relinquish "postmodern" language to the nay-sayers.

I came to the term via Alfred North Whitehead's compelling treatment of modernity in his *Science and the Modern World* (1925). Whitehead's criticisms effectively "deconstructed" modern assumptions, for me, but did not stop there. He offered something constructive in their place. This was a "philosophy of organism," as he called it, in which the brilliant but flawed achievements of the modern world—both intellectual and practical—could be put in context and incorporated into a wider, more adequate worldview. It would not turn the clock back but move on to more comprehensive understandings inclusive of, but more satisfying than, modern metaphysics and epistemology.

The modern worldview prefers quantity to quality. This is expressed in many ways, including the cult of quantification in modern science, in which nothing is accepted as understood until it can be reduced to a mathematical formula. Qualitative considerations were first ignored as negligible, then dismissed as unreal. A whole orthodoxy of "primary qualities" (mathematically measurable weights, shapes, velocities, etc.) invidiously compared with "secondary qualities" ("merely" qualitative colors, sounds, smells, etc.) became established, as we saw, in modern epistemology. Modern capitalism and modern socialism both celebrate the "bottom line" in the quantitative terms of material productivity.

In this worldview in which "objective" weight and size are primary, "subjective" odors and colors secondary, it is not surprising that matter takes precedence over mind. The "realists" are those who keep their concern focused on metric tons and leave worry about stinking ugliness to the "bleeding hearts." If qualities have no home in the real world, and if the mind alone is the domain of quality, then we start to wonder where in the real world the mind belongs—if it belongs at all. Beginning with dualism, we eventually find ourselves pressed into a space-time continuum wherein minds and their values have no intelligible place at all. Therein languishes what I called the modern agenda: viz., to find room in reality for mind and its qualities. This has still not been accomplished within the limits of modern assumptions and values.

Atoms, like the early Wittgenstein's atomic facts, are fundamental for the modern worldview, and it is assumed that atoms (like atomic facts) are just what they are without regard to anything else. They are thought, in Whitehead's language, to be "simply located." Some philosophers took this as the very definition of "substance": namely, to be thinkable, and to be able to exist, without reference to anything outside itself. This would make all relations external and secondary for substances. "Rugged individualism" would be a social manifestation of such a worldview. Community (and certainly govern-ment) would become derivative, mere means. Following its logic to the ex-treme, the "free market" of abrasive competition among impenetrable units of self-interest would become the dominant metaphor for human relations.

Appropriate to atomism of this "simply located" sort, analysis takes priority over synthesis as the preferred mode of thinking. To pull things apart is to reveal the real substances underneath. To pull ideas apart is to unveil their meaning. The characteristic educational institutions of the modern world—schools and universities with proliferated specializations pursued through highly departmentalized curricula—are the typical manifestations of these modern values. Synthesis, where it occurs, is additive and secondary, not holistic and primary. Controlled experimentation, in which deliberately simplified situa-tions are thoroughly analyzed and held constant while selected elements are subjected to rigorously determined manipulation, becomes the paradigm of inquiry. Hierarchical control becomes standard in the quintessentially modern organizational charts of business, education, medicine, and government.

Against these characteristic intellectual preferences and institutional structures, many important movements have been active in the latter part of the twentieth century. They express their uneasiness with—or, stronger, their rejection of—central modern presumptions. They have raised the conscious-ness of many, in no uncertain terms, to the prospect that the modern era has outrun its course and is now toppling, burdened by its own huge technologi-cal successes as well as by its inherent valuational flaws. Among these op-position movements are the "post-structuralist" thinkers, centered in France but widely disseminated from there. These have been the ones most publicly and vociferously proclaiming the coming of the "postmodern" age. Every-thing modern is anathema, scorned and repudiated, including (oddly, I think) the large project of thinking steadily and whole about *why* modernity is so flawed. The deconstructive postmodernist voices declare the end of meta-physics, the end of epistemology, and the end of philosophy—all, they say, are "hegemonic" and "totalizing," and thus fit only for the dustbin. I differ at this point, since I see no requirement that looking at a big picture forces the viewer into a small frame. Large vistas can be liberating, though I grant that typical modern worldviews (e.g., Newton's) have been used coercively. Still, the poststructuralists' celebration of particularity, plurality, and playful-ness; their openness to differences, to freedom, to quality; and their resistance to quantitative reduction—these I find important straws flying in the gale that is battering modernity. Even though I prefer moving beyond their deconstructive efforts to a more constructive (or reconstructive) mode of postmodernism, I am reconciled to sharing the concept of the postmodern with these difficult allies, whether or not they would be inclined to return the favor.

Other significant movements sapping the foundations of modernity include liberation theology, which questions the established assumptions of modern society on behalf of social justice and respect for persons, however weak and forgotten they may be; feminism, which tends to stress the importance of cooperation, community, relationships, and holism in thought as in life; and environmentalism, which (allied with ecofeminism) strongly questions the anthropocentric and dominating attitudes of modern thought and rejects modern alienating attitudes toward nature in general. Environmentalists are, indeed, in some ways the most radical of all, since many of them not only return qualitative and valuational questions to the center of the discussion, as do all the others, but also extend issues of justice and intrinsic value to domains far beyond human consciousness or even the narrow interests of our species. Together, and in concert with other vigorous attacks on the central pillars of modern assumption, these movements are ensuring that the twentieth century will end with a strong awareness that a major transition— a transition comparable to the transition between the premodern and the modern eras—is under way. The modern era had a beginning, rose to dominate the planet and the thoughts and attitudes of vast numbers of its adherents, and now is running out of intellectual energy. The brilliant abstractions undergirding its worldview have led to perpetual impasse, both metaphysical and epistemological, and the very successes of its science and technology now pose the gravest threats to its (and the rest of the world's) survival.

Something distinctly postmodern, something neither *pre*modern nor *hyper*modern, seems urgently called for. If it is to be established securely and is to go sufficiently deep, it must be so grounded in careful science and so extended through philosophical imagination as to provide an alternative worldview. This alternative needs to be able to make room for, and unify, the values of critical movements like feminism and environmentalism, poststructuralism and liberation theology, as they seek in various directions for postmodern solutions. It needs to make good theoretical sense and to have strong empirical footing. It needs to be applicable to social problems and capable of redesigning institutions.

I believe there is an essentially postmodern science that can ground this need. It is the young science of ecology. And I further believe that philosophical extension from the methods and concerns of scientific ecology can nurture an ecological worldview adequate to the postmodern need.

Ecology is the science of relations. It studies relations between organisms and other organisms, as well as between organisms and their inorganic settings. Its central subject matter is systems, and systems of systems. It uses modern tools of analysis; it is in no way backward-looking when it comes to utilizing the advances of modernity in chemistry or physics or mathematics;

but these tools are put to work in the interest of understanding whole systems in their complex networks of mutual influence. One of the most difficult jobs for ecological scientists is defining boundaries for study (a lake, a swamp, a watershed), since all such boundaries are at best permeable and temporary. "Everything is connected to everything else" (Commoner 1972: 29-35). Scientific ecology, aware of this, remains open in principle to influences from ever-larger wholes.

Further, ecology is a science that recognizes norms. It is not in principle value-free. Concepts such as "health" and "thriving" are built into its professional vocabulary. It recognizes the difference between a threatened biome and one that is vigorous. It notices teleology in nature, built-in tendencies, needs, and interests of organisms. It does not confuse teleology with "purpose" in premodern ways, but it does not shrink—as modern science from Galileo has shrunk—from recognizing the natural "final causation" built into food-seeking, reproduction-oriented organisms.

Still further, ecology breaks through modern alienation between what is known and the human knower. *Homo sapiens* is an important player in the systems studied by ecology. For ecology, there is no avoiding the fact that humanity is part of nature, no basis for attitudinal aloofness, as so typical in modern science, between active cognizer and passive "data." We are involved—our needs, hopes, fears, and all.

The science of ecology reverses the modern trend to ever-increasing specialization. It is essentially interdisciplinary, team-dependent, and long-term. Its most important payoffs come in unfolding large understandings rather than in nailing down small predictions. This forces ecology to struggle for its soul with modern-minded, departmentally-bound, micro-project-rewarding universities and funding sources. But since systems ecology is the bellwether for postmodern science, these struggles brim with significance for the shape of the future.

A worldview needed for our future may grow from the soil of ecological science, much as the modern worldview was constructed with the help of Newton's mechanics. An ecological worldview will not *be* science, of course, any more than the modern materialist worldview (though relying on the prestige of successes in physics and chemistry) is itself science. But since speculative imagination will be used, willy-nilly, by human beings to provide some ultimate context for our lives, philosophy hoping to support an ecologically sound and thriving postmodern world could do worse than push its speculations in harmony with systems ecology.

Suppose systems make up the universe. Suppose the model of organisms-in-connection applies "all the way down," and fits even the most elementary entities there are. Suppose these least of all puffs of existence are themselves systems of relatedness, drawing character from their immediate surroundings (insofar as these surroundings have acquired definite character that can be passed on) and determining their own definiteness in momentary throbs of self-creation. Suppose selective pressures have resulted, over cosmic aeons, in the finite set of relatively stable systems we find in our universe: that is, mutually compatible subatomic particles replicating successor particles, which in turn cooperatively sustain slowly evolved patterns by clustering into atomic nuclei and into attractive-repulsive clouds of electronic pulsations.

These were some of the suggestions I made in *Being and Value*, with deep indebtedness to Alfred North Whitehead, though with some important differences. These suppositions involve reconceiving the ultimate inert "particles" of the modern worldview as, instead, ultimate active "events." Energy, not matter, thus becomes primary, although the evolution of energetic pulses, actively creating their own definite actuality, has stabilized into what we call matter. Such matter is not "dead," as in standard modern conceptions, but is composed of ephemeral dynamic events, each with the interior capacity to grasp its immediate environment and weave what is grasped into its own intrinsic character—which, in turn, becomes its legacy to successor events of self-actualizing potential. What could be called "neomatter"—that is, matter energetically conceived—is inherently capable of evolution into increasingly complex systems of relatedness. Eventually it evolves into societies of systems so complex and differentiated that sheer rhythmic repetition of wave-patterns is not the only viable option, and significant novelty of outcome begins to be possible. The capacity for relevant spontaneity is what differentiates "living" from "non-living" matter. Once living systems appear, the rate of cosmic evolution is greatly accelerated, and complexity increases exponentially. In systems we call organic, especially in those with differentiated nervous systems and centralized brains, the survival-enhancing capacity of the whole system to respond as a unity to its larger environment is enhanced by functional differentiation into sub-systems specialized (1) for receiving inputs from various aspects of the surrounding world, (2) for transmitting these inputs (appropriately processed and amplified) to a central point, a node (3) for receiving, comparing, evaluating the many inputs, and (4) for directing the organic system as a whole into appropriate coordinated behavior. The crucial nodal points are the locations where self-creating events of extremely high complexity and (thus) potential for attainment of overtly mental character can appear. But the basic structure of these high-grade events of self-actualizing energy is not fundamentally different from the structure of the events that make up the vibratory sequence of wave-patterns we call electrons or even more elementary events. High-grade events are more capable of spontaneous novelty because they occupy a richer crossroads. An environment within a living brain offers far more alternative possibilities for synthesis into interesting actuality than does the environment inside (say) a silicon atom repeating itself within a grain of sand. But both attain actuality in the same way: by grasping what possibilities are available in the immediate environment, processing them, then settling on what definite objective character shall be actualized for presentation to successor events.

What, then, is this "grasping" of the immediate environment? It is basic to the connectedness of things and to the process of causal inheritance from past to present states of the universe. It must be a dynamic process that allows characteristics to be transferred from one to another entity. It must allow characteristics actualized in the immediate causal past to enter effectively into the making of the creative present.

We have no closer clue to the nature of the universal process of "graspings" between events—how the external is internalized—than by reflecting on what underlies our own experience, most generally considered. In experience we are *in*-formed. We take what was "objective" and "other," making it "subjective" and "our own." Experience provides connection. Search as we may, the *only* connections we directly encounter are connections in experience. Sometimes experience is overwhelming and coercive, sweeping into and over us. Sometimes, for humans at least, experience can be complex, nuanced, and open to deliberate reweaving according to our aims. It always starts, however, with something that feels settled in the immediate past; and it always contains a vector toward what feels not yet completely settled in the relatively open future.

Whitehead showed that conceiving connectedness through the model of primitive experience can be extended "all the way down." We have no other model, if we try to think what connectedness can be for the entities connected. We must not, however, clutter this model with traits unique (so far as we know) to *human* experience. That would wrongly exaggerate the role of consciousness, freedom, purpose, symbolic capacity in the larger universe. These, though we tend to value (and thus notice) them above all others, are probably not even the most typical modes of experience for humans, considered across a full lifetime or even a full day, from drowsy start to sleepy end. Instead, we should try mentally to bracket these atypical powers, achieved so rarely by evolution, and go down instead to the most basic core of experience—to sheer graspings of states of affairs from moment to moment. This is what Whitehead called *prehension*, to distinguish universal, unconscious grasping from the specialized, self-aware modes of "comprehension" or "apprehension," of which only high-grade organisms are capable.

A prehensive universe is one in which ubiquitous systems hang together only because events grasp their contexts. Human events of consciousness are exceptional only in their complexity and intensity. Otherwise, they function in complete unison with all the other events of nature. Each event earns its own achieved identity; each begins to become something for itself by prehending actualized events in its immediate past; each one processes the possibilities that its past provides; and each finds a self-consistent way of bringing about closure for itself as it squeezes out incompatible possibilities to become determinate—something of achieved value—in the moment that constitutes its present.

Perhaps the preceding, telegraphic though it is, will serve as a suggestive transition to some positive proposals toward which this book has been pointing from the start. I believe that if we combine an ecological worldview (emphasizing systems and real relatedness) with a panexperientialist account of relations (understanding relations not just externally, by describing how they *appear*, but internally, dealing with what they *are* for the entities related), we will be able to locate a philosophical standpoint for deconstructing the epistemological gap. My approach will extend the ecological model into epistemology, in that it recognizes human knowing as in no way alien, despite its rarity, within the environing universe. It will extend it still further, in that human knowing will be seen as at bottom naturally relational: an immensely amplified and refined case of what (literally) holds the cosmos together. Proposing this in more detail is my goal in the rest of this book.

Such a postmodern turn in epistemology will be deeply empirical. It will start with experience and trust its starting point. This is not to deny that experience can and often does fool us. Postmodern epistemology, in solidarity with modern and premodern varieties, must acknowledge all the illusions, delusions, mirages, and hallucinations made famous in the history of epistemology. But ecological, relational epistemology will remind us that *discovery* of mistakes in experience is possible only thanks to *more and wider experience*. And such epistemology in the ecological mode further will insist that *corrections* of experience-induced errors can only be made by accepting the feed-back from *more comprehensive or more careful appeals to experience*.

This turn will involve, at the very outset, taking a fateful fork in the philosophic road, away from the position of Parmenides, which, if pursued instead, would have systematically discounted the authority of experience. The basic standard of *adequacy* will be valued in a postmodern climate no less sensitive to "differences" than to the standard of coherence. Any coherences attained will need to be accountable to experience and will not be allowed—in the long run, certainly—to override the source of their own conceptual materials.

Although the approach I will be proposing in what follows is stalwartly empirical in this most general way, it will not be "empiricist," in the sense either of the eighteenth-century British Empiricists or of their heirs, the Logical Empiricists of the twentieth. In fact, the position will begin from a basic rejection of these Empiricists' oversimplified descriptions of experience. It will resonate instead with the more complex accounts of experience given by the coherentists and the pragmatists.

The best account of all, I think, is the one given by Alfred North Whitehead, who was "in the camp" of none of the above. His finely nuanced approach distinguishes between two major poles in what we too easily lump together as "experience." In the two sections following, I shall present in my own way what derives from the bipolar Whiteheadian position. I believe it is capable of grounding a theory of experience worthy of postmodern concerns and freed from the myth of the epistemological gap.

PHYSICAL CONTINUITIES IN EXPERIENCE

What, on a "philosophy of organism" deriving from Whitehead, do we directly experience? Strictly speaking, causal inheritance comes only from the immediate environment of a prehending event. That narrows the causal environment to the living body. What is that most intimate, most direct organic experience like?

I ponder that issue one morning on a walk with my dog. The weather is cool as we set out, down our lane and across a vacant field toward the corner newspaper shop. As I turn over various possibilities for treating the topic of immediate experience for this chapter, I attend to various sorts of awareness that I usually let lie in the background when out for walks like this. I let myself be aware of what my toes feel with each step, nested in their soft cotton gym socks and spreading at each rhythmic impact of my shoe on the ground. The muscles of the legs tighten and relax pleasingly as they swing along, while inside my knees there are smooth pressures. I am glad this morning, especially about how the knees feel today, since some years ago they moved stiffly, a painful subregion of my body then inflamed with arthritis. No pain today, thank heaven, though there is a slight twinge in my left hip if I let myself notice. As I ponder these things, my right hand is aware of my dog's retractable leash, the line beginning to play out as she slows to explore some attractive odor. Though she is behind me, and out of my field of vision, I am keenly aware of her as we progress together. My ears pick up the rattle of the leash running out, and my arm and shoulder feel the sudden jerk as she insists that I wait while she sniffs, or adds her own contribution to the canine bouquet. My stomach is content, in the early stages of digestion of a recent light breakfast, riding along under the light pressure of my belt. Something liquid, doubtless my third cup of coffee, gently sloshes as I resume my stride. My eyes, I notice, are busy searching for hazards in my path across the rough part of the field, flicking up occasionally to take in the wider surroundings, the grey sky ready to rain, then over to check my dog, and once again back to the path ahead. My nose is full of the odor of fresh cut grass. I pull my attention back to the subject of direct experience and how I might approach it for this chapter.

One thing I notice, as I reflect on this small slice of experience (in reality much more complicated, of course, than I could possibly describe), is that the kinaesthetic, internal experiences—the ones I do not usually attend to—are inextricably blended with experiences beyond their own respective areas of my body and beyond my body itself. Not just the eyes and nose and ears but also the toes and knees feel beyond themselves to a world of hummocks and pebbles. The flesh of the hand feels the grip of the leash, and beyond it the coil in the handle and the line in the coil, all the way to the companionable dog in the collar. This does not all seem equally "indirect" experience (if "indirect" implies something "inferential"), although by the time my attention reaches the dog at the end of the leash, it hardly feels "direct," either.

Another point I notice, on reflection, is that it is not at all clear how centralized all this experience really is. Whitehead described human conscious selves as made up of "ruling occasions" of experience, succeeding one another rapidly in the brain, receiving from the rest of the body (funnelled through neural networks) the indescribably complex end result of huge numbers of subordinate patterns of experience constituting the whole organism. As I shall argue in what follows, this allows a plausible account of personal consciousness, how we surf the waves of preconscious experience and direct ourselves not as a single continuous substance but as a series (usually well-integrated, but sometimes not) of episodic pattern actualizations. But, reflecting on experiences such as I had on this morning's walk, I wonder whether all our body's awareness must be channelled through higher ruling occasions in the brain. If neural networks are cut, "we" as the conscious sequence of ruling events situated in the brain, lose conscious feeling from the affected places. But the body's total experience may be more than brain-processed experience. Toes and nose and knees experience themselves and their environment whether or not our central nervous system is funnelling their experience to the brain. During periods of conscious inattention, the symphony of experience within the body is playing; it is just not being transmitted to the conductor. "Direct experience," if so, is a wider concept than "personal, conscious awareness."

Be this as it may, epistemologists are especially interested in how the world environing the living organism is transmitted to the personal center of conscious awareness. On the Whiteheadian view, this is through a causal network of feelings and feelings of feelings that link physical events into complex systems we call living sense organs, which organs, with many other mutually supportive and mutually dependent organs, constitute the still more vastly complex systems that are living animal bodies equipped with bundles of nerves, along which events of experience can be transmitted, amplified, combined with others, and eventually unified in one brief but powerful moment of conscious self-definition. That moment passes, like a single frame on a rolling film projector, but it leaves its achievement of conscious definiteness to be grasped by its successor moment, possibly somewhere else in the active brain, in what Daniel Dennett calls "distributed contentful states" (Dennett 1991: 135). Each moment initially conforms to its predecessor, sometimes introducing novelty in anticipation of its own successor.

But long before the blossoming of conscious awareness in highly specialized brain-located events of conscious perception, there are throughout the living body countless millions of simpler, preconscious perceptions within and between cells, organelles, and organs. In the case of specialized exteroceptive sense organs, like eyes and ears and noses, specific features of the immediately impinging environment—light waves, sound waves, airborne chemicals, etc.—are recognized, responded to, processed, amplified; and these processed responses are transmitted to neighboring neurons, in which electrical potential is stimulated and a series of causal connections are made, either being dealt with locally, by a reflex, or leading to the spinal cord and brain. By no means is all the perceptual information that reaches the brain brought to conscious attention. The interoceptive sense organs, which provide information about the internal environment (such as hunger and thirst, fatigue, circulatory information, etc.) may rise to consciousness or may not. The brain receives information about blood pressure, for example, and makes adjustments accordingly, without bringing the information above the preconscious threshold. And proprioceptive sense organs, which provide information about the condition of joints, tendons, muscles, etc., and about balance (located in the semicircular canals of the ear), are also often "attended to" behaviorally but not "brought to conscious attention," except in special cases. In my work as an instrument flight instructor, I routinely need to bring some of these proprioceptive senses (by actual airborne demonstration) to the forefront of my flight students' consciousness. One must be aware in instrument flight that turbulence and other G-forces may induce a conflict between visual (instrument based) and proprioceptive (semicircular canal) sensory reports to the brain on whether or not the aircraft is in a turn; one must not panic when this occurs; but, if one wants to survive, one should choose to believe the instruments!

All the reports received by conscious events in the brain are the end product of many other unconscious events of complex prehension across synapses, mediated by other prehensions within chemical neurotransmitters diffused across synaptic gaps. The neurophysiological details are fascinating but not essential for this account. What is essential is that we notice the dependence of all sense perception—conscious or unconscious, exteroceptive as well as interoceptive and proprioceptive—on presensory chemical and electrical recognitions, reactions, and further responses throughout the living system. Chemicals and fibers relate. They feel their predecessor events, attain intrinsic states of their own, and pass on their attained states to successor events.

Once this is noticed, it is obviously false to claim, as many empiricists have, that all perception is limited to Aristotle's "five senses." Not only was Aristotle's list (even if one adds his "common sensibles") incomplete, omitting such exteroceptive sensations as pain, pressure, and temperature as well as all the interoceptive and proprioceptive senses; more fundamentally, the "five senses" limitation ignores the communication system within the body that brings coherent information from the various organs to the conscious events of the brain. Synapses in the optical nerve do not *see* changes in their state. Those in the olfactory nerve do not *smell* or *taste* variations in electrical potential. Reactions in the acoustic nerve are not recognized by *hearing*. It might be agreed that *touch* comes into play, but this is far from the standard empiricist "touch." A Whiteheadian will gladly acknowledge that *feeling* occurs within the neural system, that is, prehensive grasping of prior organic states by new moments of nascent actuality. Information is recognized, reacted to, processed, and passed on. Presensory perception, unconscious but essential to any sensation as it travels from event to event toward awareness, is the underlying requisite for sensory cognition. Immediate experience, it turns out, floats on depths of presensory—thus extrasensory—perception. The dogma that cognition can be accounted for on the basis of the five senses alone is blind to the kind of experience that precedes, surrounds, and makes possible the five senses themselves. A postmodern epistemology will not be intimidated by such dogmas.

I realize that in writing "extrasensory perception" in the preceding paragraph, I am in danger of losing some readers who will recoil from what they have been taught to regard as "spooky" or, at best, the domain of charlatan "mind readers." This is not at all my meaning, but I do want to defend the reality of perception that is not reducible to the standard empiricist five senses. To this point I have stressed what might be called "infrasensory" perception. The meaningful transmission of information between events of self-actualizing energy is beneath and within every sensory signal, whether it eventually becomes conscious or not. No member of the preceding chain of preconscious informational graspings is "sensory," that is, none is on the standard list of senses. Therefore, being outside the approved list, they are (in this limited context) "extra"-sensory. But I have a still wider use for the notion of extrasensory perception. I think it quite reasonable to maintain that besides *infra*sensory perception there is also *supra*sensory perception.

Indeed, I think it obvious that we live with suprasensory perception all the time. It is not clear or distinct, like the "sense contents" appealed to by Ayer, but neither is there anything spooky about it. Consider what we would have if we had only conscious exteroceptive sense contents (i.e., sights and sounds and smells, etc.) to work with. Each would be the momentary end product of a long train of brief pulsations of information, initiated at the surface of the body at a specialized sense organ and passed along, with modifications, through the neurological system to the part of the brain that is complex enough to support the momentary surfacing into consciousness of information provided by the *immediately adjacent ganglia* of its immediate environment. Sense contents alone, in other words, would be the awareness of the interior of the brain. But that is not what we experience. We do not (usually) even experience the sense organ at the surface of the body, unless we burn our tongue or feel our eye dazzled or our ear deafened. Even then we usually feel scalding *coffee* or a bright *light* or an intolerable *explosion*. Normal daily experience is of our bodies in a world. Dogs, pebbles, clouds, as well as toes and muscles, not the insides of our brains, are what we directly experience—somehow. And yet, on the strictly causal account allowed to this point, sensory experience is limited to the series of conscious events rising— and trapped—within the billions of neurons-in-relation constituting the human brain.

If this entrapment follows from the theory, but is contradicted by experience, the theory must be wrong—or at best incomplete. Even Hobbes recognized as much when confronted with the consequence of holding that conscious experience is no more than internal "vibrations" left by incoming particles. He postulated (even before Newton's law of "equal and opposite reaction") that the atoms of our conscious "phantasms" somehow must push back against incoming stimuli and in so doing project the appearance of a world outside the body. The attempt was crude, but it shows the need. A Whiteheadian account cannot do less, though it will do it differently.

Whitehead distinguished between two poles within each occasion of experience. Initially, during the phase of self-creation in which an event prehends its immediate environment and conforms itself to its intrusive past, we encounter the "physical pole" and recognize the ground of all causal transmission. But each new event, as I have indicated, comes to its own subjective satisfaction (by internal processing of available possibilities) as it becomes definite. The latter phase Whitehead called the "mental pole," by theoretical extension of this word—for important theoretical motives of overall coherence—even to entities that, strictly speaking (even from a Whiteheadian perspective), have no "minds." That a later event can feel a noncontiguous mental achievement of another, Whitehead argued, is theoretically possible and quite "natural" within his philosophy of organism.

It is not necessary for the philosophy of organism entirely to deny that there is direct objectification of one occasion in a later occasion which is not contiguous to it. Indeed, the contrary opinion would seem the more natural for this doctrine. . . . Physical prehensions fall into two species, pure physical prehensions and hybrid physical prehensions. A pure physical prehension is a prehension whose datum is an antecedent occasion objectified in respect to one of its own *physical* prehensions. A hybrid prehension has as its datum an antecedent occasion objectified in respect to a *conceptual* prehension. Thus a pure physical prehension is the transmission of the physical feeling while hybrid prehension is the transmission of mental feeling (Whitehead 1978: 307–8).

I have for the most part been describing pure physical prehensions, thus far, which (in the universe as we find it) are the most common mode of information transmission. In our own "cosmic epoch," at least, this is the dominant "species" of prehension. But this is a contingent matter of fact, not a theoretical necessity. Thus, Whitehead writes, "There is no reason to assimilate the conditions for hybrid prehensions to those for pure physical prehensions. Indeed the contrary hypothesis is the more natural" (Whitehead 1978: 308).

Moreover, adequacy to actual experience requires that such a theoretical place for suprasensory transmissions be given respectful attention, Whitehead notes, though he gives only two examples. "This conclusion has some empirical support, both from the evidence for peculiar instances of telepathy, and from the instinctive apprehension of a tone of feeling in ordinary social intercourse" (Whitehead 1978: 308).

I shall come back to the issue of telepathy at the end of this chapter. Now it is more pertinent to note—and extend—Whitehead's appeal to the widespread sense of "instinctively" apprehending "a tone of feeling" in ordinary social settings. Perhaps some will recall stepping into a room crackling with hostility. Other happier moments of awareness may bring the instinctive sense of merriment, or quiet acceptance, or love. Whitehead does not discuss this, but the powerful effects of group psychology may be grounded also in hybrid physical prehensions, the direct feeling of primitive mental states that allow normally decent people to "go along with the crowd" in actions or emotions that would usually horrify the individual—and do, perhaps, haunt and puzzle the person afterward, for years to come. We do not need to experience a lynch mob to realize that "instinctive apprehension" of many other minds united in frenzied social purpose can invade our psyches in surprising ways; an ordinary football afternoon, or attendance at a boxing match, may do almost as well. Perhaps, from this epistemological point of view, one important justification for Quaker meetings, or other gatherings for worship and deliberate social concentration on finer, more delicate modes of mentality, may rest on this phenomenon. Certainly something about the *shared* character of meaningful beauty experienced with others in the theater and at concerts is important, too, over and above the genuine values of solitary viewing and hearing.

We should not over-interpret what hybrid physical prehension means, cognitively. It is not a matter of "reading minds" if by that is meant perceptions of clear thoughts, especially thoughts symbolized and made precise by language. It is more a matter of "sharing moods" or of feeling subjective tones that are spatially at some remove from the insides of our brains. As Whitehead warns, "Hence it will only be in exceptional circumstances that an immediate hybrid prehension has sufficient vivid definition to receive a subjective form of clear conscious attention" (Whitehead 1978: 308).

Though vague and usually submerged under the normal sensory inflow of the more potent complexities provided through the central nervous system, suprasensory experience still provides a vital background tonality of "thereness" and importance for the world beyond our cerebral cortex. Whitehead himself does not emphasis this, but I think hybrid physical prehension provides a significant escape route from entrapment inside the brain. The concrete content of remote events can be felt through the unbroken continuity of causal transmission, but hybrid physical prehension reaches directly outward, beyond the firings of neurons in the contiguous organic environment of the momentary event of conscious awareness. Without supra- as well as infrasensory perception, we would lack vital direct feelings by our brains of our bodies and, in particular, of our sense organs—interoceptive, proprioceptive, and exteroceptive—as well as the richly definite mental poles of entities constituting the "world outside."

We must be careful. The mental poles of prior infrasensory events (in synaptic transmissions, for example) are not "minds," and they do not have "thoughts," such that hybrid physical prehensions could "read" them; but on the present world-hypothesis, each causal transmission *always* involves in its later phase some minuscule subjective satisfaction from the creation of definiteness out of its prior phase of indeterminate possibility. And there are many, many of these small subjective satisfactions, tiny intrinsic states of self-valuation, to be found within the intimate environment of neural networks (and elsewhere) in the living body. From there they are to be found in myriad chains of causal continuity to and beyond the impacts on the surface of the body, on outward into the causally connected greater environment of systems we feel as our world.

This will have obvious implications for solving the problem of induction, but as that problem is usually posed, it belongs in the final section of this chapter. I am here confining my discussion to issues of experience far closer to immediate life—"closer than hands and feet." And, speaking of feet, it is worth noting that on the prehensive theory I am proposing, the toes, not only the brain, feel the intertwined messages of infra- and suprasensory transmission. The toes do not only send messages through the central nervous system to the foci of consciousness (where they are sometimes attended to, usually ignored); they also feel for themselves their context in the foot, in the sock, in the shoe, on the ground. Most of this is transmitted simply causally, by pure physical prehensions, in the dominant manner habitual for this cosmic epoch. But along with those primary causal pressures (including not just external pressures such as I have already mentioned, but also internal blood pressures, continual growth and repair work, aeration, nourishment, etc.), there also throb the low but massive tonalities of subjective achievements in the concrete actualities noncontiguous with the cells and fibers making up the inside of the toe. Since the events making up the inside of the toe cannot "think," they cannot "know" that there is a sock "out there," beyond them, or a shoe, or a grassy field interspersed with stones. But in an entirely preconceptual, nonlinguistic, unconscious way, the toe feels its connections—to the body and beyond the body. It feels a world. Tickle a toe and a reflex arc explodes. The toe does not recognize a feather as a feather. For that, causal signals need to be sent up the spinal column to the brain, where other senses, memories, concepts, will be put into play and events of conscious recognition will name the source of the tickle. But the toe feels a world through the feather without needing the brain to name its tormentor.

Experience of this primal order is even lower on the spectrum leading to consciousness than Bradley's "mere feeling," adduced in his search for and example of multiplicity without qualitative distinctions. Perhaps, though, his "mere feeling" can now be interpreted in terms of the preconscious deliverances of physical and hybrid physical prehensions. There is no reason to limit these to the human brain coming out of deep sleep or anaesthesia, as I did in my earlier illustrations. There is no reason to limit them to the human body—though these are all to which we have direct causal linkage. There is every reason to suppose, continuous with our own deeper experience, that animals feel a world and feel, perhaps with greater reliability than humans (so hyper-dependent are we on symbolic abstractions open to error), the subjective tonalities of the surrounding and noncontiguous environment. There is indeed no theoretical reason, on this ecological-prehensive view of the world, to "draw lines" beneath which entities have a zero degree of feeling for their environments. Ethical implications obviously follow, but these will be postponed to the final volume of this trilogy.

One interesting ethical-epistemological implication need not be postponed. That is the insight of Duns Scotus that unless there is some direct experience of "*haecceitas*" beyond the universal qualities of things—some real experience of the unique "thisness" of an individual—we are forced by epistemological theory to deny the deep intuition that somehow we are genuinely connected with the one we love. The awareness of a world full of real entities, not just abstract qualities in various configurations, is too powerful to be overridden by a theory that only sense contents (Ayer) or ideas (Berkeley) can possibly be before the mind. Where theory and experience clash so profoundly, the demand of adequacy requires that theory be corrected. Duns was right. We do experience *haecceitas*. He was also right that these experiences are murky, vague, and hard to point to in sharply defined concepts, though we may not wish to lay the blame for this, as he did, on "original sin." A prehensive philosophy of organism shows how these facts of experience can be reconceived in a more comprehensive theory involving both pure physical and hybrid prehensions.

Not only love, emphasized by Duns, but also all the other deep emotions—fear and anger, revulsion and admiration, etc.—characterize the subjective awareness of entities within their relevant environment. Basic experience, in other words, is laced through and through with valuing; positive and negative, valuing is bundled with prehending, as the most basic fact of relatedness. Valuing "up" or "down" is as ubiquitous as the antibodies in our bloodstream, recognizing and destroying invader microbes. The medley of valuing in a living organism provides the undercurrent of its existence. Not simply positive, not simply negative, the underlying matrix of valuational feeling—resultant of billions of ongoing preferences—provides our experience of the world its deepest organ tones of sensed importance.

Importance and solidity, awareness of looming presences behind bright surfaces, these are contributions from the physical pole of the experiencing event. These may be the more frequently neglected features of experience, but of course they are by no means the whole of it. In addition, there are indeed the bright surfaces, the clear qualities, the mathematically calculable elements. These are contributed by the other great source, to which we next turn.

CONCEPTUAL CONTINUITIES IN EXPERIENCE

When I write about "sources" of experience, I do not want to be misunderstood. These "sources" are not like separate telephone lines coming into a home; they are more like brightness and contrast in television reception. They should be conceived as distinguishable features within a single event, or series of unitary events. They are mixed and mingled in real life, always more or less, never all or none. But they are important for us to notice if we want an empirical (not "empiricist") epistemology based on an adequate description of experience.

Many of my examples in the previous section have shown the inevitably mixed character of the physical and conceptual poles of experience, though I have intentionally emphasized vague but "weighty" conformal physical feelings rather than relatively clear and distinct qualities like redness or roundness. Perhaps more illustrations from the domain of reflexes will make the polarities still clearer.

In our evolutionary bag of tricks there is something called the "withdrawal reflex." If we touch a red-hot poker, for example, our arm and hand twitch away from the dangerous object *even before the pain-signal can get to the brain.* This immediate withdrawal is governed from the spinal cord, which simultaneously might cause other limbs to move so as to keep the body's balance during the emergency. This event is about as far toward the physical pole as I can imagine. The body is experiencing and responding without thought, before "central management" even knows it has a problem. But then the pain hits. It comes in waves of increasing intensity, demanding attention. Sometimes consciousness simply shuts down, the person faints. Short of this, the eyes focus on the scene, note the glow of the poker, and as the brain processes a cascade of such signals through the deluge of pain, the conscious agent begins to recognize the situation. This is the first step toward remedial action, for example, plunging the burned hand into cold water, or the like. Perhaps an emergency telephone call follows, reporting a serious burn and requesting ambulance service, giving the address and other needed information. At this point concepts are being communicated through language. "Hot," "poker," "burned," "pain," etc., are all words carrying abstract meanings encoded in a series of conformal electrical pulses along telephone wires to a decoding apparatus and a hearer who can calmly understand and efficiently respond. Perhaps this end of the example approaches the other extreme of experience, at the conceptual pole, although emergency workers (however toughened by life's challenges) have feelings, too. Or perhaps a still better example of experience near the conceptual pole would be reflected in the consciousness of readers now completing this paragraph.

There was, I trust, no physical discomfort involved in reading the previous paragraph—no withdrawal reflex, no surges of pain, no frantic efforts at remedy. Black marks on white paper were the primary visual stimuli, but meaning blossomed from them. The "event" recounted was at no particular time or place, happened to no particular person, injured no particular hand, left or right, and was caused by no particular poker, heated to no particular heat. There is a considerable range of temperatures, any of which would count as "red-hot," ranging from dull black-orange glow, through cherry red, to nearly white. There is an even wider range of things that could count as "pokers." These are all *determinables,* capable of being fully satisfied by an indefinite number of *determinates.*

The reader's experience of the "burn" was entirely by way of concepts, learned earlier in closer proximity to the physical pole. My example was almost entirely an abstract play of ideas. And yet, though it was far toward the conceptual pole, I would not be surprised if, because of thinking about it, the reader's heartbeat was slightly elevated as adrenal glands, useful for survival, kicked in.

This is the context, I believe, in which the age-old issue of "universals" should be approached. General characteristics are an obvious aspect of experience. The problem is in giving an adequate account. What are these characteristics? Are they Platonic forms, capable of existing by themselves? Are they Aristotelian forms, existing only in substances? Are they simply general ideas in someone's mind? Are they no more than particular words we use to label groups of particulars?

My answer begins by pointing back to experience. Daily life is full of recurrent features. If there were no repetitions, no routines, no "hello again!" experiences, there could be no *re*cognitions. Without recognitions there would be nothing to which a name could be attached for deployment at different times and in different places. Even the most nominalist account needs to acknowledge that there are general, that is, repeatable, features of particulars that attract enough attention to acquire a name.

What are these "features"? In the previous volume, I called them "possibilities for actualization" or "forms of definiteness" (Ferré 1996: 344–45). They are what the energetic pulses of self-actualization make actual. In language introduced above, they are the abstract determinables that concrete entities manifest determinately. This sounds chillingly remote, but nothing could be more warmly familiar. Take, for example, the hot poker in my earlier example. The concept "hot," in this context, designates a range of temperatures, vaguely bounded at the lower end, where "warm" leaves off, and with no upper limit short of this metal's melting point, when there would be no more use for talk about a "poker." The concept of "hot" for the poker is a determinable that will be satisfied by any particular degree of heat within this range. There will always be one or another particular degree, which, using sophisticated instruments, we can "name," to a high order of precision, with numbers spelled out in many decimal points. That particular degree of temperature is the determinate "form of definiteness" (with respect to the determinable, "hot") taken by the particular physical events actualizing the poker at that particular time. Determinables become actual only in determinate forms of definiteness. We never experience "hotness in general," though we usually do not know (cannot name) the exact degree without going to considerable trouble—and even then, with our most precise instruments, there remains a "margin of error," a smudge factor in our capacity to provide a label that would cover this *and only this* quality of heat. Going to a few more decimal points would reveal further variations in range. And one can always, in principle, call for more decimal points. Our names, even for what we treat as determinates, then, remain general.

In the world of daily experience we have names for huge numbers of features that have caught our linguistic community's attention. This is the strength of the nominalist's account of the features that pervade experience. At the same time, not all the features of things can possibly be fully named. If we choose determinable words that are vague enough, like "colored," we can cover everything visible. But within the determinable "colored," there are many obvious determinate colors to be distinguished and named, according to the interests of our linguistic community. "Blue" is one determinate, with respect to "colored," but is itself a determinable which allows within its scope a number of determinate (and incompatible) shades—as everyone who has tried to match blue fabrics learns with frustration. That the features of things are not equivalent to the names we give them is vividly illustrated by that frustration. General features come first and have the last laugh as we try to get them under conceptual control.

Forms of definiteness are possibilities for actualization. They are not reducible to our talk or to our thoughts, though we can deal with possibilities (as nonactual) only in thought. When actualized, these possibilities retain their formal character—that is, they have definitely this exact quality or that precise relation, which in principle can be actualized an indefinite number of times in indefinitely many events—but in becoming actual they have squeezed out the vagueness, the smudge of tolerance, that possibilities offer for incompatible determinations under the same determinable.

With Whitehead (and Aristotle), I affirm the ontological principle that actuality is primary over possibility. To the extent that forms of definiteness are possibilities, a disembodied "realm" of these forms makes no sense. Fortunately, such a realm is not needed. Every actuality is the embodiment of many general characteristics; it is the manifestation of determinable properties in a specific set of determinates. And to the extent that mentality is a genuine, functioning part of our worldview, nonactual forms of definiteness— pure possibilities—have a place in the universe, too. Whitehead himself thought that the entire set of pure possibilities, what he called the "eternal objects," needed a single actual entity in which to be held. He postulated a Primordial Nature in one great actual entity, God, to perform this function, which he believed to be theoretically required. In the first volume I expressed my doubt that such a requirement really holds. In a cosmos in which every event has a mental pole, possibilities—the forms—would seem not to need a single, unique repository to account for them. It is the primary function of the mental to deal with possibilities, to take account of the absent as well as the present. Lower grade events, in which the mental pole is of negligible importance, deal with realized possibilities in mainly conformal ways, through causal inheritance. For them, that is, for the vast bulk of the physical universe, abstract possibilities are neither real nor relevant. Higher grade events, however, are able to evaluate inherited possibilities in contrast with alternatives not physically present. The richer the inheritance, the more possibilities the mental processes have to play with. Hybrid physical prehension, too, functions more powerfully where mentality is more developed, releasing such events from complete dependence on the contiguous environment as source of all conceptual materials for creative recombination.

Add to this the thought that forms of definiteness may not need to be "eternal," as Whitehead (in the Platonic tradition) believed. In a self-creating universe, I favor allowing for genuinely new possibilities. This is clearly the case with "real possibilities," as Whitehead also saw. There are always limits to what is really possible within a given state of the universe. One millisecond before an automobile crash, there is no real possibility of avoiding the collision. A minute before, even ten seconds before, there had been other real possibilities, now gone. The reverse is also the case. In the year a baby is born, there is no real possibility of the infant's writing a great symphony. In the next year, still none to speak of, but new real possibilities can gradually be created, especially by application of steady purpose, as shown by Leopold Mozart. When his son, Wolfgang, actualized these newly created real possibilities in his symphonies, he was at the same time creating new formal possibilities of musical beauty. Must we hold that Mozart's symphonies were "eternal," having some standing in the universe even before he was born? It is a way of speaking in praise of great art that it is "eternal," but in some ways it diminishes the creative achievement (and clutters the ontological landscape) to insist that Mozart just "discovered," and wrote down, forty-one out of an infinite number of possible "Mozart symphonies," the pure possibility of which had forever been previsioned by God. Instead, I prefer to think that in Mozart's act of creation, new formal entities—hitherto nonexistent forms of definiteness—were added to the universe. These would take their place among what in the previous volume I called "temporal formal entities" (Ferré 1996: 329).

Be this as it may metaphysically, it is clear epistemologically that an inverse ratio exists between the degree of realization of possibilities and the quality, or complexity, of mentality. That is, when forms of definiteness are overwhelmingly *present*, forcing causal conformity and rhythmic repetitions, as in the pulsations of atomic structures, mentality is least significant; when the relevant possibilities are *remote*, taken account of as pure possibilities, mentality is at its highest. The more distant a possibility is from realization, the greater the role of mentality.

Of all known processes produced by the evolutionary self-ordering of our cosmos, human thinking is by far the most capable of dealing with remote possibilities. It is our most distinctive capacity, affecting everything we do, think, and are. It allows for distant goals and the deliberate creation of new real possibilities in practice (e.g., writing by word processor) and in thought (e.g., planning and composing a series of chapters or books). It makes moral responsibility possible. It allows us to take account of our own death, and is the ground of poetry and religion. Without it there could be no civilization. For better or for worse, human mentality has made a huge difference to the planet that spawned it; perhaps mentality will have consequences yet unimagined for the solar system and the greater universe.

This power for dealing with pure possibilities is our pride, our joy, and (in some contexts) our downfall. I shall save discussion of the ethical issues for *Living and Value*. Here we should notice the impact of this special human talent on philosophical accounts of experience, both for good and ill.

When we humans start to attend most closely to immediate experience, as philosophers do when attempting to ground theories of knowing, we tend quite understandably to pay most attention to the clearest, brightest, steadiest aspects. These are taken as normative. Plato led the way, with his admiration for the perfect Forms, ideal qualities luminous in their intellectual accessibility, satisfyingly *intelligible* for the exercise of our distinctive human powers. The rest of experience is second-best for Plato: murky, worthless for knowledge. Only if we focus all our attention on what stands out as changeless— eternal—will we find success, he thought, in the cognitive quest. The body, together with all its organs of need and sensation, must be left behind by the true philosopher. In some moods, as we saw, Plato recognized the body's role in providing a sensory ladder of love toward the increasingly mental; in other moods he suggested that the body should be fought and abandoned as soon as possible. In Plato's account of experience, the conceptual pole was to rule supreme; the physical pole was to be suppressed.

Aristotle pulled back from this extreme, but only a little. He was a genuine disciple of Plato in his admiration for the Forms as the only aspect of experience that could lead to knowledge of the best sort. He was not entirely dogmatic about this, as we saw, when he allowed some status for empirical physicians, like his father, and therefore some place for knowledge of individual cases. But the human powers of ideal contemplation were treasured by Aristotle no less than by Plato, and his account of human experience was heavily in favor of forms of definiteness over physical prehensions. And through the ages following, the joint influence of these great philosophers dominated medieval epistemology, as we have seen. John Duns Scotus was the only major exception to the orthodoxy privileging the conceptual pole over the physical pole in experience. Even the nominalists, toward the end of the premodern period, emphasized clear modes of experience: viz., those that can be well and truly *named*.

Preferential treatment for the conceptual pole in experience continued in the modern era. Only Hobbes and Locke were not entirely silent or negative on the physical pole. Hobbes, we saw, remarked on the felt reciprocal outward "pressure" of mental phantasms, evidence of their causal source in a world outside the body and its organs. Locke, we noticed, included the "we know not what" of substance beneath and supporting the clear but lifeless ideas he identified as fundamental to experience. He also accepted "powers" in things, though unfortunately these escaped detection except through the qualities they generate for our ideas.

Except for these rather awkward acknowledgements, however, modern epistemology tilted almost entirely toward our species' pride and joy, the clear, abstract conceptual pole in experience. Descartes would trust only clear and distinct ideas as giving us anything at all worthwhile. He went far beyond Aristotle by dismissing even the most vivid colors or qualities of odor as "secondary," ultimately worthless in cognition. Only those aspects of experience that are subject to mathematical treatment—Galileo's "primary qualities"—were genuinely "clear" and "distinct" for Descartes. And in the end the whole knowable physical universe became for him simply *res extensa*, a plenum of pure extension itself, which his newly invented Cartesian coordinate system was able to translate into algebraic formulae. All the rest of experience was temptation to error.

Despite their many differences with Descartes, Berkeley and Hume both accepted the clarity and distinctness criterion for normative human experience. They both represent a more moderate return toward Aristotle, of course, in their greater respect for the unquantifiable qualities in direct experience. Still, a Berkeleian idea must be completely determinate. There was in his account of experience no penumbral area, except, perhaps, for the direct "notion" (not an idea) of what it is to be an active spirit. But regarding the world, there could be no ideas allowing ambiguity or admitting causal powers of their own. Every perception must be completely determinate, a sharp idea, a passive definiteness.

Hume accepted the same principle, taking "impressions" as normative for experience. These he distinguished by their "force and liveliness" from mere "ideas," which have less of both and are mere "copies" of the impressions that gave them birth in our experience. Unfortunately, even regarding impressions, whether of sense or "reflexion," Hume made no real use of either "force" (he denied that we can experience any "force" between events, external or internal) or "liveliness" (he said they have no living organic powers). As a result, even impressions were treated as mere sense contents, clear for conceptual recognition, but so "distinct" as to be entirely "loose and separate."

This became the "phenomenal world" Kant left as his legacy to modern epistemology. He recognized that absence of substance and causality would make a real world impossible, and science futile. To supply what was missing in the British empiricist account of experience, however, he did not redress the tilt toward the conceptual pole by adding accounts of the physical pole, organic, unclear, intimate, and powerfully filled with intimations of importance. On the contrary, he thought that solving the problem could be accomplished by placing even more emphasis on the conceptual. He proposed to solve Hume's problem of an experientially causeless phenomenal world by making causality an a priori category of *reason*. Scientists will always find causes for events, he asserted, because our *minds* guarantee it. No challenge was launched against the one-sided modern account of experience. In this he definitively widened and confirmed the epistemological gap.

EXPERIENCE: SPECTRA AND BIPOLARITIES

The actual situation in human experience is far from pure. In wakeful, alert life, the conceptual pole may dominate, with clearly delineated qualities drawing most of our attention. But even at our most alert and concentrated, this kind of awareness is punctuated with vagueness, momentary daydreams, visceral messages of all sorts—from toes and knees, bladder and bowels, stomach and lungs, to sore thumb. Our experience, as David Gelernter puts it in his insightful challenge to orthodox assumptions in the artificial intelligence community, is on a spectrum.

> Here is my argument. Human thought is laid out in a continuous spectrum. Every human mind is a spectrum; every human mind possesses a broad continuous range of different ways in which to think. The way in which a person happens to be thinking at any given moment depends on a characteristic I'll call "mental focus." Focus can be high or low or medium; it changes throughout the day, not because the thinker consciously changes it, as he might consciously raise his arm, but in subliminal responses to his physiological state as a whole. Fatigue (for example) makes focus go lower. Wide-awakeness makes it go higher (Gelernter 1994: 4).

The trouble with most artificial intelligence research, Gelernter argues, is that virtually all attention has been paid to emulating (very) "high focus" functions, like mathematical calculation, as in the "counting out" of alternative possibilities in chess playing. Since these are what I have called conceptual pole activities, the vast majority of computer scientists and artificial intelligence researchers (unsurprisingly, in light of the pro-conceptual-pole bias in the history of epistemology) have assumed unquestioningly that these functions represent the only "important" kinds of thinking and have placed exclusive emphasis on them. Gelernter is a happy exception. He recognizes that our culture has made a value judgment favoring these "high focus" powers, but that the judgment is one-sided and incomplete. As he puts it, "Making high-focus thought the norm, setting it at the center of our cognitive universe, is the supreme and defining achievement of the modern mind" (Gelernter 1994: 76). He does not mention it, but he might have supported his case by pointing to the chemicals preferred in modern society. Most approve adding to our bloodstream chemicals that induce wakeful (conceptual pole) states of experience—above all, caffeine, through coffee, tea, and cola drug-delivery systems—and many harshly disapprove of those, such as alcohol or *Cannabis sativa*, with opposite effects.

Gelernter proposes a broader appreciation of the full range of human experience and thought. Poetry and religion, grounded in the "lower focus" of human mentality, he takes with seriousness and appreciation. These lie in the domain of creativity, where great affective metaphors link together unexpectedly to reveal new connections. He quotes the poet Shelley: "Reason respects the difference, and imagination the similitudes of things" (Shelley 1966, in Gelernter 1994: 80). What we call spirituality, Gelernter continues, must not be held in contempt, as the dominant values of the modern era have prompted us to do. Jewish mystics, and even the secular Sigmund Freud (Gay 1987: 17), were right to give it priority.

> The essence of the phenomenon might be a sense of *connectedness*—among the creatures, objects, and events of the outside world, and between this outside world and the inner world of the thinker; the spiritual state of mind is preeminently the sensation that "all life is linked . . ." (Bokser 1981, 1). I say *sensation* on purpose. No-one has to convince you that the sky is blue—you perceive that it is; and the mind in a spiritual state perceives a kind of all-encompassing connectedness, the "undefined sense of connectedness" that Romain Rolland, among many others, "took to be at the heart of religious sentiments . . ." (Gelernter 1994: 93).

Computer scientists, Gelernter argues, will never succeed in finding the key to human mentality, much less to synthesizing it by machines, no matter how powerful, without finding a way of paying adequate attention to the full spectrum of experience, from high to low. His own Yale University laboratories are at work, taking first tentative steps exactly in this direction.

It was a horrible irony that this exceptional scientist (whom I would compare to a postmodern Moses, trying to lead cognitive science out of its bondage in modernity) bore the brunt of the Unabomber's uncomprehending, antimodernist fury.

Other nascent postmodern scientific work supports the general account of a spectrum of human experience, ranging from low-focus, highly affective perception close to the physical pole, toward higher-focus, more neutral, critical thought closer to the conceptual pole. At the annual meeting of the American Psychological Association held August 13, 1995, Jonathan Bargh presented findings that all perceptions come initially laden with values. "We have yet to find something the mind regards with complete impartiality, without at least a mild judgment of liking or disliking" (Bargh 1995: B-5). Value judgments are basic and inescapable near the physical pole of experience. We feel the world preferentially. Our world, far prior to conscious awareness, is a vast field of values and disvalues, adversions and aversions. This state need not remain dominant, however, as experience comes increasingly close to the conceptual pole. Thinking in explicit concepts distances us from the immediate pulls and pushes of preference. According to Bargh, "The more you think about an opinion, the weaker the influence of these automatic judgments" (Bargh 1995: B-9). Similarly, "If you tend toward . . . bias, you can override it by conscious thought" (Bargh 1995: B-9).

Alfred North Whitehead's account of actual mixed human experience also maintains the two poles in constant interactive tension. He calls our normal wakeful state "symbolic reference." The physical pole, where "causal efficacy" occurs, provides the massive sense of *thereness* and *importance* in experience. The conceptual pole, the source of "presentational immediacy," manifests our power of dealing with pure possibility, that is, with forms of definiteness in their disembodied generality. In normal sense experience, we prehend realized possibilities from our environment; we physically process, amplify, transduce, and transmit them organically to events of consciousness. This is the physical pole that provides our feeling of the "weight" of the real world over-against us, invading us with its presence and with what Bargh calls its inescapable preconscious values. It gives us what Gelernter refers to as the "sense of connectedness." But it is vague in its affective richness. Overlying this background, wakeful human experience also weaves a foreground, thanks to the conceptual abilities of human mentality, full of geometric shapes, crisp colors, and all that goes into what Hume called the vivacious impressions that give rise to ideas. On the present account, it is our capacity for dealing with ideas that makes possible the vividly distinguishable impressions in experience. We refer features received vaguely by physical prehension back onto the canvas of the powerfully felt world; but in this symbolic reference, we experience these features in clarified, sharpened, and deracinated versions, sanitized from the affectively potent actual events that brought them to us, and projected onto the extensive continuum of geometrical time and space. This we take to be our contemporary world. Evolution has proven this projective capacity highly effective for species survival. But of course it is capable of letting us down. As in any symbolic reference, the symbol is not the thing symbolized. Prehensions at the physical pole are too deep and immediate for the issue of "error" to arise. But causal prehensions are always of the immediate past, not of the present. When we attribute qualities to a world taken as contemporary, we may be wrong. Gazing at the planet Mars at night, we need to be reminded that this is not exactly how Mars looks *now*. It took several minutes for the light from that planet to reach our eyes. Some celestial objects seen with the naked eye may show themselves as they were hundreds of years ago. Some stars twinkling in our sky may actually have exploded long ago. The same thing is true, in principle, of the familiar walls of our room. There is a *practically negligible* but *theoretically vital* gap between immediate past stimuli prehended in our body and brain, and the wall experienced as contemporary. Features (qualities, forms of definiteness) organically received from our immediate past, processed and purified, geometrized, and projected, are what we attribute to the contemporary wall.

This bipolar interplay usually works well enough. Normally we are justified in neglecting what is practically negligible. But not always. Those long-famous illusions, delusions, and hallucinations do occur. We humans open our door especially wide to them by our own great talent for dealing with pure possibilities. Vivid possibilities, when taken as actualities, may let us down. This state of affairs seems worth enduring, however, since the alternative to the opportunity for error would be the dull infallibility of unthinking things. The capacity to be mistaken is something to be claimed with pride.

I am still referring only to perceptual mistakes, not to theoretical ones, which will need to be considered in connection with knowing, not experiencing. Much more could be said about the bipolarities of human experience, drawing, perhaps, on the "tacit" and "focal" dimensions distinguished by Michael Polanyi (Polanyi 1966, 1964). But Polanyi's views will figure in the next chapter, as such bipolarities relate to thinking. Thus, although more could be added, perhaps enough has been presented here to suggest an alternative account of experience, empirical but not empiricist, that can offer benefits for a postmodern epistemology. The first, and greatest, benefit is fuller adequacy to the complete range of data that should be included in any account of human experience. A corollary of greater adequacy (as the next chapter will show) is recognition of such continuities between body and mind, world and experience, that obviate the epistemological gap itself. Other benefits, I shall argue, include (1) the escape from old conundrums, such as

Hume's problem of induction (and Kant's misdirected "solution" of it), and (2) the provision of newly thinkable possibilities for extended ranges of experiential data that might provide postmodern psychology (and postmodern ethology) with new and fascinating research programs. These two topics will conclude the present chapter.

BIPOLAR EXPERIENCE: SOME BENEFITS

One of the most intractable of all modern philosophical issues is the justification of inductive expectations. In common life as well as in the most abstract reaches of science, we suppose that we are not irrational to anticipate that future experiences will confirm what we have learned to expect from past experiences. Ordinary people become aware of regularities (and pass them on as recipes or rules of thumb); scientists since Kepler and Galileo have worked hard to show the mathematical form of these, as well as many more subtle regularities, in expressions they eventually promulgate as laws. Thanks to the network of such recipes and laws, ordinary people and scientists draw inferences about likely matters of fact—which normally happen as predicted. Surely this is one of the most reasonable activities we humans engage in, is it not?

It is not, if Hume and the vast majority of modern philosophers who accept the empiricist account of experience remain unchallenged. That account, as we saw, holds that in the clear, crisp moment of a present sense impression—its description heavily biased toward the conceptual pole of universal qualities, whether secondary or primary—there is no detectable direct experience of past or future, no feeling of causal connection. Every event of experience, on this account, is completely cut off from every other, except by such external characteristics as resemblance, contiguity, etc.; thus every event in the world is condemned to be "entirely loose and separate." On this standard modern account, there can be no basis for a meaningful expression of causal connection that would warrant the real limitation of events in the present by their immediate past, or ground future events on the actual achievements of the present.

Hume offered, in place of the experience of real casual connection, only our experience of habituated expectation, a subjective substitute for the objective connections between things. But even this concession was too much if all events are to be considered "entirely loose and separate." Are our thoughts *constrained* by our habits? Then even Hume is admitting, by the back door (as Whitehead suggests) that there are feelings of causality, where the accumulated past thrusts itself into the present, whether we like it or not.

No philosopher really holds that this is the sole source of information: Hume and his followers appeal vaguely to 'memory' and to 'practice,' in order to supplement their direct information, and Kant wrote other *Critiques* in order to supplement his *Critique of Pure Reason*. But the general procedure of modern philosophical 'criticism' is to tie down opponents strictly to the front door of presentational immediacy as the sole source of information, while one's own philosophy makes its escape by a back door veiled under the ordinary usages of language (Whitehead 1978: 174).

Hume's appeal to "habit" is one such back door escape from the implausible purity of his bias toward the conceptual pole as completely describing experience. The bias is utterly basic in modern preferences. Only the conceptual pole in experience is open to the clarities of mathematical treatment, and this only for the minority portion of it treasured as the "primary qualities." But the strong preference for this sort of clarity was enough to convince Hume and most moderns that this pole, with its fruit of abstract presentational immediacy, should be taken as normative for what counts as "real" experience. The rest—messy, vague, fluid—was unworthy of serious philosophical notice.

If Hume had been more willing to consider the organic context of human experience, including reflexes and the other bodily functions I have emphasized earlier in this chapter, the famous problem of induction might never have risen to haunt modern philosophy. In experiencing reflexes, we are close to the physical pole. We feel ourselves causally constrained to jerk our hand away from the hot poker before we feel the pain. A Humean account misdescribes experience in such cases. Hume argued that all we can mean by "causal connection" is derived from our experience of mentally connecting clearly defined impressions. When we have learned to associate event B (pulling our hand away) with event A (touching a hot poker), we expect, when an A-type event occurs, that a B-type event will follow. This felt expectation linking well-defined event-types is all we can mean by "cause," he maintained. Clarity of formal properties (like "hot" and "hand") is presupposed, as is the explicit recognition of the situation. This description may apply reasonably well to our visual observation of one billiard ball approaching another, and our expectation that the second will be put in motion in usual ways. But none of these conceptual-pole clarities are present in reflex behavior. Since real experience is mixed experience, some conceptual elements will always be found, but more important will be immediate feelings of causal efficacy. Whitehead proposes another example. Imagine a man sitting in the dark and suddenly having a bright light turned on. He blinks. This happens very rapidly, practically simultaneously, though the flash of bright light is experienced as coming first. Hume would have argued that *all* we directly experience is this temporal sequence, first the flash and then

the blink, and that we merely expect cause from becoming accustomed to repeated instances of this sequence. But this is not accurate description. It
leaves something utterly vital out of the inventory of experiences.

According to the philosophy of organism, the man also experiences
another percept in the mode of causal efficacy. He feels that the experiences of the *eye* in the matter of the flash are causal of the blink. The
man himself will have no doubt of it. In fact, it is the feeling of causality which enables the man to distinguish the priority of the flash; and
the inversion of the argument, whereby the temporal sequence 'flash to
blink' is made the premise of the 'causality' belief, has its origin in pure
theory. The man will explain his experience by saying, 'The flash made
me blink'; and if his statement be doubted, he will reply, 'I know it,
because I felt it' (Whitehead 1978: 174–75).

The immediate past, objectively present, is prehended causally in the
event of awareness. The present is the duration in which the experiencer's
world loses the last of its unrealized possibilities. At the physical pole, experience conforms to the actualities of circumstance. Thus events are not
"loose and separate," as Hume claimed. Far from it, present events are what
they are because of the pressure of the causal past on their opening (physical)
phases, and future events are limited to a finite range of real possibilities
because of present events' achievements of definiteness.

This unabashedly metaphysical account of how we can ground an epistemology that makes sense of our awareness of causal connection helps make
science reasonable again, along with our everyday recipes and rules of thumb.
This is because finding laws within the observed regularities of nature is just
learning how the evolved stabilities of the universe perpetuate themselves,
eliminating mere logical possibilities and delimiting every future by the massive
actuality of past achievements. It is reasonable to expect laws of nature,
carefully observed and formulated, to "work," because at any given moment
there is a real world objectively imposing itself on, and limiting, the energies
of the present.

This appeal to causal experience does nothing at all, of course, to
"solve" the spurious question, "Why must the future always be like the past?"
This query has been taken, by some, as a possible route to the justification
of induction. If only it could be proved that the future must always be like
the past, then the conclusion of this proof could be taken as a universal
premise in a great deductive argument demonstrating that anything that has
behaved in a regular way in the past must continue to do so. This deduction
would then vindicate our instinctive trust in all the laws and recipes and rules
of thumb by which we think and live. The modern impasse over induction—

and a large consequence of the mythical epistemological gap—would be elegantly overcome.

But on my proposed postmodern worldview, overcoming the riddle of induction has nothing to do with guaranteeing that the future will always be like the past. Why should it be? There is nothing but Platonic prejudice to argue for the notion that the regularities of our cosmos are more than temporary and local. Methodologically, admittedly, it would be much harder to feel secure about the results of (say) cosmological science if one were to take seriously the likelihood that physical regularities themselves have gradually been evolving as our universe has cooled and swirled. Our best yardsticks could turn out to be made of rubber. But this is only a methodological (perhaps emotional) complication. And perhaps we should not take the results of cosmological science so solemnly, after all. It may be more epistemologically appropriate to take current "constants" (e.g., the rate of expansion of the universe) *cum grano salis.*

What is important is the reality of regularity. These may be local (applicable, for example, only to plants or to plasmas) and may be temporary (applicable, for example, only during adolescent years). There seem to be some immensely widespread regularities, extending also far back into the history of the evolving universe (so far as our methods and assumptions can tell). These are what Whitehead called the "habits" of the physical universe in our own cosmic epoch. These habits are immensely strong. It does not pay to bet against them. The patterns of interaction established by atomic and subatomic elements, so far as we can tell, rule the physical order, despite occasional randomness. Our laws describe these patterns—in mathematical abstractions, whenever possible, of great power and wide applicability.

Other lesser regularities are also of great interest and importance, even though (again, as far as we know) such behaviors may be limited to the surface of the earth. The habits of living organisms, the habits of social organizations of living organisms, the habits of neurons, and especially ganglia of neurons associated in immensely complex brains, also offer regularities for confident study. Martian life, if there is any, may not have evolved the same regularities as terrestrial life. If so, that will be of great interest, since (putting it in a different way) different laws will apply, at least in part. But this will not represent a "breakdown of induction." The world should only be expected to be as orderly as we find it to be. Laws are not ghostly "things" that "rule" the events of nature. On the contrary, nature's self-actualizing events, constrained within the boundaries of their concretely evolved environments, adapting to these realities, occasionally undergoing a fortunate mutation, filling new niches, improvising new patterns of mutual accommodation—or perishing—these are the pulsing events that allow for human recognition, formulation, prediction, and (sometimes) control.

The modern "problem of induction," then, is an artifact of an inadequate, though pervasively accepted, account of experience. This account is under the thrall of excessive admiration for the conceptual pole alone—which, admittedly, is for human beings exceptionally developed and important. A properly bipolar approach to experience, however, will recognize that high-focus, abstract, conceptual-pole experience, for all its fascination, clarity, and practical usefulness, floats on a sea of physical-pole experience. It is in that sea, whose waves sometimes break into conscious awareness, but usually not, that we find the deep causal pressures that make us so certain (when we are not philosophizing with Hume and his many followers) that we are alive in a lawful but creative world that holds, nourishes, punishes, and connects us.

Connectedness is the key. As indicated earlier, there are, according to Whitehead, two sorts of prehensive connectedness. *Pure physical feelings* are the first sort, the kind I have been concentrating on in the preceding half of this section. These require that the prehending event be immediately contiguous with physically felt events, experienced *after* their full actualization (i.e., in the mode Whitehead calls "superjective"). The other sort are *hybrid physical feelings*, which are noncontiguous prehensions of the conceptual poles of other events *before* their complete actualization, experienced therefore as partially ideal. The great benefit to postmodern epistemology of recognizing *pure* physical feeling is the disappearance of the "problem" of induction. The corresponding benefit of recognizing *hybrid* physical feeling is the reasonable availability of the resource of telepathy.

Modern epistemology has no place for telepathy. It is the paradigm case of what must be absurd for materialism and even for more moderate sense-organ empiricism. It involves the heretical idea of mind as active and—at least as regards universals or forms of definiteness—being free from spatio-temporal simple location, that is, from being an event cooped up in one tiny spot somewhere among a mass of firing neural fibers. But, as we saw, what I earlier introduced as suprasensory experience is not at all absurd for a postmodern organismic worldview grounded in the Whiteheadian system of thought. First, *all* sensory experience depends on extrasensory (infra- or suprasensory) experience. Second, the further activities of mind, from sorting out alternative possibilities for actualization, to psychosomatic influences on the organism which it guides, are obvious features of human experience. And, third, available abstract possibilities—"forms of definiteness"—themselves independent of spatial location, are also a primary ingredient of this worldview. If minds are capable of grasping such universals at all, it is not a priori obvious that such acts of grasping must be limited to the narrow spatial environment in which their pure physical feelings must be located.

This would be the metaphysical basis for awareness of "contemporary events." Such events could not be causally felt by pure physical prehension, since they are at a distance and thus beyond the range of causal efficacy, however rich in continuity the causal chain between a spatially remote environment and a perceiving event. But, regardless, we are aware of a contemporary-but-distant world surrounding us, rich with qualities and heavy with presence. The heaviness of presence can be interpreted through the dim modes of causal efficacy, pressing, penetrating, informing experience; the richness of qualities, felt for contemporary as distinct from contiguous events, needs another avenue. This would be the avenue of hybrid physical feeling, direct mental-pole to mental-pole influence free from the spatial limits of pure physical causation. This is the avenue I have called telepathy, understood not as a spooky exception but as a pervasive natural phenomenon.

Assuming that a fully-developed postmodern psychological science would take seriously the possibility of telepathy, many new topics would beg for study. Whitehead gives no hint, for example, of the range over which noncontiguous hybrid physical feelings might occur. Could direct feelings of the conceptual poles of other events occur over very wide distances? Are they more likely to occur within the same room? The same city square? The same town? Is there a regular rate of dissipation of the strength of hybrid physical feeling, as in the inverse cube or inverse square laws known in physical science? Are other factors, entirely independent of spatial location, more significant? Are biological twins, or lovers—or enemies—more likely to manifest telepathic communication?

However interesting, these are empirical questions not suitable for the present discussion. Research into the topic has settled little; but this is not to the present point. More important is getting clear on what telepathy would (and would not) be for a postmodern philosophy of personalistic organicism, and how it might advance epistemological opportunity in various domains if it were to become part of the postmodern scientific arsenal.

First, it is crucial to remember that the word, "telepathy" comes from the Greek for *distant feeling*. Hybrid physical feeling is still *feeling*, even though it may be the direct feeling of conceptual elements—universal characteristics like sensory qualities (colors, tones, odors, etc.), emotional states (fear, hope, love, etc.), or even geometrical shapes (square, circular, triangular, etc.). This means that on this view telepathy would not in principle support linguistic communication of complex "messages," such as were reportedly attempted by the former Soviet Union (and perhaps by the United States military, as well) during the Cold War (Ostrander and Schroeder 1970). The development of language and propositional knowledge falls into a still later and more complex phase of cognizing events, and will be examined only in the next chapter. Telepathy, as I envision it, is far more primitive. It is the feeling of qualities across space. Since only the mental can take account of qualities when they are spatially absent, the phrase, "mental telepathy," is redundant.

This means that the importance of giving and receiving qualitative information at a distance will vary with the level and complexity of the mentalities involved. A hybrid physical prehension is the feeling of a form of definiteness in the mental pole of the felt event. Where there is little or no novelty arising in the creativity of events, that is, where the contribution of the mental pole is negligible, hybrid physical prehensions play no significant role. Therefore in the domains of physics and chemistry I would not expect important research findings of telepathic effects. Patterns of objective transmission based on pure physical feeling, as described earlier, rule these huge regions.

The situation is significantly different, however, at the levels of complexity reached in living organisms. The creative events of such societies, even in simple living cells, are many orders of magnitude more complex, involving correspondingly much more significant mental poles, than are the events of inanimate chemistry. Postmodern psychology might well anticipate, therefore, that organized societies of living cells, like plants, might share internal telepathic feelings as a normal part of the efficient causes shaping their growth and health. Telepathic communication, at an unconscious level, between plants (as in a forest environment, or a prairie) may be discovered to contribute to ecosystem stability. It might be possible, along these lines, to expect that plants could receive telepathic feelings from animal species with which they are closely involved, and that such receptions might have influence not only on general health but also on the course of evolutionary change toward symbiotic modifications.

Plants, by hypothesis, are not so organized as to have a single dominant event, animus, or psyche, such as on my view gives unity and mental individuality to animals as wholes. Therefore postmodern psychology would not anticipate that an individual plant could send telepathic information qua individual. There is no place in this theory for having a true conversation with a plant (Tompkins and Bird 1974). But it is not out of the question that low-level, mutually reinforcing telepathic transmissions from the many cells of a plant, or, still more probably, from the combined force of weak hybrid prehensions generated within a great forest, might be powerful enough to provide animals who attend to their telepathic prehensions a significant tone of feeling.

Discussing animals, however, brings discussion to another threshold of mentality, at which, on postmodern psychology, the presence of hybrid prehensions should be encountered with much more force and frequency. In animals, even relatively simple ones, there are somatic means for the amplification of experiences and ways of responding actively to the world experienced. This focuses still more importance—by many orders of magnitude—on mental poles of the creative entities making up the animal organism. More and sharper contrasts among actualities, and between actualities and possibilities, are open to animal psyches. Particularly when developed sense organs and neural systems come into play, the likelihood of telepathy, on this theory, would be increased.

"Individuality," however, need not be defined in terms of free-standing nervous systems. It would be interesting for postmodern science to consider the possibility that a single bee, for example, is not the most relevant psychobiological unit. It may be that the hive, instead, is a telepathically unified individual organism, with the queen bee providing the spatial localization for the hive's unconscious psyche. This approach would interpret a hive of bees analogously to a multicellular organism, but with these differentiated "cells" equipped with sense organs, means of locomotion, and nervous systems, all feeding into the common life of the organism. Taking telepathy seriously in this way might bring revolutionary new understanding, not only of insects but also of bird migration and many other phenomena.

The higher mammals—horses, dogs, cats, elephants, dolphins, chimpanzees—are of course still more obvious centers of mentality, where postmodern psychology (or ethology) should anticipate the likelihood of important telepathic events. Here might be found rich research possibilities for telepathy between animals of the same species, among animals of differing species, and between animals and human beings. Such research would be the opposite in moral tone from typical animal research procedures condoned by modern science, since postmodern attitudes would tend to enhance respect for the mentality of other species and underscore the many linkages between us all.

Finally, among humans, postmodern psychology will anticipate the greatest likelihood of advanced telepathic encounters. Human mentality, on this worldview, is still more orders of magnitude of complexity and refinement beyond even the highest of the nonlinguistic species. Postmodern psychology has no need to require, a priori, that consciousness arises only in human beings; but full consciousness seems to flicker so sporadically even in high human culture, that it seems a risk to attribute it to animals who lack the linguistic vehicles in which to soar to the freedoms only humans, so far as we know, can reach. It seems quite likely, indeed, that human consciousness is itself the evolutionary product of culture. Perhaps our sharp, modern sense of private individuality was not even typical until the invention of writing, history, and civilization (Cobb 1967: chapters 1–4).

Whether absolutely unique or not, human consciousness represents another qualitative threshold in mentality that would justify postmodern psychology in devoting research effort to the telepathic effects that hybrid physical prehensions may have among people. Here is an opportunity to give theoretical coherence to vast amounts of merely anecdotal material. Mothers saving their children because of mysterious intuitions of danger—as happened twice in my own family—are genuine events, but inexplicable on the modern worldview. Careful attention freed from modern prejudices may open up new possibilities. In this context it should be noted that David Ray Griffin, in a daring book published in this series, celebrates these possibilities with enthusiasm (Griffin 1997). He pushes far beyond telepathy, to proposals I find difficult to square with my own understanding of a Whiteheadian worldview (Ferré 1994), but these debates throw new light on many fascinating issues in epistemology, metaphysics, and ethics. Some of these—particularly the environmental and social ethics implied by taking telepathy seriously—will occupy me further in *Living and Value*.

Vastly more needs to be said about all of the above. But the entrancing themes of this chapter need to stand aside for the equally urgent issues of the next. Here I have attempted to reexamine experience, drawing attention to some of the features that tend to get short shrift in the discussions of orthodox modern empiricists. I have reminded readers of the postmodern intimations of a worldview suggested in *Being and Value*, and have shown in this context how a generally Whiteheadian perspective can interpret the complexities— the unclarities as well as the clarities—of actual concrete experience.

9

THINKING THE WORLD

We experience our own thinking, of course, but thinking goes beyond experience, at least in the usual senses of the key words. My plan for this chapter
is to follow this process of extension from experience to thinking, and from
thinking to truth. I hope to suggest helpful reforms in the way all these key
concepts should be defined, in contrast to both premodern and modern
epistemic norms.

The process of transition is not at bottom discontinuous. There is (as we
have seen) an important conceptual pole in experience and (as we shall see)
an indispensable experiential contribution to conceptual thinking. But the
situation does not *look* smoothly continuous. A significant shift in the center
of gravity occurs as we put more and more weight on the conceptual end of
the experience-thinking complex. In a finely balanced aircraft, the load may
be shifted slightly forward or aft with no great changes in flight characteristics; but, after a while, the qualitative result of small linear changes in one
direction can be sudden and dramatic. Such a highly dramatic change occurs
vividly in human mentality whenever we speak and theorize.

Readers of this page, for example, are *attending to thoughts*—of an
aircraft in flight suddenly becoming uncontrollable due to small shifts in its
center of gravity, and of similar dramatic qualitative changes coming from
apparently trivial quantitative differences—and are not just *looking at black
marks* on a white surface. Beyond even the useful capacity to recognize the
perceived shapes of these marks as familiar, as constituting significant clusters (words), normal readers are thinking thoughts *through* the words. Even

the specific words themselves do not matter absolutely (though without some set of them, nothing would be conveyed). As I write, I am keenly aware that I could use other words to generate the same reflections—perhaps more effectively. This is why I feel free to revise and revise, searching for just the right combination, not of black marks nor even regular clusters of black marks, but of thoughts, to make the point most economically and effectively. In this I feel a freedom that is even more basic than simple word production. I am guiding my choice of words with the prior purpose of expressing the themes of this chapter. Words are indispensable. Without the availability of words I would never have gained the ability to become interested in such thoughts, and without relying on words I would never be able to articulate (even for myself) what I am trying to think. But I am conscious also of the process of searching for a word. This familiar process is not exhausted by words; rather, it is a disciplined mental capacity to pass various words in review and reject or accept them according to a prior sense of what is needed to advance my thought. Likewise, I can tell when a word I have written is wrong for my thought. My thoughts, though served up in words, spill over and beyond the words that convey them.

Readers enjoy an analogous freedom, attending *beyond* and *through* the marks on the page and *beyond* and *through* my specific words to thoughts that may or may not be mine. They may be better than mine. Such thoughts may involve a prearticulate wish that the words on the page had been different ones. Then the reader's prearticulate wish may trigger the process of passing in review other words that might have been. When the better words are found, fresh thought has been articulated. This is the hope of every author who admires Socrates and loves dialogue. It marks the process of creative reading, which (like creative writing) is simply a form of creative thinking.

Such creative thinking, using the human mind's freedom—in ways disciplined by method—to select alternative symbolic forms for articulating thought, is located far toward the "dramatic change" side of the continuum ranging from primitive causal feeling to genius. As I indicated earlier, at first blush it hardly seems a continuum at all; but while qualitatively there are huge consequences from many incremental tilts to the center of gravity, the presence of genius in the world, however rare, is no intrusion from another cosmos. It is grounded in the common structure of the fundamental entities that make up everything that is. These entities, on the Whiteheadian worldview I have been recommending, are brief, self-developing events. They are units of energy, conditioned by the real possibilities presented in their immediate environment and selective of their own concrete actuality. The process of becoming concrete—Whitehead called it *concrescence*—has a structure that runs through all grades of complexity and gives the hugely diverse realm of nature its underlying unity, from sub-electronic occasions to Einstein's mind.

I hinted at this in the previous chapter, but before I can discuss the continuum from causal experience to creative thinking, I need to lay out in a little more detail the unifying pattern shared by all events.

THE PHASES OF CONCRESCENCE

The first thing to remember about the process of concrescence is that on the proffered worldview it is fundamental to everything that can be taken as real. Though it is a temporal process, it is not *in* physical time (as though time were something independently flowing through the universe as in Newton's vision of things), but, rather, concrescence is the *basis* for time itself. Time, on this view, is a quantum phenomenon. Its fundamental, all-or-none units are these events of concrescence. Time does not "flow"; instead, the universe pulses with tiny units of creative energy concrescing at various speeds. We do not know what the briefest unit of time may be, but whatever its duration, it must make one-tenth of a second seem like centuries. Whitehead speculates that the duration of an average human event of awareness may be about one-tenth of a second—too short to feel discontinuous (any more than the frames in a cinema seem separate), but much longer than the duration of (say) a photon propagating periodically through space.

The reason I begin with this rather abstruse topic is to emphasize one point that is immensely difficult for many to grasp: namely, the temporal indivisibility of the process of concrescence. Though it has phases, "earlier" and "later," these phases are not isolable into "past" or "future," external to each other. To hold otherwise would be to make abstract time more basic than concrete becoming. In concrete becoming, the push of early phases is ingredient in the later phases, and the pull of later phases is ingredient in the earlier phases. In Aristotelian language, "final causation" is fully active in fundamental concrescence. The event's destination, in other words, makes a difference even at the starting gate.

As I have already tried to make clear, the event is headed toward its own unification, toward a weaving of available possibilities into a fresh integration in which the multiplicity of objective starting conditions becomes a final unity of subjective satisfaction. I say "subjective," here, because each event (the many unconscious ones as well as the few conscious ones) is something for itself. During its brief moment of self-actualization, its interiority matters, at least to itself. It is its own creation: *causa sui*, in traditional premodern language. I say "satisfaction," as well, because when an event becomes fully determinate and thus something objective for the next generation of events to prehend, its task is done. The drive from possibility to actuality has achieved another small victory. Something definite—what Whitehead calls an actual occasion—has been created.

Since in this indivisible quantum of duration the end, is influential even at the beginning, the drive toward integration—toward self-consistent actuality—requires that whatever is impossible to integrate must be excluded from the initial data demanding synthesis. This means that there will be negative prehensions at the outset. And their presence as negative feelings may make a significant difference throughout the process. As Whitehead put it:

In this process, the negative prehensions which effect the elimination are not merely negligible. The process through which a feeling passes in constituting itself also records itself in the subjective form of the integral feeling [at the "end" of the process]. The negative prehensions have their own subjective forms which they contribute to the process. A feeling bears on itself the scars of its birth; it recollects as a subjective emotion its struggle for existence; it retains the impress of what it might have been, but is not. It is for this reason that what an actual entity has avoided as a datum for feeling may yet be an important part of its equipment. The actual cannot be reduced to mere matter of fact in divorce from the potential (Whitehead 1978: 226–27).

Still more important, however, are the positive prehensions from the immediate past environment that provide the main positive content of the concrescing event. These are very many, of course, even in simple environments, and beyond any schematic description. Suffice it to say that the earliest phase of concrescence is what I referred to in the previous chapter as the physical pole in experiencing the world. Immediately past actual entities enter this first phase, providing both the feelings of solid connectedness with a world and the actualized forms of definiteness (the general characteristics) that just became concrete in immediate past occasions—at least as far as these are accepted (not turned away with negative prehensions) as material for fresh unification in the new moment rising.

The next phase, what Whitehead called the phase of conceptual feelings, involves the processing of the input received through these physical feelings. This processing may be extremely simple. But, simple or complex, it always involves contrasts. The first contrast is between the environment causally felt, in its concreteness, and the same environment felt in terms of its general characteristics in their capacity for universality. Thus, at the start of the conceptual phase there occurs a conceptual reproduction of the physically felt world. The next contrast is between at least some of these general characteristics, now felt as possibilities rather than actualities, and different but related general characteristics which might have been (or might be) otherwise. Relevant alternatives are at least briefly entertained, with a positive or negative valuation as part of the feeling. Whitehead refers to these two sub-phases within the early conceptual phase of concrescence as conceptual reproduction and conceptual diversity, or "conceptual valuation" and "conceptual reversion" (Whitehead 1978: 248–49).

In very simple contexts, it may be that the conceptual pole in concrescence is exhausted by this degree of conceptual contrast. For example, the oscillating character of our universe of electrons, photons, etc., may be accounted for, Whitehead suggests, as a regular and repeated valuation of the total contrast between one form of wave pattern (the positive pulse) and its opposite (the negative pulse). An electronic event physically prehends its immediate predecessor in one phase, then through conceptual reversion actualizes its exactly inverted form. This pattern of continual sign reversal from electronic event to electronic event would combine the utmost in simplicity (the pattern itself is not changed except from positive to negative) with the utmost in vividness of contrast. This would result in the maximum of intensity of subjective satisfaction for each event, as it attains its own fresh integration in sharp contrast with its past, but with the minimum of decay in the pattern itself—thus helping to account for the massive stability of the physical universe as it has evolved over uncountable generations of concrescent events. Each actual entity helps to secure a mutually supportive environment for others in its own environment. Electrons support the continuation of their species, and also support mutual interaction with, for example, the nuclei of hydrogen atoms. As Whitehead puts it:

> Thus just as the members of the same species mutually favour each other, so do members of associated species. We find the rudimentary fact of association in the existence of the two species, electrons and hydrogen nuclei. The simplicity of the dual association, and the apparent absence of competition from other antagonistic species accounts for the massive endurance which we find among them (Whitehead 1925: 111).

But in a universe that has evolved to the levels of richness and diversity we observe, physical stability through causal inheritance and mere conceptual reversion can only be part of the story. The other part is the creative capacity of nature to evolve toward novel possibilities. Whitehead continues, referring to individual concrescing events in his special sense as "organisms":

> The other side of the evolutionary machinery, the neglected side, is expressed by the world *creativeness*. The organisms can create their own environment. For this purpose, the single organism is almost helpless. The adequate forces require societies of coöperating organisms. . . . The riddle of the universe is not so simple. There is the aspect of

permanence in which a given type of attainment is endlessly repeated for its own sake; and there is the aspect of transition to other things—it may be of higher worth, and it may be of lower worth (Whitehead 1925: 111–12).

Among the many obvious phenomena that have evolved in this surprising universe are living societies of events, mutually supporting one another by forming self-repairing tissues and interactive organs (including sense organs connected through central nervous systems) that make up intelligent species. In the brains of some members of these species are types of events that have evolved so as to integrate huge masses of causal input and, in some cases, to manipulate their conceptual prehensions in such ways as to become symbol-using persons.

Although it is admittedly a breathtaking jump from electrons to conscious thinkers, the basic structures of concrescence, on the present view, are only enhanced and elaborated, not abandoned. The primary phase remains causal (as shown in the previous chapter), feeling the data of the immediate past as transmitted through the neural network. The next phase, for persons as for electrons, continues to be conceptual, starting with the recasting of the concrete given in its contrasting universal aspect, then feeling the contrast of these universals against relevant possibilities not physically given. But for electrons and other relatively simple events, the conceptual phase ends there, for all practical purposes, with unitary but unsubtle subjective satisfactions. For the indescribably richer and more complex events occurring in critical brain-locations, there is stimulus to still more contrasts, and contrasts of contrasts, before the final harmonization and integration occurs.

Richer environments, especially those found within living organisms, allow a more advanced type of contrasts which, though not yet necessarily conscious, are located well toward the mental pole and (for the first time) are subject to questions of truth or falsity. In view of their subject-predicate structure, Whitehead calls these *propositional feelings*. They are the felt contrast between *(a)* the form of definiteness (the "eternal object") that has now been reproduced or reverted and *(b)* the immediately past physical world stripped of its qualitative character and felt as a bare (but still real) logical subject. A proposition, that is, constitutes a felt connection between a *predicate*—a whatness—consisting in a pure possibility, limited only by reference to a particular context, with a *subject*—a thisness—which provides the limiting context. "This is green," as a simple singular proposition, is itself abstract and formal. In itself (apart from its assertion by some subject) it is not even true or false, since it has been provided no actual context and is not functioning to refer to anything. So far, it is merely a formal possibility for a judgment. When an actual subject, however, uses it to judge (assert) that it is in fact applicable to a particular context, then it is fair to ask whether it is true or false, depending on the actual character of the physical environment at the time of the assertion. Under these circumstances it has the function (and what Whitehead calls the "subjective form") of an empirical judgment.

Philosophers traditionally pay a great deal of attention to this use of propositions, and there is an overwhelming preference within this use for true judgments over false ones. But this is an extremely narrow approach to propositional feelings. Taken in itself, a propositional feeling is simply the feeling of unity-in-contrast between an uncharacterized locus and an unlocalized character. The *locus* is the felt manifold of the experienced world stripped of all but its capacity to support characters; the *character* is a possibility (favorably or unfavorably felt) for characterizing the entities of this time and place. The main function of propositions, quite apart from their occasional ability to be judged for truth or falsity, is as enhancement for intensity of feeling through offering the excitement of novelty.

Sheer conceptual feeling, prior to the propositional phase, loses this excitement because it *refers* to nothing. It is simply bare possibility and, as an empty abstraction, fails to generate much emotional power. But intensity of feeling increases when bare possibility is put into bright contrast with particular actuality. Whitehead expresses his central insight (with an interesting anticipation of what would become a major theme of the later Wittgenstein) by insisting on the multiplicity of uses for propositional formalisms, noting that:

> [The] ordinary logical account of 'propositions' expresses only a restricted aspect of their rôle in the universe, namely, when they are the data of feelings whose subjective forms are those of judgements. It is an essential doctrine in the philosophy of organism that the primary function of a proposition is to be relevant as a lure for feeling. For example, some propositions are the data of feelings with subjective forms such as to constitute those feelings to be the enjoyment of a joke. Other propositions are felt with feelings whose subjective forms are horror, disgust, or indignation (Whitehead 1978: 25).

My examples have presupposed consciousness, but countless propositional feelings occur, in humans as in other intelligent creatures, far below the explicit level of awareness. They allow, for those entities complex enough to enjoy them, the painting of possible hues on a world held as a blank canvas. They are the vehicles of imagination, the channels of novelty, the springs of error. Since we find error and novelty far below the level of what plausibly could be considered conscious—where fish engage in elaborate deceptions, for example, and macaques learn new behaviors—propositional feelings (though negligible in the inorganic world) must be widely distributed in organic nature.

False propositions—attributing forms of definiteness to contexts where they do not conform—are likely (at least in the short run) to be more interesting than true ones. For better or worse, they add new possibilities to the world. All fiction, all films, all hopes and dreams, all creative novelties, are based on the power of false propositions. But the fundamental significance of false propositions runs even deeper:

> When a non-conformal proposition is admitted into feeling, the reaction to the datum has resulted in the synthesis of fact with the alternative potentiality of the complex predicate. A novelty has emerged into creation. The novelty may promote or destroy order; it may be good or bad. But it is new, a new type of individual, and not merely a new intensity of individual feeling. That member of the locus has introduced a new form into the actual world; or, at least, an old form in a new function (Whitehead 1978: 187).

The transformation of this widespread source of unconscious novelty into a conscious thought, on the Whiteheadian account, depends on one final set of contrasts. Just as a *propositional feeling* rests on the contrast between a possible predicate and an abstract subject, so what Whitehead calls an *intellectual feeling* reflects the contrast between a propositional feeling and the world to which the proposition refers. Intellectual feelings are conscious. They represent, at last, the phenomenon of thinking. This level of "complex comparative feelings" is where Peirce located the essence of the scientific method, and where poets find poignancy in longing. It is where critical awareness is born from the intercourse of actuality and possibility, whose complex patterns of felt interplay stimulate the concrescing subject to new heights of subjective intensity.

The final state of concrescence (as terminus, it is hardly a "stage") is, as I indicated earlier, its *satisfaction*. This satisfaction may be very simple. In principle there must be many simpler events than electron-occasions, for example, the events we designate as "empty space." Here the satisfaction of each concrescence would presumably be merely conformal repetition, utterly dull, with negligible internal intensity—a unity without contrast, with virtually no subjective vividness, holding hardly any value for itself. Still, even the most trivial event of empty space draws into its own unity whatever data it finds; if the satisfaction is slight, it is because the prehended data are not only few but also boringly lacking in contrast. Harmonizing such data is easy, since each event could truthfully sing, "I got plenty of nothin'."

For the pulsing universe of sub-atomic particles, however, there is available the comparative richness of definite energetic pattern (what we call a wave-function) and the social structure of an atomic environment to receive, revert, and actualize. This allows satisfactions that maximize a type of vividness provided by total contrasts between oscillating phases. The harmonies are boring, sheer reversal of field over and over again, but they have enough internal intensity to be extremely stable.

At every level of complexity, satisfaction involves the synthesis of many into one. The more contrasts offered in the many initial prehensions, the richer become the harmonies possible in the final satisfaction. And the richer these final outcomes, the greater the value for itself of the concrescent event. Achieving actuality, over and over again, is the point of the process. Wholeness at the end of each pulse of this process is a given, since every concrete entity must be self-consistent. But the quality of the wholeness is a variable. This depends on the complexity of the environment and the creative energy of the event. In every case the event's underlying subjective aim is to maximize the richness of its final satisfaction, bringing initial differences into unified harmony. This may be done blandly, by excluding much of the initial environment through negative prehension, or it may be done excitingly, by including dissonances and contrasts and relating them in interesting ways. Solving a problem of competing claims to a limited resource, for example, can be done narrowly, by treating the situation as a zero-sum game, or it can be done by widening the frame and including all claims in a new context that expands the resource. Each concrescence poses such a problem, "writ small," for the event in process. Each event must inevitably eventuate in one solution or another. The internal drive of each one is to find a solution, within the limits of its finite duration and its impinging resources, which will maximize its own intrinsic richness by the moment of its concluding wholeness, thus leaving something of instrumental worth to successor events in the transcending future it feels immanent within its process. We shall see that this universal demand, rooted in the microstructure of the cosmos for richness and wholeness, has crucial implications for epistemology and for ethics. Discussion of the ethics I must postpone until the next volume, *Living and Value*, but the epistemological implications are now nearly ready to unfold.

Much more could be said about the process of concrescence in general, of course, but this much should be enough for my present purposes since the rest of the chapter is meant to flesh out the final phases—what happens in human events of conscious thought. On the theory I am presenting, such events arise only rarely in the known universe, at the complex culmination of concrescing events occurring within the incomparable informational richness of living human bodies. Still, though human thinking is astonishingly amplified, the theory serves to emphasize the continuities "all the way down," from events of consciousness, through animal organisms, to phases within the energetic pulses that fuel the stars, and even to empty space. I hope this moderately technical excursus into the microanalysis of individual concrescent occasions will provide useful background as I now turn to a considerably broader treatment of the path to conceptual thinking, truth, and (in the next chapter) knowing.

THE PATH TO CONCEPTUAL THINKING

After all that, the hardy reader will not be shocked to learn that in my view conceptual thinking springs from something pervasive, from processes found in inorganic as well as organic nature. I anticipated this much in the opening reflections of this volume, where I drew attention to the importance of recognition (including my dog's ability to recognize people, places, and furniture) and to what I there referred to as "memory knowledge." This is not an amnesiac universe. The habits of electrons and protons are perpetuated; elastic substances return to previous states; the antibodies in our immune systems recognize microbes as friend or foe. One might go on to describe these phenomena as inevitable consequences of a prehensive universe in which causal inheritance links past events to present ones, and in which the past makes a real difference—but giving such an account is unnecessary here. The point merely is that grasp across time is real and basic. Inheritance happens. Recognition occurs. And this is the basis on which concepts are gradually formed.

Before conceptual cognition, there winds the long path of preconceptual recognition. The curves of this path would be interesting to explore in themselves, but I shall need to straighten them rather abruptly if we are to reach the human level without too much delay. A good model to follow is Michael Polanyi's economical treatment of the stages of animal learning.

Polanyi distinguishes three levels of "inarticulate intelligence" (Polanyi 1964: 71–77). The first level is *trick learning*. Here a good example would be the capacity of a rat or a pigeon to recognize a lever as something that can be pushed or pecked to provide food. At first, when the animal is introduced to the situation, there is a period of random exploration. An accidental activation of the food-mechanism occurs. The animal eats. Later there is another such accident, and learning sets in. The behavior becomes more frequent and can be plotted on a predictable curve. "Finally the rat becomes engaged assiduously in lever-pressing and pellet-eating; and the process of learning is complete" (Polanyi 1964: 72). There is a direct inductive causal relation between pushing the lever and receiving the food. The animal has discovered a means-end relationship, all without words or even signs to mediate.

Signs come at the second level of inarticulate intelligence. A dog, for example, can react to a bell or buzzer as though to a more normal life-situation. Ivan Petrovich Pavlov (1849–1936), for example, showed that dogs could learn to respond, by salivating, to a bell which, by many repetitions, had become associated with food. The bell alone, after a while, was enough to stimulate a physical reflex which, without the learning process, would have occurred only in the presence of food itself. The bell became a sign for food. Animals live naturally in a world of signs, not simply those contrived in the laboratory. H. H. Price delightfully discusses sign cognition in many contexts, both human and animal. "To the cat, the loud sound of a bark is a sign of the presence of a dog. It is also a sign *for* running up a tree or taking other evasive action" (Price 1953: 91). Or, again:

> Here we may notice another curious feature of signification. There is often a kind of conflict between its cognitive aspect and its practical aspect. When A is a sign *of* B, it is often a sign *for* an action which will prevent B from happening. The sign 'releases' an action which falsifies the signified proposition. . . . Still more often, the sign releases an action which prevents the signified proposition from being verified by the sign cognisant. This happens whenever the sign is a sign for a movement of escape or of concealment. A mewing sound signifies the presence of a cat. By running away into its hole or under the dresser, the mouse prevents itself from having experiences which would verify the signified proposition (Price 1953: 91).

The very fact that signs can be falsified, as they often are, emphasizes the mediated character of sign cognition. Where there is room for error, we have reached an important point on the path to conceptual thinking. Still, sign cognition requires the physical presence of a signifier in the causal environment of the interpreter. It is not "free" thinking, but tied to the domain of perception.

The third, still higher, level of inarticulate intelligence Polanyi calls *latent learning*. It goes beyond direct inductive connection and habituated sign cognition, which are tied to specifics. Instead, it is the interpretation of a situation, the capacity to solve general problems. Polanyi's example is the ability of a rat to learn flexible appropriate responses to a maze.

> Thus a rat which has learned to run a maze will show a high degree of ingenuity in choosing the shortest alternative path when one of the paths has been closed to it. This behaviour of the rat is such as would be accounted for by its having acquired a mental map of the maze, which it can use for its guidance when faced with different situations within the maze (Polanyi 1964: 74).

This is the "latency" of such learning: that it can be drawn upon in an indefinite number of new circumstances. I would not want to guess how far down into the animal kingdom this third and highest level of inarticulate intelligence might extend. Anyone who has watched a spider spinning—or, better, repairing—a web may be inclined to credit it with a remarkable grasp of three-dimensional spatial relations as the animal solves new problems of tension, stress, and balance. The issue of downward extent is not the main point, however; preconceptual intelligence of all three kinds is certainly found plentifully in nature. More to the point of this chapter, the same three kinds are also found conceptually in human beings.

> Our three types of animal learning are primordial forms of three faculties more highly developed in man. Trick-learning may be regarded as an act of *invention*; sign-learning as an act of *observation*; latent learning as an act of *interpretation* (Polanyi 1964: 76).

How does this come about? We are not born thinking conceptually. Human infants start out very much like other primates, though perhaps a little slower at the beginning in learning tricks. The difference is made by human culture and in particular by the rise of symbolic intelligence including, but not limited to, language.

This process begins in parallel with the rest of the prehensive universe; that is, with the physical capacity to *feel forms of definiteness* and the conceptual capacity to *distinguish, remember, and recognize repeated characters* that transcend the flux of the immediate moment. Just as a rat or a pigeon can recognize a lever in its presence, so as to notice and push it, so a human infant has "hello again!" experiences of many sorts, probably beginning with the mother's breast. This is not an amnesiac world, and human babies are among its busiest recognizers. As weeks and months pass, babies without language learn tricks (means-end inductive causal relations between things in their environment) and signs (associations between things present and things absent) and even how to interpret general situations—just as do other intelligent animals. For all three of these types of preconceptual learning, the necessary condition is an experienced world that is full of repetitions, loaded with characters that present themselves again and again in more or less regular patterns. Some of these characters, or patterns of characters, stand out for recognition with special intensity. They are connected from the start with strong evaluational content, positive or negative. The warm, sweet wetness of mother's milk; the discomfort of hunger (or gas) pangs; the glad gestalt of a loving face; the disagreeable chafing of dirty diapers—all these and more become features prominent in a world of nameless but significant entities and processes. To achieve this status, the forms of definiteness involved need not only to be *regular*, that is, repeatedly presented to experience, but also to be *frequent, valuationally relevant*, and on a *comprehensible* spatio-temporal scale neither too prolonged nor too brief, neither too large nor too small, for notice.

The rise of symbolic thinking follows the same pattern. The forms of definiteness that become symbols begin for the child, after all, simply as more features of the recognizable world. Practically anything can become a symbol. A particular old tree, for example, can be a symbol for a group of environmentalists. Whitehead defines human symbolic thinking inclusively:

> The human mind is functioning symbolically when some components of its experience elicit consciousness, beliefs, emotions, and usages, respecting other components of its experience (Whitehead 1927: 8).

But while this is a good definition for symbolic thinking, it is not specific enough for language. An ancient tree may be a powerful symbol, but it does not make a useful word. A tree is fixed in one place, extremely hard to manipulate, and impossible to produce at will. Other quite different components of experience need to be relied on for providing the linguistic symbols that make possible human conceptual intelligence and distinctive human culture.

What must such components of experience be like? If they are to be noticed, distinguished, recognized within the flow of a child's immediate experience, they (like all the other contents of the child's emerging world) need to be regular, frequently repeated, valued as important, and spatio-temporally comprehensible.

The *regularity* requirement places an interesting limitation on language: namely, that it must manifest a grammar. Regularity, as we have seen, is a necessary condition of recognition. A grammar is simply the specific regularity that has become habitual in the linguistic community concerned. There must be *some* such regularity for there to be language at all. It is no miracle, and certainly no coincidence, that all languages exhibit grammaticality. Babbling without any structure would be naturally selected against, never capable of becoming language at all. Whether or not one needs to postulate some "depth grammar" in the human species is an entirely separate question, to be decided empirically by reference to degrees of similarity among independently developed social habits of linguistic expression. On a Whiteheadian view, where even the laws of physics are seen as reflecting the stabilized habits of socially interactive entities, not as mysterious transcendent causes prior to social behavior, grammaticality in language could be anticipated without postulating further hypothetical structures.

The *frequency* requirement has other interesting implications. The components of experience that can become linguistic symbols must be relatively few, so that they can be repeated again and again. If a vocabulary were to be too large and varied, it would take too long for a given potential symbol to come around again. This would make it extremely hard to notice and remember it. Michael Polanyi calls this the Law of Poverty in language.

> Suppose you wanted to improve a language by increasing its richness indefinitely. We can get an idea of the enormous number of printed or written words that could be formed by different combinations of phonemes or letters, by envisaging the fact that from an alphabet of 23 letters we could construct 23^8, i.e., about one hundred thousand million eight-letter code words. This should allow us to replace each different sentence ever printed in the English language by a different printed word, so that this code word (which would function as a verb) would cover what that sentence asserts. This millionfold enrichment of the English language would completely destroy it; not only because nobody could remember so many words, but for the more important reason that they would be meaningless. For the meaning of a word is formed and manifested by its repeated usage, and the vast majority of our eight-letter codes words would be used only once or at any rate too rarely to acquire and express a definite meaning. It follows that a language must be poor enough to allow the same words to be used a sufficient number of times. We may call this the Law of Poverty (Polanyi 1964: 78).

A corollary of this Law of Poverty is the necessity for generalized reference in language. Linguistic symbols, if they must be relatively few to be meaningful, must be useful for many contexts, many purposes. To this inevitable generality in concepts I shall return soon, in connection with the logic of definition.

The *importance* requirement, that the components of experience that can serve as linguistic symbols need to be attended to as relevant and vital, somehow, seems something that nature supplies in the developmental repertoire of the human child. "Language readiness" is another way of referring to the fact that children simply do take a special interest—for a limited number of years—in the linguistic world in which they find themselves. I am not denying that species other than human may be able to learn linguistically, especially with the sustained help of human beings. Evidence seems increasing that language is not exclusively a human preserve. But human infants are vastly more inclined than those of other species to pay positive attention to, show interest in, and value the components of experience they later come to name as "words."

Words, spoken or written, are excellent ways of satisfying the final requirement of *spatio-temporal comprehensibility*. Spoken words are long enough to be noticeable but not so prolonged (as in the hour-long phrases of whale songs) as to lose their definite form within human attention spans. Written marks are equally easy to keep within manageable scale. Moreover, unlike ancient trees, they can easily be produced and reproduced at will. Our vocal cords are always handy, traveling with us, and functional wherever we go. Shapes on the ground or on other substances are not difficult to scratch. Sounds and shapes, further, can be sharply distinguished, an advantage for accuracy of recognition. This rests on the fortunate fact that the senses of hearing and vision are both capable of fine discriminations—unlike the senses of taste and smell, in which human neurological equipment permits fewer discriminations (and in which domain we are certainly even more limited as to the variety of flavors and odors we can emit at will).

Our ability to produce clearly differentiated sounds and visually recognizable marks leads to exciting consequences. In the domain of generally symbolic intelligence, it allows us to break free of what the environment happens to provide. The three sorts of preconceptual learning I distinguished earlier are all tied to the immediate perceptual field. (1) Trick learning, in my example, requires *encountering, in the actual environment, the presence of the lever* by which to procure desired food. There is, admittedly, a certain degree of "taking account of the absent," even in this kind of preconceptual inductive learning. After the trick is learned, the *absent food* is attended to (and obtained) by paying attention to the *present lever*. Since I earlier characterized mentality itself as the capacity to take account of the absent (as well as the present), mentality is already at work here, in learning and performing the trick, even though the function of mentality at this level is to overcome the absence of the symbolized term as quickly as possible. (2) Sign learning is also tied to a feature of given experience, by which the sign interpreter takes account of something else that may or may not also be given in immediate experience. The meowing sound must actually be heard for the mouse to attend to the likelihood of a cat in the general neighborhood. Sign cognition, learned by the conjunction—sometimes practically simultaneous (as nearby lightning and thunder) sometimes delayed, sometimes falsified—of sign with thing signified, continues to be dependent on the environment's *actually providing the sign*, whether it be the sight of a boiling black cloud signifying impending rain to birds, or the odor of a leopard signifying danger to a herd of gazelles. (3) Even in latent learning, as in the maze example, although the symbolic map elicited is more complex and allows more flexible applications, there must be *perceptual cues actually present* to the interpreter who has learned the maze.

Linguistic symbols are different. They are no less physically perceptible (at least at first), since they are recognizable sounds and marks. But
because they are the sorts of sounds and marks *we can produce anywhere*,
without waiting for our environment to present them, they free us to that
extent from the givens of the immediate physical context. Human infants
normally find themselves in an environment offering many features worth
noticing, remembering, and recognizing—including regularly repeated sounds
produced by important beings who feed, clean, and cuddle. These sounds
gradually become signs, recognized in their physical presence and thus "elic-
iting emotions respecting other components of experience" (as Whitehead
might have put it). But as the infant vocalizes, producing random sounds,
soon these self-emitted sounds themselves start to be remembered and recognized; and though there may be little control at first, the great day eventually
dawns on which some of these distinguishable, self-generated sounds (especially the ones that were followed by reinforcing excitement from those doting
sound-emitters in the social environment) can be repeated more or less reliably ("Da! Da!," "Ma! Ma!") to general jubilation and reward.

The line from preconceptual signs to verbal symbols is not sharp. But
there comes a stage at which a child recognizes that the sounds it produces,
and the sounds its care-givers produce, are significantly similar. Language
rises from its general prelinguistic symbolic matrix when this significant,
recognizable similarity is reliably appreciated as offering shared symbolic
reference. My "Da! Da!" noises and your "Da! Da!" noises "elicit consciousness, beliefs, emotions, and usages" regarding the same scratchy-faced entity
(perhaps, at first, all scratchy-faced entities with low-toned voices); my "Ma!
Ma!" noises and yours elicit references to the same warm, comfortable milk
provider. Important repeated features of experience thus have been recognized and linked with other important repeated features of experience, not
just privately but in a shared vocabulary. And to make this even better, if I
am the infant, the shared vocabulary can be produced by me anytime, anywhere. I do not have to wait for the physical environment to provide signs
for my attention. I can now yell "Ma! Ma!" in the middle of the night, with
no one physically present. I can in this way take account of the physically
absent, important to me, whenever I feel like it. And others can share my
meaning. This is much better than simple crying, which may get attention but
is highly amorphous in message. If I am thirsty and want "wawa," it does no
good to be burped.

On this view, then—to summarize thus far—symbolism names the most
basic process of mental functioning. *Symbolism* is the process in which one
feature of a subject's experience elicits taking account of another feature
(absent or present), if only in action or emotion; *mentality* is a subject's
capacity to take symbolic account of the physically absent, as well as what

is present, if only by seeking (or longing) for an absent feature, such as food or water. *Signs* are "found" symbols by which subjects take mental account of absent or present features; *words* are symbols subjects can produce for themselves, independent of the current physical context; a *language* is the set of words and habits of usage such subjects share with other symbol users.

Two quick remarks on the consequences of my approach to language might be in order before I go on. First remark: there is no problem on this view with "private" words. If one chooses, quite apart from anyone else, to link a recognizable feature of one's experience to a certain sound or set of marks, one is certainly free to do so. Many children do seem to make up private words (doctrinaire denials by followers of Wittgenstein to the contrary), and there is no reason to doubt that such associations between recognizable components of someone's private experience may work for them perfectly well. In the middle of the night, alone, they can utter their private word and thereby elicit emotions or thoughts respecting the other component of their experience. This qualifies, so far, for conceptual thinking, though of an extremely limited sort. But when one teaches one's private word to a brother or sister, a new language is born. The word is private no longer; real language (no matter how small its community) is operative. Language is always social ("public," in this sense); words usually are.

Second remark: wherever there are words, on my view, there are concepts. (I shall shortly develop this connection as I turn to the logic of concept definition.) This, if so, has two important corollaries. First, most (but not necessarily all) concepts are public, that is, social artifacts. Second, where we find the marks of mentality operating without words, we are normally in the presence of preconceptual modes of intelligence. I admit that any "line" between the conceptual and the preconceptual is blurred and arbitrary, but it is useful to be able to distinguish *(a)* the kinds of often impressive intelligence that operate *dependent* on the givens of the physical environment, from *(b)* the kinds of intelligence that operate *independent* of such circumstances through the power of symbolic (word) production. Finally, using the term "symbolic" here may set off alarm bells for certain readers. Some prefer to reserve "symbol" talk for high-order linguistic functions. There is much usage to support this preference. We speak of "symbolic logic," "mathematical symbols," and the like. But no alarm is in order. On my proposed usage, we are free to continue to speak as usual. The symbols we manipulate in logic or mathematics, the symbols we revere in religion, the symbolisms of daily life, such as patriotic respect for the flag—all are indeed symbols. But I prefer my proposed wider usage, precisely *because* it relates symbolic activities such as these, functioning at the explicit level of human consciousness, to the pervasiveness of symbolic functions stretching indefinitely outward in nonhuman nature.

Epistemology, however, as I noted in the first chapter (and as has been manifest throughout this book), is especially interested in human thinking. At its most distinctive, this is linguistic thinking. The rest of this section, consequently, will focus on the rising and defining of linguistic concepts.

Concepts are in the main social artifacts. Even in the rare cases when they might be private, they are parasitic on the prior awakening of language, which is always social. If a person's "language readiness" fails to be activated by some social environment in which recognizable vocalizations are associated with other recognizable features of experience, there is little likelihood that such a person would start to associate his or her private vocalizations with anything at all. Therefore, putting aside the "private word-cum-concept" as a mere waystation between animal (and infant) sign learning (which clearly can be private) and free theoretical thinking (which clearly requires society), we can now concentrate on the social origins of linguistic meanings.

At the root of every linguistic concept lie community assessments of value. Here important continuities between linguistic and prelinguistic thinking are obvious. For sign cognition to occur, for example, the rat or dog or infant must first *take an interest* in a relatively few features selected from the enormous manifold of experience, notice them, then consider them important enough to remember, to recognize when repeated, and eventually to associate together so that one evokes the other. Equally, linguistic thinking has its genesis in *judgments of importance*. What is *worth* naming? Fortunately for both processes of sign and concept making, relations of worth are at the heart of all experience. This is the shared insight behind Robert Neville's excellent "axiological hypothesis" about thinking (Neville: 1981 12–29). As he shows, "thinking is founded in valuation" (Neville: 1981: 12). Whitehead offers the basic reason for this: the initial causal prehension of the environment is value-laden. Likewise, the early conceptual phase of reversion, in which the causally given forms of definiteness are contrasted with relevant possible alternatives, is one in which a "valuing up" or "valuing down" occurs. In less technical terms, our experience, long before it reaches consciousness, swims in an ocean of attractions and repulsions. Some of these are obviously biology driven. Human beings are early (and universally) positively interested in our mothers and in food, water, warmth, and the like; we are, contrariwise, negatively interested in what might consider *us* as food, and in other dangers to survival and contentment. These features of experience, for every human society, are eminently worth naming, and they do appear, in one way or another, in all languages. This is not surprising. A warning of the hungry sabre-tooth tiger, lurking outside the cave, needs to be given—as specifically as possible. It does not matter just *which* sounds are regularly uttered to evoke appropriate attention to this other, highly unwelcome possible content of experience, but *something* needs to be agreed on. Likewise, in common tasks, such as hunting or finding berries, it is highly worthwhile to build a common vocabulary. Building together (in this and many other ways) is at the root of the word "community": "com-" is from *cum* (the Latin for "with" or "together") and "-munity" derives from *muneo* (the Latin verb "to build"). For some community purposes, meaning can be carried without larynx-generated words. A distinctive whistle will do, or sounds deliberately produced on instruments. My mother established with her children that a certain whistled phrase would mean "Come running!" The double-bass warning theme in *Jaws* comes unmistakably to mean "shark!" during the course of the film—even to the point of being used at unexpected times for clever artistic deception.

Different communities find different regularities of experience, or different combinations of features, worth naming. Various ways of life, carrying with them different needs even within highly similar environmental regularities of experience, make various features stand out; once named, such distinctive features or combination of features will thenceforth still more likely be recognized. Rather than illustrating this in standard ways—for example, the number of different words the Polynesian Tuvaluan language has for distinguishable forms of coconut (Finegan and Besnier 1989: 21)—I shall take one example from my father's culture, and one from my wife's. My father grew up in Sweden. There he learned a word he could never translate into English, though it was important to him, and he used it often to describe his state of mind. He was, he would say, *snopen.* We children, from the context of its repeated use, learned that Daddy was feeling somewhere between embarrassed and bewildered, with just a dash of self-deprecating amusement thrown in. We of the English language community seem never to have considered just this combination of feelings socially important enough to name. Even the Germans apparently fail to share this judgment of importance with the Swedes, I realized, after consulting a Swedish-German dictionary in which the German translations stress the amazement or perplexity of being *snopen*, but miss the charm, amusement, and self-deprecation also contained in the concept. But the Germans do have the wonderful concept of *Gemütlichkeit*, which their language community considers important enough to have noticed and named. Since German is my wife's native tongue, I have learned from her how crude the Anglo-Saxon social experience must be, cut off from those special depths of coziness and supportive fellow-feeling that her language community's adjective, *gemütlich*, draws together and evokes in one untranslatable conceptual glow.

The normative judgment of importance—that a certain recognized regularity (*R*) is something *worth* symbolizing with its own sound or shape (*S*)—is at the start of conceptual thinking, but other normative judgments are essential throughout. We need to judge both whether this is an *authentic* case of R and whether we (or others involved) have *successfully* produced S. There is no objective formula for deciding this. Every case of R is likely to be a little bit different. How different can it get and still be authenticated as a case of R? Likewise, every pronunciation (or visual shaping) of S is likely to have its own sound or slant. How far off can an utterance or a shape be allowed to stray and still qualify as an instance of S? A child's baby-talk may be perfectly clear to parents involved with the daily evolution of this speech, but utterly unintelligible to outsiders. Parents need to listen with great alertness, prepared to authenticate that this or that utterance is really intended as this or that word. The child, likewise, must vocalize observantly, hoping to hit "well enough" within the range of acceptable sounds and looking to parental encouragement (or blank stares) for guidance. Gradually sounds come under control and are produced more accurately within the normative range, but there are no sharp boundaries between "pass" and "fail." We must simply judge that this is "well enough" in range so as to qualify for S.

This requirement that we evaluate and authenticate our own and others' speech performances is never outgrown, though our awareness of it may fade when all seems to be going well. It is expressed in such normative questions as: *Should* I have used that word? Is it the *right* word? Is there a *better* way of expressing what I want to say? And, for those (like myself) with marginal penmanship, it is continuous with such questions as: Is this a *good enough* rendering of my words so as to be intelligible to others (or even to myself at a later time)? I must, alas, ask this if my purposes in writing are not to be frustrated. Unless I do, even I, preeminent connoisseur of my own handwriting, may not be able to make out my notes when I need them.

Analogous to the normative ranges of pronunciation and written appearance of words, the normative range of meanings of most words in real languages like English, Swedish, or German is picked up, most of the time, from experiencing their repeated use in actual contexts, not by explicit definition. We learn the meanings of these terms, what they imply and what they rule out—their logic—from such repeated experience. It is a straightforward a posteriori matter, linking some aspects of our experience (word sounds or shapes) with other aspects (other word sounds or shapes). But from this a posteriori source, we learn analytic truths, such as that being a bachelor rules out being married, or that being a sister requires being a sibling. This informal logical structure is of great importance in daily life and reasoning, and gives the answer, at last, to the question posed in Chapter 1, whether the "analytic a posteriori" box has any contents. Of course it does. The syntactical robustness of all natural languages depends on these contents. But for purposes of careful thinking, and certainly for theoretical purposes (a topic for the next chapter), explicit definitions are often needed. I shall therefore conclude this section with some reflections on the highly normative logic of the definitional process.

All linguistic meaning begins in ordinary usage. This is the case for so-called "natural" languages, like English or German, where, as we have seen, socially negotiated value judgments by listeners and speakers alike tend to push speech toward central norms in pronunciation, orthography, grammar, as well as meaning. This is no less the case for "artificial" languages (codes, logics, mathematics), as well, which are at bottom parasitic for their existence and intelligibility on natural languages. Some philosophers have recognized the enormous significance of ordinary language and embraced it as their final norm for philosophy, but this is going too far. Ordinary usage gives us an essential start, but it is no stopping place.

This is especially obvious in connection with the "difficult" concepts that provide the red meat of philosophical thinking. Earlier in my career I needed to wrestle with making philosophical sense of such elusive terms as "religion" (Ferré 1967b: chap. 2), "technology" (Ferré 1995: chap. 2), "nature" (Ferré 1995: chap. 2), and "intelligence" (Ferré 1995: chapters 3 and 4). The key words for all these topics are found in daily usage. In ordinary life, for example, we are capable of dealing appropriately with the question: "What is your (his) religion?" As standard English speakers we are aware that our answer on a personnel questionnaire could appropriately be chosen from such possibilities as "Protestant," "Catholic," "Jew," or "none"; and we are equally well aware that an answer chosen from the group "street sweeper," "carpenter," or "housewife," would betray a misunderstanding of the question: namely, the confusion of a question about religion with a question about occupation. The same sort of thing could be said about technology. We can distinguish an instance of technology, for example, a watch, from the empty heath on which it might have been found. Nature, too, is something we can talk about without confusion most of the time. The empty heath is an instance of it, in contrast to the watch we may have stumbled on. Likewise, it takes only average intelligence to be able to use the word "intelligence" more or less appropriately in many contexts. This is guaranteed by the fact that, as we saw, ordinary usage is itself an edifice of averages. This does not mean, however, that the concepts involved are clear—as anyone who has tried to think in a sustained way about any of these words will have discovered.

Ordinary usage gives us something to go on, then, before we even begin to reflect philosophically about how we should think about religion or technology, nature or intelligence. In a sense, learning our language immerses us in a vast, but not trackless, sea of meaning at the outset. We are not utterly at a loss about what we mean by these words before we define them. And this is fortunate, since without this prephilosophical push in one direction rather than another, we would not even know where to start searching for an adequate understanding.

Search, however, we must. Ordinary usage may be able to point us in a general direction, but it soon becomes a fickle compass. When relied upon too heavily, it turns out to be ambiguous, contradictory, and blind.

The *ambiguity* of "religion" and its derivatives in ordinary usage (to take one example) arises, as in the case of all ambiguous terms, from our readiness to apply such words to referents with quite different characteristics. Ordinary usage recognizes not only "He is religiously ill-informed" (i.e., ignorant with respect to Christianity, Hinduism, or the like) but also "She is religiously punctual" (i.e., extremely careful about meeting appointments on time). Ordinary usage applies "religious" to activities as vastly different as the contortions of a tribal shaman's war dance, the meditations of a Tibetan monk beside a prayer wheel, the eating of a Passover meal, the self-flagellations of a medieval hermit, the labors of an agricultural missionary to distribute fertilizers, the shouting and leaping of a Pentecostal with "the gift of tongues," the silent sitting at a Quaker meeting, the begging of a Buddhist priest—and on indefinitely. Ordinary usage permits us to refer confidently to Christianity or Taoism as "religion"; but usage also sometimes allows us to say, "Her face is her religion" or "Making money has become a religion for him." Are these metaphorical uses? All we know now is that they are *uses*. What, though, of Communism or Fascism or Humanism or Nationalism? Does ordinary usage permit us to use the word "religious" of them? Is not Communism a vastly different complex phenomenon from, say, Christianity? And yet, the usage does occur—sometimes. Is it proper? Improper?

From just such ambiguities arise the *contradictions* that undermine ordinary usage as a dependable guide for thought. It is perfectly possible, for example, to listen to a political speech on Saturday denouncing Communism as "militantly opposed to all religion" and on Sunday to hear a sermon containing an equally strong attack on Communism as "a false and idolatrous religion." Both usages are recognized and fairly common; but contradiction is the death of clarity. Again, we began by noting the fairly clear distinction in popular usage between religions and occupations; but we have acknowledged recently that another usage allows making money to be considered intelligibly as someone's religion. What shall we do? Ordinary usage seems to be pointing us in different directions at once. "Religion" in ordinary usage sometimes seems self-stultifying almost without limit. And this is intolerable if any kind of precision in thinking is our aim.

But if there must be limits, how shall they be determined? The *blindness* of ordinary usage to rules of "proper" or "improper" applications of language prevents us from expecting much help from this source. Usage simply is what it is. As Gilbert Ryle correctly noted, "There cannot be a misusage any more than there can be a miscustom or a misvogue" (Ryle 1953: 174). Ordinary usage provides us with facts which enable us to begin; but facts alone, without general rules, are "blind" in two important senses.

First, usage alone is unable to determine whether a *new* phenomenon (about which there is as yet no usage) shall or shall not be considered "religious." Nothing in established usage—*unless it be generalized somehow into a rule of decision*—can guide usage that has yet to be established. But, it may be objected, when (for example) the Ba'hai movement was first encountered in the nineteenth century there was no popular hesitation to call it a "religion" even though its scriptures were not the Bible, its prophet was not Jesus or Mohammed or Moses, and its doctrines were not those of any previous religion. This objection, however, illustrate precisely my point. The decision to call Ba'hai a religion must have been based on an at least implicit rule: perhaps the rather specific rule that having scriptures and a prophet and doctrines qualifies a new movement to join the company of religions, or perhaps only the general rule that new phenomena bearing some basic resemblance to other phenomena covered by a standard usage may share the usage. The job of making explicit, specifying, and refining such rules for the *extension of usage* is one important thing that we do when we formulate a definition for any term.

Second, usage alone is unable to tell us how to resolve the confusions that arise when existing usages are unclear or actually in conflict. In order to think critically about religion (to continue the example) we must have something definite to think about; we must be able at the very least to banish contradiction from our employment of "religion"-terms, either by rejecting one of two mutually incompatible usages or by discovering some means of showing that prima facie equivocation or contradiction in usage is only apparent. But appeal to ordinary usage, to the mere facts of the linguistic behavior of standard speakers in a language, has no such power. Again some rule is needed to serve as a basis for judgments among competing usages. Such a rule cannot usefully serve its function if it is entirely irrelevant to all ordinary usage, but neither can it be the slave of the usage it is called upon to judge. The ticklish business of formulating and establishing such rules for the discrimination of usages is another thing that we do in the process of defining any term, and it should now be abundantly clear how important are value judgments in the defining process.

We need to consider more clearly the general purposes, potentials, and limits of making definitions. Definitions, as rules for the discrimination and extension of usage, are essential for clear thought; but what, more precisely, are we doing when we seriously propose one of these rules? What kind of activity is the formulation, application, and evaluation of rules?

In the first place it is important to notice that the logical status of a rule—any rule, including a rule for language—is significantly different from that of a descriptive statement. We *lay down* rules, but we *search* for descriptions. We *obey* rules, but we *believe* descriptions. We *break* rules, but we *doubt* descriptions. We *abandon* rules, but we *disprove* descriptions. We attack or defend rules through assessment of their *consequences,* but we attack or defend descriptions through assessment of their *probabilities.* As a result of the logical status of rules, we are much freer to do as we please in proposing rules than in framing descriptions. Much of the confusion of tongues—in philosophy and elsewhere—because of the multiplicity of rival definitions for key terms stems from the freedoms inherent in the rule-making process. *In setting up definitions every person becomes a legislator.*

But what is such a person "legislating" about? We have seen earlier in this chapter that this legislation has to do with the use of words. More specifically, a definition is a rule connecting words with other words—finally with terms associated with regular, recognizable features in experience, "forms of definiteness," that is, properties and relations—and therefore it is a rule connecting a word usage with whatever possesses the set of properties or characteristics named by those terms. For example, if our accepted definition of "triangle" is a "three-sided plane figure," we have resolved by accepting this definition to admit the word "triangle" for anything which has the general characteristics named by "plane figure" and "three-sided"; and we have also accepted the rule not to apply the word "triangle" to anything that lacks these forms of definiteness. Similarly, if we decide to define "murder" as simply "the act of killing," we are committed thereby to calling anything that is so characterized (in this case including stepping on an ant or chopping down a tree) "murder." Our decisions to accept definitions may accord with society at large (as in the first instance), or they may be idiosyncratic (as in the second), but in all cases we are determining how we shall regularly use words with respect to various collections of general properties and relations. The definition-form "*X* is a *yz*" translates: "Call a thing *X* only if it possesses the characteristics *y* and *z*; and if anything possesses *y* and *z*, call it *X*." Given the rule, then, our usage is put under authority; but whether or not we accept the rule—or what the rule we accept shall be—is for us to decide. And, although this is not by any means the whole story, at this point we are "our own boss."

Let us examine briefly what is involved in being "one's own boss" in the choice of definitions. It presupposes (1) that *every explicit definition is an artifact,* not a natural object. We may not have constructed it ourselves, but some person or group of persons did make every definition. Further, it means (2) that *every definition is the product of decision.* We may not have "decided" consciously ourselves (though examples of explicit decision may be observed, as in the stipulative introduction of new words or in the provision of old words with new or more precise meanings), but we must "agree" at least implicitly—that is, at least as exhibited in our usage—to every definition before it has a claim on us. Together, these principles mean that if we prefer not to go along with the decisions of others concerning the definitions they will employ, we are at liberty to be different. We cannot (on the first principle) be forced by any "natural connection" between words and what they represent; neither the sound nor the shape of "cat" has any natural connection to the soft purring animal by the fireplace. Even onomatopoeic words, like "buzz" or "ding-dong," which were once doubtless *suggested* by occurring sounds, are conventional today—as can quickly be confirmed by considering how many other ways different languages have found to refer, by their own conventions, to the same sounds. And (on the second principle) we cannot be forced into conformity out of fear that our different definition will be proved "false"; the adjectives "true" or "false" have no proper application to a definition. A definition, after all, is the index of one's determination to use words in certain ways and not in others. It is a rule one adopts to govern one's behavior with respect to a human artifact. If one decides to use the sound "fish" to refer henceforth only to feathered flying things, this may be extremely odd; but it is not false. It would indeed be false to assert (the descriptive claim) that the standard use in English of "fish" is to refer to feathered flying things. But in proposing to employ the word this way oneself, one is not describing anything that could possibly be false or true any more than the command "Right face!" could be false or true; one is not even asserting one's intention to obey one's own rule, although this latter assertion (which *could* be either true or false) is one that might reasonably be assumed to follow.

Talk *about* definitions may be true or false, then, but definitions themselves are neither. They are not themselves assertions or descriptions but, rather, rules of meaning on the basis of which assertions or descriptions can be uttered and understood. Does this suggest, then, that "anything goes"? If definitions are acts of will, are we lost in the shoreless swamps of the purely arbitrary? Have we begun to search for standards only to find that because "we are the boss" there can be none?

There is no need for despair. Although it is essential for an understanding of the defining process that we learn well the first half of the lesson, that half must be carefully tempered by the whole. Much skepticism about "mere definitions"—especially disputed ones of terms like "religion"—may be due to learning not wisely but too well some of the principles we have noted. But these common attitudes are premature reactions to a partial analysis. Definitions, in good logic, cannot be *true or false*; but this does not mean that all definitions are equally *good*. Every maker of a definition becomes a legislator; but if legislation is to be useful, even the legislator must acknowledge limits to sovereignty. Certainly "we are the boss"; but even bosses (perhaps especially bosses) are required to be practical.

Any rule worth making is laid down with the hope that it will achieve some end or other. Definitions, as we have seen, are rules made for the purpose of stably connecting words with other words designating general properties or relations and hence with anything possessing those specified properties and standing in such relations. And if this is the aim of the defining enterprise, then several practical standards for successful definitions appear.

First, since language is essentially social, blatant violations of common usage will almost certainly be self-defeating. There are two general reasons for this warning, both illustrated by our earlier I'll-show-the-world-I'm-free definition of "fish." One obvious defect of defining the word in terms of the characteristics named by "feathered" and "capable of flight" is that it is *unnecessary*. Another word, "bird," already exists, which does a similar job quite well enough. The two are not quite synonyms, of course, since proper English usage of "bird" (wisely) includes animals that are neither feathered (e.g., chicks before they have grown their feathers, a plucked goose) nor capable of flight (e.g., penguins, ostriches); and since unliving flying feathered things, like many arrows and most badminton shuttlecocks, would on this definition be classified with robins as "fish"!

But this simply illustrates the second defect of this odd definition, namely, that it is *confusing*. There is nothing true or false about the decision, as we have seen, but *since it is true that "fish" in ordinary English already means something quite different*, the new definition would run against the insuperable practical handicap of having to change firmly established habits of usage. Even if we, or a small group of speakers, were to try to obey the new rule represented by this definition, we would in all likelihood find ourselves slipping unconsciously back and forth between the new stipulated use and the old familiar one. Thus the proposal, like all proposals in utter defiance of normal usage, tends toward anarchy in language and thought—especially if we happen to be mariners or ornithologists—rather than toward the stability at which we had aimed. And all this for what meager accomplishment? Merely to have a word for application to all things, from arrows to angels, that have feathers (if angel wings have feathers) and fly.

This last reflection leads us to a second extremely important practical standard for successful definition: since a definition is a rule intended to establish stable connections between the term being defined and a group of defining characteristics, those characteristics chosen must be the *crucial* features for the primary purpose at hand or the definition will fail to advance that purpose. Several points must be made about this standard of "cruciality." First, it is clear from what has been noted already about our freedom in making definitions that it is logically possible to cut up our conceptual cosmos in an unlimited number of ways. But it is also true that there are discoverable uniformities or resemblances in our experience, with various degrees of pervasiveness, obviousness, or importance for shared human interests. These are the regularities which have been considered important enough to have been noticed and given names, and it is at the major intersections of such regularities that we are likely to find our most crucial interests delineated.

To make this notion less abstract let us compare the entire universe of our experience with a roast turkey, sitting on the table ready for the carving. With a sharp enough knife it would be *possible* (though odd) to carve the turkey as though it were a roast of beef, cutting slices of the bird containing light meat, dark meat, cross-sections of bone, stuffing, and all. Indeed, this cross-section might be exactly what is needed (except for the stuffing) by a zoologist for some special work. But most of us have a rather different practical interest in cutting up the turkey. We have discovered certain uniformities in our experience of the creature which we consider noteworthy: leg and wing and breast and thigh, and the like. And therefore we consider it useful to carve so that these different uniformities are separated from one another but kept themselves distinct.

In like manner, our definitions will be useful only if they help us to slice the universe at what for our purposes are its "natural" joints. When we establish our rules for speech and thought, we want whatever properties we use as principles of division to carve out a noteworthy segment of the universe. This can be accomplished only if the properties are indeed "crucial" to whatever is being defined.

Consider the definition of "the human being" as "the lachrymal animal." If we accept this as an adequate definition, we shall be bound to apply the word "human" to anything that possesses both the characteristic of being an animal and the characteristic of being able to cry, and we shall be equally bound to refuse the name to any being not possessing both properties. Should we so legislate? There is of course no way of judging this definition, or any other, "true" or "false"; are we simply to make up our minds arbitrarily? No; at this point we may appeal to the standard of "cruciality"; and here at last issues of truth or falsity do become relevant: Are there animals, *besides* the two-legged uniformities we are interested in, which possess tear ducts and use them to weep? Do "human beings" (as the phrase is commonly used outside this definition) sometimes lose the capacity to weep, either through psychological or physiological defect? Suppose the answers to these two questions should be: "Yes, an obscure type of lemur is capable of using tear ducts to weep under situations of stress or bereavement; and, yes, some human beings lose their ability to cry." Then, armed with relevant facts about the world of our experience, we can make our decision. If we are determined to do so, we are still *free* to take this as our definition of "human," but now we know that "human," on this usage, will include some lemurs and will exclude (perhaps) one's friend or one's next-door neighbor. This discovery, while not "refutation," is a consequence so grossly unhelpful as to be patently disqualifying. The definition has not in fact found a "natural joint in the cosmos."

But what if the answers to our factual questions had been otherwise? If it had turned out that *only* humans weep and that *all* humans weep, would the definition then be an adequate one? Again our answer could be negative. Definitions are not summaries of fact but indexes of our intentions to use language in all possible situations. It does not matter, then, whether *in fact* all humans are capable of tears, if in our judgment we would still be determined to call our neighbor a human being *even though* (as is conceivable, at least) the neighbor were to lose all lachrymal capacities. And the moment we have made such a determination, we have grounds to reject the proffered definition. We have made an important value judgment. The proposed characteristic, we judge, is *insufficiently crucial* to constitute a good defining property. If all humans happen to weep, and only humans happen to weep, this is an interesting fact about humans. But if it is not an important enough uniformity about the world to constitute a *defining* characteristic, we shall call such a property a "constantly accompanying characteristic." The test to distinguish "constantly accompanying" from "defining" characteristics is always a normative judgment. Is the questionable property so *important* that I would wish to exclude from the defined class all objects which might fail to possess this property when the facts happen to turn out this way? If the answer is "yes," the property is a defining characteristic; if "no," then it must be no part of our definition.

Two important facts about definitions are implicit in the foregoing. First, it is clear from the nature of the situation that we must have some idea of what it is that we are interested in *before* the formal defining process is completed. We could not otherwise make a judgment of relative importance concerning various characteristics as they are presented. We would not be able to decide, for example, whether "ability to weep" was important enough to "human beings" to be made a defining characteristic unless we had some preliminary idea—independent of our definition—of what "human" means. This fact bothers some, who suppose that the whole meaning of a word should flow exclusively from its explicit definition; but it should not upset us, in view of what we have recognized earlier about our being "immersed in a sea of meanings." Simply by learning our language we are given the "something to go on" that makes the refinement of meaning possible. And that "something" is likely to repay serious attention, even though it may suffer from all the defects we noted earlier. Any usage that has become imbedded in common speech rests somewhere upon the recognized regularities in experience that are "crucial" at least for some purpose. If the distinctions in ordinary language failed utterly to "carve the universe" at some "natural joint" or other, the usage would hardly have survived the mechanism of natural selection which weeds out the unfit for linguistic, as surely as the unfit for biological, perpetuation. If a form of language survives, it serves a function.

Second, it is equally clear that the refinement we achieve through definition is inescapably based on determinations of value. To decide what is "crucial" is to make a judgment on relative importance. And this is the case for every definition in every field, however hard-headed, or however suspicious its practitioners may be of "value judgments." The scientist who, in concert with colleagues, decides that the uniformities in experience represented by the chemical properties of an element are more important for defining purposes than differences of atomic weight, and so calls two substances with different atomic weights but shared chemical properties "isotopes of the same element" rather than "different elements," makes a value judgment for scientific purposes no less than the humanist who makes value judgments, for example, which are the literary works of a given century most worth studying, for the literary domain. Value judgments necessarily undergird all clear thinking; and if this should seem shocking, perhaps the blame for this lies on the common but uncritical assumption that value judgments must by nature be irrational, arbitrary, and uncontrollable.

The fact that determinations of cruciality can and must be made about any subject prior to, and during, the process of defining, leads to the third major standard for success in this process: resolutions of *scope*. The defining characteristics adopted must be not only crucial but also chosen so as to carve out a segment of the universe that is *neither too large* to be handled *nor too small* to be satisfying for the purpose at hand. To illustrate: suppose someone clumsily attempted to define "furniture" as "any material objects used for sitting or sleeping." The definition quite obviously will not do. It is *too restrictive*, in one respect, since furniture is something used for many purposes (such as holding food or giving illumination or decorating interiors) besides those specified; and it is *too inclusive*, in another respect, since we may use an indefinite number of material objects besides furniture (such as haylofts or trees or rowboats) for sitting or sleeping.

We must now notice the interplay among all three of our practical standards of definitional success illustrated in this last simple example. *Common usage* is what gives us our preliminary knowledge of the subject being defined, and it is on the basis of that knowledge that we make our determinations of *cruciality* (in this case, that what we do with furniture besides sitting or sleeping on it is too important to be eliminated) and our judgments of *scope* (that it would simply be too confusing to call haystacks, and so on, "furniture"). In a sense, then, all our current discussion of standards points to one general principle: *We judge definitions on the basis of a set of preliminary minimum ideas on what the definition shall include and exclude.* It will be useful to give these ideas a name: let us call the whole set our "predefinitional resolutions." Those predefinitional resolutions, of course, are never themselves beyond argument or criticism. But their argument or defense will be carried on in terms of the value laden standards we have now isolated.

One last important standard should at least be noted, though it is not so much relevant to definitions themselves as to our use of them: If definitions are to succeed in their function, *we must be faithful to them.* A definition, we have seen, is essentially an expression of our linguistic determination; but (it almost goes without saying) indexes of determination are vitiated if the determination itself is missing. Occasionally, however, even respected thinkers fail to obey their own explicit linguistic rules and so make a mockery of the entire definitional enterprise. Quite clearly this is one more instance of the general truth that those who have freedom—as we all do in the definitional enterprise—have also a concomitant responsibility. There is a morality, as well as a technique, to the conduct of thought.

Defining the True

One widely accepted moral obligation for thinking is to think truly about what is true. Not everyone feels this imperative with equal force, of course; but for scientists and philosophers it has been a central goal, and we have seen how epistemologist have long debated theories of truth. My approach, in the interest of sorting out what should be meant by "truth" and "true," will start by applying the principles of definition outlined at the end of the previous section. This should help to clarify these "difficult" words—heavily loaded, as they are, with emotional freight and epistemic consequences—and to lay groundwork for a theory capable both of recognizing strengths in premodern and modern approaches and of going beyond presently available approaches in a reconciling way.

"Truth" is an abstract noun; to get down to the concrete we must examine the more homely adjective "true," which when attributed to an assertion makes the basic claim. To say (vaguely) of a proposition that it contributes to or is part of "the truth" is to say (much more immediately) that it deserves, somehow, to be called "true." "The truth," conceptually speaking, is the class of all statements qualified for that crucial adjective, "true."

What we must do, then, is to get clear on what—most generally of all—"qualifies" something as true. Here it is important to adopt a sufficiently inclusive predefinitional *resolution of scope.* "True" is a word that functions meaningfully in many more contexts than philosophers normally have noticed. If we are to escape from the well-worn ruts that have constrained the wheels of epistemological thinking about truth for too long, we must recognize that "true" has a number of uses besides the theoretical ones with which philosophers usually have been happy to stop. Perhaps we can get a hint concerning the basic force of "true" by broadening our focus beyond conceptual truth for a moment.

We speak, for example, of "true" love, or the corner of the roof being "out of true," or a marksman's aim being "true," as well as of "true" propositions, "true" likenesses, "true" stories, and the rest. Is there a common bond that unites these uses? Yes, in each case the adjective "true" indicates that its object noun *does not need to be corrected, requires no emendation*, is (in its own context) *reliable*.

The "true" lover does not need to mend his or her ways; the "true" aim is one that hits the mark; the board or angle that is "true" has been corrected or adjusted to the purpose at hand and needs no more improvement. Nonconceptually as well as conceptually the "true" is what does not disappoint, what will not let one down relative to one's interests.

Our interests as philosophers are, of course, conceptual and theoretical. But the hint we discover from the context of these other uses of "true" proves helpful. The "true" in thinking, as in other areas, will at least be the *conceptually reliable*: that is, the truth of a thought is finally to be determined by its capacity not to need correction, not to fail us in performing the logical function or functions we appropriately expect of it.

Reflecting on the contexts uncovered by this resolution of scope draws attention to some predefinitional *resolutions of cruciality* worth making explicit. First, it is crucial that "true" remain a "success" word. In all its natural contexts there is a positive evaluative content carried by the term. It is a paradigmatic "got it!" word. If the true were to turn out to be something toward which we could be entirely indifferent, it would not be what we are looking for. Second, and closely related to the first, it is crucial that "true" remain a term of praise. We need to remember, as we approach the subject, that being true is a quality that in some contexts has been taken with the utmost seriousness. It has sometimes been considered worth killing for, and worth dying for. Outraged lovers and holy martyrs have been known to care deeply—even to the point giving or receiving death—whether the object of their interest is true. Scientists and philosophers spend their lives in search of the true. Children beg to know whether a story is really true. It seems to make a difference. There needs to be a way to account for the fact that sometimes truth has been treasured almost to the point of sacredness. And, despite this, sometimes we need to be able to say that something is "true but trivial."

Third, relating to this last point, it is crucial that "true" is an adjective capable of degrees. A marksman's aim may be more or less true. A joist may be more or less out of true. A "little white lie" may not be wholly untrue. Assertions may be partially true, and so may theories. But, fourth, and related to the third resolution, it is equally crucial that true be a limit-term, at least in principle. When something is "just, plain true," it has hit the mark and cannot be improved in that respect. Perhaps it can be enriched or repeated or connected (improvement in every respect is by no means ruled out), but in its own terms it is final. It may be a small hit, but it is nonetheless objectively a hit. If our measuring capabilities improve to the point where we find that Robin's arrow was just slightly off from the center of the bull's-eye, then his aim was not quite true after all. To be completely true is to be perfectly on the mark. Sometimes—usually—it may not matter whether that limit is reached; sometimes it may matter a great deal, whether or not the achievement can be perfectly measured.

What shall we do with these predefinitional resolutions? Accepting them will commit anyone seeking a theory of epistemic truth to consider what counts as "hitting the mark" in various context of thought. Our inclusive resolution of scope reminds us that determining what is true will at bottom be a measure of *reliability*, but standards of reliability differ with differing purposes. We check with a carpenter's square, for example, whether the angle of a joist is true; this is not how to check whether a lover's love, or an archer's aim, is true. Our resolutions of cruciality additionally remind us that the true will be open to degrees of *importance*—sometimes intense, sometimes trivial—as an estimate of success in some enterprise, but also that such successes are subject to *gradation* in degree short of the final limit.

To which theory or theories of epistemic truth will these predefinitional resolutions be hospitable? I believe the answer could be "all the major theories" or "none of the major theories." The pragmatic theory of truth would certainly find comfort in the emphasis on purpose and success; the representational-correspondence theory would take cheer in the acknowledgment of a final goal in which something objective is genuinely hit; the holistic-correspondence theory would be happy with the acknowledgment of grades of truth and would see nothing excluding its special emphasis on these grades depending on completeness of systems of assertions.

My own view, however, is "none of the above." The basic true-indicating property, as I described it earlier in this chapter, rises at the propositional phase in the concrescence of a high order, or intelligent, event of experience. In that phase, the abstracted, reverted, and compared formal characteristics affirmed by intelligence as actually present in the causally prehended world are either conformal with that world or not. Likewise, in the case of conceptual prehension or hybrid conceptual prehension, the forms of definiteness concerned are either conformal or not. If the mental predicate in a physical prehension is conformal to its physical subject, or if the mental predicate in a hybrid prehension is conformal to its mental subject, then to that degree it is true; if nonconformal, then to that degree it is not true. The micro-level basis of "truth," on this account, is *conformality* rather than "correspondence," which carries with it the inescapable suggestion of representational distance between knower and known. Conformality, in other words, is not mirroring (*pace* Rorty 1980); it is intimate and intertwined. Conformality is grasping and being grasped, feeling and being felt, fitting or not fitting. It is penetrative. It allows room for error, in the mode of impending dissonance, but no room for an epistemological gap between knower and known.

The basic authority over thought, on this view, is conformality to fact. This does not at all deny that our propositions and theories are human constructs (as we shall see in the next chapter), but it does mean that these constructs, when used for the *purpose* of conceptual reliability (rather than for entertainment or for considering amusing or frightening alternatives or simply for enhancing intensity of experience), are open to discipline by the concomitant *obligation* to be true—a standard of success dependent on the world's being more conformal with some assertions than with others.

The world, as conceived in this trilogy, is a domain of possibilities and actualities. The actualities are concrescing entities realizing abstract possibilities in pulsations of creative energy. These energetic events, in the moments of their self-actualization, are related to one another, by both internal and external relations (Ferré 1996: 316–38). Some are more strongly determined by their internal relations, some less strongly, but all, low-order or high, are something in and for themselves. Besides their public behavior, they also have an inside, a subjectivity, which carries a subjective tone, however simple, and which is something of value, however minuscule and fleeting.

Given this, the complete fact that should ultimately authorize thought would be the whole universe of these entities, including the full, complex relations that have evolved among them at the time of the thinking, together with (at the abstract extreme) the penumbra of all currently unactualized possibilities and (at the concrete extreme) the inner, intrinsic values of every actual, related entity. Thought conformal to all this would be the ultimately true thought. No one could suppose that human beings have access to such truth, but I mention it because the approximations to true thinking we do encounter in fallible, limited human realms of discourse are all implicit in this stupendous, unattainable limit. To illustrate, I shall run through the major familiar varieties of truth from the most abstract to the most concrete.

First, *logically (mathematically) true* statements function in the domain of symbols as they relate to other symbols. Conceptual reliability relative to the order of symbolic abstractions is determined by inquiring whether a set of symbols is in fact functioning conformally to stipulated rules. When language is successful in this function, not needing correction, this is what logicians call "logical truth," sometimes loosely translated "consistency," but normally involving not only the rule of consistency but also rules of transformation and implication, rules defining proper syntactical form, and the like. In the end, what makes a logical truth true is the conformality of the symbolic forms themselves to one another. This means that the rule of identity, "A is A," finally undergirds logically true statements, where identity of form must be simply grasped, and the responsible act of grasping must be self-authenticated by the thinker.

Within the secure framework of logical truth, purely possible forms of definiteness of many more varieties than mathematical can be thought, including even sensory possibilities, as long as they are considered generally, independent of any spatio-temporal actualization. The abstract properties of all sorts of forms of definiteness can be interestingly related and discussed, as in the ever-elusive question of how we know whether anything can be both green and red all over at the same time, a topic on which, long ago, I published my first article as a very "green" philosopher (Ferré 1961a: 90–94).

Second, symbols like "red" and "green" would not be intelligible or form part of our language, with its contingently evolved rules of grammar, if we did not also make and interpret statements that are *empirically true*. Conceptual reliability relative to the order of empirical assertions is determined by whether the linguistic symbols we have created, by noticing and remembering regularities in experience, help us satisfactorily in anticipating further experience. A primary function of empirical statements (when the context of their use is for providing information, not for playing a game, or telling a story, or the like) is to assist in forecasting experience. If we can anticipate the behavior of something, as Comte and James agreed, to that extent it ceases to be an absolute mystery, even though we still might not understand it in many further respects. Discovering dependable regularities in our environment, once given our conceptual ability to abstract certain features of that environment (e.g., "smoke," "fire") and to fix symbolically their mutual relations in empirical generalizations (e.g., "Where there's smoke, there's fire"), is an extremely important way of introducing form into our apprehension of what we must cope with as conscious, active beings.

Empirical assertions function as informal hypotheses. These hypotheses are best, of course, when our expectations of observations can be formulated into the precise symbolism of mathematical language. But this precision is not necessary. When I assert that dinner is ready, I am telling myself and others that *if* I go to the dining table, I shall find food there, ready to eat, and so will anyone else who may be willing to make the same trip. My assertion is verified as empirically true when conceptual anticipations of these further experiences, excited by the symbols I have uttered, evoking dinner in absence, are actualized by causal prehension.

Here, on the conformal theory of truth, there are two sorts of conformality to be distinguished. The most basic one, on which the very meaning of "true" rests, is the conformality between *(a)* the actualized possibilities in the world (the complex relations of possibility that are actual in swordfish steak, for example) and *(b)* the abstract concepts affirmed of the situation (that there is swordfish on the table). This first conformality constitutes the underlying truth-situation—the conformality of proposition with circumstance—that our experiment in coming to the table seeks to verify. But there is also a second conformality involved, between *(b')* an abstract symbol entertained with expectation and *(a')* an actual concrete experience *judged* similar enough to satisfy the normal range of expectations evoked by the symbol. It is up to us, as certifiers of our own experiential capacities and judges of the acceptable range allowed for determinable concepts (like "dinner" or "swordfish") to *decide* on the degree of conformality and therefore on the degree to which our empirical propositions are true.

This is the natural home of the correspondence theory of truth. The correspondence theory, I believe, draws its great intuitive strength from the fact that in ordinary practical life we are acutely interested in the conformality of our representations of things, whether pictorial or purely verbal, with what they are alleged to represent. This is inseparable from our confidence in the reliability of our conceptual-perceptual apparatus as it functions to help us anticipate and cope with new experience. If we claim it true that Smith's house is painted green, a large part of what we mean is that the expectations evoked by the proposition, "Smith's house is green," are not in need of correction in the light of actual standard experience of the appearance of the house. We must note, however, that this appearing, too (like the expecting), is a mental event. What we are comparing is the event of expecting an experience with the event of experiencing itself. In this limited sense there may be said to be correspondence between "thoughts" and "things"; here, however, "things" are in no sense divorced from "thoughts" but are also involved within the mentality that all experiencing involves. The main point, though it could be indefinitely developed, is simple. It is that the "correspondence of thought to reality" is nothing more than a special case of conceptual reliability grounded, we hope, in the more basic conformality of the properties entertained in our thought with the properties of the things to which our thought refers.

Third, this same hope may persist when we go beyond the logical and empirical truth to the *theoretically true*. The aim is still for conformality—now between systems of assertions and those limited systems of actualities making up portions of the universe in which we are interested. But the methods of testing for the likelihood of such conformality are different. Conceptual reliability in *logical* truth rests ultimately on *consistency* or identity; conceptual reliability in *empirical* truth rests mainly on *correspondence* between expectations evoked and experiences obtained; but conceptual reliability in *theoretical* truth rests on *coherence* woven from both of these. I shall save fuller discussion for the next chapter, where I make my proposals about theoretical knowing. But already it should be clear that while theory without logical consistency is useless, without empirical correspondence it is irrelevant. For a limited theory (e.g., one from science), to be true is to be at least self-consistent and empirically well-informed. But its function goes beyond these levels. A theory's function is to account, somehow, for its data. It needs to interpret its elements and move them beyond the status of "brute facts." Its type of conceptual reliability, and its type of truth, needs to show connections and to clarify or create intelligible linkages. The greater the success in this, the stronger a theory's conceptual reliability in performing its function, and the firmer we judge its claim to be theoretically true.

This preliminary mention of theory and its functions points ahead to the final chapter. But before reaching the level of theory again, we must first work through more levels of contrast-embracing continuity within the domain of knowing proper. This chapter has continued to contribute to the deconstruction of the myth of the epistemological gap by attempting, constructively, to show connections where disconnection is often supposed to lurk. Just as Chapter 8 focused on continuities of *experience* linking events at every level of complexity to the objects of their prehensions and, in particular, comparing human experiencers to object-grasping events in nature generally, so this chapter has focused on continuities of *thinking*. Understood in full Whiteheadian generality, symbolic mentality is the seed-bed for language. Widely functioning in nature, it makes linguistic thinking possible as a special case of concrescence, highly refined and powerful. Language, as it grows naturally out of prearticulate intelligence, however, never outgrows its roots in value-laden experience, biological need, and social purpose. Obviously, the achievement of free linguistic symbols marks a huge qualitative shift in conceptual center of gravity for adult, fully socialized human thinking. This occurs, however, in a seamless evolutionary process that liberates us from oppressive modern fears of epistemological gaps. Since the keyword is "continuity" for experience and for thinking, my constructive deconstruction of the epistemological gap only awaits completion by finding still more continuities within the domains of knowing.

10

KNOWING THE WORLD

The myth of the epistemological gap should by now be losing its power. On this book's ecological worldview there are no gaps; instead, one finds continuities everywhere. If (as has been wisely said) the only way to get out of solipsism is never to allow oneself to get into it, then it is fair to say that the only way to get across the epistemological gap is never to permit such a gap to open at all. Instead, one should deconstruct it, undermining its power with a fuller account of what is involved in experience, thought, and knowing.

What is needed, if we are finally to be liberated from myth of the epistemological gap, is a recognition of continuities "all the way down," but continuities that allow for important differentiations. There are, after all, evident differences in modes of knowing. We could not be happy with an epistemological position that required homogenization, any more than we could accept a theory that ends with hopeless fragmentation. The start of this last chapter seems a good place to address, now in full context, those unresolved issues of epistemological pluralism raised in the first chapter.

Let us first tackle epistemological dualism. There are plenty of grounds for a sympathetic look at dualism. The most fundamental duality, on which other modes of dualism tacitly depend, is the deep contrast between what I called the "Greek" and "Hebrew" approaches to the cognitive act. The first stresses *contemplation* as the model and ideal. It rests on metaphors of vision, calling for emotional coolness, appropriate distance, standard illumination, and an unchanging object to observe. The second prefers the images and ideals of *intimacy*. It calls on metaphors of sexual intercourse, emphasizing closeness, penetration, and emotional warmth, and it requires neither external light sources nor static passivity from the object of its attention.

The account in Chapter 9 of the phases of concrescence accommodates both these ideals as rooted in the bipolar character of self-actualizing events in general, and of human cognitive experience in particular. The first pole is that of physical feeling, when the immediate contiguous environment invades the newly forming event. This is the profoundly emotional, value-laden moment of causal prehension that characterizes all internal relatedness and that continues to characterize human experience and thinking. But, as the previous two chapters have shown, this moment in human experience tends to be submerged under the highly developed (and intensely valued) second pole, which is that of conceptual feeling—something that in human thinking becomes increasingly abstract entertainment of pure possibilities, forms of definiteness, characters, properties, eternal objects, in their relatedness to one another and to a highly abstract logical subject. We of the would-be *sapiens* species tend to place our emphasis on the pole in which we take most pride. Especially for philosophers, this has been the conceptual pole, the pole within our continuously bipolar experience that comes closest to the ideals of contemplation.

We would do better, as philosophers and as a species, if we were more balanced in our emphasis. The physical pole gives us far less clarity, but it makes up for its murkiness by delivering causal continuity and importance. Both Greek and Hebrew aspects are genuine and essential. Both are grounded in the ultimate character of things.

The epistemological gap is implicit in the representational theory of thinking. This involves another form of dualism, between the representation and the object represented, the image and the reality. Again it is important to recognize how compelling representationalism can seem. In visual perception (the paradigm of the contemplative ideal of knowing), inverted images, painted by photons focused on the retinal lining of the eye, are transmitted to the brain for general interpretation. The image in our experience is different from the image in our eye (e.g., in experience it is not inverted), and the image in our eye is different—in a different place, of a different size, different orientation, etc.—from the object imaged. Given the strong preference for the contemplative ideal of cognition, the representational theory of thinking, in which thoughts are likened to images distanced in many ways from their referents, feels almost inevitable. And there is an honorable place for this representational aspect of human thought in the bipolar account. The image of the contemporary world around us (as I have argued above) is a mental projection, generated in the final phases of the conceptual pole and painted onto a highly simplified canvas of the real world that, a moment before, had been attained causally, in all its richness, through the more basic physical pole. Whitehead called this mode "symbolic reference" (Whitehead 1978: chap. 8). It is *symbolic* inasmuch as one aspect of experience evokes other aspects, opening a space for error to intrude. It is *reference* because one thing (for example, a shade of color) is used to refer to another thing (for example, a wall in a room). This is the home ground of the representational theory. It is where the epistemological gap, if allowed, would start to open.

But on the bipolar understanding, the gap never starts to threaten, since representation is only half the story. *Of course* there are differences between images and their objects. *Of course* there may be errors of perception and conception that creep in through these differences. This is allowed for, expected, on the conceptual side of the polarities involved. It is, indeed, a good thing that there can be these distances, since without them we would be entirely under the control of the causally given. Without some breathing room from the contiguous environment, we could never take account of the absent, would not be capable of valuing relevant alternatives, would have no openings for novelty. Error is the mark of mentality at work. But the (happy) possibility of error does not open a dangerous epistemological gap in the bipolar context. The world remains felt, prior to and beneath all characterizations. It may turn out to be mischaracterized, but this is relatively a minor matter, open to correction by deeper or wider experience and thinking. Error is not an enemy, it is a stimulus and a goad. True, it may be dangerous, even fatal for individuals who take the unreliable for the reliable. But in the larger picture, for the species, this risk is part of the natural selection process. The possibility of error is no invitation to skepticism, no warrant for epistemic despair.

As for the other types of pluralism discussed in the opening chapter, it seems clear that there are indeed many forms of knowing, significantly dissimilar in character. Historical and mathematical knowing, scientific and ethical knowing, knowing a face, knowing a wine, knowing the sacred—all these, and more, are distinct in many ways. Hard epistemological pluralism would hold that they are irreducibly different; hard epistemological monism would insist that at bottom they are all exactly the same. Moderate pluralism, which I shall defend in the remainder of the book, celebrates the genuine differences but also finds family resemblances—and even underlying genetic sources— that can justify the common application of the word "knowing" to them all. Moderate pluralism recognizes a kind of ecology of knowing, a webwork of differentiated domains, interactive and mutually dependent, finally grounded in real relations. The basic relation, as I have argued, is prehension. The basic genetic source of knowing is recognition.

There are more commonalities, but before I try to draw these out any further, it would be well to explore three importantly different kinds of knowing that are often rightly contrasted. These are *practical* knowing, *observational* knowing, and *theoretical* knowing.

PRACTICAL KNOWING

Knowing *how* to accomplish something implies nothing at all about understanding what is going on in the circumstances. Once rats or pigeons have learned how to obtain food pellets from pushing or pecking at a dispenser, for example, we may legitimately say that they "know how" to do it, though they have no idea of the internal workings of the mechanism they control. We may say this (nonmetaphorically), that is, if we find, consulting our own and others' intuitions of ordinary usage, that this sort of language is within the recognized range of normal speech in this limited context. It is probably outside that range, however, to speak of such animals as possessing "knowledge." "Knowing"-language seems to include a somewhat wider domain than "knowledge"-language. "Knowledge" is the conceptualized deposit of many events of knowing of all kinds. It may not require *theoretical* foundations (there is such a thing as purely practical knowledge), but it goes beyond mere trick learning. Still, rats and pigeons and many other species successfully learn to *know how* to do many things. Preconceptual organisms, that is, can learn method, and method is the secret of practical knowing.

Method requires mentality. A method, after all, is something general. It is an abstraction that is underdetermined by (not merely equivalent to) any finite set of instances that exemplify it. It involves linking recognizable and repeatable elements within the flux of experience. "Push here, get food," is beyond a rat's power to formulate in words, or probably to consider at all in the absence of the lever of the food dispenser. But once having learned the connection between a recognizable behavior-type and a value-laden result—all this depending on sensory discrimination, memory, and recognition—the animal gains mental grasp (at least when the lever is presented to perception) of a general method of getting food, one that can be applied again and again, in slightly varying circumstances, sometimes to the point of exhaustion.

This is what Michael Polanyi called "trick learning." In a sense, all methods are tricks for getting something done. Whitehead called method a "dodge" (one recognized meaning of a "dodger" is one who uses clever or resourceful devices). All such devices are in the service of some end. A method "starts as a dodge facilitating the accomplishment of some nascent urge of life" (Whitehead 1929: 18). The basic urge of life, illustrated at all levels of mentality, Whitehead says succinctly, is threefold:

> (i) to live, (ii) to live well, (iii) to live better. In fact the art of life is *first* to be alive, *secondly* to be alive in a satisfactory way, and *thirdly* to acquire an increase in satisfaction (Whitehead 1929: 8).

Methods are discovered and adopted in much the same way by rats and humans. There is a stage of unsatisfactory experience (hunger, thirst, or something more sophisticated) in which the mentality of the organism operates at random. The mental pole, after all, is the organism's way of taking account of the absent; it is not wholly under the control of the immediate perceptual environment; it is therefore the anarchical principle, a worm of "might be" in an otherwise solid block of "is." In the first, restless stage, the organism emits behaviors apparently at random. A lucky hit occurs, bringing about some degree of satisfaction. The rat pushes at a lever and finds a pellet of food. This is not yet a method, it was just a happy accident. But after several such anarchical accidents, the capacity of living organisms to grasp particular events shot through with formal similarities, to remember features, to establish associations—this capacity begins to work. Recognizing common characteristics that are important enough, regular enough, frequent enough, and on a scale comprehensible enough to notice, the organism that previously had no routine now has a new general pattern—a method, a trick, a dodge—at its disposal.

Practical knowing requires the same normative or self-certifying implicit judgments as we encountered in the previous chapter on learning and using words. That is, having and using a method requires judging, each time, that a new situation is similar enough to a previous situation to count as an instance of the general pattern; it requires self-certification of memory as trustworthy; and it requires judging this performance of pattern recognition as good enough to warrant the attempt to generate a new example of a general type of behavioral response in the presented circumstances.

Discovering and applying method is difficult but immensely rewarding. The difference between lacking and having a method may well be the difference between life and death. Anarchic behavior can be life-threatening. To survive (the first urge of life) in this world of threats and risks is difficult enough even with methods to help find food in the woods or water in the desert, or to help mitigate the dangers of crossing busy streets. Methods are valuable because they discipline the anarchic tendencies of pure mentality. Since methods are the mental products of noticing, remembering, and associating, it is fair to say that method in general—learning an effective routine way of doing something—is the self-discipline of mentality. Unfettered mentality, the principle of pure "might be," is a danger to a living organism. In consequence, one response to the urge of life for survival is to use mentality to put fetters on mentality.

Further, once a method is discovered, it is precious. It allows the organism equipped with method to enhance its satisfactions, to live well. Rats and pigeons show by their behavior, once their trick is learned, how intensely they value their methods of gaining vastly increased access to food. The craft secrets of the medieval guilds (like those of today's multinational corporations) were closely guarded methods. It is hard to imagine human life shorn of the deposit of methods, from making fire to growing crops, which gradually differentiated the tricks of early *Homo sapiens* from those of other species. Knowing how to make pottery, how to work with metals, and the like, took thousands of painful and patient years to acquire, remember, and refine.

This is the basis for the well-justified conservatism of practical knowing. "If it ain't broke, don't fix it!" "Leave well-enough alone!" These are the understandable defensive reactions of practical people to dangerous tinkerers. The mental fetters of tradition are welcomed in light of the alternatives— anarchy and ruin. Method controls the wildness of which mind, when free to play with possibilities, is inherently capable. Method assists the urge of life to survive and to survive well.

But what of the third part of Whitehead's tripartite formula: "to live better"? Traditions can be heavy-handed. Method is better than no method, but sometimes old methods get in the way of better methods. Fortunately for the urges of life, mentality is never quite exhausted by the methods it invents to control its own appetite for anarchy. Mentality remains at bottom the capacity to deal with unrealized possibilities. From the mental pole of organisms, especially from those with more complex and vivid mental lives, flow not only new methods but also vital criticisms of old methods that mind has made.

This critique of methods springs from the same urges that motivate them in the first place. If the aim of life is for survival, for satisfaction, and for ever-better satisfactions, then a method that realizes fewer satisfactions than another will be subject to practical criticism. The legendary method that achieved the gustatory satisfaction of roast meat by burning down the barn each time a feast was planned is, on this criterion, inferior to other methods that allow the satisfactions both of enjoying roast meat *and* of continuing to use the barn. This, on the level of practical knowing, is the criterion of richness: As many satisfactions as possible, please! The more the merrier!

But satisfactions, helter-skelter, have a way of getting in each other's way. Still better methods would allow more satisfactions by overcoming conflict. Lesser methods, by clashing with each other, may block satisfactions, all of which might be goals of life. A better method, then, might be a larger method capable of turning a "win-lose" into a "win-win" situation for an individual or a group. This, on the level of practical knowing, reflects the criterion of wholeness. To know how to turn a zero-sum game into a nonzero-sum game becomes the apogee of practical wisdom. As we shall see in *Living and Value*, integrity in personal life, and flourishing in society, both depend on its cultivation.

Richness and wholeness (adequacy and coherence) have now reemerged in a new context. It is a context that could lead to an entire philosophical stance toward technology, or provide a fruitful meeting point between epistemology and ethics. But for all its richness of ethical promise, the present epistemological context has been limited. It is restricted to knowing *how to do* something judged worthwhile. So far it does not (as I mentioned at the start) imply anything about understanding the circumstances in which practical knowing-how is set. For humans, of course, at least after the earliest days of infancy, there is no such thing as "pure" practical knowing. We come to our methods, in part, by trying this and that in light of what we suppose we *understand* is going on. And we criticize our methods by subjecting them to *observational* tests concerning likely outcomes, supposing we do this or supposing we do that. Both these dimensions, understanding and observation, go beyond the purely practical. We need to add them to our collection of "knowings."

OBSERVATIONAL KNOWING

Observing goes on throughout the animal kingdom. My dog is not always actively engaged in her perceptual world. Often, muzzle on paws, she just lets the world go on around her, watching intently. Squirrels, for her, are not necessarily things to be chased. Sometimes they are just interesting things to observe.

Sign cognition, as we saw in the previous chapter, is the basis for developing a sense for the regularities to be expected in experience. One item of experience is taken as a sign for another probable item. Seeing a lightning flash becomes a sign for hearing a peal of thunder soon. Red sky in the morning becomes, for sailors, a sign of rain before nightfall. Shorter days, for those in moderate latitudes, become a sign for colder weather due after a while. For antelope, the sight of a patch of tall grass waving on a windless day becomes a sign for the possible sight of a hungry cheetah springing out from cover. Some signs, as H. H. Price points out, are short-range (the lightning and the thunder) and some long-range (the red sky and the rain); some signs are strong (the thunder and the lightning) and some weak (the red sky and the rain, the grass and the cheetah); some are short-range and weak (the grass and the cheetah); some are long-range and strong (the shortening days and the colder weather); most long-range signs are weaker than short-range signs (Price 1953: 102–10).

At the biological level, most observational knowing is "interested," as opposed to "disinterested." Survival depends on taking precautions, and eternal vigilance demands taking account of even quite weak signs if there is some likelihood that life is at stake. At the same time, in contrast to practical knowing, which is always "interested" in outcomes, observational knowing has another important aspect that distinguishes it from practical knowing. It can, at least sometimes—often for humans—be "disinterestedly" satisfying. Perhaps this extends well into the animal kingdom, too. It is impossible to be sure, but I think it likely that sometimes my dog is "interested" in her perceived environment in the other sense of the word: that she finds her world simply *interesting*—worth attending to, satisfying to see and smell just for the intrinsic pleasures involved.

Human beings observe their world with both motives. We find intrinsic satisfaction in watching waves rolling in at the beach. There we see stately regularities spiced with infinite detailed differences. We enjoy observing patterns in the flames dancing in the fireplace. Many love to watch and identify birds and their busy ways. Others observe the stars at night for the sheer pleasure of it. Tracing forms in clouds is endlessly fascinating. As Aristotle said, we take joy "in our perceptions, which we cherish for their own sakes, quite apart from any benefits they may yield us" (Aristotle 1951a: 67). Especially joyful are the perceptions that allow us to anticipate other perceptions, and the delights of fulfilled general expectations laced with delicious detailed surprises.

With human language, wordless sign cognition gives way to the linguistic framing of empirical hypotheses. These, too, may be of both intrinsic and instrumental value. The sheer delights of fulfilled anticipation are no less satisfying when the anticipations involved have first been expressed in words. On the contrary, for observational scientists skilled in the formulation of complex, sophisticated anticipations, the thrill of the pursuit of subtle regularities in nature may be among life's most treasured intrinsic values. But of course our observational hypotheses, commonplace as well as specialized, are also of enormous instrumental value for our practical methodologies. Methods themselves are among the second-order objects for observation—how regularly do they work?—and of course first-order regularities within the perceivable natural order are important to notice since when noticed and formulated they may become either the basis for a new method or a key element in the criticism of an old one.

The framing of observational hypotheses, informally or formally, requires just the same mental rhythms as the adopting of methods. There must first be the prehension of a causal environment characterized by forms of definiteness. There must be memory, linking these present prehensions to others so that recognition of the "same again" can occur. One must be capable of the experience of "hello, again!" when another A comes along, and likewise capable of greeting another B with similar familiarity. Then the association of B-after-A must itself, as an abstract relation, become familiar. And in all of this, there is the requirement that we certify our acts of recognition and memory as good enough to rely on. Other judgments are equally essential: for example, that this aspect of experience is a sufficiently normative instance of an A to warrant its classification under that general heading; and that this other aspect of experience is a sufficiently authentic instance of B to deserve the title. Then we need to judge how strong the link of expectation should be. Is this a case of weak signification? Is it short-range or long-range? Is it weak but short-range and important enough to deserve intense concern? Is it long-range but in need of preparation, that is, finding the umbrella?

The anarchical capabilities of mentality provide power in principle for an unlimited number of hypotheses about possible observations. This means that mind needs to fetter itself with method to keep its own superabundant creativity under control. Such method, generally speaking, is often called the "logic of confirmation," in contrast to the mercurial "logic of discovery."

Here we are on the familiar turf of standard modern philosophy of science, which has refined the logic of confirmation more than any other topic. The main force of the verificational approach to philosophy, too, treated in detail in Chapter 5, above, falls on this domain. Consequently, I now need only to recall highlights for this new context.

What are the objectives of observational knowing? One aim, I have argued, is sheer satisfaction in experiencing the fulfillment of expectation. I do not mean, by "observation" here, simple grateful gazing at beautiful objects (I shall return to the aesthetics of knowing in the final section), but, rather, "observation" in the stronger sense—as the inductive process of carefully coming to appreciate sequences of experience in their regularities, great and small, and to enjoy the power of predicting for its own sake. Such enjoyments are enhanced by recognizing small variations when they occur against the background of greater predictabilities, then finding still more minute regularities within those small, surprising variations, and so on indefinitely. The other aim, more often noted, is the enhanced capability of interacting with a world whose regularities can be correctly anticipated. If the first type of satisfactions are intrinsic, the second type are instrumental—in the service of critique and/or development of practical methods. Once again, when through careful observing we come to expect basic regularities along with their finer variations, and when we further learn to expect the mini-regularities within these variations, we can refine methods of practice that in turn provide vast ranges of other satisfactions.

Both aims, intrinsic and instrumental, demand as *many* observational regularities as possible—both long-term (as seasonal patterns) and short-term (as which way a deer is about to run)—and as many regularities among the variations on regularities as possible too. Here is a reappearance of the demand, once again, for richness, for fullness, for adequacy. The more the merrier! Noticing, recognizing, naming, associating, and anticipating elements of experience constitute a process with no maximal limit. Both intrinsic satisfaction and practical success depend on endless gathering and attending. This is one side of the logic of confirmation.

When, though, is a hypothesis likely to be successful in allowing us to anticipate the future? What, in other words, is the range of its applicability? Can the circumstances be specified in which a hypothesis is regularly reliable? Are there other circumstances in which it is not to be trusted? Life may depend on learning such meta-hypotheses about the conditions of defeasibility of lower-order hypotheses. For example, it is a pretty good hypothesis that experiencing a lion on the savannah will be followed by experiencing being attacked and torn to pieces; but in case the lion is experienced as lying down with a distended stomach and other signs of recent feeding, the original hypothesis may (fortunately) not hold. The same sort of delimitation of the range of applicability of empirical laws is an important function of scientific investigation. Snell's Law on the refraction of light through various substances, for example, satisfies expectations quite reliably in many contexts, but not in all (Toulmin 1953: 75–88). All empirical hypotheses have unstated ranges of applicability that must be externally supplied by still other hypotheses. For the most part we consider these ranges obvious (e.g., that assertions about many properties of iron hold for the earth but not for the center of the sun), but that does not change the logical point.

In this process of forming observational hypotheses about hypotheses, we are both adding more to our total stock (as the criterion of adequacy, or richness, demands), and we are organizing hypotheses into mutually related *patterns* of hypotheses. The wider-ranging hypotheses provide inductive guidance concerning which narrower-ranging hypotheses to trust under given observational circumstances, and which to ignore. Just here, functioning to assist the aims of observational knowing as part of the logic of confirmation, we find again the criterion of coherence. Confirmation, to be effective in assuring regularities of satisfaction, needs not only to seek out smaller and smaller variations for noticing and naming (as demanded for adequacy); it also needs to relate lesser contexts of observation to larger contexts, to generate and test wider and wider patterns of regularity (as demanded by coherence). The ideal of confirmation in observational knowing would be to have a system of expectations both *full* and *whole*, both *rich* and *related*, both *complete* and *integrated*.

Real life falls far short of such an ideal. Our powers of attention are imperfect; our capacities of memory are limited; our abilities to relate and correct are finite. As maintained earlier in this chapter, there is inevitable (and in some ways welcome) error in observational knowing. Error enters when expectations based on observation are disappointed. I am not here discussing the perceptual errors of illusion or hallucination. Those "errors" are only errors if they are believed. Illusions are quite normal events of perception. They are standard events complicated by nonstandard environmental conditions. They can be counted on (e.g., by painters, architects, and magicians); they can be corrected for (e.g., by swimmers, pilots, or camel drivers). The illusion of the "broken" oar in the water can be predicted by Snell's Law of Refraction, and those who have perfected techniques of spear fishing know how to compensate for the standard illusions caused by passage of light from the medium of air to the medium of water. Hallucinations, too, are standard perceptual events, but these are complicated by nonstandard conditions in the perceiving organism rather than in the environment. Elevated levels of alcohol in the bloodstream or LSD in the brain can be anticipated to have perceptual effects of fairly well-defined sorts, though the complexity of living organisms and the psychological uniqueness of human persons makes detailed predictions unfeasible. Perceptual errors of these sorts, however, are, qua experience, simply perceptions. They illustrate the cognitive distance between the conceptual pole in conscious concrescence, on the one hand, and the surrounding world of causal efficacy prehended at the physical pole, on the other. As I have indicated earlier, this is predictable, correctable, and no ground for epistemological panic. The fact that we can speak of "error" at all in such contexts shows (1) that we have the intersubjective means of detecting the nonstandard conditions affecting perception in such cases, (2) that we know how to identify illusion and hallucination when it occurs, and (3) that we know better than to trust such nonstandard perceptual experience.

Errors not based in illusion or hallucination also need attention. It is quite common to find ourselves making an inductive leap to an expectation that lets us down. On the boardwalk yesterday I was smiled at by an attractive stranger; again this morning I was smiled at by this stranger. My hopes, my self-esteem, predispose me to anticipate more smiles and . . . perhaps more than that. But am I wise to weave hypotheses about possible future elements of experience from such flimsy perceptual signs, even if the stranger's smile was neither optical illusion nor chemically induced hallucination? No, but people weave them all the time. Sometimes their hypotheses are happily rewarded; sometimes they are falsified with crushing disappointment.

Error in observational knowing must be expected not only in such extreme cases of cognitive long shots. By its very character—thanks to the mediation of the conceptual pole in the simplifying and organizing of experience—hypotheses must allow the logical possibility, at least, of error. "If this is a case of X, then I should anticipate Y," is put at risk (1) by the possibility that I have misidentified a habit of the universe, (2) by the possibility that circumstances are such that I am outside the range of application of a genuine but contextually limited habit, (3) by the possibility that something nonhabitual—something spontaneous or genuinely novel—will occur, and (4) by the possibility that I have misrecognized or misclassified the event X. It may not be a case of X, after all; or it may be a case of X_1 or X_2, subvarieties of X with subtly different habits.

Since these sources of error are always possible, in principle, even the hypotheses of the most rigorously verified "hard sciences" must take account of error. This can be done in two distinct ways, logically equivalent but strikingly different in affective tone. The first, most common, way is to state the hypothesis in categorical terms—e.g., "$A = \frac{1}{2}T^2$," pure, exact, absolute— but add, separately, a statement of the range of observational error since (as noted earlier) nothing ever comes out *exactly* on a number. Because decimal points are infinitely expansible, there will always need to be a "rounding off" and "cleaning up" of perceptual approximations within the domain of conceptual absolutes. A second, less chosen, way would be to state all hypotheses in probabilistic mathematical form from the outset. This would be less pretentious, more modestly in line with the actual practice of scientific observation; but it would be mathematically messier and harder to handle, and above all, it would be less suggestive of a perfect mechanical order, hence less supportive of powerful ideals of the cosmos.

My worldview is messier—more polycentric, evolutionary, dynamic— therefore I welcome the inevitability of error. Taking error more *seriously* would incorporate it into our methods of formulating our observational laws; taking it more *positively*—as liberation both from ideally imposed absolute concepts and (as noted earlier in the chapter) from total submergence in the immediate perceptual environment—would open us to an ecological worldview of provisional stabilities, emergence, and novelty. Here is another place in which epistemological preferences, this one for dealing with the common facts of imperfect observational knowing, may have heavy bearing on metaphysical outlooks. (Or is it the other way: that metaphysical preferences have influenced our epistemological policies for conceiving observational error? I suspect the influence is mutual and self-reinforcing.)

My discussion is inevitably being drawn from observational to theoretical knowing, but before I allow the magnetism of that topic to pull me entirely out of this section of the chapter, I need to make two concluding remarks on empirical hypotheses: first, on their pervasiveness (and linkage to sheer perception), and, second, on their truth.

I have defended the important distinction between "perception" and "observation." *Perception*, as described in the previous chapters, is the direct experiential processing of the world through phases of concrescence, sprouting in pure physical prehension and flowering in symbolic reference. *Observation*, as here delimited, is learning the linkage of perceivable elements across time, so that regularities are noticed and expected, even when not directly experienced. Both perception and observation allow error (fortunately), but neither allows an epistemological gap of any frightening sort.

Now I need to qualify the distinction. Often we report on our immediate perception in singular statements of grammatically categorical form, such as "Ronald's hair is black." This does not seem on its face hypothetical, but I believe that under its grammatical surface it is just that. Our learning of the appropriate words to carry our meaning is a social process requiring throughout, as I have argued, self-certified normative acts of judgment. Beneath this process is always the implicit "if," presupposed by any act of public discourse. *If* I have learned the appropriate perceptual context for the use of "black" as a type of sound- or shape-production, and *if* I have learned the appropriate perceptual context for the use of "hair" as another type of sound- or shape-production, *then* when I utter, "Ronald's hair is black," I shall be understood, under standard conditions in an English-speaking community, as asserting that Ronald's hair is black. Any of those hypotheticals could prove wrong, in which case I would need to withdraw and reconsider.

Beyond this inevitably vulnerable level of all linguistic assertion, what is asserted, as the Logical Positivists maintained, can be interpreted by an indefinite set of hypotheses about what I, or any normally situated observer, would perceive under various conditions. One possible empirical meaning might be: "*If* I (or anyone) were to examine Ronald's hair follicles all the way to their roots, perceptions of them would continue prehending the eternal object, black, with respect to them." (Ronald has not used a dye or rinse to alter the color of his hair.) Another might be: "*If* I (or anyone) were to step into standard sunlight, perceptions of Ronald's hair would continue prehending the eternal object, black, with respect to that portion of the visible environment." (No one was suffering from optical illusion due to nonstandard lighting effects.)

All empirical assertions, in this way, are conditional. Sometimes they are proven false by subsequent experience. In principle, any such assertion can be false, because symbolic reference is occurring. There is a logical difference between the conceptually configured, clarified, and simplified predicate at the conceptual pole of experience and the causally transmitted, powerful, but vague logical subject at the physical pole. The "contemporary" world we paint with our brightened conceptual pigments is not, in reality, quite contemporary. Some time has elapsed in the physical transmission. In extremely rare cases, as in looking at a distant star, the temporal distance can be extremely significant. In most cases, transmission time is negligible, and we properly neglect it. Still, whatever their grammatical form, empirical propositions are hypotheses, for better and for worse. For worse, we can be tripped up in our expectations. Our spear may miss the fish we think we see right there. We may be embarrassed—or worse—by having hypothesized too much about an attractive stranger. Both are cases of false expectation. Both lead to dissatisfaction.

The facts of stable material structures, functioning societies, and flourishing organisms indicate that dissatisfaction is the exception, not the rule. Without an undergirding network of fulfilled expectations, there would be no world, no ordered cosmos of recognitions and regularities, in which mistakes and disappointments could occur. Dissatisfaction is parasitical on satisfaction. Or, in other words, false expectation depends on a context of normally true expectation.

For something to be "true," as I argued in the previous chapter, is a matter of *relevant conformality*, the test for which is *long-run reliability*, of the sort appropriate to the context at hand. In the context of empirical hypotheses, the relevant conformality is between the forms of definiteness to be manifested by the world at a specified future time, and the forms of definiteness entertained mentally as expectations for that future. When the forms fit (within the somewhat flexible range of acceptable variation), cognitive satisfaction is achieved. The specific prediction is "verified" (from *verus*, Latin for "true"), and so far forth, the hypothesis underlying the prediction is strengthened in its claim for conceptual reliability. As is well known, no finite number of such verifications can finally seal the verdict that the hypothesis itself is absolutely true with no logical possibility of exception. This inference is barred by the fallacy of Affirming the Consequent (i.e., *"If P, then Q; and Q"* proves nothing about P, since it allows for an indefinite range of *other* possibilities. That is, even if it is true that "If this is a cow, then it is a mammal"; and it is true that "This is a mammal," such verification still does not rule out that "This is not a cow," since it might be a dog or cat or person). But, deductive fallacy notwithstanding, the best test for observational knowing is long-run reliability, where endlessly repeated experiences of satisfied conformal expectations trend asymptotically toward the ideal limit where "immensely likely" would touch "is so."

Asymptotes never touch their limits, of course. For this reason, ideals of absolute knowing in empirical matters are logically out of place. Plato was right to exclude the observable world of becoming from what he stipulated that "knowing" must be. He was wrong, as I shall argue in the next section, to demand such an absolute epistemic norm for theoretical knowing, but it must now be clear from this book as a whole that observational knowing must not be held to any such norm. At the same time, the inappropriateness of absolute epistemic norms in this domain ought not to spark explosive overreaction. There are in fact observational laws. Admittedly, there is and can be no sharp line dividing observational laws from observational hypotheses. Hypotheses may be extremely probable; laws are subject to revision, though rarely. On my proffered worldview, this is as it should be, both metaphysically and epistemically. Empirical laws, metaphysically, are no more than the settled social accommodations, the habits, of evolved energetic events. Hypotheses long unshaken we call laws. We possess a huge stock of observational knowledge, both individually as organisms and vastly more as a species, of which we have no good grounds to suspect that it is not true.

Many observational hypotheses, in contrast, we do (for good reasons) suspect are not true. They may, as we have seen, be weakly predictive (as the waving grass in the African savannah). Often we may ardently hope they are not true. We may attend to them and take precautions against their coming true, feeling relief when they turn out to be false. But all these are exceptional cases, vividly claiming attention against a solid, if vague, taken-for-granted background of conformality between expectations and outcomes—thanks to which specific focus on problematic hypotheses can be narrowed, precautions be implemented, vigilance be extended.

In this way, in simple as well as highly sophisticated ways, observational knowing of regularities, both in our experience and conformally in our world, leads to methods enhancing the urge to live, to live well, and to live better. Practical knowing, the mental disciplining of anarchical mentality by method, itself is placed under higher discipline. Items of observational knowing, once learned, can criticize less effective methods from the standpoint of a more reliable grasp of what can be expected under what relevant conditions. And, linked to practical knowing by the shared ends of living well and better, observational knowing can help invent new kinds of know-how: new methods, techniques, implements, and technologies for practical flourishing.

To summarize: practical knowing is *knowing how* to accomplish something worth doing. Observational knowing is *knowing what* is going on— what is worth noticing, recognizing, and relating—in the otherwise buzzing confusion of raw experience. "Knowing what" is immensely helpful for "knowing how"; and, reciprocally, experiments in "knowing how" add usefully to the fund of "knowing what." Neither, however, in the relatively pure forms I have presented, has been involved with *knowing why*. Theoretical knowing, my next topic, depends on knowing both how and what. It goes beyond both; at times it is in tension with both; but part of its influence cycles around not only to illuminate but also to transform practice and observation. Still, as a function of human mentality, it shares many traits with practical and observational knowing. In the ecology of knowing, we should expect to find as many continuities, here too, as differences.

THEORETICAL KNOWING

The fundamental continuities that tie theoretical knowing to previous modes of knowing and experiencing are rooted in the basic phases of concrescence shared by every actual event. Since theory is primarily a function of conceptual construction, requiring highly developed linguistic abstractions, the emphasis of theoretical knowing will naturally fall on the latter phases of concrescence, in which complex comparative feelings dominate experience. Here, close to the conceptual pole and relatively insulated from the insistent importances of the physical pole, the anarchical tendencies of mentality are in their element. Theoretical knowing is born in speculation, free from the constraints of the given immediate environment. Theorizing, whether seen in the early stages of Greek speculation or in beginning students, has a certain wonderful wildness to it. Whitehead spoke of the prophets and seers and acknowledged the temptations of "charlatanism" built into the unconstrained making of theories. Just as "knowing how" requires the mental self-discipline of practical methods, and just as "knowing what" demands the mental self-discipline of experimental methods, so "knowing why" has a built-in need for self-constraint. As Whitehead put it:

> The world's experience of professed seers has on the whole been very unfortunate. In the main, they are a shady lot with a bad reputation. Even if we put aside those with some tinge of insincerity, there still remain the presumptuous, ignorant, incompetent, unbalanced band of false prophets who deceive the people. On the whole, the odds are so heavily against any particular prophet that, apart from some method of testing, perhaps it is safer to stone them, in some merciful way (Whitehead 1929: 67).

The answer to this need was the invention of logic, in the larger sense: that is, the self-imposition of method on speculation for the sake of its own well-being. At every level, then, mentality, free from determination by the given environment, introduces wildness into the concrescent event. At every level, mentality learns to channel itself by inventing methods: of acting, of observing, of theorizing. *Practical* methods are abstract models for action in general ways for the sake of achieving satisfying outcomes. These methods are subject to criticism, by practical intelligence itself and by observational knowledge, on the criteria of richness and wholeness. *Observational* methods are abstract rules for attending, noticing, remembering, recognizing, and associating elements of experience for the sake of reliable satisfactions in expectations. These methods, too, as we saw, are subject to criticism on the criteria of richness and wholeness. Shortly I shall explore the character and limitations of theoretical methods. No one should be surprised to find plenty of parallels in the new context.

First, however, it is useful to notice how theorizing is both dependent on, and in conflict with, the other two modes of knowing. Theorizing depends heavily on practical knowing. As an exercise in the manipulation of linguistic symbols—the construction of patterns from abstractions—theorizing is a rarity in the universe. It is an activity, so far as we know, of only one recently evolved species. Even among the minority of human beings who achieve sophisticated competence in symbolic abstractions, theorizing is a flickering candle in a drafty room. The practical possibility of theoretical activities depends (like every life process) on a supportive environment. Specifically, in this case, there needs to be enough leisure so that such thought, unbound to the practical needs of the moment, may take place. Until practical "knowing how" has succeeded in defending life at a good level, there will be no theorizing. This means that practical knowing should be thanked for inventing the social methods—libraries, monasteries, synagogues, salons, universities—that have protected the flickering flame. One should never underestimate the importance of great institutions, the social technologies that further our practical aims to live, to live well, to live better.

Theorizing is also deeply dependent on "knowing what" is going on in the buzzing world of experience. At one level (as we saw in the previous chapter), language itself depends on observing regularities. Without observational knowing there could be no recognition of features, no noticing of repeatable sounds, no associations, no social meanings. Given language, theorizing needs the established regularities discovered by observational knowing as its fodder and its check.

But to note this need is also to recognize two of the ways in which theoretical knowing might come into conflict with—show itself distinct from—observational knowing. For observational knowing, the regularities we call empirical laws are the end result, the triumph, the satisfaction of mental efforts to describe. For theoretical knowing, in contrast, these laws are just the beginning of the struggle to understand. It is fine that B can be counted on reliably to follow A. But *why* does this happen? Satisfied with description alone, the advocates of observational knowing (e.g., Auguste Comte and his followers) reject the question. But those seized by the urgencies of theoretical knowing (e.g., Albert Einstein reluctantly parting company with Ernst Mach) go on asking. Here lies a deep conflict. It is a conflict in values. One unmoved by the claims of theoretical satisfaction will be unlikely to be persuaded by anything the theorizer has to say. The same can hold in reverse. There have been theorizers so enamored of their theories that they prefer them to the grubby descriptions of observational knowing. Some (e.g., Parmenides) have gone to the length of discarding observation altogether, rejecting it as a form of knowing and relegating it to a Way of Seeming.

Theoretical knowing can and does conflict also with practical knowing. Practical methods that work satisfy urges of life to live and to live well. Large investments of energy and emotion may have been made in these methods.

The alternative to method is anarchy. Practical mentality therefore is inclined to defend the precious methods it has laboriously noticed, protected, and institutionalized. Practical mentality tends to discourage criticisms of its achieved methods. As we saw above, "If it ain't broke, don't fix it," is a basic practical maxim. But theoretical mentality functions differently. *Why* does this method work? Let us analyze this element out, try something else and see if this idea is right, scrap the whole thing for a new concept. . . . Again the value-conflict is deep. Theoretical intelligence seems sometimes to want to bite the hand that literally keeps it fed. Theory sees practice as obscurantist; practice sees theory as rash.

Resolving such conflicts can only be an ongoing ecological process of checks and balances. Here there are no static solutions. Theoretical mentality needs to be allowed to be the terror of practical complacency, the implacable critic of limited hypotheses. But, at the same time, theoretical mentality needs to be curbed by something. This "something," broadly speaking, is its logic; and its logic must include both the other modes of knowing, as enhancements and controls. Logic, after all, is the product of theoretical mentality. It is the formal understanding of the processes of reliable (normative) theorizing. It is the freely invented conceptual self-disciplining of the conceptual pole at its freest. It is not just the careful arrangement of symbolic formulae, although it includes that. When fully developed, the ecological worldview will doubtless develop its own reformed logic, less inclined toward disjunctions and more sensitive to relations than typical modern logics.

On this understanding of logic, a great deal has already been said about the logic of theoretical knowing. It is now only necessary to draw these topics together in an explicit construction fit for the habitation of our minds. Theory-making, including the present theory of theory-making, is conceptual construction, "all the way down." First we make the bricks. The bricks of theory are linguistic symbols. Words, as described in the previous chapter, are made from the material of sign cognition, which is itself grounded in the universal processes of prehension and recognition. These words become the socially shared abstractions we entertain, dismiss, relate, and appreciate in the further work of making that is theory construction. Like all making, theory construction is motivated by purpose. It is done for the sake of the mental satisfactions of understanding.

We construct theories in all sizes and shapes. Some are very small. If I find gouge marks in the cheese and little black particles scattered around the cupboard shelf nearby, I may construct a theory that there is a mouse somewhere behind the wainscot. The theoretical entity, "mouse," serves to help me understand, make sense of, the observations. The mouse is in this case a theoretical entity, since I have not seen it. Being a theoretical entity by no means precludes being observable under the right conditions. If, following my theory, I set a mouse trap, I may succeed in transforming my theoretical living entity into an observational dead one. But at first, at the stage of theory construction, I am adding something freely drawn from my repertoire of concepts to what is presented to perception. I add the concept of "mouse," which I have learned (from observational regularities and repeated social contexts) is the term for something that likes to eat cheese, has teeth that produce gouge marks, and leaves behind little black particles. Adding the concept "mouse"—constructing a theory including it along with concepts of "gouged cheese" and "black particles"—makes sense of the observed cheese and particles by going behind them, tying them conceptually together as the effects of a single familiar causal agent.

Going behind observed regularities to tie them together in a unified way is what theory construction aims to achieve at every level of generality or complexity. Polanyi's rat in the maze, capable of drawing on what seems to be a mental map connecting elements which from the rat's perspective can only be perceived in fragments, is engaging in the pre-conceptual analogue of theory making, allowing it, once the map is constructed, to behave understandingly when familiar routes are blocked. My theory of the disappearing cheese; a detective's theory of the case; a scientist's theory of what is behind and explanatory of Snell's Law of Refraction; Plato's theory of reminiscence; Kant's theory of the noumenal world—all alike are efforts at transcending the immediate perceptual environment by constructing conceptual maps on which otherwise disconnected elements are given intelligible connection, and on which otherwise brute facts are provided luminous, or at least plausible, places in a unified pattern.

How wide the pattern, how comprehensive the theory should be, will be relative to our purposes. For a narrow context, like that of the diminishing cheese in my cupboard, a limited range of elements is appropriate. The unity constructed from these elements may be minuscule, though still satisfying if the context is kept proportionately small and the aim kept low. What "rich" means has always depended on the neighborhood, and "whole" is relative to the riches requiring integration. The wider the subject matter, the higher the definition of "richness" and the more challenging the achievement of "wholeness."

Maximal comprehensiveness comes with "theories of everything." Ironically, physicists who use that phrase (and suppose that theories from pure physics may qualify for such a job) are implicitly adopting a *meta-physical* theory—that everything is a matter of physics—but are usually guilty of omitting from their theory the all-important arguments for such a view, overlooking or denying data about mind, purpose, quality, and value. Thus genuine "theories of everything" (if really completely comprehensive) are inevitably philosophical and theological. More precisely, they are to be found at the open-ended horizon where philosophy and religion, knowing and valuing, merge.

This recognized, Plato's locating the goal of ultimate knowing in the Form of the Good, where the True, the Beautiful, and the Real unite, makes sense; but his choice of epistemic norms for actual human knowing does not. That choice was, as we saw throughout the first two parts of this book, a fateful stipulation: namely, that absolute certainty and incorrigibility must be achieved before the laurel crown of "knowing" could be bestowed.

I shall return at the end of this chapter to discuss what was right about Plato's insight into the union of knowing and valuing, but here it is important to disclaim what has been for millennia a mistaken standard. On my evolutionary, relational, ecological account of knowing, the static, eternal perfections of the Forms can be seen as deriving from the fallacy of misplaced concreteness. Plato's is a "top down" epistemology; mine is "bottom up." Concepts come from noticing features of experience felt as important, recognizing repetitions, naming them, relating them, and, often enough, revising them. The dynamic of revision is vital (quite literally, rising from the processes of life) and renders inappropriate the epistemic norm of perfect certainty. Our powers of noticing, we now realize, are vastly subject to change. The most important enhancements of our abilities to notice, recognize, and name have been contributed by practical knowing married to theoretical knowing: viz., scientific instruments of all sorts, from telescopes and microscopes to supercolliders. The content of observational knowing, that is, located at the fertile meeting point between craft and curiosity, has been revolutionized many times, and we must expect continuing revolutions. The "richness" criterion presents a moving target.

Not only do our powers of noticing change but also our sense of what is *important* to notice, distinguish, and remember. As theories evolve, they redirect our attention to new places, and often we find new things important to observe. Alternative values and purposes may draw us toward different standards for the theories, too. As Alexander Rosenberg puts it:

> Part of the task of the philosopher of science is to reconcile alternative epistemologies with actual scientific theories and the methodological rules scientists employ, for these alternative epistemologies are in effect specifications of the goals of science. By setting out definitions of knowledge, they prescribe the conditions that must be met to attain it (Rosenberg 1992: 13).

Epistemic norms—standards of success sought by theories—are subject to change, and with them the aims and efforts of science change as well. More deeply yet, mentality's naturally wild streak is capable of criticizing and proposing improvements in logic itself. Logic, as I have maintained, is a mentally invented method for the mind's self-discipline. Logic is important for canalizing thought, but it never exhausts the creative powers of mind; sometimes even a good logic can stimulate rebellion in favor of a better. Like every method, the logic of an era may work reasonably well but still be in need of critique and reform. In the last two centuries the history of logic has been extraordinarily dynamic. As long as mind is buzzing, we should not expect its gadfly sting to cease. As mentioned earlier, an ecological logic might well be expected to accompany and complement a postmodern epistemology and metaphysics.

For all these reasons, Plato's premodern epistemic ruling in favor of static perfections of certainty as the necessary marks of knowing—a ruling adopted by Descartes and most of the moderns—must be replaced in a postmodern epistemology. I propose that moderate pluralism be adopted instead. The theory of moderate pluralism I have been constructing recognizes a range of knowings, each with its own way of being conceptually reliable and, consequently, each with its own way of being true. I have now dealt with practical and observational knowing with these issues in mind. When we come to theoretical knowing, what needs to be added?

First, as we saw in the previous chapter, there are two distinct senses in which a theory can be true. One sense (which I shall from now on call $true_1$), reflects the applicable *test* of what "true" means practically; that is, that our conceptual construction has not let us down, does not need correction, has proven itself conceptually reliable for whatever functions we employ it. In this sense a theory is $true_1$ the way a lover's love or a marksman's aim is true. This is an enormously important sense, since in the end we have no other test. The other sense (which I shall from now on call $true_2$), reflects the applicable *definition* of what "true" means metaphysically, that is, conformality. The lover's actions are $true_2$ if and only if they conform to the ideal pattern of how lovers should behave; the marksman's arrow is $true_2$ if and only if it conforms to the exact spot defined as the goal of the arrow; the theory is $true_2$ if and only if its forms of definiteness—the features, qualities, and relations of the theory—are conformal to the features, qualities, and relations of its objective subject matter.

My friend and pioneering constructivist, Ernst von Glasersfeld, maintains that I have no right, in a constructivist epistemology, to add my definition of conformality ($true_2$) to my test of conceptual reliability ($true_1$). The notion of conformality presupposes an objective world of features, qualities, and relations, which he abjures. Conceptual reliability is all we can have, he argues. He admits that some constructs are more reliable than others, and that this needs an explanation.

[We] shall have to account for a difference in conceptual constructs which, even as constructivists, we would not like to miss: the difference between knowledge that we want to trust as though it were objective, and constructs that we consider to be questionable if not downright illusory. Needless to say, this constructivist 'objectivity' should be called by another name because it does not lie in, nor does it point to, a world of things-in-themselves. It lies wholly within the confines of the phenomenal (von Glasersfeld 1995: 119).

But von Glasersfeld's whole position rests on his belief that the epistemological gap between the phenomenal world and the world of things-in-themselves is absolute. He remains caught in Kant's trap. The main hope motivating these last three chapters, however, has been to offer von Glasersfeld and the many others in his predicament a way out. To his challenge, "that those who maintain that we *do* receive objective information through the senses, come up with a plausible model to explain *how* such a communicative transfer might work" (von Glasersfeld 1995: 116), this book is an extended reply. The required model is Whiteheadian, naturalistic, empirical, ecological. It offers a way to deconstruct the epistemological gap.

I acknowledge that it is impossible to test whether a theory is conformal to objective reality (is $true_2$) aside from whether it is conceptually reliable (is $true_1$), to which topic I shall soon return. But the definition of $true_2$ is not an empty one. It is quite possible to understand what conformality between the features of a world and the forms of our thinking would be. It would be a world really characterized by many of the features that also characterize our experience. The impossible task, rather, is to imagine or think a world exhibiting *no* such conformality. Into this epistemological abyss thought simply disappears.

Note that this is not a question of "correspondence," which presupposes ontologically isolated entities resembling or mirroring one another. I argue instead for "conformality," which presupposes an interpenetrative, ecological ontology allowing for mutually shared characteristics. I suspect that many of the characteristics of our experience and thought (e.g., causality and triangularity) do conform with characteristics of the objective world, though many (e.g., tickles and pains) may not. The fun for explorers is finding out which are more likely to be which, and which patterns in thought are more likely to characterize the patterns among things. Over the long run, the most *reliable* ($true_1$) are the best candidates for being the most *conformal* ($true_2$). At no point in time, since experience is open-ended, can this be finally demonstrated, but it can be hoped or feared.

Hope and fear may at first seem odd categories to apply to many kinds of theoretical knowing. On my view, however, there is always some degree of concern about the truth of one's theory. In some cases, admittedly—for example, small contexts or highly abstract ones—one's emotional investment in the outcome may seem quite minor; in some lines of work—for example, banking or analytical chemistry—professional training involves deliberate suppression of affective categories. In other cases, however, especially where the subject matter comprehends the thinker and where deeply important values are at issue (as in metaphysical or theological theories), there is obviously much about which to hope or fear.

While the human cognitive situation—at one with the character of the universe in being temporal, creative, unfinished—precludes ever being absolutely certain, as Plato and Descartes demanded, that our theories are $true_2$, we do have tests for conceptual reliability that allow us to estimate how $true_1$ our theories are. These are the tests of richness and wholeness that we have found functioning at all the other levels of life and thought. This is no coincidence. They are built into the aims of life and the functions of intelligence. If the aims of life are survival ("to live"), growth ("to live well"), and continuing qualitative improvement ("to live better"), then a certain threshold of richness of satisfactions (at least enough to eat, drink, breathe, etc.) is entailed by the basic aim, and additional satisfactions—but satisfactions organized, so as not to block each other or destroy the living organism—are required in order to fulfill the next two. *Richness* is the primary imperative, always relative to the context. *Wholeness* is the functional necessity, relative to the richness attained. Wholeness works to optimize what the demand for richness tries to maximize.

The richness requirement in theoretical knowing is what I have often called "adequacy." Adequacy is always relative to the context of subject matter and purpose. As noted earlier, some contexts may be quite small. We never know for certain the limits of relevance, even in small contexts (since new laws may be discovered, or conceptual revolutions occur, changing what needs to be considered relevant), but at any given time, adequacy as a test of conceptual reliability calls for completeness—for inclusion of *all* that is judged relevant evidence. A conceptual construction that systematically leaves out chunks of relevant data is more likely to let us down, to show it is not $true_1$, than an alternative construction that makes sense out of everything the first included, plus the additional evidence previously ignored.

This principle of inclusion, of completeness, is field-dependent, since some fields are broader than others; but for all fields, for all degrees of comprehensiveness, adequacy is a basic measure of theoretical reliability. The passion with which opposing lawyers argue over the "admissibility" of different items, and the "relevance" of testimony, shows its importance. The entire theory of a case may depend on keeping some of the evidence excluded from consideration. Items that do not lend themselves to harmonization with a favored theory—undigestible bits—make selling the jury one's story (a conceptual construct) considerably harder.

This is one of the important reasons, also, why selling philosophers on a comprehensive vision is so difficult. Adequacy is field-dependent, and the philosophical field has no boundaries. Everything is relevant. All experience counts. Whitehead's classic formulation of the richness requirement is almost comical in its insistent litany:

> Nothing can be omitted, experience drunk and experience sober, experience sleeping and experience waking, experience drowsy and experience wide-awake, experience self-conscious and experience self-forgetful, experience intellectual and experience physical, experience religious and experience skeptical, experience anxious and experience carefree, experience anticipatory and experience retrospective, experience happy and experience grieving, experience dominated by emotion and experience under self-restraint, experience in the light and experience in the dark, experience normal and experience abnormal (Whitehead 1933: 226).

Adequacy of this sort is an ideal that none of us can attain, though Whitehead's own system scores much higher than most in meeting his requirement. Still, such adequacy is one of the great ideals, functionally reflecting the aim of theory to construct a conceptual map that leaves nothing out that will ever be important for understanding the territory. It is much easier for philosophers to be selective from the start, keeping the jury from hearing some kinds of testimony, and arguing fiercely that some seeming evidence (e.g., moral experience, intentional states, secondary qualities, etc.) should be ruled inadmissible. On the level of high theory, this is the equivalent of the humble negative prehension, assuring unity of concrescence by excluding in advance what, it seems, cannot be harmonized into a final satisfaction.

This reference to "satisfaction" reminds us that satisfactory mental harmonization of all relevant concepts into *unities* as rich as possible is the other built-in aim of theorizing. The unity or wholeness requirement in theoretical knowing is what I have often called "coherence." This criterion is field-dependent as well. Sometimes it is called "simplicity," frequently in connection with theories in physics or in other fields that deal with many entities that beg for grouping in conceptually comprehensible ways. There is no single meaning for simplicity, since it can be attained in many ways, but however attained, it is in the service of coherence. At other times, especially in mathematical or other formal theories, it is called "elegance," which usually involves some mode of simplicity as well as an aesthetic element that provides joy to those who can appreciate it. Elegance, too, is a form of coherence and marks success in achieving a noteworthy harmonization of elements in a satisfying way. Modern methodologists of science have sometimes been puzzled or embarrassed by the role of simplicity and elegance in theoretical knowing. They need not have been. Both are reflections of achievements in wholeness that are one of the marks by which we can judge whether our theories are conceptually reliable. When present, they show that the coherence-making functions required by theory are being achieved. When so characterized, our theories are to that extent more likely to be true$_1$.

Satisfactions in richness, satisfactions in wholeness, are the marks of theoretical knowing. Most of the time we can stop with that. A comprehensive, growing coherence is normally all we ask, when "comprehensive" is relative to limited subject matters, like mice in the cupboard or even quasars in the sky. But there is one context, the horizon context, where the completely comprehensive theories of philosophy and religion function, that demands even more. At this conceptual horizon, even coherence that is open to all the relevant data and responsive to the addition of more data is not enough to bring final satisfaction. The speculative gadfly of mentality never rests: Why is *this* the coherence of all relevant data rather than some other equally coherent system of concepts? To this querulous, insatiable refrain there is no purely theoretical end. The underlying reason is that mentality is the principle of dissatisfaction with anything actual. If we achieved a final coherence, the very actuality of its achievement would set speculative mentality into its negative mode. In many ways, we should be grateful for this irrepressible gadfly sting. It saves us from obscurantism, from premature closures, from settling for "good enough" methods—whether in craft traditions or in the latest logics—by pressing its queries against every completed construction. But it undermines final satisfaction, too, as long as we stay on its terms.

There is one way beyond. That is to add to the explanatory satisfactions of richness and wholeness the additional satisfactions of goodness and beauty—to enter the domain of what might be called the "religiously true" (Ferré 1967b: 402–3) Here Plato was right. The ultimate fulfillment of knowing would be finding that the True is Beautiful. The answer to the endless queries of free, speculative mentality is not to end them but to make them less querulous. The ideal would be to continue to probe earnestly but without anxiety, in the conviction that what is finally *so* is intrinsically *acceptable*. The theoretical open-endedness of the ultimate horizon itself, if we could approach it cognitively, would bother inquirers only to the degree that it were felt as arbitrary, oppressive, a "brute" fact. If it were felt to be not brutal but benign, not ugly but radiant with loveliness, it would offer compensatory, overriding satisfaction beyond the dissatisfactions of the "insatiable why."

THE KNOWING OF BEAUTY AND THE BEAUTY OF KNOWING

What I am proposing is an aesthetic resolution of this age-old epistemological impasse. Beauty is self-justifying. By its nature, beauty involves contrasting, even conflicting, elements but resolves their conflict by making them internal to a satisfactory synthesis that retains the elements, adjusted to one another so that they enhance the whole.

A good example might be drawn from the often-neglected beauties of food and drink. Sweet-and-sour sauce is a simple but effective synthesis of conflicting elements which, together, enhance gustatory experience more intensely than either cloying sweetness or mouth-puckering sourness alone can do. Together, mutually adjusted and with other elements (such as salt and other spices), sugar and vinegar enhance one another without ceasing to be what they are or to perform their characteristic functions. Intrinsically satisfying experience comes from the harmonious synthesis of discordant ingredients. Intrinsically satisfying experience is what I mean by "beauty" (Ferré 1996: 358).

The higher beauties of the palate are based on the same principle. Distinguished chefs labor to bring their guests maximum intensities of satisfaction by finding just the right balances of herbs, sauces, textures, etc., in the foods they carefully prepare, as well as in the sequencing of the various courses in the menus they construct. The beauty of the taste of great wine, similarly, lies in the subtle contrasts between its elements—tannin, acid, sugar, etc.—blended in organic harmonies beyond full analysis, even by experts who devote their lives to the task. More, with the harmonies of aroma and taste, from both food and drink, are integrated the additional visual beauties of the table. Contrasting colors on the plate; the bloom of red wine through sparkling crystal; the warm ambiance of candlelight illuminating the background of white linen and glowing silver; and, at best, the stimulating mix of different personalities among the diners, providing rich conversational variety—these disparate elements are unified by the experiencing subjects who thereby enjoy a truly beautiful evening.

Our human bias toward eyesight—perhaps because of our highly developed optical-neurological system—draws us too quickly (and sometimes even exclusively) to the visual, to paintings, landscapes, sunsets, rainbows, or comely people, as instances of what it is to know beauty. These offer excellent examples; but, for a change, I am inclined to consider music. Music, like poetry, drama, the novel, and film, wears its temporality on its sleeve. The beauty of a painting is no more timeless and static than that of a string quartet, since both are appreciated only in a span of time, but a painting's physical form, complete once and for all within its frame, may make it seem nontemporal. Music and poetry are more paradigmatic of the kalogenetic—beauty-making—process (Turner 1985: 237–66, and Ferré 1996: 339–70).

The process is grounded in the fundamental character of experience which, on my panexperientialist worldview, involves even the most evanescent event of concrescence. My focus here, however, is on human experience. The previous chapters have expressed my view, summarized as follows: In every brief event of experience, data in vast multiplicity are prehended physically; these data are simplified and further enriched conceptually; finally, they are harmonized into a determinate subjective unity, which is the objective ("superjective") heritage left to be prehended in the next moment. The "satisfaction" of an event of concrescence in this unitary climax is its value for itself. However rich or poor its quality, that degree of satisfaction—from drawing a variety of possibilities into a unity for actuality—is its creation of beauty, such as it is.

This final qualifier suggests that we can know many grades of beauty. I take this as an obvious fact of experience. Just as the satisfactions of dining are not always filled with moments of wonderfully harmonized elements, but often only with the grosser urgencies of hunger overlaid with physical satisfactions of organic needs, so the satisfactions of music are often not particularly high-grade. Contrasting pitches, timbres, volume changes, rhythms, and melodic lines may be boringly simple. The insistent periodicity of a drum delivers the contrast between moments of sound and moments of silence, and builds expectation of the contrast between the present and the immediate future. Some kinds of "disco" music offer only a few distinct qualities of sound, minimal rhythmic contrast, and few melodic surprises. These allow syntheses of elements constituting minor moments beauty, of a sort. But, at the other extreme, a great symphony orchestra can supply almost unlimited variety in instrumental tones, dynamic ranges from barely audible to deafening, and music carefully devised for it (by composers as intent as any master chef on evoking intensity of experience from the blending of many contrasting elements) may include the delights of subtle dissonances and rhythmic variation taken up and resolved in endlessly engaging ways. Distinct themes can be toyed with, repeated in different registers, inverted, made to clash with other elements—all within the capacities of human experiencers to distinguish, remember, recognize, associate, learn to anticipate, feel the satisfaction of expectations confirmed, feel the stimulating jolt of expectations playfully postponed, and feel the sweet surprise of expectations met in unexpected, still more interesting ways.

These we recognize as the capacities of thinking in general, which can be diminished by illness, fatigue, and drugs—or enhanced by training and cultivation. Close attention, motivated by feelings of importance, can lead to noticing and naming subtle differences in the regularities of such experience.

Once they are noticed and named, and once we become thereby equipped with a common language within an attentive community (however small), the availability of linguistic symbols can, reciprocally, abet further discriminating and recognizing of significant forms of definiteness, whether these are found in the odors of herbs, or in the aftertaste of wine, or in the exciting rivalries of brass with woodwind sonorities, or in obbligati, syncopations, or fugues. To discriminate differences is to enrich awareness, thus enhancing intensity of satisfaction by pushing toward ampler, more complex unities. Once again we encounter richness and wholeness, now the standards-in-tension for beauty, as we saw them to be for truth$_1$ also. It is possible to achieve minor occasions of beauty (like trivial truths) by eliminating discordant elements and leaving only a few to be harmonized in perfunctory unities. Most occasions of beauty, like most occasions of truth, are likely to be flat. But it is also possible to draw a rich diversity of elements into inspiring coherences, full of the piquancy of complexity and capable of overcoming the tensions of dissonance in resolutions of higher harmony.

My position entails that there are genuinely higher and lower orders of beauty, finer and coarser satisfactions, greater and lesser expressions of music, depending on the character and complexity of its blend of richness and wholeness. It does not, however, entail that there is such a thing as "absolute" music or art—or "absolute" meals or wines. On the contrary, just as there are multiplicities of ways to achieve great culinary satisfactions in different cultural traditions, using different ingredients, in different ways, there must be room for generous pluralism in what rightly counts as great beauty in poetry, visual art, and music. As one who has played both, I am sure that there is great jazz as well as great symphonic music, for example. There must also be room for future advances in all these domains, room for open-ended enhancement of experience by ever-finer discriminations of elements, thus creating real possibilities of ever-growing coherences in ever-more-intense satisfactions.

Why should a book on epistemology discuss the merits of jazz and symphonic music? My answer: because knowing is the music of thought. The knowing of beauty, wherever found, is our best access to an appreciation of the beauty of knowing.

There are parallels between making music and all three of the types of knowing. *Practical* knowing innovates, doodles around, lucks into something neat, tries it again, likes the effect, repeats it, and repeats it some more. Music making, unstudied, is just a way of making sounds and silences and stumbling on methods that work somehow to please. *Observational* knowing watches the natural rhythms of things; associates and relates disparate perceptual elements in patterns across time; finds satisfaction in resolutions according to expectation. Music making, attended to, notices, recognizes, and associates distinguishable sound qualities, rhythms, harmonies; it finds "laws" in scales and keys and harmonies that tend regularly to evoke moods of sadness, joy, militancy, romance. These parallels could be greatly expanded.

But my primary interest here is in *theoretical* knowing and therefore in analogies between the composition of music and the construction of theories. Both are abstract, symbolic activities. A composer and a theorist must often be satisfied with something mundane, just a simple little ditty or a minor scrap of theory. But sometimes great works beckon. The composer may assay a symphony; the theorist may tackle a wide-ranging scientific problem or even hope to build a philosophical system.

In both cases, there will be vastly more elements available than can possibly be given their due. There must be selection, subordination, thematic configuration, internal relation—all organized around a few central ideas. There will be a mood set, a key. This need not remain unchanged throughout—it should not, since the spice of variety is craved, for example, flashes of humor, even in a serious work—but the unity of affective tone underlies all other, lesser unities that make up the work as a whole. If the work is to be rich, it needs tension between elements that rival each other for notice and for dominance. If the work is to be whole, the tensions need to be resolved, over and over again, in lesser resolutions that spark larger tensions, finally finding full voice in a climax that offers acknowledgment, acceptance, peace.

"Coherence" is the dreary word some philosophers use for the unity that ought to offer peace to theory. This, I have argued, is not enough for final satisfaction if a thought system is not also felt as beauty. For a few, perhaps for Brand Blanshard and William James, this is exactly what a sufficiently rich coherence would provide. The complexity of its unity would offer such intensity of mental fulfillment as to provide its own justification. But I have doubts that just any all-comprehensive system, given sufficient coherence, would serve. There are coherences and coherences, systems and systems, just as there are symphonies and other symphonies. Not all are on a par. We may not wish to dismiss any. We may agree that all are great achievements. But some may move and inspire more than others. There are some symphonies we might choose to dwell with often. There are some philosophical thought-worlds we might choose to dwell in for a lifetime.

Philosophical systems are constructed as possible habitations for whole persons. This involves conceptual satisfaction, of course, but also satisfactions for feeling and acting. And not only for isolated individuals. There are no isolated individuals in an ecological worldview. Theoretical knowing at its most comprehensive is not full enough if it does not comprehend society. The satisfying system would unite not only the fragmented knowledge of the sciences in a harmony of cognition; it would also draw together ethics and religion, humanity and nature, technologies and institutions worthy of a common life. These are topics for the final volume of this trilogy, *Living and Value*.

Before turning to that volume, however, there is one last epistemological issue to be resolved. What happens to truth? When theory is seen as music, shaped for the satisfaction of living minds, is truth made irrelevant? If theory is constructed for the sake of satisfaction, and finally in the interest of beauty, all theorizing becomes interested. Is there no place left for the virtues of disinterested theory, the pursuit of unvarnished truth wherever the path might lead?

All theory is inevitably, in one broad sense, "interested." If this were not so, there would be no theoretical activity, since theorizers must first be interested in theorizing if they are going to bother to engage in it. This does not mean that all thought must be pragmatic, as if praxis were the only genuine human interest. Often, perhaps usually, we seek to know for the sake of practical satisfactions; but sometimes, at least, we seek to know for the sheer joys of its intrinsic satisfactions. Even the most "disinterested" thinker seeks the stoic beauty of cognitive closure, though the heavens fall. We admire this steely quest, but let us not suppose there is no interest there.

What, though, of fiction? Might fantasy not give as much or more zing to the mind than fact? If intrinsic satisfaction—intellectual beauty—is the goal of system, why suffer the pains of inquiry in search of the true, which may not be half so beautiful as wishful thinking? I answer that in some contexts, fiction may be far more interesting, and more rewarding to the mind, than the dull deliverances of the immediate objective environment. This is why we enjoy films, novels, theater, opera, and even daydreaming. The arts of fantasy are honorable. They feed the mind with possibility. They expand awareness and increase the capacity for sympathy. They enrich life.

Moreover, imagination and fantasy are at the heart of all worldviews, including the one I favor, and the risk of error is high for all comprehensive theories, including the one I offer in these volumes. This is a healthy feature of postmodern insight into the ludicrousness of all pretention to finality. To realize that every theory is a conceptual construction is to be liberated from hegemonic oppression by anyone's ideas—including one's own. It is to remind every author of such a theory to keep a light heart.

At the same time, theories may be better or worse. The modern era was a time of brilliant abstractions guilty of excessive omissions. Many have tried to dwell in the metaphysics and epistemologies of modernity. Many have been diminished. Many have lost confidence in the legitimacy of mind and value in modern metaphysics, and many have lost confidence in their powers of knowing in modern epistemology. These problems are obviously linked. The alienation of mind from nature underlies them both.

My theory, gratefully drawn from Whitehead's, is (like all theory) in large part fanciful. The large ideas—experience as concrescent, prehensive connection, etc.—that provide its structure and its principles of selection and relation, are imaginative creations. They are a manifestation of the wildness of mentality at the level of speculative play.

But what of truth? Are comprehensive theories, worldviews, only to be judged on their capacities to provide aesthetic satisfaction? Are they *just* speculative play? Are they not to be taken seriously? I believe they should be taken with the utmost seriousness although they are play. They are play on which our lives depend. The character and quality of our personal selves, the institutions and activities of our social structures, are deeply shaped by the ultimate stories we tell ourselves and others about who we are, what the world is like, and how we can know it.

Therefore the question of truth matters. It matters whether a would-be comprehensive story leaves out huge domains or whether it includes them. It matters which domains are highlighted, which are left in relative shade. It matters what the basic imaginative ideas are that organize and select what is taken as real and important and possible. It matters, not just practically (as we shall see in the next volume), but also because, over the long run, the tests of what theories are likely to be $true_1$ give us our only ground for guessing what may reasonably be hoped to be $true_2$.

Modern metaphysics and epistemology have had a fairly long run in which to reveal their strengths and weaknesses. They are not disproven. That is not what happens to comprehensive theories. But they are weakened by increasingly felt inadequacies and incoherences, those that the first two volumes of this trilogy have narrated. To this extent, these theories are defective in the conceptual reliability called for, over time, to justify holding that any great theory is largely $true_1$.

We want to judge whether theories are $true_1$, finally, because we hope or fear that they may be $true_2$. These hopes may not be particularly pressing in the case of many lesser theories. In some domains of theorizing, we may be able to adopt a purely instrumentalist attitude, using a theory merely as a tool to anticipate and control events, not caring whether objective reality shares the properties of the concepts we employ to gain our cognitive purchase. But in the domain of comprehensive theories, especially where the question of other subjectivities is at stake, it does matter whether what is objectively so shares the features that our best-attested theories attribute to it. If I love you, for example, it matters to me whether my theory that solipsism is crazy—and that you are really a subjective center of thought and feelings who can love me back—is $true_2$ or not. It is not good enough that you behave *as though* you love me, if in fact you are feeling nothing. The instrumentalist verification of my theory will not do in this case. I may not be able to prove that you are another personal subject. Solipsism is a comprehensive worldview, and such theories are not disproven. Instead, when they are as profoundly dissatisfying as solipsism, they are legitimately set aside. But one can understand, and fear, what a solipsist world would be like, if true$_2$. One can also understand what it should be for one's beloved to be a personal subject, not a (behaviorally indistinguishable) automaton devoid of internal thought and feeling. One can hope, that is, that one's very personal theory, however well confirmed as true$_1$, is also true$_2$.

In similar manner, I cannot prove that my kalogenic theory of the universe is true$_2$. It lies at the opposite pole from solipsism. It acknowledges the objective reality of subjectivities everywhere. The best I can hope is (1) that over the long run, something like the panexperientialist naturalism I advocate can be shown, relative to its alternatives, to include more and exclude less from the boundless sea of experience, and (2) that its key ecological ideas—prehension, internal relatedness, evolving social organization, etc.— will be continually more capable of organizing a unified view of the world so lucid, coherent, and attractive that it illuminates understanding, nourishes persistent personal hungers, and supports virtuous institutions for a postmodern world.

From its humblest origins to its highest aspirations, knowing is mingled with value. Experience arrives in a flood of affective tone; its earliest glimmerings, rising from preconscious states, are already selective, busy with affirmations and negations. Praxis is motivated by the urge to learn methods for the sake of survival and for the flourishing of life. Sign cognition depends on intuitions of importance among discriminated regularities in experience and on normative judgments that memory is reliable, that sign tokens fall within the acceptable range of sign types, and that associations are fruitful. Concept formation rests on what is deemed worthy of noticing and naming. It is no mere coincidence that one of the meanings of "significance" is "importance," and that one of the meanings of "meaningless" is "trivial." Conceptual meaning, language itself, thus reflects judgments of importance, and every definition of every word implies resolutions of scope and cruciality, community norms of usage, and the reciprocal obligations of communication. Observation is shaped not only by the affective stream of bodily experience and implicit judgments of what is important and intrinsically interesting to notice, but also by social preferences that have shaped the language of observation and by the shifting urgencies of praxis. Theory construction is always interested. From the smallest construct that helps make sense of momentary experience to the grandest theories of science and philosophy, theories use value-generated concepts to interpret value-organized data drawn from value-laden experience. Theory justification, finally, rests on satisfaction: first, on satisfaction of the criteria of richness (appropriate to the domain) and of wholeness (relative to the richness), and, finally, on the intrinsic satisfaction of understanding. Understanding is knowing's highest value. But this value is not static. It contains the restless dynamic of mentality, the principle of unrest and creativity in the universe. It calls for closure that is never closed; it calls for satisfaction that is always a prelude to fresh satisfactions; it calls for dissonances to be resolved in harmonizations that themselves resolve into ever-richer harmonies. Knowing finds fulfillment, but not a stopping place, in beauty.

WORKS CITED

Anderson, Douglas R. 1995. *Strands of System: The Philosophy of Charles Peirce.* West Lafayette, Ind.: Purdue University Press.

Anselm, Saint. 1958a. *Monologium.* Translated by Sidney Norton Deane. La Salle, Ill.: Open Court.

———. 1958b. *Proslogium.* Translated by Sidney Norton Deane. La Salle, Ill.: Open Court.

Aquinas, Saint Thomas. 1948. *Summa Theologica.* In *Introduction to Saint Thomas Aquinas*, translated and edited by Anton C. Pegis. New York: Random House.

Aristotle. 1951a. *Metaphysics.* Translated by Philip Wheelwright. New York: Odyssey Press.

———. 1951b. *Nicomachean Ethics.* Translated by Philip Wheelwright. New York: Odyssey Press.

———. 1951c. *Psychology* Translated by Philip Wheelwright. New York: Odyssey Press.

Aubrey, John. 1898. *"Brief Lives," Chiefly of Contemporaries, Set Down by John Aubrey, between the Years 1669 and 1696.* Edited by Andrew Clark. 2 vols. Oxford: Clarendon Press.

Augustine, Saint Aurelius. 1961. *The Confessions of Saint Augustine.* Translated by Edward B. Pusey. New York: Washington Square Press.

———. 1964a. *Against the Academics.* Translated by J. J. O'Meara. In John A. Mourant, *Introduction to the Philosophy of Saint Augustine.* University Park, Pa.: Pennsylvania State University Press.

———. 1964b. Letter 120. Translated by Thomas F. Gilligan. In John A. Mourant, *Introduction to the Philosophy of Saint Augustine.* University Park, Pa.: Pennsylvania State University Press.

———. 1964c. *On Free Choice of the Will.* Translated by Anna S. Benjamin and L.H. Hackstaff. Indianapolis: Bobbs Merrill.

———. 1964d. *The City of God.* Translated by Marcus Dods. In John A. Mourant, *Introduction to the Philosophy of Saint Augustine.* University Park, Pa.: Pennsylvania State University Press.

———. 1964e. *The Literal Meaning of Genesis.* Translated by John S. Taylor. In John A. Mourant, *Introduction to the Philosophy of Saint Augustine.* University Park, Pa.: Pennsylvania State University Press.

————. 1964f. *The Trinity.* In John A. Mourant, *Introduction to the Philosophy of Saint Augustine.* University Park, Pa.: Pennsylvania State University Press.

Ayer, A. J. 1940. *The Foundations of Empirical Knowledge.* London: Macmillan.

————. 1946. *Language, Truth and Logic.* 2d ed. London: Victor Gollancz.

————. 1956. *The Problem of Knowledge.* London: Penguin Books.

Bargh, J. 1995. Reported by Daniel Goleman. *The New York Times.* 8 Aug.

Berkeley, George. 1962. *Treatise Concerning the Principles of Human Knowledge.* In Walter Kaufman, *Philosophical Classics: Bacon to Kant.* Englewood Cliffs, N.J.: Prentice-Hall.

Blanshard, Brand. 1939. *The Nature of Thought.* 2 vols. London: George Allen & Unwin.

————. 1968. Kierkegaard on Faith. *The Personalist* 49 (Winter): 5–23.

————. 1975. *Reason and Belief.* New Haven: Yale University Press.

————. 1980a. Reply to Frederick Ferré. In *The Philosophy of Brand Blanshard,* edited by Paul Arthur Schilpp. La Salle, Ill.: Open Court.

————. 1980b. Reply to Nicholas Rescher. In *The Philosophy of Brand Blanshard,* edited by Paul Arthur Schilpp. La Salle, Ill.: Open Court.

Bohm, David. 1980. *Wholeness and the Implicate Order.* London: Routledge & Kegan Paul.

Bokser, B. Z. 1981. *The Jewish Mythical Tradition.* New York: Pilgrim Press.

Bradley, F. H. 1893. *Appearance and Reality: A Metaphysical Essay.* Oxford: Clarendon Press.

————. 1914. *Essays on Truth and Reality.* Oxford: Clarendon Press.

Burnet, John. 1961. *Early Greek Philosophy.* 4th ed. Cleveland and New York: World Publishing Company.

Cicero. 1974. *Academica.* Translated by A. A. Long. In *Hellenistic Philosophy: Stoics, Epicureans, Sceptics.* London: Gerald Duckworth.

Cobb, John B., Jr. 1967. *The Structure of Human Existence.* Philadelphia: Westminster Press.

Commoner, Barry. 1972. *The Closing Circle: Nature, Man, and Technology.* New York: Bantam Books.

Copleston, Frederick. 1962. *A History of Philosophy.* Garden City, N.Y.: Doubleday.

Dennett, Daniel. 1991. *Consciousness Explained.* Boston: Little, Brown.

Descartes, René. 1958. *Meditations on First Philosophy: In Which the Existence of God and the Distinction in Man of Soul and Body are Demonstrated.* Translated by Norman Kemp Smith. In *Descartes: Philosophical Writings,* edited by Norman Kemp Smith. New York: Random House.

————. 1960. *Discourse on Method.* Translated by Laurence J. Lafleur. Indianapolis: Bobbs-Merrill.

Diogenes Laertius. 1974. *Diogenes Laertius.* In A. A. Long, *Hellenistic Philosophy: Stoics, Epicureans, Sceptics.* London: Gerald Duckworth.

Einstein, Albert. 1949. *Albert Einstein: Philosopher-Scientist.* Vol. 1. Edited by Paul Arthur Schilpp. New York: Harper & Brothers.

Epicurus. 1974a. *Kuriai doxai.* Translated by A. A. Long. In A. A. Long, *Hellenistic Philosophy: Stoics, Epicureans, Sceptics.* London: Gerald Duckworth.

————. 1974b. *Letter to Herodotus*. Translated by A. A. Long. In A. A. Long, *Hellenistic Philosophy: Stoics, Epicureans, Sceptics*. London: Gerald Duckworth.

————. 1974c. *Letter to Pythocles*. Translated by A. A. Long. In A. A. Long, *Hellenistic Philosophy: Stoics, Epicureans, Sceptics*. London: Gerald Duckworth.

Eriugena, John Scotus. 1962. *De Divisione Naturae* In Frederick Copleston, *A History of Philosophy*, vol. 2, pt. 1. Garden City, N.Y.: Doubleday.

Ewing, A. C. 1934. *Idealism: A Critical Survey*. London: Methuen & Co.

Ferré, Frederick. 1961a. Colour Incompatibility and Language-Games. *Mind* 70 (277): 90–94.

————. 1961b. *Language, Logic and God*. New York: Harper & Row.

————. 1967a. Analogy in Theology. In *The Encyclopedia of Philosophy*, vol. 1, edited by Paul Edwards. New York: Macmillan.

————. 1967b. *Basic Modern Philosophy of Religion*. New York: Charles Scribner's Sons.

————. 1971. The Ethics of Belief. *Philosophic Exchange* 1 (2): 95–100.

————. 1980. Brand Blanshard on Reason and Religious Belief. In *The Philosophy of Brand Blanshard*, edited by Paul Arthur Schilpp. La Salle, Ill.: Open Court.

————. 1990. Reflections on Blanshard, Reason, and Religion. *Idealistic Studies* 20 (2): 122–39.

————. 1994. Whitehead and the Advance Beyond Modern Mindlessness. *Journal of the American Society for Psychical Research* 88 (April): 147–66.

————. 1995. *Philosophy of Technology*. Athens, Ga.: University of Georgia Press.

————. 1996. *Being and Value: Toward a Constructive Postmodern Metaphysics*. Albany, N.Y.: State University of New York Press.

Feyerabend, Paul. 1975. *Against Method: Outline of an Anarchistic Theory of Knowledge*. Atlantic Highlands, N.J.: Humanities Press.

Finegan, Edward & Niko Besnier. 1989. *Language: Its Structure and Use*. New York: Harcourt Brace Jovanovich.

Fisch, Max, et al. 1982. *Writings of Charles S. Peirce: A Chronological Edition*. Bloomington, Ind.: Indiana University Press.

Gay, P. 1987. *A Godless Jew: Freud, Atheism, and the Making of Psychoanalysis*. New Haven, Conn.: Yale University Press.

Gelernter, David. 1994. *The Muse in the Machine: Computerizing the Poetry of Human Thought*. New York: Free Press.

Genesis. 1952. *The Holy Bible*. Revised Standard Version. New York: Thomas Nelson and Sons.

Griffin, David Ray. 1997. *Parapsychology, Philosophy, and Spirituality: A Postmodern Exploration*. Albany, N.Y.: State University of New York Press.

Hanson, N. R. 1953. *Patterns of Discovery*. Cambridge: Cambridge University Press.

Heisenberg, Werner. 1958. *Physics and Philosophy: Revolution in Modern Science*. New York: Harper & Brothers.

Hobbes, Thomas. 1839. *Leviathan*. In *The English Works of Thomas Hobbes of Malmesbury; Now First Collected and Edited*, edited by William Molesworth. London: John Bohn.

————. 1955. The Third Set of Objections. In *The Philosophical Works of Descartes*, translated and edited by Elizabeth S. Haldane and G. R. T. Ross. Cambridge: Cambridge University Press.

————. 1986. *Autobiography*. In Arnold A. Rogow, *Thomas Hobbes: Radical in the Service of Reaction*. New York: W. W. Norton.

Hume, David. 1888. *A Treatise of Human Nature*. Edited by L. A. Selby-Bigge. Oxford: Clarendon Press.

————. 1902. *An Enquiry Concerning Human Understanding*. 2d ed. Edited by L. A. Selby-Bigge. Oxford: Clarendon Press.

James, Henry, ed. 1920. *The Letters of William James*. Boston: Atlantic Monthly Press.

James, William. 1957a. The Sentiment of Rationality (1880). In *Essays in Pragmatism*, edited by Alburey Castell. New York: Hafner Publishing Co.

————. 1957b. The Will to Believe (1896). In *Essays in Pragmatism*, edited by Alburey Castell. New York: Hafner Publishing Co.

Kant, Immanuel. 1966. *Critique of Pure Reason*. Translated by Max Müller. Garden City, New York: Doubleday.

Kaufmann, Walter. 1962. *Philosophical Classics*. Englewood Cliffs, N.J.: Prentice-Hall.

Kierkegaard, Søren. 1936. *Philosophical Fragments*. Translated by David F. Swenson. Princeton, N.J.: Princeton University Press.

————. 1941a. *Concluding Unscientific Postscript*. Translated by David F. Swenson. Completed and edited by Walter Lowrie. Princeton, N.J.: Princeton University Press.

————. 1941b. *Training in Christianity*. Translated by Walter Lowrie. New York: Oxford University Press.

————. 1954. *Fear and Trembling: A Dialectical Lyric*. Translated by Walter Lowrie. Garden City, N.Y.: Doubleday Anchor Books.

Kuhn, Thomas S. 1957. *The Copernican Revolution: Planetary Astronomy in the Development of Western Thought*. New York: Random House.

————. 1970. *The Structure of Scientific Revolutions*. 2d ed. Chicago: University of Chicago Press.

Lakatos, Imre. 1977. *The Methodology of Scientific Research Programmes*. Cambridge: Cambridge University Press.

Liddell & Scott. 1953. *A Lexicon*. Oxford: Clarendon Press.

Locke, John. 1956. *An Essay Concerning Human Understanding*. Edited by A. S. Pringle-Pattison. Oxford: Clarendon Press.

Long, A. A. 1974. *Hellenistic Philosophy: Stoics, Epicureans, Sceptics*. London: Gerald Duckworth.

Mach, Ernst. 1976. Sensation, Intuition, Phantasy. In *Knowledge and Error: Sketches on the Psychology of Enquiry*, edited by Irwin N. Hiebert, translated by Paul Foulkes. Dordrecht, Netherlands: D. Reidel.

Mill, John Stuart. 1868. *An Examination of Sir William Hamilton's Philosophy and of the Principal Philosophical Questions Discussed in His Writings*. 2 vols. Boston: William V. Spencer.

———. 1873. *The Positive Philosophy of Auguste Comte*. New York: Henry Holt & Co.

Mourant, John A. 1964. *Introduction to the Philosophy of Saint Augustine*. University Park, Pa.: Pennsylvania State University Press.

Neville, Robert C. 1981. *Reconstruction of Thinking*. Albany, N.Y.: State University of New York Press.

Nietzsche, Friedrich. 1954. *The Portable Nietzsche*. Edited by Walter Kaufmann. New York: Viking Press.

Ockham, John. 1957. *Ockham: Philosophical Writings*. Edited by Philotheus Boehner. Edinburgh and London: Thomas Nelson & Sons.

Ostrander, Sheila & Lynn Schroeder. 1970. *Psychic Discoveries Behind the Iron Curtain*. Englewood Cliffs, N.J.: Prentice Hall.

Peirce, Charles Sanders. 1995. The Fixation of Belief. In Douglas R. Anderson, *Strands of System: Philosophy of Charles Peirce*. West Lafayette, Ind.: Purdue University Press.

Philodemus. 1974. On Signs. In A. A. Long, *Hellenistic Philosophy: Stoics, Epicureans, Sceptics*. London: Gerald Duckworth.

Plato. 1937a. *Protagoras*. In *The Dialogues of Plato*, vol. 1, translated by B. Jowett. New York: Random House.

———. 1937b. *Theaetetus*. In *The Dialogues of Plato*, vol. 2, translated by B. Jowett. New York: Random House.

———. 1954. *The Republic of Plato*. Translated by Francis Macdonald Cornford. New York and London: Oxford University Press.

———. 1985a. *Meno*. Translated by A. C. Guthrie. In *Greek Philosophy: Thales to Aristotle*, rev. ed., edited by R. E. Allen. New York and London: Free Press and Collier Macmillan Publishers.

———. 1985b. *Phaedo*. Translated by R. Hackforth. In *Greek Philosophy: Thales to Aristotle*, rev. ed., edited by R. E. Allen. New York and London: Free Press and Collier Macmillan Publishers.

———. 1985c. *Symposium*. Translated by R. E. Allen. In *Greek Philosophy: Thales to Aristotle*, rev. ed., edited by R. E. Allen. New York and London: Free Press and Collier Macmillan Publishers.

Polanyi, Michael. 1964. *Personal Knowledge: Towards a Post-Critical Philosophy*. New York: Harper Torchbooks.

———. 1966. *The Tacit Dimension*. Garden City, N.Y.: Anchor Books.

Price, H. H. 1953. *Thinking and Experience*. Cambridge, Mass.: Harvard University Press.

Quine, Willard van Orman. 1980. Two Dogmas of Empiricism. In *From a Logical Point of View*, 2d ed. Cambridge, Mass.: Harvard University Press.

Rescher, Nicholas. 1992. *A System of Pragmatic Idealism*. Vol. 1 of *Human Knowledge in Idealistic Perspective*. Princeton, N.J.: Princeton University Press.

Rogow, Arnold A. 1986. *Thomas Hobbes: Radical in the Service of Reaction*. New York: W. W. Norton.

Rorty, Richard. 1980. *Philosophy and the Mirror of Nature*. Princeton, N.J.: Princeton University Press.

Rosenberg, Alexander. 1992. *Economics—Mathematical Politics or Science of Diminishing Returns?* Chicago: University of Chicago Press.

Russell, Bertrand, & Alfred North Whitehead. 1927. *Principia Mathematica.* 2d ed., 3 vols. Cambridge and New York: Cambridge University Press.

Ryle, Gilbert. 1953. Ordinary Language. *Philosophical Review* 62.

———. 1984. *The Concept of Mind.* Chicago: University of Chicago Press.

Sartre, Jean–Paul. 1957. *Existentialism and Human Emotions.* Translated by Hazel E. Barnes. New York: Philosophical Library.

Schilpp, Paul Arthur, ed. 1949. *Albert Einstein: Philosopher-Scientist.* New York: Harper & Brothers.

Scotus, John Duns. 1962. *Opus Oxoniense.* Translated by F. Copleston. In Frederick Copleston, *A History of Philosophy*, vol. 2, pt. 2. Garden City, N.Y.: Doubleday.

Shelley, Percy Bysshe. 1966. *The Selected Poetry and Prose of Shelley.* Edited by H. Bloom. New York: Signet.

Tompkins, Peter & Christopher BIRD. 1974. *The Secret Life of Plants.* New York: Harper, 1974.

Toulmin, Stephen. 1953. *Philosophy of Science.* New York: Harper & Brothers.

———. 1961. *Foresight and Understanding.* Indianapolis: Indiana University Press.

———. 1972. *Human Understanding: Collective Use and Evolution of Concepts.* Princeton, N.J.: Princeton University Press.

Turner, Frederick. 1985. *Natural Classicism: Essays on Literature and Science.* New York: Paragon House.

Von Glasersfeld, Ernst. 1995. *Radical Constructivism: A Way of Knowing and Learning.* London: Falmer Press.

Whewell, William. 1858. *Novum Organon Renovatum.* London.

Whitehead, Alfred North. 1925. *Science and the Modern World.* New York: Macmillan.

———. 1927. *Symbolism, Its Meaning and Effect.* New York: Macmillan.

———. 1929. *The Function of Reason.* Boston: Beacon Press.

———. 1933. *Adventures of Ideas.* New York: Macmillan.

———. 1978. *Process and Reality: An Essay in Cosmology.* Corrected ed. Edited by David Ray Griffin and Donald W. Sherburne. New York: Free Press.

Wittgenstein, Ludwig. 1922. *Tractatus Logico-Philosophicus.* Edited by C. K. Ogden and translated by F. P. Ramsey. London: Routledge & Kegan Paul.

———. 1953. *Philosophical Investigations.* Translated by G. E. M. Anscombe. Oxford: Basil Blackwell.

NOTE ON SUPPORTING CENTER

This series is published under the auspices of the Center for Process Studies, a research organization affiliated with the Claremont School of Theology and Claremont Graduate University. It was founded in 1973 by John B. Cobb, Jr., Founding Director, and David Ray Griffin, Executive Director; Mary Elizabeth Moore and Marjorie Suchocki are now also Co-Directors. It encourages research and reflection on the process philosophy of Alfred North Whitehead, Charles Hartshorne, and related thinkers, and on the application and testing of this viewpoint in all areas of thought and practice. The center sponsors conferences, welcomes visiting scholars to use its library, and publishes a scholarly journal, *Process Studies,* and a newsletter, *Process Perspectives.* Located at 1325 North College, Claremont, California 91711, it gratefully accepts (tax-deductible) contributions to support its work.

Names Index

Subject Index

Abduction, 251
Academy: 40, 41, 43, 47, 50, 53; New, 59
Adequacy, 3–5, 9, 57, 123, 168, 258, 275, 297, 347, 349, 350, 364–65. *See also* Experience
Animal learning, 4–6, 314–16, 322, 329, 344. *See also* Trick learning
Anthropocentrism, 5
Anthropomorphism, 170
Apology, 29
Artificial intelligence, 291–93
Ataraxia, 52, 56
Atomic facts: 178–79, 180–81, 183–84 203, 205, 207, 217, 234, 269; and propositions, 180–81, 198; statements, 223
Atomism, 99, 113, 127
Atomists, 52, 99, 121, 176
Axioms, 16, 216, 218–19

Beauty: 8, 17, 33–34, 282, 355, 365, 366–73; harmonization of, 366–69, 373; and knowing, 366–73; and music, 288, 366–70; and painting, 366, 378; and poetry, 366–68
Belief: 36, 56–58, 70–72, 85–86, 205–6, 219, 224–25, 242, 250–52, 257–58, 260, 262–63; Christian, 56, 77, 88; and faith, 70; religious, 235, 258, 260, 261; and shared experience, 434; of taste, 366; of theoretical form, 8; and ultimate reality, 258–60; visual, 366; in witchcraft, 222

Causality, 82, 155, 158–60, 207, 291, 295–97, 300, 317
Christianity: 55–59, 66, 67, 241, 326; and God, 72; and Platonism, 67; platonized, 65
Conceptualism, 76
Cogito ergo sum, 107, 136
Cognition: 9, 14, 26, 36–37, 47, 53, 64, 83, 161, 167, 183, 184, 226, 234, 290, 314, 342, 358, 369, 372; and animal learning, 314–16; sign, 315, 322, 347–48. *See also* Knowledge
Coherence: 3–4, 17, 18, 28, 123, 125, 152, 168, 170, 185, 205–6, 209, 215–20, 230–31, 242, 245, 253, 260, 340, 347, 350, 355–56, 364–65, 368; and analysis, 253; and constancy, 152; and elegance, 364–65; and harmonization, 364; and incoherence, 254; mathematical, 224; and tension, 369; and unity, 83. *See also* Experience
Coherentism, 18, 203, 204, 211, 214, 219–22, 230, 233, 234, 235, 267, 276, 367
Concrescence: 306–14, 340, 342, 355–56; and actuality, 308, 313; and environment, 308–9; and harmony, 310, 312–13, 364; and prehension, 308, 364; and satisfaction, 312
Consistency: 3–4, 9, 10, 121, 210, 338–40; and inconsistency, "madness," 243